THE
GOSPEL
OF
Matthew
AND
ITS
READERS

Howard Clarke

THE

GOSPEL

OF

Matthew

AND

ITS

READERS

A Historical Introduction to the First Gospel

INDIANA University Press

Bloomington & Indianapolis

Publication of this book is made possible in part with the
assistance of a Challenge Grant from the National Endowment
for the Humanities, a federal agency that supports research,
education, and public programming in the humanities.

This book is a publication of

Indiana University Press
601 North Morton Street
Bloomington, Indiana 47404-3797 USA

http://iupress.indiana.edu

Telephone orders   800-842-6796
Fax orders   812-855-7931
Orders by e-mail   iuporder@indiana.edu

The paper used in this publication meets the minimum
requirements of American National Standard for Information
Sciences—Permanence of Paper for Printed Library
Materials, ANSI Z39.48-1984.

Manufactured in the United States of America

Library of Congress Cataloging-in-Publication Data

Clarke, Howard W.
  The Gospel of Matthew and its readers : a historical introduction to
the First Gospel / Howard Clarke.
     p. cm.
Includes bibliographical references and index.
  ISBN 0-253-34235-X (cloth : alk. paper) — ISBN 0-253-21600-1
(pbk. : alk. paper)
1. Bible. N.T. Matthew—Commentaries. I. Title.
  BS2575.53 .C58 2003
  226.2'07—dc21

                                    2002152283

1 2 3 4 5 08 07 06 05 04 03

For Ursula

Contents

Preface

This is, yes, another commentary on St. Matthew's gospel, and like the others it is nothing more than a connected series of footnotes to the gospel text. But it is different from the others—different, indeed, from any biblical commentary known to its author. For one thing, its annotations are something of a mixed bag. They are not written from a denominational point of view, nor are they the work of a theologian, clergyman, or Bible scholar. Nor do they adhere to the historical-critical tradition that has shaped Bible scholarship for the past two hundred years. Instead, they reproduce what appear to be contemporary scholarship's majority interpretations (if interpretations so often questioned, debated, and revised can ever command a majority, much less a consensus), and they then expand their explications with a random sampling of materials from the reception of Matthew, that is, from the ways it has been read, understood, and applied over the last two millennia. Better: "some" of the ways, for few books have had this gospel's manifold influences, and any survey of its afterlife can only hope to be inclusive but not integral, illustrative but not exhaustive, selective but not systematic.

Behind this approach lies the persuasion that an essential way to understand—or experience—a text is to see it not only as a passive field for academic investigation but also as an active and creative force in the lives of individuals, in their religious communities, and in the events of history. One problem with scholarly inquiries into the Bible is that for all their sophistication and erudition they sometimes fail to convey the power of Scripture, the ways in which over the centuries people have been inspired, transformed, and in some cases mystified or even appalled by its hallowed words. So while other commentaries refer *back* to the text's composers, this one refers *forward* to its readers, since, as has been often observed, ideas have consequences, and the books that express them can exist as fully in the minds of their audiences as in the minds of their authors. Hence, it exploits that tension between what Matthew may have intended (as understood today) and the quite different, indeed often eccentric or bizarre ways his intentions have been received, assimilated, and sometimes manipulated over the centuries; it shows how the Christian denominations have adopted and adapted his words for their theologies and liturgies; it appeals to every reader's natural curiosity to know how other readers in other times have reacted to the first gospel; it testifies to the richness of Matthew's message, or perhaps to its ambiguities and elasticity; and it reminds us that many of our own "established" interpretations may seem equally odd or irrelevant to future readers of this influential text.

Furthermore, this commentary does not use as its source the best—i.e., the most accurate—of Bible texts and translations (currently the New Revised Standard Version), but that classic of English—or Tudor—translation, the King James Version, or KJV (commissioned in 1604, completed in 1611), also known as the "Authorized Version," though it was never officially authorized, only "appointed," or permitted, for use in English churches. The KJV was unheralded at its publication, unpopular in its early lifetime, and unoriginal, sometimes wrong, in its renderings; yet it has acquired a stature its composers could have hardly envisioned ("The Bible God uses and Satan hates"). It was based on few and defective manuscripts and has often been edited and amended, but it has been, for better or for worse, the Bible read by many of the figures cited here, and it is still the most familiar and available version today. And although more acceptable renderings will be noted here when the KJV is obscure or defective, in its obvious limitations the KJV remains a useful reminder of how approximate and provisional is any rendering of those distant Greek and Hebrew originals. It is another of the curiosities of this masterpiece that the first gospel was largely the work of William Tyndale (1494–1536), whose 1534 translation was only lightly revised by King James's appointees. The absence of Tyndale's name from its prefatory remarks is one of the great injustices of literary history, and since it is estimated that 84 percent of the New Testament is his, it is important to acknowledge his contribution to the creation of English prose.[1]

Finally, this work also differs from all other Bible commentaries in that it offers some—if not equal—space to those who have questioned, rejected, or even ridiculed Matthew's messages. In his Bible Sir Walter Scott wrote of such readers (lines Byron later copied): "And better had they ne'er been born, / Who read to doubt, or read to scorn." So this is not the part of the Bible's influence that comforts most believers (and Voltaire, Thomas Paine, and Robert Ingersoll are almost never mentioned in standard commentaries).[2] But Bible-bashing, like Bible-thumping, is a historically significant part of the experience of reading Scripture, and though its practitioners favor some of the same techniques—a narrow selection of texts, a calculated exclusion of alternative explanations, a numbing literalism, a willful disregard of context—that they deplore in their opponents, their comments have been widely influential and deserve to be recorded, especially since much of Christian orthodoxy was created in response to dissenters from the faith. So this approach necessarily entails many of the alleged misreadings of Matthew, and some of the following pages will mention interpretations, legends, and traditions that are discounted, disparaged, or dismissed by modern scholars—what Matthew Arnold, translating Goethe's *Aberglaube,* called "extra-belief."[3] The most egregious of these uses is, of course, the historical appropriation of the Hebrew Bible by Christians concerned to see in its sentiments, episodes, and personalities a foreshadowing of their own faith. The practice of typology (for so it is called) may often be arbitrary and anachronistic, but it is a large part of the historical record and should not be ignored. It is also important for understanding religious art, and visitors to museums and galleries as well as to European churches (the OT mosaics in Rome's Santa Maria Maggiore are a good example) will often see artworks and sculptural decorations that juxtapose scenes from the two Testaments. Another use of Scripture that dominates its reception is "proof-texting" (or, less charitably, "text-mongering"), the use of single verses, sometimes parts of verses, usually out of context, in an attempt to support, even establish, often conclusively, points of doctrine and morality. The proof texters' picking and choosing was calculated and tendentious, as will be evident as we follow Matthew through the centuries; and though this may not be a popular practice today, it is again a large part of the historical record and should not be ignored.

Here are some examples from that record. Many readers know that 16:18 ("Thou art Peter . . . I will build my church") is basic to Catholicism's claims for the papacy. But how many know that 9:2-7 is a foundation text for Christian Scientists? Or that Matthew, the only gospel to use the word *church*, is a central presence in Mormonism, and that "pearl of great price" (13:46) became the title of one of the Mormons' basic texts? Or that 5:34, forbidding oaths, was a fundamental provision of Quakerism? And that the "Harrowing of Hell" (27:52-53), found only in Matthew and often disregarded, has a special place in the art and spirituality of Eastern Orthodoxy? As for Judaism, in the late Middle Ages, a Jew called Shem-Tob created a Hebrew version of Matthew to assist his people in their disputes with Christians, who had for too long used another Matthean verse, the "Cry of the People" (27:25), to justify their anti-Semitism. Historically, 4:17 not only provided the opening salvo of the Reformation, but in the same verse the translation of just one of Matthew's words, as *repent,* ended for Protestants the century-old tradition of auricular confession as well as the sacramental status of penance. And ubiquitous in Reformation writings is their "Call of the Savior" (11:28-30), which seemed to sum up all they found wrong in Romanism—though Matthew's accounts of baptism and the Eucharist also accounted for bitter divisions among the Reformers. The meaning of Jesus' words on divorce and adultery is still debated (recall how 5:28, on lust in the heart, almost derailed Jimmy Carter's presidential campaign in 1976). And 5:39, which helped change Tolstoy's life, has become as much a staple of Christian pacifism as 10:34 is for the militants of liberation theology. The "Christian perfectionism" of 5:48 has inspired both monks and Methodists, and it lurks behind most Christian cults and heresies. In Western culture, Matthew gave the Christmas scene its eastern star, its wisemen, and its "Flight into Egypt"; an allusion to Matthew helped Hamlet to resolve his tragic dilemma; and the first gospel continues to infiltrate our books and films. The hell that is preached to us is largely Matthean, and in the gospel's final lines rests Scripture's only formulation of the Trinity while also establishing the basis for Christianity's missionary enterprises. Matthew is everywhere.

The following pages, then, will consist of a collage of secondary readings that testify to the constant vitality of Matthew, historically and culturally, in the lives of the Bible's readers. Their selection inevitably reflects the personal and professional orientation of their selector, who is a Roman Catholic and also a classicist, comparatist, and generalist; and its viewpoint is necessarily orthodox and conservative, if only better to highlight the variety of responses by those who redefined or rejected the traditions they had inherited. The consequence, then, is a miscellany of understandings and interpretations, and it is hoped that their sheer diversity and heterogeneity will dilute any, even unconscious, biases. The concern here is marginally postmodern, not to argue a thesis or establish some disembodied Truth, but to document historical meanings that reflect a variety of competing ideologies and subvert any complacent reading of Matthew as a master narrative of Christian orthodoxy. For it remains a fact that Scripture, so piously honored as master, has too often been employed as a servant in thrall to many an alien agenda. So we must often leave open the question of whether the Bible, and Matthew in particular, has directly enlightened and inspired or simply offered its readers an arsenal of proof texts to sanction ideas and positions conceived independently or inferentially.

This book is intended for the general reader, whose experience of the Bible today is usually fitful and fragmented, more likely to come from references and allusions in modern writers than from a systematic study in churches, synagogues, or schools. It is an endeavor to give in one volume, devoted to one gospel, some substance—if only randomly and superficially—to that hoariest of platitudes: that the Bible, "The Greatest Book Ever Written," has been the most influential book in Western civilization. And to its more restrictive corollary: that the King James Version has deeply influenced English writers. True enough, and here is one attempt to show how.

I cannot end these prefatory remarks without gratefully acknowledging my indebtedness to the office staff of the UCSB Department of Classics, Betty Koch, Anna Roberts, and, for her word processing skills, Liz Frech.

Introduction

> The Christian's Bible is a drug store. Its
> contents remain the same, but the
> medical practice changes.
> —Mark Twain

Scripture

The Bible is not a book, it is an anthology, a library, a literature—that is, a collection of books, and of books so different from one another in size and style and content that it might be compared to a newspaper, where we have quite different expectations of what and how we will be reading as we look at the headlines, the sports pages, the editorial cartoons, the classified ads, the society columns, the comics, and the straight news stories. Of course, the situation with the Bible is both simpler, since its books are more closely related than newspaper articles, and more complicated, since they are ancient works composed in unfamiliar languages and often alien in their references and opaque in their expressions. Furthermore, the books—originally scrolls—were not written all at one time, and so we cannot date their subjects as securely as we can the events described in a daily newspaper. And even if we could apply approximate dates to the Bible's various books, we would still have to make allowances for the times when the events in the books might have taken place; the times they were first reported; the times during which reports were passed along orally; the times when they were recorded in writing; the times during which the writings were copied and edited, combined and collated; and, for those reading the Bible in translation, the times when they were rendered into different languages, each with its own verbal peculiarities and syntactic conventions, prepared for publication, and, finally, printed. And since historical, cultural, and social circumstances change along with the times, readers have to assess how much these varying conditions might have influenced biblical writings at each stage in the process from the original event to the words on the pages they turn today.

Many readers will feel that since the characters and events of the Bible have had a special, indeed sacred, status in history, as the people and workings of God, theirs is a divinely inspired, revelational, and authoritative record (including those genealogies?)—one that was passed along with a special care and concern for accuracy, perhaps even enjoying a grace of preservation. Others will wonder to what extent human weakness and willfulness may have intruded into this process, and they will draw attention to those passages that seem incompatible or inconsistent, if not directly contradictory, or that appear to betray the divine revelation they are meant to record and proclaim. And although many readers will insist on the "truth" of the Bible, most will have to admit that its truths operate on different levels; are not uniformly cogent; and have been variously selected, understood, and applied over the centuries. Similarly, even the most orthodox or pious reader of Scripture, the most fervent believer in its "oracular authority," "plenary inspiration," and "verbal inerrancy," will also concede that its words, all of which have been translated, sometimes have to be taken "in context" or less than literally. Hence, the preference of some of the Bible's defenders to speak, not of its inerrancy, but of its infallibility, its trustworthiness, its credibility, and its authority, at least as far as its spiritual content is concerned.

But putting the Bible "in context" raises more questions than it answers. Since the Bible's composers, like everyone else, inhabited several contexts, which are relevant? And how large the context? Must each verse be seen and interpreted as part of its chapter, each chapter as part of its book, each book as part of the Bible, the Bible as part of the civilization of the ancient Near East, the ancient Near East as part of the Western world, with the significance of each passage modified by these successive frames and locations? Must readers constantly refer each sentiment in the Bible to its authorial, theological, literary, or historical settings? But how to distinguish among settings so diverse that they encompass most literary genres and more than a thousand years of history? What to make, for example, of first-century Judea with its multiple and overlapping contexts: Hebrew in religion, Aramaic in language, Greek in culture, Roman in administration, urban and rural, orthodox and sectarian, peaceful and hostile? And how do our own early twenty-first-century contexts affect our understanding of the Bible's contexts? But will all of this contextualizing not relativize Scripture by ascribing and reducing it to a variety of composer concerns and a succession of social settings, each with its special pressures? Or is Bible study something more than cultural anthropology? Are there some portions so eloquent, so inspiring, that they transcend, even annihilate, context, becoming genuinely representative of the whole, capturing the true spirit—whatever that is—of Scripture? Can these passages stand alone as timeless, exemplary, and autonomous manifestations of God's eternal truth ("The Bible teaches us that . . ."")? If so, which passages are they? And do they offer only incandescent moments of spiritual enlightenment, or can they also be stitched together as "proof texts" into a patchwork quilt of doctrines? Can, for example, the Sermon on the Mount be excerpted from Matthew's gospel and offered as "the charter of Christianity," or should it be regarded as a collection of Jesus' sayings that were probably never delivered at one time (hence the apparent inconsistencies)? And should it be read alone or in the light of the other gospels (in Luke's gospel, it seems to take place on a plain)? But even if readers concede that this Sermon was never actually delivered as a sermon, and that the Mount is a reference to Mt. Sinai in Exodus rather than to a physical feature of Galilean topography, do these concessions in any way detract from the significance, the importance, the truth of what Jesus preached? But how are readers to account for the divergent conclusions drawn from these words?

These are all troubling questions. Indeed, considerable ink—and even blood—has been spilt over them for hundreds of years, and it still remains the business of biblical scholars to sort them out and even presume to answer them. This they do in an annual flood of commentaries and books and articles that shows no sign of abating and that offers a dismaying prospect to any ordinary reader who consults them—which ones to choose?—in order to find out what is "really going on" in the Bible and how its contents should be understood. Today it is customary in a secular setting such as a public university to evade the "sacredness" of the Bible, its presence among us as what Coleridge aptly called a "believed book," and to claim that we are reading and interpreting it "as literature."[1] But the Bible, for all its human interest, narrative power, and rhetorical artistry, is not literature (if anything, it is closer to history or legislation), at least not in the ordinary sense of an imaginative work of art that we can attribute to a single author who was composing at a particular time in history; and it has traditionally made—and still makes—the kinds of "truth" claims on us that literature does not. That is, in invoking divine inspiration for its human compositions, it claims a residual authority and purports to tell us some ultimate and determinative truths about who made the world and why, how we should conduct our lives in the light of those truths, and what will happen to us if we fail to do so. This is how most people first come to know the stories of the Bible—for their doctrinal content and within the confines of church or synagogue worship. Readers may choose to question or qualify or even reject such claims, but they cannot deny that they are present in the Bible and have to be reckoned with.

Another sensitive area in Bible study and commentary is nomenclature, since names have ideological implications and can readily reveal prejudices and evoke passions. Should the Bible be seen as comprising the "Old Testament" and the "New Testament"? These are traditional and generally acceptable terms, in use since the second century (and will be retained here), though the English words suggest a last will or bequest that is unilateral, not a covenantal relationship between a loving ruler and His people; and Jews rightfully object to the implication that what is called "old"—their testament—has somehow been superseded by what is new. So they—and many others—now prefer "Hebrew Bible" and "Christian Bible," though some might understand the former to mean a Hebrew-language Bible (though some small parts are in Aramaic). A simple alternative is to call them "Scripture(s)," which suggests the writing down of words that were normally read aloud, though it conceals the fact that the major faiths have different selections and arrangements of books.

There is also the problem of BC ("Before Christ") and AD (*Anno Domini* or "In the Year of the Lord"), divisions introduced in the sixth century by a Scythian monk named Dionysius Exiguus. These are clearly Christian designations, even though they have been used so long that most people are not conscious of their sectarianism, so many modern writers have begun to use BCE ("Before the Common Era") and CE ("Common Era"). It is too soon to say if these religiously neutral abbreviations will be generally adopted (and the year numbers themselves still mark Christ's birth-date as the great turning-point of world history). So in these pages the traditional abbreviations will remain in use.

One other convention will be retained that has now almost disappeared: the capitalization of pronouns referring to the deity of the Old Testament. It is old and respected, like the KJV itself, and it can often contribute to the clarity of written comments. Finally, in an area like Bible studies, where little is certain, much is contested, and there is no shortage of reasonable alternatives, all dates are approximate, all opinions tentative, and all conclusions provisional; and those weasel words, "seems," "appears," "probably," "perhaps," and the like will run riot through the following pages.

Gospels

Christianity's earliest documents are St. Paul's, all composed around the middle of the first century, so it is with them that the Christian Bible should logically begin.[2] But it also makes a great deal of sense to begin with the stories of its founder's life and ministry, even though—or perhaps because—the four evangelists present us with four rather different pictures of Jesus Christ, pictures that are closer to artists' portraits than to photographers' snapshots. This should not be surprising, since subjects always present different appearances to different portraitists, and it is never easy for artists to separate interpretations from representations, impressions from realities. The same holds for literary artists, particularly when, as in the Gospels, the authors are also drawing on an oral tradition and trying to combine history, biography, and theology (Muslims separate "The Life of the Prophet" from their holy book, the Koran). In addition, the four evangelists had to deal with the problem of picturing someone who was for them both Jesus and the Christ, man and God, human and divine; and it appears likely that none of them knew Jesus personally during his ministry, and hence all had to rely on various kinds of sources. Also, each of them was writing forty to sixty years after Jesus' crucifixion and inevitably saw his life in multiple perspectives: first, through the climactic events of Passion Week; then through the ensuing generation of (largely unrecorded) reaction, discussion, and preaching; and finally in the light of current concerns, both their own and those for whom they were writing. And as Jesus' followers they were composing narratives designed to express their convictions about Jesus as Messiah and Savior, versions of Jewish ideas that they had to translate—and how much was lost or distorted?—into the language of Greek pagans.

A gospel, then, is history and biography as interpretive narrative, as apology, as faith-confession, even propaganda (in a positive sense); it is not neutral or impartial or disinterested, and the evidence it offers for its own authenticity is only probable at best. The story it tells, though generally chronological, is often fragmented, discontinuous, and episodic, reflecting the various incidents of Jesus' life and preaching as they were recalled by those who had known him during his ministry, passed along orally or preserved in various literary formats (which constitutes the "dominical tradition"), and finally recorded by the four evangelists in full conviction of the reality of the resurrection and the divinity of Jesus. Furthermore, it is a story told for those who were "second-generation" Christians in the evangelists' communities; hence, it is often deficient in background information, especially for the crucial period before the Romans' destruction of the Jerusalem temple in AD 70, or it fails to address issues of interest to readers in subsequent ages. But however inconsistent, implausible, or tendentious the narratives may seem, no one has ever produced any factual evidence to prove that what the evangelists report of Jesus' public life did not happen; and that creation of modern scholarship, the elusive "Jesus of history," though often advertised as the "real" Jesus, stepping out from behind the ecclesiastical facade of myth and dogma, too often turns out to be the Jesus of whatever revisionist feels tempted to reinterpret the gospels. Investigators concerned to establish the facts of Jesus' life find little straw for their bricks as they come up with "agreed results" or "critically assured minimums" that are meager and diverse. Their consensus is always being revised, and little is left of Jesus' story if controverted words and deeds are excised from the narrative. Hence the inevitability of expansion, speculation, and interpretation—and all too often, a weakness for remotely plausible alternatives and fashionable revisions. In the end, readers can only say about the events of Jesus' life what has been said about his miracles: they are easy to deny, hard to disprove.

Of the four gospels, Mark's is the earliest and briefest, and if we can trust the tradition that he knew Peter, his is the most "apostolic" of the gospels. He presents Jesus as a man in a hurry, with event following event in rapid succession. Nothing is said of his birth or childhood, and his ministry is a vivid narrative of busy activity and crowded scenes (words for "crowd" appear more than forty times), with his divine sonship only reluctantly revealed until it has been verified by his resurrection from the dead. Matthew's Jesus is a teacher, preacher, and lawgiver in the tradition of Moses, whose career offers precedents for episodes in Jesus' own life, particularly his infancy and his Sermon on the Mount. But Matthew goes on to present Jesus also as the fulfillment of Israel's messianic hopes, which seems to have been a significant issue for his own community. Many contemporary readers find Luke's portrait of Jesus has the most universal appeal of the four. Not only is it well written and supplemented by the Acts of the Apostles, but it shows a Jesus responding compassionately to the marginal figures of his time such as women, lepers, and the poor. The Jesus of John's gospel, written toward the end of the first century, is, by contrast, a remoter figure, more at one with his Father in heaven than with the crowds on earth. It is up to each reader, then, to decide how—or if—these four approaches to the Jesus of history and the Christ of faith cohere in a unified, convincing, and even inspiring impression. Or, as Matthew (22:42) puts it: "What think ye of Christ?"

For some the Gospels are, ultimately, the products of divine inspiration (variously understood); for others, of human invention with all its failings. But for both there is the problem of disagreements, inconsistencies, and contradictions among the four authors; and Muslims later made much of these variations in both Testaments, arguing that similar—and calculated—alterations had been made to eliminate references to Muhammad. In a relentlessly modern Protestant church called "The People's Liberal," in Peter DeVries' novel *The Mackerel Plaza* (1958), the "first split-level church in America," there is a "worship area" with a pulpit consisting of "a slab of marble set on four legs of four delicately differing fruitwoods, to symbolize the four Gospels and their failure to harmonize."[3] The same situation was faced early on, and Origen (185–254) characterized the discrepancies as "different sounds" from "one saving voice," while St. John Chrysostom (347–407) made them a powerful argument for gospel veracity: "For if they had agreed in all things, exactly even to times, and place, and to the very words, none of our enemies would have believed but that they had met together, and had written what they wrote by some human compact."[4] Or as William Paley (1743–1805) put it, the Gospels have enough variety "as to repel all suspicion of confederacy," and enough agreement "as to show that the accounts had one real transaction for their common foundation."[5] And in his classic defense of Christianity, *The Analogy of Religion* (1736), Joseph Butler (1692–1752) pointed out that nature, God's other great book, exhibited similar disharmonies.[6] Hence, the difficulties in the narratives became signs of their authenticity, evidence that there had been no concerted effort to concoct a story too good to be true. This is not a very compelling argument, but it allows disagreements as well as agreements to confirm the reliability of the Gospels.

But why should there be precisely four portraits of Jesus? There were others circulating in the early church that are now grouped among the NT "pseudepigrapha," such as the *Gospel of Peter,* and the *Infancy Gospel of Thomas,* and the *Protevangelium of James,* sometimes called "secret," "lost," or "hidden" gospels.[7] They are secondary compositions, but they once filled more pages than do the canonical texts, they contain popular and devotional materials (along with various anomalies), and they have led a kind of half-life in the shadow of the canonical writings. Most are obviously late and derivative, though they may still reflect early and aberrant traditions, and they continue to intrigue those readers who like to imagine that they may contain startling and subversive revelations about Jesus that the ecclesiastical establishments want to conceal (in this melodrama the Vatican is usually the villain). They do not.

Finally, in the second century a writer named Tatian harmonized the four into one continuous narrative called the *Diatessaron* ("Through the Four [Gospels]"), based largely on Matthew and now surviving only in quotations, though it was very popular, often translated, and long used in Syriac-speaking churches. But there still seems a special rightness in the standard four portraits, and Irenaeus (140–202), an early bishop of Lyons, found an appropriate, if fanciful, universality in their number: "The Gospels could not possibly be either more or less in number than they are. Since there are four zones of the world in which we live, and four principal winds, while the Church is spread over all the earth . . . it fittingly has four pillars."[8] The Gospels are often associated with four of the church's earliest centers: Rome (Mark), Antioch (Matthew), Athens (Luke), and Ephesus (John), their authors thought to be "apostles" and hence reliable witnesses to the faith. Or they can be matched with the four elements: air for Luke, the longest of the gospels; earth for Matthew with the incarnation implied in his infancy narrative; fire for John, the most spiritual of the four; and water for Mark, which begins with Jesus' baptism. Or they are identified with the four living creatures of Ezra 1:10 and Revelation 4:6-7, each the highest in its own area: man with Matthew because he begins his gospel with Jesus' human genealogy; the lion with Mark because he begins with the roaring voice of St. John the Baptist; the (sacrificial) ox with Luke because he begins with St. John's father, the priest Zacharias; and the eagle with John because he begins with the soaring quality of the Word. Or they represent the four covenants: with Adam, Noah, Moses, and Jesus; or the four Major Prophets of the Old Testament: Isaiah, Jeremiah, Ezekiel, and Daniel.

Even though their story is told in four versions, which were first collected and given their traditional ascriptions in the second century (the earliest complete NT manuscripts date from the fourth century), the evangelists, writing in Greek, could provide only a biographical introduction to the faith that Jesus founded, the essentials (in their view) of a ministry that was to become a religion. And since they were in part adapting the tradition to their own circumstances, telling their audiences what they wanted them to know, they often fail to tell us modern readers what we would like to know. Hence, it was left to the Greek and Latin fathers in Christianity's early centuries not only to propagate his teachings in other languages but also to describe, define, and systematize them and then to defend them against dissident voices in their own ranks as well as against spokesmen for the powerfully competing systems of Judaism and paganism. They had to create a "Christology," that is, show how Jesus could be both God and man, and that he was indeed the messiah that seemed foretold in at least some OT texts and awaited by at least some Jews. They had to create a "soteriology," that is, an account of his earthly life in terms that would make of him not just a teacher and prophet but the Redeemer of mankind (however "redemption" might be understood), bodily resurrected from the dead and ascended into heaven. They had to create a Trinity, that is, reconcile their traditional insistence on God's unity with the evangelists' scattered references to a triad of divine powers. They had to create some sort of organization, both temporal and spiritual, that would faithfully continue the work of their Master and that could survive in a Mediterranean world that still acknowledged the gods of Mt. Olympus and officially worshiped the emperors of Rome. They had to create a system of sacraments that would liturgically witness to God's continuing presence in their churches and would serve worshipers as conduits of His graces. And since Jesus had not returned after the resurrection and the world had not ended or even changed, they had to establish the kingdom of God both as a spiritual reality in the hearts of the faithful, attainable through repentance and belief, and as a hope for the future, whether it be near or far, in this world or the next. And all of this had to be done on the basis of Jesus' words, often inconsistent and enigmatic, and his actions, often unreliably witnessed and imperfectly recorded, which were then passed on in languages he did not speak. They were given directions; they had to create a road map.

Matthew

Voltaire aptly called Matthew "the most circumstantial Gospel that we possess."[9] It is also the best known of the canonical four, so comprehensive in scope that it is called, paradoxically, both "the church's gospel" and "the Jewish gospel," and so influential—if not always popular—that it must count as one of the most important books in world history. It is also a book of proverbs, both memorable and quotable, even in translation; and when we think of our unappreciated favors as "pearls before swine," or separate the "sheep from the goats," or praise someone as the "salt of the earth," or burn the midnight oil, or brand a hypocrite as a "Pharisee," or wait until the "eleventh hour," or beware of wolves "in sheep's clothing," or hope to be one of "the chosen few," or note the "signs of the times," or complain of "the blind leading the blind," or point out that someone's left hand doesn't know what his right hand is doing, or keep to the "straight (better: strait) and narrow," or warn that those who live by the sword will die by the sword, or regret that "the spirit is willing, but the flesh is weak," or "wash our hands" of something we are dismissing, or just "make light" of it, or are willing to go that extra mile, then we are quoting Matthew. It is from his Gospel, not Luke's, that we take our familiar versions of the Beatitudes and the Lord's Prayer. And even when words or sentiments are quoted that the Synoptics share in common, it is often assumed—as will happen in the following pages—that Matthew, the "teaching gospel," is the primary source. In fact, it is probably not an exaggeration to say that despite an undistinguished Greek style, words from Matthew have been pronounced, prayed, and intoned more often than those of any author we know; and when we hear "the Bible says," we will hear more often from Matthew than from any other book of Scripture. This kind of eminence was confirmed by Matthew's having the first place among the *NT*'s writings, the only Synoptic attributed to an Apostle. Long thought to have been the first written, it lost that distinction to Mark in the late nineteenth century; and even though Mark's current priority may seem to imply superiority, Matthew still retains its authority and prestige as the canonical exposition of Jesus' teachings and an early record of a community being formed on the basis of those teachings. He stands with John and Paul as one of the three great creators of a Christian identity, and, like theirs, his message has not always been welcomed.[10]

Matthew's gospel divides into three or four parts: the introduction of Jesus by way of his genealogy, birth, baptism, and temptation in the desert (1–4, though perhaps the infancy narrative, 1–2, should be separate); his public ministry in and around Galilee (5–16:20); and the last days in Jerusalem, with his passion, death, and resurrection (16:21–28:20). But at the heart of Matthew are the discourses of Jesus, which alternate with narrative sections and can be roughly divided into five groups (sometimes seen as corresponding to the Pentateuch, the first five books of the OT): the Sermon on the Mount (ethical), 5–7; the Mission Charge (apostolic), 10; the Kingdom of God Parables (kerygmatic, or revelational), 13; Community Discipline (ecclesiastical), 18; and the Second Coming (eschatological), 24–25. Each ends with a similar "completion" formula: "When Jesus had finished. . . ."

The gospel's author is unknown, although its status has always benefited from its attribution to the Apostle Matthew (called "Levi" in Mark 2:14), the tax collector of 9:9. But this attribution seems improbable since the author never adverts to his being an eyewitness of his gospel's events (nor does he ever indicate an eyewitness source), and it would leave unexplained his apparent dependence on Mark, who was not an apostle. Still, it is convenient to use

"Matthew" to designate both its composer and its contents, just as "Homer" is both an unknown author and also shorthand for what goes on in the *Iliad* and the *Odyssey*. Some conclude from his knowledge of Judaism that he was a converted Pharisee or rabbi, and he may resemble the good scribe of 13:52, a Jewish official but now "instructed unto the kingdom of heaven."

As for his sources, most commentators now accept the "Two-Source Hypothesis": that in addition to some 210 verses of his own material ("special Matthew"), the author-editor used Mark as a basis and narrative outline, retaining over 90 percent of its verses, and that an analysis of what was retained, omitted, revised, or added can often reveal the contours of his own (and sometimes inconsistent) theology. He also used another source, whether oral or written, now called *Q* (from the German word *Quelle*, "source") or the "Sayings Source," in Aramaic or Greek. First proposed in 1838, it was thought to be composed mostly of the sayings of Jesus. Dating from the 50s, it is a document that does not exist but has had to be invented to explain the materials— about two hundred verses—shared, often verbatim, by Matthew and Luke that are not in Mark, though there is also the possibility that Luke took these verses not directly from *Q* but from Matthew. And to thicken the mix, there is the remoter possibility that the Apostle Matthew may have been the original source of a document that underwent considerable editing and expanding before reaching its present form toward the end of the first century, that at one early stage there was an Aramaic Matthew, and that Mark is a later and abridged version of that ur-Matthew.

As for the date of Matthew, if the destroyed city mentioned in a parable at 22:7 looks back to the destruction of Jerusalem in AD 70, then the gospel we read today may have been composed around 85, perhaps in a town in Galilee, where it has Jesus spend almost all his time, or more likely in Antioch, capital of the Roman province of Syria, the city where Jesus' disciples were first called Christians (Acts 11:26). Matthew is first cited by Ignatius, Bishop of Antioch, in the second century; Syria is mentioned in 4:24; and the prominence the gospel gives to Peter may reflect his importance in the Antioch church, where one tradition made him a bishop before his removal to Rome. Composed in *koine* ("common") Greek, the lingua franca of Rome's Eastern empire, its intended audience seems to have been an urban community of Greek-speaking Jewish converts living in an environment of sectarian tension as they sought to position themselves as a separate and competing faction within the new world of synagogue Judaism.

The Romans had forced this new world into being in 70 by their destruction of the temple in the course of crushing the first Jewish revolt. As a consequence the Jews, once more dispersed in exile, had to reestablish their faith around their local synagogues and under the immediate leadership of the scribes and the Pharisees. The position of Jewish Christians within these synagogues must have become exceedingly difficult if not impossible, especially after the rabbis reformulated for the synagogue liturgy a prayer, the "Twelfth Benediction," that in some versions apparently included Christians among the heretics it cursed. Thus, in this gospel Matthew sought to define their situation as followers of Jesus by giving them an account of his life and teachings from birth to resurrection and also by locating their crucified leader within the Jewish tradition as the culmination of Israel's history and the fulfillment of her messianic hopes. His story is of Jesus' rejection, but although he can portray a Jesus harshly critical of Jewish officialdom, particularly the Pharisees (the Reformers would later find the virulence of chapter 23 useful in their attacks on the Catholic hierarchy), Matthew's references remain largely Jewish. By stressing the continuing authority of the Mosaic law, he warns his followers not to regard their new faith as a reason to scandalize other Jews: they should still pay their temple tax (17:24), honor the Sabbath (24:20), and heed the "scribes and the Pharisees" (23:2-3). But he also wants to amplify and extend their national tradition, showing Jesus both as a second Moses and as the Messiah, the son of David, and, especially, the "fulfillment" of OT prophecies (his sources are various, often from a version of the Septuagint, the third-century translation of the Old Testament into Greek, and his citations are mostly from the Prophets), a point he deliberately makes some eleven times, mostly in the beginning and middle of his gospel. This enables him to see in certain NT events the completion or validation of events from the Old Testament, an important consideration for his Jewish-Christian audience; and for many Christians prophecies have more evidential power than reports of miracles, since their fulfillment can be demonstrated. Some have even argued that Matthew deliberately chose incidents that would illustrate key OT texts, but it seems more likely that he added these references to the narrative, choosing some himself and taking others that were current among Jewish Christians and may well have been invoked by Jesus himself. John Updike has noted that it is Matthew "who handles Christian belief's awkward lumber—the threats of hellfire and outer darkness and the, to a modern reader, irksome insistence upon Christ's life as a detailed fulfillment of Old Testament prophecies."[11]

Since it is a fact of history that a church is emerging from the synagogue, Matthew's Jesus must create a "Christianity," warning the Jews that "The kingdom of God shall be taken from you, and given to a nation bringing forth the fruits thereof" (21:43). So what Jesus tells his disciples is often what Matthew wants to tell his community fifty years later: that they are to do the will of God, a commitment that might be summed up by what he repeatedly calls "righteousness," a word not found in Mark. Matthew's sense of community is strong (he is the only evangelist to mention a "church"), so its members must also learn how to treat one another and how to defend against false disciples in their own ranks (ch. 18). But that is not all, for their Jewish sect is about to become a universal religion, "catholic" in its literal sense. So eventually they must turn to the Gentile world, and as they pursue their missionary work they must define and defend their beliefs, all of this as they look forward to an end time and a second coming that seem forever delayed. Hence, Matthew finds himself at a divide of worlds, between a Judaism that is in transition and a Christianity that is still in its beginnings, between a law that is absolute and a law that will be superseded, between a righteousness that is external and one that is internal, between a salvation that is merited by good works and one dependent on faith, between a faith that is monotheistic and a leader who is the Son of God, between a community that is Jewish and an empire that is Roman. Thus, his gospel is inclusive, catholic, embracing both the contrarieties of human experience and the paradoxes of a faith in which God became man and the Prince of Glory died a criminal's death. Matthew witnesses all the contrasts, tensions, inconsistencies, and even contradictions that heterogeneity entails as it not only looks back to Israel and the Old Testament for its validation, but will also look forward in its final lines to "all nations" of the world.

THE

GOSPEL

OF

Matthew

AND

ITS

READERS

1

The Infancy Narrative

The first part of the infancy narrative is a presentation of Jesus' "family tree." Then at 1:18 the genealogy becomes narrative as Matthew describes Jesus' miraculous birth. Chapter 2 tells of the "troubled" Herod and the visit of the magi, followed by an angel's advice in a dream to Joseph that the family take flight into Egypt. A second such dream, again to Joseph, takes them back to Judea, where Herod's son Archelaus is ruling; and a third warns them to go to Nazareth in Galilee, where Jesus will spend his youth and young manhood, of which nothing is reported.

Tell all the truth but tell it slant.
—Emily Dickinson

The Christian Bible begins with Matthew's version of Genesis, as if he were commencing a new version of Scripture and a new era in human history. Like Luke, he includes a genealogy and an infancy narrative, and although the two evangelists differ in their choice of forebears and events (they do seem to agree on the dual sonship of Jesus and his virgin birth), they both want to satisfy converts' understandable curiosity regarding Jesus' background, both personal and familial. They also want to demonstrate that his status as the long-awaited Messiah—and, indeed, as the Son of God—was assured at and before his birth, not conferred at some point in his ministry or acquired after his death (since Paul's Epistles might give the impression that it was his death, crucifixion, resurrection, and ascension that alone confirmed Jesus' divinity).

Matthew's genealogy cannot be harmonized with Luke's, and for those rationalists, ancient and modern, who regarded contradiction as the unforgivable sin, the Gospels lost their credibility in the first lines of Matthew. Today they are generally accepted as theological constructs, with some characterizing Matthew's genealogy as "royal" (mentioning Solomon) and Luke's as "priestly" (mentioning Levi). What other information the first Christians had on the early Jesus and his forebears was undoubtedly fragmented and anecdotal, read back into his obscure beginnings from the known events of his later ministry and buttressed by "predictive" testimonies from the Old Testament. All of this Matthew uses, with the result that his gospel acquires a structural symmetry, not only balancing Jesus' birth and death but also employing certain motifs —even words—associated with the nativity that will recur during his passion, as at both points of his life Jesus must confront the local Jewish and Roman leaders.

There are difficulties in assessing the sources and the historical validity of these two infancy stories, since there could have been few eyewitnesses to their events, and certainly not the gospel composers or the apostles before them. There was a Christian tradition that made Joseph the source for Matthew, Mary for Luke; and there were precedents in antiquity for ascribing wondrous qualities to the births and childhood activities of great figures. So all is not lost, and the Bible's readers should remember that only significant events generate legends and that legendary traditions, particularly those as moving as the Christmas stories, can often provide as much material for theological and spiritual reflection as the spare facts of history. Thus, Matthew prefaces his infancy narrative (most of which the KJV translators took directly from Tyndale) with a genealogical outline of Israel's legendary history. Unlike Luke, he begins with "begats"—thirty-nine of them. By commencing Jesus' lineage with Abraham and David, father and king, Matthew emphasizes his historical position, Jewish identity, and royal descent, even though the bloodline comes through Joseph, who was not really Jesus' father (hence the switch to Mary at v. 16).

Since an orderly and prestigious lineage mattered deeply to the inherited monarchies of medieval rulers, Matthew's "Tree of Jesse," David's father, was reproduced in illuminated manuscripts and in the stained glass "Jesse" windows of Gothic cathedrals, notably the great western front window of Chartres (1145). The proof text was Isaiah 11:1: "And there shall come forth a rod out of the stem of Jesse, and a Branch shall grow out of his roots," recalled in the fourth stanza of the popular Christmas carol "O Come, O Come, Emmanuel!" Illustrations generally showed a tree growing out of Jesse's loins, with Matthew's figures pictured among its branches and Christ at its crown. It helped too that the Latin Vulgate's word for "rod," *virga*, so closely resembled *virgo*, "virgin," though Protestants have preferred to see the "rod" as Jesse himself. Hence, these figures are also represented among the antecedents of Jesus in the decorative statuary of Gothic cathedrals, notably at Chartres, Reims, and Amiens.

Matthew also likes triads, so his lineage presents three groups of fourteen generations each (and in Hebrew number lore, the value of the three consonants in "David" is fourteen). The first is from Abraham to David, the second from Solomon to the Babylonian deportations of the sixth century, and the third (actually with only thirteen generations) ending with verse 17 and the birth of Jesus, here given the messianic title "the Christ." Since this is also the beginning of what would be a fourth group, it suggests that at this point a significant event is occurring, that this is in fact both the climax of Jewish history and a new beginning.

On the first page of the first Bible translation printed in English (1525), Tyndale glossed the genealogy: "Saynct mathew leveth out certeyne generacions," an acknowledgement that these verses may be of Matthew's devising, freely and selectively adapted from 1 Chronicles 2–3 and contrasting with Luke's genealogy (3:23-38), which traces Jesus beyond Abraham to Adam himself.[1] On the female side the unnamed Bathsheba, married to the Hittite Uriah, joins Tamar, Rahab, and Ruth as somewhat notorious women. The reason for their presence is unclear (where are Sarah, Rebekah, Rachel?), but they were also quasi-foreigners, an early indication of the inclusiveness of Jesus' ministry; and the fact that they had unusual marital relationships also foreshadows the union of Mary and Joseph. Matthew's figures were represented in the now-fragmentary mosaics (13th century) on the south wall of Bethlehem's Church of the Nativity; and today visitors to the Sistine Chapel in Rome can see Michelangelo's versions of the genealogy's figures, now colorfully restored, in lunettes above the windows along the upper walls, their names on tablets at the peak of each lunette. Just as the genealogy establishes a past continuity for Jesus, its counterpart at the end of the gospel, the Great Commission of chapter 28, offers the future prospect of a continuing community. Thus, Matthew's view of salvation history is both transitional and universal, moving from Abraham to the Gentiles, and from Israel to "all nations" (28:19).

But why was Jesus born at this particular juncture? Some early Christians looked to the six days of Creation (Gen. 2:2) and to Psalm 90:4 ("For a thousand years in thy sight are but as yesterday") to estimate that the world would last six thousand years, which might make Jesus' death part of the beginning of the end time. This dread event is eloquently foretold by John the Baptist at 3:2, and chapter 27 recounts the three hours of darkness, the rending of the temple veil, the opening of graves, and the resurrection of the dead, all phenomena associated with the last days. For the first Christians, a preoccupation with the world's ending—or at least with a violent change in their own situation—is understandable, since throughout history there seems to be a persistent obsession among groups that are small, marginalized, and persecuted that soon they will experience a general cataclysm in which their troubles will end, their foes will be routed, and they will be gloriously vindicated. So it must have appeared to some of his followers that Jesus' birth was ordained to usher in history's grand climax and that he would return soon after his resurrection. But it did not happen, and with the delay of the Parousia (Greek for "presence," the technical term for Jesus' second coming) much of the scriptural record had to be spiritualized, and end time events had to be allegorized as referring to aspects of Jesus' ministry or legacy, not to the end of the space-time universe. There is some evidence that Christians were disappointed by their baffled expectations, but they seemed to feel little need to revise or reject those verses in the Gospels—and there are many—that appeared to foretell an imminent Parousia. Even today the most notorious example of apocalyptic writing, Revelation, continues to intrigue and inspire the Bible's readers.

The forty-two generations of Matthew's genealogy also equal six "sevens" or weeks, which again recalls the days of Creation, though fanciful interpretations saw the three groups as replicating the waxing, waning, and waxing of the moon or as foreshadowing the Trinity; and the fourteen generations as equaling the Ten Commandments plus the four gospels. It may be hard to imagine that such fancies could contribute to a philosophy of history, but the fact that each generation lasted thirty years helped a Cistercian monk and visionary named Joachim of Fiore (1135–1202) decide that in the thirteenth century the "Age of Christ" would end and yield to the "Age of the Holy Spirit." He had devised a historical scenario, based on the Trinity, that was optimistic, even utopian, whereby a Gospel of the Holy Spirit was about to succeed the Gospel of the Father or the Law (OT) and the Gospel of the Son or Grace (NT). Hence, he moved beyond Matthew's method of using the Old Testament as predictive of the New Testament to see both as predictive of future history, with the Christology of the New Testament to be followed by the "pneumatology" of the Holy Spirit, as human history divided into three successive—and progressive—stages in a scheme that expanded the familiar sequence of Old and New Testaments. These stages were symbolized by the family (the Father's creation of Adam and Eve), the clergy (the Son's creation of the church and the priesthood), and the recently founded monastic orders (the Holy Spirit empowering the monks). Hence, the laws of the Old Testament and the faith of the New Testament would evolve—after the appearance and defeat of the antichrist, who would end the second age—into a third age of general joy, freedom, and love so spiritually enlightened, so morally perfected, that it would have no need of a church with its hierarchy, sacraments, and all-too-worldly institutions.

Joachim was always respected as a faithful Catholic, and Dante put him in his *Paradiso* (13.140) as a prophet. But his revolutionary theories, revived after his death and sometimes called the "Everlasting Gospel" (Rev. 14:6), of how the Trinity provided a pattern for history, were condemned by the Fourth Lateran Council in 1215 and by Pope Alexander IV in 1256. Still, the notion of ushering in the "Age of the Spirit" in direct communion with the Holy Spirit has been an unfailing inspiration for religious visionaries, reformers—and, yes, crackpots. Joachim has had other descendants in those ideologues who have seen in the modern world a "third" period that would in effect put an end to history (Communism, that would succeed feudalism and capitalism; even Hitler's Third Reich).[2]

The real beginning of the first gospel is at 1:16-18, and *Christi . . . generatio* ("birth of Christ") at verse 18 provided one of the most elaborately illuminated pages (the "*Chi-rho* page") in the magnificent Book of Kells (800; now in the Trinity College Library, Dublin), with *CHRI* in ornately stylized Greek letters. When the "begats" stop, Matthew turns to Mary, who, we are told, "was found with child of the Holy Ghost." Again, the life-giving action of the Holy Spirit recalls the activity of the "Spirit of God" in Genesis 1:2: a new world is beginning. (Unfortunately, the shift in the popular meaning of *ghost* from "life" and "spirit" to a sort of ectoplasmic spook undermined its seriousness, and the substitution of Holy Spirit for Holy Ghost was the most striking change in the Revised Standard Version of 1881–85 and the American Standard Version of 1901.)

Matthew sees Joseph as Jesus' adoptive father, though he is never called "father." One Jewish story had Jesus fathered by a Roman soldier called Panthera, a common name and oddly close to the Greek *parthenos,* "virgin." It appears in the Hebrew legal commentary, the Talmud, and it was earlier invoked by Celsus, a second-century Platonist who was one of Christianity's earliest critics (1.32). Since it diluted Jesus' Jewishness, it was revived by those German Nazis who claimed to be Christians.[3] Luke 3:23, another proof text for the virgin birth, refers to Jesus as the "supposed" son of Joseph; and Mark 6:3 omits Joseph entirely and calls Jesus only "the son of Mary." But Mark's gospel might have had, and lost, an infancy narrative of its own.

The KJV's "virgin" (23) is a direct translation of the Greek *parthenos* that Matthew found in the Isaiah (7:14) of the Septuagint, a third-century Greek translation of the Hebrew Bible. It is more specific than the Hebrew "young woman" and is paralleled by Luke 2:7 ("And she brought forth her first-born son"). In a second-century "debate" between the Latin father Justin Martyr (100–65) and his opponent, a Jew he called Trypho, the latter charged Christians with a deliberate mistranslation—and the meaning of this word is still a sensitive issue for NT commentators.[4] Though it is nowhere mentioned apart from the two infancy narratives, Jesus' virgin birth, as specified in 1:23-25, has always been a Christian tradition, presumably originating from Mary herself. It was enshrined in the Apostles' Creed, established as dogma at the Councils of Ephesus (431) and Chalcedon (451), and accepted by Luther, Calvin, and Zwingli. (Actually, it should more accurately be called "virginal conception," since virgin birth refers to Jesus' emergence from Mary's closed womb and nothing is said of her subsequent virginity.)

In the cited passage, Isaiah, who had no developed conception of a royal messiah, seems to have been explicitly referring to a son of the Judean King Ahaz (ca. 735–15), not to his mother, so Matthew's allusion must be taken as a controversial "secondary interpretation," "creative misreading," or with Butler's *Analogy*, a "further completion."[5] Here, as often, he is less interested in the quotation's original context than in its applicability to the present circumstance, and as usual, he assumes that OT prophecies are really predictions. There is no evidence that the Jews expected that a virgin would bear their messiah, and the "till" of verse 25 has been at the basis of a long—and probably unresolvable—controversy regarding Mary's virginity. Was it perpetual (traditionally the Catholic position and accepted by Luther and John Wesley), or did Joseph subsequently resume relations with Mary? Some copyists, concerned to preserve the orthodox position, omitted "her firstborn" from their manuscripts.

→   The doctrines of Jesus' virginal conception and birth have often been dismissed as "mythical," but although Greek mythology has examples of strange but divine impregnations (Danaë by Zeus in a shower of gold, Leda by Zeus disguised as a swan, Alcmena by Zeus impersonating her husband) and unusual births (Dionysus from Zeus's thigh, Athena from his head), all the women had sexual relations of a sort, and their stories were not important for their children's subsequent careers. Although it was reported that Apollo was Plato's father and that Alexander the Great was conceived before his parents consummated their marriage, these Hellenistic tales were not part of Matthew's culture, and it is hard to imagine that first-century Christians, whether Jewish or Gentile, would adapt minor pagan legends to the birth of Jesus. But the existence of these legendary parallels has also been seen, paradoxically, as an argument for the authenticity of the virgin birth. For according to a unique sort of plagiarism, Greek thought, both mythical and philosophical, was originally derived from Moses, who while he was in Egypt, may somehow have happened to meet Homer. Or else Plato on his visit to Egypt in the fourth century found a copy of the Pentateuch, the first five books of the Old Testament. For the apologist Justin Martyr, the pagan mythmakers were led astray by demons, and "hearing what was said by the prophets they did not necessarily understand it."[6] Thus, Orpheus, the mythic musician who enchanted forests and animals and brought Eurydice back from the dead, prefigures Jesus, who "alone has tamed man, the most intractable of animals" and the music of whose words revives souls deadened by sin.[7] In addition there was the "Egyptian gold" argument, based on Exodus 12:35, recounting how the escaping Israelites took gold and silver vessels from the Egyptians, and interpreted as also justifying the taking of pagan wisdom from the Greek and Roman classics.[8] Hence, there are two scriptures in God's unified revelation, the supernatural revealed to the Hebrew people and a second indirectly revealed to pagans, a useful if less exalted version and one that brought them to Christ as surely as the law did for Jews. They often garbled and misunderstood what they had been given, but at their best they enjoyed a preview of Christian truth, and their myths of wondrous impregnations were God's way of preparing the world for the greater mystery of the virgin birth.

So Jesus' virgin birth became the miraculous event at the beginning of his life, one that has its counterpart in the miraculous resurrection at the end. In Christian art, it is sometimes symbolized by a window in Mary's room, representing the image of Jesus emerging from her womb like light through a glass. Another image likened the baby's birth to the shedding of rays from the sun; another, recalling the words spoken by the angel in Luke 1:28-33 (the "Annunciation"), saw Jesus conceived through Mary's ear. But the American patriot Thomas Paine (1737–1809), who was a deist (believing that after God created the world, He took no further part in its workings) and an eloquent and influential critic of biblical Christianity, preferred to sneer, "What is it the Testament teaches us?—to believe that the Almighty committed debauchery with a woman engaged to be married: and the belief of this debauchery is called faith."[9]

Although there is no OT episode prefiguring Joseph's situation, he does have a counterpart in the Joseph whose story ends Genesis, and like him he goes into Egypt, provides an example of chastity under pressure, and is similarly receptive to cautionary dreams, a narrative device found only in Matthew. He is also a kind of Moses, who was ordered by the Lord at Exodus 4:19 to take his wife and sons to Egypt. But since he was neither martyr nor saint and says not a word in the Gospels, he was given little attention by the church fathers, and John Chrysostom took the absence of "to you" after "bring forth a son" (21) as a proof text that Jesus was not Joseph's natural son.[10] His anomalous position—he will quickly disappear from the gospel story, perhaps through an early death—has led to the inevitable (and anachronistic) speculations. Here he is a "just" man (1:19; a term Matthew likes), but the apocryphal gospels *Protevangelium of James* (8–13), from the second century, and *Pseudo-Matthew* (10–11), from the eighth or ninth century, were the basis for the tradition of the "Doubting" or "Troubled" Joseph, the aged cuckold who appears as an almost comic or pitiable character in the medieval English mystery plays ("I am beguiled—how, wot I not, / My young wife is with child full great").[11] However, it is to Joseph's credit in Matthew that he is so impressed by Mary's goodness that he does not want her pregnancy to expose her to public humiliation and punishment. He is usually pictured in art as an older man—according to the apocryphal tradition he was a widower—sometimes with a crutch suggesting advanced years or even impotence; and a body of legends grew up around him. The influential *Golden Legend*, a thirteenth-century collection of saints' lives and legends by an Italian Dominican, Jacobus de Voragine (1229–98), popularized the tradition that he was chosen as Mary's spouse after a heavenly voice had ordered suitable candidates to "bring a branch to the altar." Because Joseph's branch sprouted a flower and a dove alighted on it, typologists connected this branch with the "rod" that came "out of the stem of Jesse" in one of Christianity's favorite Messianic passages (Isa.11:1).[12] In his great painting *The Marriage of the Virgin* (1504, Milan), Raphael gave prominence to a young suitor so disappointed that his rod did not flower that he is shown breaking it over his knee. Eventually Joseph was canonized, and devotion to St. Joseph was revived in the sixteenth century. In 1624 he was named patron saint of Canada (rising above the slopes of Mount Royal in Montreal is an impressive church dedicated to him); and in 1870 Pope Pius IX, honoring Joseph as the protector of Jesus and Mary, declared him "Patron of the Universal Church." His feast days are March 29 (the day the swallows traditionally return to Capistrano) and May 1 ("St. Joseph the Worker").

Before Jesus is born an angel appears to Joseph in a dream and announces that his name will be Jesus (1:20-21). *Nomen est omen,* and Christians saw in his name and titles indications of his nature and purpose. Like Joseph and John, Jesus was a fairly common name. In the Septuagint it is the rendering of "Yeshua," as he was called in his lifetime, or "Joshua" ("Yahweh helps," later understood as "Yahweh saves"). Matthew added "from their sins" from Psalm 30:8, and although here he does not say how this will be effected, the words "unto remission of sins" will recur at the Last Supper (26:28) and will play a crucial role in Christian theology. *Christos,* Greek for "anointed," was added to render "Messiah," first as a title (16:20, 26:63: "the Christ"), then gradually becoming a second name, as it appears in the gospel's first line. In one of the earliest pagan notices of Jesus, the Roman writer Suetonius (69–140) misunderstood this as "Chrestus," a common name for slaves. There is also Emmanuel ("God with us"), reprinted on countless Christmas cards and immortalized in the familiar carol, "O Come, O Come, Emmanuel!" (a hymn more about the second coming than the nativity), and foreshadowing Jesus' final words, promising always to be "with" his disciples. The name itself is from Isaiah (7:14), the prophet most favored by Matthew and the church because of what they saw as passages predicting the messiahship of Christ; and in the "Jesse window" of Chartres Cathedral, Matthew is seated on Isaiah's shoulders. Its assurance of God's presence will recur at the very end of the gospel (28:20: "I am with you always").

In addition to his name(s), Matthew uses significant formulas to characterize Jesus. As Mark is interested in Jesus' miraculous exercise of his messianic powers, Matthew, writing for a Jewish audience and seeing Jesus' life against the background of Jewish history, is interested in his fulfillment of messianic promises. Hence, Matthew calls Jesus "son of David" nine times; Mark only three; and Luke not at all. But it remains an odd fact that although Jesus' name occurs some one hundred and fifty times in Matthew, none of the human characters uses it in addressing him.

The "JC" of Jesus Christ has become a favorite indicator for modern writers creating characters modeled after Jesus. Examples are Hans (Johann) Castorp, the young hero of Thomas Mann's *Magic Mountain;* Jim Conklin, the "tall soldier" in Stephen Crane's *Red Badge of Courage* who dies with a wound in his side; Jim Casy, the ex-preacher turned labor agitator in John Steinbeck's *The Grapes of Wrath* who "sacrifices" himself to save Tom Joad, the novel's ex-convict hero; and Joe Christmas, the illegitimate son of a black father and white mother in William Faulkner's *Light in August.*

The Incarnation

> When you care enough
> to send the very best.
> —Joyce Clyde Hall

It testifies to Matthew's art that his infancy narrative, like an operatic overture, touches on themes that characterize his gospel: a full revelation of Jesus' divine identity, and the responses of acceptance and rejection that it evoked. Theologically, it is one scriptural authority for the later doctrine of the incarnation (for another, see 9:6), that is, that not only was Jesus the "Word made Flesh," but he was both "true God and true man," two distinct natures joined in "hypostatic union."[13] This was a difficult formulation (unthinkable in Judaism, and in Islam considered beneath God's dignity), since the early church fathers in often acrimonious debates had to balance the gospel narratives of Jesus acting like a man, particularly in his suffering and death, with those where he performed the miracles and proclaimed the message of a god. One serious problem arose when Nestorius, Bishop of Constantinople (428–31), argued that the "young child" of 2:13 constituted a proof text that Mary was the mother only of Jesus' humanity, and that the human and divine natures in Jesus were separate and only conjoined, with God living within Jesus as in a temple. His argument was that Mary could hardly have conceived in time a being who had existed from all eternity, and that she was therefore *Theodochos,* the "Receiver of God," not *Theotokos,* the "Bearer of God" (another of those theological disputes that centered on one or two letters). In opposition, Cyril of Alexandria (d.444) argued for the full humanity (and divinity) of Jesus, defending what became the orthodox position: that Mary "bore God," not a man onto whom divinity had somehow been grafted, and that God and man are united "hypostatically" in Jesus' one nature. Cyril had an influential supporter in Pulcheria, the powerful sister of the Emperor Theodosius II, who regarded herself as a champion of Mary; and with her help and the support of an entourage of fifty bishops from Egypt, his views were confirmed as orthodox at the tumultuous Third Ecumenical Council held at Ephesus in 431 and published in 433 as the "Formula of Union." Cyril was acclaimed, while Nestorius was vilified as a new Judas, deposed, and exiled into Egypt. But Nestorianism did not die at Ephesus; it became a dogma of the church in Persia and lives on in the small "Assyrian Church of the East." Today tourists to Ephesus in Turkey can visit the remains of the church where the council met, and in Rome they can see a monument to Cyril's victory, for in 432 Pope Sixtus III celebrated Mary's status by beginning construction there of the great basilica of Santa Maria Maggiore ("St. Mary the Greater").

Finally, the last of the church's creeds (the Reformers preferred to call them "confessions") was formulated at a council held in 451 at Chalcedon, a town on the Bosphorus opposite Constantinople. It affirmed that Jesus was "truly God and truly man," and "Chalcedon" or "two natures in one person" has since designated the church's definition of christological orthodoxy, though it is complicated by the theory of "anhypostasia"—that Jesus took on human nature but not a human personality—not a doctrine congenial to those fascinated by the Jesus of the Gospels.

The non-Chalcedonians, that is, those who later rejected the 451 "Formula of Reunion" on the grounds that it overvalued Jesus' humanity, are the "Oriental Orthodox Church." But the controversies persisted, and orthodoxy ("Dyophisitism" or "two natures") also had to overcome the competing theories—later heresies—of Docetism (that Jesus was a divine spirit, only seeming to be human and hence not really suffering and dying), Adoptionism (that at one point in his life God chose Jesus as His son and granted him divine powers), Apollinarianism (that Jesus was human in body and soul but divine in intellect), Sabellianism (that God temporarily manifested himself as Jesus and as the Holy Spirit), Eutychianism (that Jesus had only one nature, which was divine), Monothelitism (that Jesus had two natures but only one will), Monarchianism (that Jesus was one mode of God), Nestorianism (that in Jesus human and divine were only conjoined, like husband and wife), and Arianism (that Jesus was not co-eternal with God). Theories claiming that Jesus' human nature was absorbed by his divine nature were generally called "monophysite" ("one nature"), and its adherents were—and still are—particularly numerous in the Christian churches of Egypt, Syria, and Armenia. So it remains a nice question whether these theories, varieties of which have periodically recurred in church history, were the aberrant products of Christianity's fringe elements, destined to wither and die, or alternative theologies unfairly suppressed by the orthodox establishment. Celsus noted these divisions among the faithful who had once been united but in his time had little more in common than the name "Christian." Origen, who recorded Celsus's criticisms, agreed, adding that the gospels showed that they were not united even in Jesus' lifetime, but, he went on, no more divided than were the members of the Greek philosophical schools.[14]

But it was Gnosticism (that Jesus was a divine messenger and guide who took on human form to bring enlightenment and salvation to a fallen world), or varieties of gnostic beliefs, both Jewish and Christian, that most troubled the church early and later; and for the church historian Adolf von Harnack (1851–1930), "the Catholic church had its origin in the struggle with Gnosticism."[15] The gnostics were dualists and hence had the advantage of basing their theories on the obvious antinomies of ordinary experience, such as dark and light, matter and spirit, body and soul, earth and heaven; whereas Christians had to deal with the elusive categories of sin and grace, hope and faith. And they were spiritualists, which meant that they did not have to deal with the stubborn facts of history. Theorizing that material creation was the work, not of a good God, but of a rebellious angel called the Demiurge, they could "solve" the problem of evil by positing a God so transcendent that He was not responsible for this sorry world. Fortunately, the gnostics' "good" God provided a secret but saving "knowledge" (*gnosis* in Greek) whereby individuals could become enlightened and illumine the divine spark within. This would enable them to transcend their earthbound selves and achieve, in stages, personal salvation, the blessedness from which they had once "fallen." For Christian gnostics the agent of their redemption was Jesus Christ, whom they regarded as a pure spirit who only *appeared* to take on human flesh. Hence, basic to all forms of Gnosticism were a dualistic cosmology and a theology of individual redemption from the confinements of nature. Christianity's response was to insist on both the goodness of God and the goodness of the world He alone had created. It was not esoteric or speculative insights that would lead to salvation but faith in God through the atoning ministry of Jesus Christ, personal behavior, and participation in the sacramental life of the Church. Orthodoxy was based, not on secret or hidden doctrines, but on a public record derived from the apostles, contained in the Scriptures and accessible to all.

Gnosticism appealed to Greeks since it endorsed a quasi-Christianity that was philosophically oriented and was divorced from Judaism, with its Scriptures and laws, and from the historical Jesus, whom it came to regard not as a Redeemer but as a teacher or "revealer." For gnostics the "kingdom of God" was not to be found in any text, but was to be discovered within by each believer. These notions reappeared in nineteenth-century Theosophy, and the gnostics' alienation, individualism, elitism, and promise of "liberation" have given them some recent appeal. Speculations that the gnostics might have been more liberal and more sexually permissive than orthodox Christians, particularly in their letting women serve as priests and prophets (though they seem to have had no religious institutions), have generated a good deal of interest; and some have found in New Age movements, with their emphasis on transformed consciousness and self-realization, contemporary counterparts of Gnosticism.

Interest in Gnosticism has been principally fueled by a Bedouin's accidental discovery in 1945 at Nag Hammadi, three hundred miles up the Nile from Cairo, of a small library of fourth-century texts, thirteen papyrus codices containing fifty-two works. Some were only fragmentary, and the contents of others were already known, but some forty were new. These were fourth-century translations of earlier works from Greek into a Coptic that was written in Greek letters and were of unknown origin or purpose. The most controversial among them is the "secret" *Gospel of Thomas,* a nonnarrative collection of 114 sayings attributed to Jesus, supposedly collected by one Judas Thomas. Some parallel Jesus' sentiments in the canonical gospels, others rehash gnostic theology, and many are obscure, esoteric, or bizarre. Before this find at Nag Hammadi, information about Gnosticism came largely from church polemicists, particularly Irenaeus, made Bishop of Lyons in 177, who attacked them in a five-book tract, *Adversus Haereses* ("Against Heresies"). Such defenses of the faith had the meritorious effect of causing the early church to define and explain its own doctrines of God and man, good and evil, body and soul, faith and knowledge.

Many Christians have had difficulty conceiving of a being who is simple in substance but double in nature, both divine and human. With the increasing skepticism regarding the factual reliability of the Gospels, some modern believers still revert to versions of these ancient heresies, preferring to see the historical Jesus as a "manifestation" of God's power and love; others want to see in Jesus a man who enjoyed a unique and exemplary relationship with God, rather like the Jewish prophets, or else as a sage, rather like the Buddha, offering enlightenment and inspiration. These and other reservations were first voiced in antiquity by Celsus and by Porphyry (233–304), who anticipated many of the great historical objections to the Christian message.[16] Celsus, for example, found it hard to reconcile the Christians' human God, who was born and matured, with their divine God, who was supposed to be one and unchanging (4.14); or to understand why, if God wanted to reform humanity, he chose to descend and live on earth; or how his brief presence in Jerusalem could benefit all the millions of people who lived elsewhere in the world or who had lived and died before his incarnation (4.2–8).

There was also an analogy between the incarnation and Scripture, and in his 1943 encyclical *Divino Afflante Spiritu* ("Under the Inspiration of the Holy Spirit") that did so much to encourage biblical studies and ecumenicism among Catholic scholars, Pope Pius XII pointed out that both "words" are simultaneously divine and human, with the human element, flesh and text, veiling the divine, God and His message. "For as the substantial Word of God became like to men in all things, 'except sin,' so the words of God, expressed in human language, are made like to human speech in every respect, except error."[17] This relation can be illustrated by medieval and Renaissance paintings of the annunciation, where Mary holds an open book (usually Isaiah) as the angel Gabriel announces that she shall "bring forth a son" (Luke 1:31). Analogously, this also alludes to the ancient theory of "condescension," first formulated by Chrysostom, that God often had to resort to the imperfect words of men to render His ineffable truths. Hence, biblical narratives might not be factual in the literal sense, but they were God's way to communicate, and their occasional naivete is a divine accommodation to the limited understanding of Scripture's listeners and readers.

The incarnation can also serve as a precedent and justification for Christian art, for as God became flesh in Jesus, so divine truths can be materialized in painting and sculpture. At 13:16, Matthew added another proof text for the legitimacy of Christian icons ("But blessed are your eyes, for they see: and your ears, for they hear"), though iconoclasm never became for the Western church the divisive issue it was for the Eastern, where it divided Orthodoxy from 752 to 842 and caused a wholesale destruction of icons. Orthodoxy still gives their holy icons, with their flat and stylized figures in richly colored vestments, a quasi-sacramental status, whereas it rejects naturalistic paintings as well as statues and crucifixes.

The early church historian Eusebius put Christ's birth in the year 5200 after the Creation, but its exact time is still unknown. The "death of Herod" (Matt. 2:15) in 4 BC or 750 AUC (*Ab Urbe Condita,* "From the Founding of Rome") fixes Jesus' birth in that year or shortly before—which means that Christ was born "Before Christ." The tradition of dating subsequent events as AD (*Anno Domini,* "In the Year of the Lord") began with Dionysius Exiguus ("Denny the Dwarf"), who around 533 devised a liturgical calendar that put Jesus' birth 753 years after the founding of Rome; and an adjustment in 1582 by Pope Gregory created our "Gregorian" calendar. BC ("Before Christ") for previous dates was the work of Isidore of Seville (570–636), but it did not become widespread until the seventeenth century.

The Western church's date of December 25 for the birth of Jesus was a fourth-century arrangement whereby the Nativity would offset the Roman Saturnalia festival and the "birth of the unconquered Sun." This was the date of the winter solstice as set by the solar calendar introduced by Julius Caesar in 46 BC and was a holiday established in 275 by the Emperor Aurelian (270–75), a monarch who liked to associate himself with the power and brilliance of the sun. The cult of the sun was continued by Emperor Diocletian (284–305) and the early Constantine (324–37), and its vague monotheism represented one of the last gasps of Olympianism. It even infected Christianity (surviving in English in the "son-sun" pun). A mosaic in a mausoleum on Vatican Hill shows Christ as a sun god in his chariot, recalling the pagan deities Apollo and Helios. The winter date (which Chrysostom called "the birth of the Sun of Justice"), combined with a springtime Easter, also had the merit of harmonizing the church year with the rhythm of the seasons—at least in the Northern Hemisphere. It was also nine months from March 25, said to be the Day of Creation, and it was given its own "Lenten" preparation period, the forty days of Advent ("Coming" of Christ). The medieval historian Otto, Bishop of Freising, was among those who found a special appropriateness— even inevitability—in the timing of Jesus' birth. Earlier, he would have been too close to the descendants of our sinful first parents, and so God first provided the Mosaic law, then the power of Rome to unite the world, and finally the wisdom of the pagan philosophers so that "the minds of men were suited to grasp more lofty precepts about right living."[18]

Still, Christmas ("Christ's Mass") was a minor part of church life until 1223, when for midnight Mass at Greccio, St. Francis of Assisi received church permission to set up a manger surrounded by Matthew's magi, Luke's shepherds, and the animals—St. Francis's were live—from *Pseudo-Matthew*. The animals also recall Isaiah 1:3 ("The ox knoweth his owner, and the ass his master's crib: but Israel doth not know"), words foreshadowing Jesus' rejection, although their immediate purpose was to warm the newborn baby with their breath. With this crèche, St. Francis humanized the incarnation and created the emotional, even sentimental associations that make December 25, especially as described in the Lukan account, the high point of the liturgical year for most Christians (Calvinists were an important exception) and the subject of our fondest celebrations and best-loved hymns. Yet to be added was Santa Claus from St. Nicholas (with the title "Santa" oddly feminine), candy canes in the shape of his bishop's staff, and the evergreen Christmas tree, its candles or lights said to be Luther's innovation when he saw the stars shining through the branches of a tree while he was out for a walk on Christmas Eve. Finally, for a truly "Victorian Christmas" British Druids supplied the mistletoe, suggesting new life, while the red holly berries foreshadow Jesus' blood and their sharp leaves his crown of thorns. Readers who wanted a nativity story in all its picturesque, if imagined details first found it in the late-thirteenth-century *Meditations on the Life of Christ*. Said to be the work of the Franciscan St. Bonaventure, it is an immensely influential narrative that fills out the gospel stories with invented dialogues and edifying homilies.[19] So our Christmas, like other Christian commemorations, is a jumble of scriptural events and local customs, raising the question whether the tendency to assimilate these various traditions, legends, and usages is a sign of Christianity's weakness or its strength.

Matthew and Luke agree that Jesus' birthplace was Bethlehem, Joseph's home and David's, but Matthew's house differs from Luke's manger, which was actually a feed trough, or from the cave that is symbolized by the semi-dome over the apse behind the altar of many Catholic and Orthodox churches. The first mention of the traditional cave appears in the second century in the apocryphal infancy narrative called the *Protevangelium of James* (18.1) and in Justin Martyr ("a cave is shown in Bethlehem where he was born"); it also foreshadows the cave-tomb of his death.[20] Caves were often associated with pagan divinities in Judea, and there was one in a grove that once lay beneath Bethlehem's Church of the Nativity, built by Constantine in 330 after his mother, St. Helena, had visited the Holy Land to locate the sacred places of her son's adopted faith. Her church was rebuilt by the Emperor Justinian in the sixth century and was subsequently damaged, looted, and altered. But its outlines are still recognizable, and Christian hearts are invariably humbled as they stoop to negotiate the tiny entry, a low door originally meant to keep out mounted Muslims, that leads to the place of Jesus' great entry. Another Bethlehem cave entered Bible history when St. Jerome moved there in 384 and under the patronage of St. Paula and her daughter Eustochium is said to have written his letters, tracts, and, especially, his Latin translation of the Bible in one of the local caves. This was the famous "Vulgate" Bible, declared "sacred and canonical" by the Council of Trent in the mid-sixteenth century.

Mary

Although the New Testament in general says little of Mary's personal life or her relationship with Jesus, she is, in the simplicity of her faith and devotion, the incarnation's human face; and it is her presence in Luke that gives his infancy narrative such charm and appeal. If Jesus is going to suffer on the cross, then Mary (an anglicized form of Miriam) will suffer under the cross—"There stood the sorrowing mother" being the first words of the famous Latin hymn "Stabat Mater." Her obedience here contrasts with Eve's disobedience in Genesis and foreshadows Jesus' own acceptance of his Father's will; and the virgin birth meant a fresh start for humanity after it had failed with the newly created Adam. On the other hand, Mary's submissiveness and docility (at least as recorded in Scripture) as well as her exemption from sexuality and physical childbirth has alienated her from some feminists, who rather identify with the mother goddess of pre-Christian fertility cults.

Interest in Mary's purity had begun with legends collected in the *Protevangelium of James,* which tells how she spent most of her childhood in the temple, where she spun the threads for the veil that would be rent at the crucifixion (27:51). It was there that a messenger from the Lord announced her betrothal to the aged and widowed Joseph, whereupon the narrative concludes with a retelling, from Matthew, of the virgin birth, the magi, and the massacre of the innocents. It is almost universally observed that the Latin "Ave" of "Ave Maria" ("Hail Mary") was the reversal of "Eva." Later writers could multiply the paradoxes—Mary as "Virgin and mother, daughter of thine own son" (Dante, *Paradiso,* 33.1), and "Thy Makers maker, and thy Fathers mother" (Donne, "Annunciation")—as they explored those uncharted territories suggested by her place in Jesus' life but meagerly represented in Scripture.

Mary also has a significant role in the Koran, where she is mentioned more often than in the New Testament.[21] In its version of Jesus' birth, she is told by God (or by His emissary) that despite her virginity she will conceive and bear a child who will be a prophet and "a sign to mankind." The birth occurs "in a distant place" under a palm tree that drops ripe dates to nourish her, an event that seems derived from the flight into Egypt as recorded in the *Pseudo-Matthew.* The details of the annunciation are from Luke, not Matthew; and that Mary is called the "sister of Aaron" suggests that her name is confused with that of the OT Miriam. The Koran also charges that Jesus regarded Mary as divine, a status Muslims reject along with the divinity of Jesus (5.114).

Although she was also celebrated, paradoxically, as the Bride of Christ, Mary's virginity served as a model of Christian asceticism (some argued that she did not even menstruate); but more important theologically was her maternal importance in underscoring Jesus' human nature. The notion evolved that in the scheme of salvation her position in heaven was next to Jesus, where she came to function as a mediatrix, an intercessor for sinners, her mercy leavening his divine justice. By the fourth century, the cult of Mary ("Mariology," or, for its opponents, "Mariolatry") was ready to become one of the great cultural phenomena of Western civilization ("Symbol or energy," wrote Henry Adams, "the Virgin acted as the greatest force the Western world had ever felt"[22]) and as a counterweight to Christianity's occasional fulminations against the "daughters of Eve" or women in general ("the devil's gateway," according to Tertullian). In assimilating Mary to the celestial woman of Revelation 12:1-6, who was seen as incarnating the church and giving birth to a "man child who was to rule all nations," it created cathedrals ("Notre Dame de" Chartres, Paris, Reims, Amiens) and inspired artworks and devotions. Her prayer, the "Ave Maria" ("Hail Mary"), ranked with the Lord's Prayer; Saturday was her day, since she believed in Jesus' divinity before he was resurrected; and since it was believed her body was assumed into heaven, she has no special shrine. Instead, she is everywhere, universally honored in the rosary and appearing in visions, usually to people of pure and simple faith. Indeed, she seems sometimes to usurp the role of the Holy Spirit in Catholic experience. Her youth became the stuff of legends; and her relics, particularly vials of her "milk," were highly prized, preserved in reliquaries, and sent on tour in relics road shows.

That Mary's heavenly role as co-redemptress diluted the importance of Jesus as the one mediator between man and God troubled the Calvinist Reformers, who also noted that the materials of her cult, from rosaries to cathedrals, were all of human origin. James I of England (1603–25), a monarch who fancied himself a theologian, hoped that Mary had other things to do in heaven "than to hear every idle man's suit and busy herself in their errands, whiles requesting, whiles commanding her Son."[23] So with its charms and its excesses, its sanctities and its superstitions, its fervor and its fanaticism, Mariology exemplifies what separates the biblical record from popular piety, or, denominationally, Protestants from Catholics. What was imported arbitrarily from outside, what developed logically from within?

In the modern world, controversies have centered on the "immaculate conception," a dogma regularly confused in the secular world with the dogma of the virgin birth. According to this, Mary, "by a singular grace and privilege" was, like the first Eve, conceived without the taint of original sin. The immaculate conception was proclaimed as Catholic dogma in 1854 (and although Luther had accepted it before it became dogma, most Protestants maintained that it diminished Christ's share in sinful humanity and undercut the doctrine of his universal redemption). Controversial, too, was her "assumption," whereby at her death she was "assumed body and soul into heavenly glory," in part because she had in life enjoyed a unique "consortium" with her son and in part because she was exempted from the death that is the legacy of original sin. The assumption was proclaimed as dogma in 1950.[24]

The Magi

The second of the three infancy sections (2:1-12) features the magi and a "star in the east." Matthew's is a story that, like two other dramatic masterpieces, Aeschylus's *Oresteia* and Shakespeare's *Hamlet,* begins in the dark. Like the Greek tragedy, with its fiery signal announcing the fall of Troy, the good news is symbolized by light out of darkness—though both stories will lead to suffering and death, and when Jesus is crucified there will again be "darkness all over the land" (27:45). The star is purely Matthean, since there would be no room for the magi's visit in Luke's infancy narrative, where their place is taken by the shepherds. Astral wonders were often associated with the births and deaths of ancient leaders, most notably the spectacular daylight comet of 44 BC that appeared at Julius Caesar's funeral and was interpreted as a sign that he had been made a god. But here the "fulfillment" citation, which surprisingly Matthew does not quote, perhaps because he had doubts about the story's historicity, is Numbers 24:17 ("There shall come a Star out of Jacob"), a prophecy by Balsam, a seer-magician who foreshadows the magi. Its memory is preserved in Orthodoxy's liturgy, where the priest uses a star-shaped object with bent tips to cover but not touch a particle of the communion bread; and it has given its name to the Masonic Order of the Eastern Star.

There has also been a long tradition of attempts to verify the star story through astronomical data, whether they showed a conjunction of planets, a comet (since it seems to move), or a supernova.[25] This still leaves unexplained the odd fact that the always-suspicious Herod did not notice it, though it "stood over where the young child was" (2:9). This, in turn, raises the possibility that it was not a star but a sign that the magi—if they were astrologers—interpreted as presaging the birth of a messiah. Popular piety expanded these wonders: one legend had the star take on the appearance of a child's shining face with scepter and cross; another held that it showed the Greek designation for Christ, chi-rho (*XP*). From Ignatius of Antioch, early second century, the first churchman to quote Matthew, came the story that all the other stars, including the sun and moon, formed a ring around this star, only to be outshone by it so much that all magic, witchcraft, and diabolism ceased, for the power of death was about to be destroyed.[26] In satirizing the medieval obsession with relics in his *Decameron,* Boccaccio (1313–75) has one of his churchmen list those he was privileged to see while in Jerusalem: the finger of the Holy Spirit, a vial of the sweat of St. Michael shed while fighting the devil, some of the sound from the bells of Solomon's temple, and rays from the star that the magi saw in the east.[27]

Matthew's dramatic juxtaposition of "King of the Jews" (2:2), referring to Jesus, and "Herod the king" explains why the Romans' puppet ruler is "troubled," though it is unclear why "all Jerusalem" is troubled with him. This prefigures the "kingship" of Jesus that will recur during his confrontation with Pontius Pilate (27:11, 29, 37), who in AD 26 became the third prefect of Judea after the Romans' removal of Herod's ruthless son Archelaus in AD 6. As for the "little town of Bethlehem," the prophet Micah (5:2) foretold that out of it would come a "ruler in Israel," but its main significance for Matthew is that it was David's town, and he is fond of giving Jesus the messianic title "Son of David." Bethlehem is now almost a southern suburb of Jerusalem, and its Church of the Nativity has a crypt called the "Grotto of the Nativity," though there is great uncertainty as to the exact site of Jesus' birth, if in fact it took place in Bethlehem and not in Nazareth, as many scholars believe. Nazareth was of even less importance than Bethlehem, generally unmentioned outside the New Testament (John 1:46: "Can there any good thing come out of Nazareth?"). Until excavations in 1955 proved otherwise, it was believed not to have existed before the fourth century BC. Its biblical remains are sparse and questionable: a crypt said to contain parts of Mary's house under the modern Church of the Annunciation; "Mary's Well," still in use; and St. Joseph's Church, over what is reputed to have been his house and workshop.

The magi are traditionally three in number, to correspond with their gifts, and have been given the exotic and melodious names Caspar, Melchior, and Balthasar. They are usually portrayed traveling by camel and wearing royal or priestly robes, often with conical "Phrygian caps" folded forward at the peak. Their exotic attire adds a picturesque effect to the rustic settings of so many "adoration of the magi" paintings, and Christmas card buyers reportedly prefer Matthew's magi to Luke's shepherds, though many artists include both contingents. They are occasionally said to be descended from Noah's three sons; hence, they can represent the three known continents (Balthasar is sometimes pictured as black) or the three stages of life. Their three gifts can symbolize Jesus' royalty (gold), divinity (frankincense used in worship, more commonly in the Eastern church and not until the fourth century—or for the more pedestrian purpose of masking the smells of the stable, though here they are in a house), and humanity or, ominously, death (since corpses were anointed with myrrh, a mixture of aromatic resins); and one story had them receiving Jesus' swaddling clothes as a return gift. Or, according to the *Golden Legend*, in terms of the givers, the gifts represent love, prayer (since incense in church services rises as a fragrant offering to God), and self-mortification (1.83). Dante in his political essay *De Monarchia* mentions—and disputes—another tradition, that frankincense and gold represent spiritual and temporal power, which Jesus would later pass on to Peter and to Peter's papal successors.[28] A sixth-century legend claimed that they were treasures brought by Adam from paradise and hidden by his sons in a cave, where they were found by the magi. But a cranky English deist, Thomas Woolston (1669–1733), objected to the gifts. "If they had brought sugar, soap and candles they had acted like wise men." And feminists have observed that if the "Three Wise Men" had been "Three Wise Women," they would have brought practical gifts and asked directions so that they could arrive in time to clean the stable and help deliver the baby. Still, each year the British monarch has two Gentleman Ushers present gifts of gold, frankincense, and myrrh to the Dean of the Chapel Royal in London, and the magi's offering of gold is a precedent for the sumptuous decoration of churches.

The popular hymn "We Three Kings" has it that they "from Orient are" (deriving from Isa. 60:3, 6 and Ps. 72:10), but the magi were probably thought of as Persian priests or Babylonian astrologers (Dan. 1:20, 2:27, and 5:15; hence "magic"), and the "star" that guides them may refer to their astrological findings. As both "wise men" (the KJV translation of *magoi* at 2:1) and Gentiles, the magi were important for the universality of Jesus' mission; and in 1894, as part of his reconciliation efforts with Orthodoxy, Pope Leo XIII cited their worship of the Christ child as the first example of "Eastern rites" in the Church.[29] They are pagans brought early to Jesus, though it may never be known whose envoys they were, why they would seek out a Jewish messiah, why they did not go directly to Bethlehem, how they must have reacted on discovering that the future "king of the Jews" was a baby so humbly born, how a star could designate a single house (despite the artistic tradition, they do not kneel at the manger), or what they made of their experience. But their obeisance before the infant symbolically foreshadows the subjection of learning to revelation, of magic to miracle, of superstition to faith, of paganism to Christianity. Even though the church, which condemns astrology for its determinism and fatalism, was uncomfortable with the star's predictive function in this story (if it was not a special star), it is appropriate that the pagan magi be informed and inspired in terms of their own astral beliefs.

Tertullian (160–225) was the first to note that the magi were also considered kings, drawing on Isaiah 60:3 ("And the Gentiles shall come to thy light, and kings to the brightness of thy rising"), both to magnify their importance and minimize their association with magic and to illustrate the subjection of temporal power to spiritual.[30] One legend had Mary and Joseph robbed of the gold by the thieves later crucified with Jesus, another that it was entrusted to Judas, who embezzled it. In attacking the Church of the Nativity in 614, the Persians were said to have spared the columns decorated with paintings of their three ancestors, the magi. Constantine's mother, Helena, reportedly brought back relics—if not the bodily remains—of the magi to Constantinople, from where they traveled to Milan and then with Frederick Barbarossa in 1164 to Cologne, where they would be visited by German kings after their coronation in Aachen. Visitors to the Cologne Cathedral can see the "Shrine of the Three Kings," a gold sarcophagus reputed to be the largest in Western Europe, though one such visitor, Martin Luther, denounced it as a fraud. Later Swinburne, in a letter to his mother, wrote: "The Priest removed a part of the head and showed me the three skulls crowned and the names written in rubies. The bare dark skulls looked strange, but not, I thought, ugly or out of place in the diadems of gold and pearls."[31] Marco Polo also claimed to have seen the magi's bodies at Saveh near Teheran in 1272, still intact and with hair and beards in place.[32] In medieval devotions the magi, who had been guided by God and saved from Herod, had a special place as protectors and intercessors.

Matthew's "Epiphany" (2:11) recalls the "revelation" ceremonies in paganism at which an image or symbol of the god was displayed to the people, and it has been variously associated with Jesus' birth, baptism, or appearance to the magi. Celebrated on January 6, it is regarded as Christmas in many Eastern churches since Jesus now appears to the wider world. It is then that the magi give children gifts, while in the West it is often the date for removing Christmas decorations. Epiphany is also known as the "Feast of the Twelve Days," since it completes the Christmas cycle begun on December 24, though Matthew does not mention Jesus' circumcision or Mary's purification (Luke 2:21-

22), which is surprising since he records Jesus' later assertion that he has come to fulfill every "jot" and "tittle" of the law (5:17–18).

But there is more to this verse (2:11): Matthew is preeminently the gospel of worship, and "fell down" also provides scriptural warrant, with Luke 5:8 (Peter "fell down at Jesus' knees"), for kneeling at prayer. The ancients generally thought kneeling was undignified, but for St. Basil it was a "way of showing by our actions that sin has cast us to the ground," and the longstanding prohibition of kneeling in Orthodox churches on Sunday and Easter is a sign "that our fall has been corrected through the resurrection of Christ on the third day."[33] In the early church the custom was to stand for collective prayer, kneel for private prayer; but for Catholic Christians one sits to listen, stands to sing, and kneels to pray. Most expressive of all is prostration, described here and again with Jesus in the Garden of Gethsemane (26:39). Suggesting the veneration due a god, it is normally reserved for priests at their ordination.

Kneeling has always been a source of denominational disagreements, particularly when receiving the bread and wine of Communion, since Jesus' disciples were probably reclining when the Eucharist was instituted at the Last Supper. One dispute concerned the "Declaration on Kneeling," which Thomas Cranmer (1489–1556), Archbishop of Canterbury under Henry VIII, inserted at the last minute into the 1552 revision of the *Book of Common Prayer* (1549). It permitted communicants to kneel for the reception of the Eucharist, though specifying that this did not demonstrate a belief that Christ's "natural flesh and blood" was present in the host and that "no adoration is done, ought to be done" to the bread and wine. But it was omitted from the 1559 edition, then shortened and reintroduced in 1632, with "real and essential" changed to "corporal." In nineteenth-century editions of the *BCP,* it became known as the "Black Rubric" when it was printed in black instead of the red print used to indicate liturgical rubrics, or directions. Conversely, the Puritans rejected this "show of papistry," and with an allusion to 11:28b ("I will give you rest") favored sitting at their "Common Table," for thereby, they said, "we signify rest, that is a full finishing through Christ of all the ceremonial law, and a perfect work of redemption wrought that giveth rest forever."[34]

One story had the star leading the magi back home, another that they were later baptized by St. Thomas the Apostle on his way to evangelize India. But the fact that they went back by "another way," reportedly to avoid Herod, has become a Christian metaphor for the radical and unsettling change in "way of life" by those "pale unsatisfied ones" who have come to Christ and experienced "the uncontrollable mystery on the bestial floor" (Yeats, "The Magi").[35] Already in the late sixth century, Gregory the Great (540–604) noted that "having come to know Jesus, we are forbidden to return by the way we came." This is also a theme of T. S. Eliot's poem, "Journey of the Magi," in which the speaker comments that "this Birth was / Hard and bitter agony for us, like Death, our death. / We returned to our places, these kingdoms, / But no longer at ease here, in the old dispensation, / With an alien people clutching their gods."[36]

The next event is the "massacre of the innocents" (2:16-18), which Jesus escapes by the "flight into Egypt"—episodes that only Matthew records and that give his narrative a dark dimension missing from Luke's message of peace and joy. The prophecy thereby "fulfilled" is at Hosea 11:1, where it refers to the exodus, thus underlining a connection between Jesus and the Israelites fleeing from Egypt. Readers might wonder what Herod had to fear from a baby, or why he was unable to find Jesus in a house marked by a star and visited by three important foreigners, or why he would order the murder of two-year-olds if he wanted only to eliminate one newly born infant. The historian Josephus (37–100), who records the bloodthirstiness of Herod, does not mention this event that has been so vividly represented in Western painting, and it is unlikely that Herod's Roman masters would have tolerated such an outrage. Even those who take it as factual concede that it might have involved no more than twenty children, whereas one martyrology put it at fourteen thousand. Some prefer to see it as an elaboration of the historical fact that Herod put three of his sons to death, and Christian moralists could take comfort in the justice of a child-murderer being repaid with terrible children of his own. The *Golden Legend* also reports that among the massacre victims was one of Herod's infant sons, who had been entrusted to a nurse (1.58). It obviously reflects the common myth that gods and heroes suffer endangered births and often have to be taken into temporary exile. Still, a shoulder-blade from one of the "Holy Innocents" was listed among the relics owned by Peterborough Abbey in England in the twelfth century, and the skeleton of another was said to be in the vast collection of relics at Wittenberg, the cradle of the Reformation, the property of the local leader and protector of Luther, Frederick the Wise. And it is appropriate that the true "King of the Jews" (2:2) conflict with the man who only *thinks* he is king of the Jews.

According to the *Golden Legend,* the Holy Innocents, "in each of whom Christ was put to death" (2.33), were accorded instant sainthood as the church's first martyrs, even though they died before Jesus' redemptive work was accomplished (a similar exception was made for the seven Maccabee brothers who led the Hebrew revolt against Antiochus in the second century BC). Their martyrdom was celebrated by the early Christian poet Prudentius: "All hail, ye infant martyr flowers, / Cut off in life's first dawning hours."[37] Their slaughter is commemorated on December 28, "Holy Innocents' Day," when in medieval times children were allowed to take over the churches during the "Feast of the Boy Bishop," the innocence of children understood as mitigating any possible offense. Their fate reappeared in the notoriously anti-

Semitic legends of Christian children kidnapped by Jews and forced, often at Easter, to repeat the sufferings inflicted on Jesus. Most famous was "yonge Hugh of Lincoln," an eleven-year-old boy said to have been crucified on August 27, 1255, by wealthy Jews in that city, his fate recorded in Chaucer's *Prioress' Tale* (232).

Verse 17 refers to Jeremiah 31:15, where Rachel, the mother of Joseph and Benjamin, is pictured in Ramah "weeping for her children," the Israelites being deported to Babylon (just as Jesus had been "deported" into Egypt), but Calvin noted that the next two verses in Jeremiah point to hope and restoration. Thomas Paine, for whom all the "fulfillments" cited in the New Testament were not prophecies but "impositions" wrested out of context, wrote: "This verse, when separated from the verses before and after it, and which explain its application, might with equal propriety be applied to every case of wars, sieges, and other violences, such as Christians themselves have often done to the Jews, where mothers have lamented the loss of their children."[38]

That the king was "exceeding wroth" (v. 16) supplied the raging Herod of the medieval mystery cycles, as recalled in Hamlet's "it out-Herods Herod" (3.2.16). In the Wakefield pageant *Herod the Great,* the king fears that he will be deposed by an alliance of these three kings and the child destined to be a king. During one liturgical drama staged in the cathedral at Padua, the attendants of the angry Herod went around the church striking clerics and worshipers with inflated bladders. And in our own time, Herod has appeared as a disillusioned liberal in W. H. Auden's Christmas oratorio *For the Time Being* (1944). His rule, he insists, has been enlightened and progressive, but he is helpless in the face of what he sees as his subjects' irrational needs and hopes— so he must reluctantly resort to force. "O dear, why couldn't this wretched infant be born somewhere else? Why can't people be sensible? I don't want to be horrid."[39] And in his 1961 remake of Cecil B. DeMille's film *King of Kings,* director Nicholas Ray, presumably out of deference to American Jews, identified Herod as "an Arab of the Bedouin tribe."

These events look before and after, foreshadowing the passion, when "the chief priests and scribes" will again help another official to find and condemn Jesus. And they recall the unusual birth of a former leader and liberator, Moses, and the slaughter of the Hebrew babies (Ex. 1:22), just as Herod plays the role of the hard-hearted Pharaoh. Similarly, the Holy Family's return from Egypt repeats the exodus experience, and Jesus' name reproduces Joshua. Matthew's fondness for these OT connections, which are not in Luke's infancy narrative, casts further doubt on the historicity of the events.

The "Egyptian Connection" (vv. 19-22), important in associating Jesus with Moses, is elaborated in the *Pseudo-Matthew* (18–20), which has wild animals reverently escorting the Holy Family on its journey, palm trees lowering their branches to do the Christ child homage and to provide the family with food, and the 365 idols in one city falling to pieces on their arrival. Although their stay there was brief, one story had Jesus working in Egypt, the traditional home of sorcerers, and learning the kinds of magical arts that would enable him on his return to Palestine to style himself as a "Son of God" (the allegation of Celsus [1.28]). Other legends are more complimentary, with Jesus helping Mary eke out a living as a spinner and seamstress while Joseph works as a carpenter, with various localities later claiming to have been their place of refuge. Scenes of the Holy Family resting on their flight into Egypt were popular with Reformation painters since they showed Mary as a normal woman, not the quasi-supernatural mediator that Luther had criticized. These countered the paintings of *Maria Lactans,* Mary nursing the Christ child, a favorite subject for those churches claiming to have among their relics vials of her milk, while theologically it presented the Catholic Mary as a source of grace. "Flight" paintings also enabled artists to add landscape settings, often classical or European (cf. Carracci, 1603–1604; Rome), and the presence of an ass and palm trees contrasted this scene of flight with Jesus' later—and triumphal—entry into Jerusalem (21:7-8). The event was parodied in the medieval "Feast of Asses," popular in France, where a young girl carrying a baby on an ass would ride into the church and braying sounds were inserted into the Latin of the liturgy. Visitors to Bethlehem can be shown the "Milk Grotto" just southeast of Manger Square, where Mary and Jesus were supposedly hidden before the flight. The sojourn in Egypt was also prophetic in taking Jesus early in his life to a land of the Gentiles; and Egypt as a place of refuge recalls the sojourn in Egypt of another Joseph (Gen. 39:2: "and he was in the house of his master the Egyptian").

The infancy narrative was amplified by a series of curious legends found in the *Infancy Gospel of Thomas* (2c). The child Jesus, sometimes oddly obnoxious or pointlessly precocious, turns clay sparrows into live birds (a detail that found its way into the Koran [3.48]); he causes the death of one boy who bumps into him, then revives another who has fallen off a roof and died. He bewilders his teachers with arcane allegories, and he helps Joseph by lengthening boards to the right size. Mark Twain parodied these stories: "A young man who had been bewitched and turned into a mule, miraculously cured by the infant Savior being put on his back, and is married to the girl who had been cured of leprosy. Whereupon the bystanders praise God."[40]

The infancy narrative then concludes with the Holy Family returning, not to Bethlehem, but to Nazareth in Galilee, a fertile and densely populated area in northern Palestine. Their purpose was to avoid Archelaus, the worst of Herod's three sons, who appears only here (v. 22) in the New Testament. On his father's death, the Romans made him "ethnarch" of Judea, Samaria, and Idumea but deposed and banished him in favor of their own governors in AD 6 when his subjects protested his brutality. The source of this "fulfillment citation" (v. 23), attributed vaguely to "prophets," is unknown, but the early Christians were called "Nazarenes" (Acts 24:5).

Legend has the actual house of Mary saved from the Arabs in 1291 and carried by angels from Nazareth to Dalmatia and then in 1294 to Loreto, Italy, where it was deposited in a laurel grove (hence the city's name) to become the *Santa Casa* ("Holy House"), a popular pilgrimage goal (Descartes visited it in 1623; Galileo, in 1618 and 1624). It is now inside the Sanctuary of the Holy House, begun in 1468, and is encased in walls by Bramante (1444–1514) that are faced with marble and richly decorated. It has no foundation, and its materials are said to be peculiar to Nazareth. But the Catholic Church, while acknowledging pious opinion, prefers to regard it only as a shrine to the house of the annunciation.

Strangely missing from the New Testament is any mention of Sepphoris, a city that Jesus must have known well since it was only three miles northwest of Nazareth, it had a multilingual population that may have reached 30,000, and it served in the first centuries before and after Christ as the capital of Galilee. Destroyed by the Romans after uprisings that followed the death of Herod in 4 BC, it was rebuilt by his son Herod Antipas, tetrarch of Galilee, and adorned with shops, public buildings, and a theater. With a large Greek-speaking population, it could well have been where Matthew's gospel was composed. Those who prefer to see Jesus as a wise man rather than a divine redeemer are tempted to speculate that Joseph might have worked on the reconstruction of Sepphoris and that Jesus might have visited it, experiencing something of its Hellenistic cosmopolitanism, and that not all of his young manhood was spent in the remote and rural Nazareth of Christian tradition.

2

The Ministry Begins

Matthew's chapter 3 picks up the story some thirty years later with the ministry of John the Baptist, the baptism of Jesus, and in 4:1-11 the temptation narrative. At 4:12 Jesus returns to Galilee, not home to Nazareth but rather to Capernaum, where he begins to enlist disciples, beginning with Simon Peter and his brother Andrew. His itinerant ministry takes him throughout Galilee, his fame extending north to Syria and attracting crowds from the Jerusalem area, from the ten cities along the Mediterranean coast, and from the other, or eastern side of the Jordan.

> Those that repent and embrace
> the Faith and do what is right
> shall be admitted to Paradise.
> —*Koran*

With chapter 3 the narrative has bypassed Jesus' childhood and young adulthood, which by the second century had become the stuff of legends. It is now the spring of AD 28 (perhaps) and a significant event occurs: the baptism of Jesus by his cousin and great predecessor, John the Baptist, now often called the "Baptizer," or, among Baptists, "John the Immerser" (or, less reverently, the "Big Dipper"). Repentance, for John, entails baptism, to which Jesus also submits ("to fulfil all righteousness"), although the event itself is not described and it is unclear what the sinless agent of God's redeeming has to repent.

John is a wilderness figure resembling Elijah the Tishbite ("an hairy man, and girt with a girdle of leather about his loins" [2 Kgs. 1:8]), preaching the need for repentance and the nearness of a mysteriously undefined "kingdom of heaven," a message Jesus will repeat at 4:17. His proclamation is so brief and abrupt that readers are not told if divine forgiveness is assured by repentance or what sort of life the repentant sinner should live after baptism. Here he appears suddenly and unexpectedly, but he will be generally absent from Jesus' ministry, though his unhappy fate, described in 14:1-12, foreshadows Jesus' rejection and his crucifixion. John was a model ascetic, and that the word of God came to him while he was "in the wilderness" (Isa. 40:3) helped justify the earliest monks when they withdrew from civilization to be "alone with God," though Calvin warned against turning John into a proto-monk.[1] It is symbolically appropriate that he performed baptism, a ceremony of transition, in the Jordan River, the traditional boundary between the wilderness and the promised land.

Baptism is something of a problem, being uncertain in its origins and meaning, unexpected in a life of Jesus, unparalleled in the Old Testament, unclear in its theology, and uneven in its acceptance and practice among Christian denominations, though it eventually came to rank with the Eucharist as the fundamental Christian sacrament. It is even questioned in its English rendering, as some would prefer "immersion," pointing out that the Greek of 3:11 is literally "in water" and "in the spirit and fire." Jews were accustomed to purifying themselves through ritual ablutions and bathing, as can be seen from the records of the Essenes or in the Dead Sea Scrolls, where the Qumran community seems to have practiced frequent washings. But quite different is the rite of baptism, which by contrast has an indelible character and is not repeatable (though baptism vows can be renewed). Thus, it may have served as an initiation for converts to Judaism who were not circumcised and needed to be cleansed of their Gentile impurities, though it is unknown when or where or why it became an initiatory rite for Christian converts. Nevertheless, Jews did not baptize other Jews, so John's insistence on its accompanying their acts of repentance must have seemed a surprising innovation. Baptism recurs at the end of Matthew when Jesus orders his disciples to baptize converts in the name of the Trinity (28:19). But there is no indication that it was formally instituted by him, and only once (John 3:22) is he said to baptize anyone himself.

Jesus' baptism is recorded in all four gospels, but the presence of the Holy Spirit suggests that his is a special Spirit-baptism, not a cleansing from sin. For ordinary Christians, it became a sacrament that would remit all sin, so it was normally delayed in the early church until candidates had undergone months of probation and instruction, particularly in the forty days of Lent that ended on Holy Saturday. It was then performed at Easter in order to assimilate its "rebirth" symbolism with the death and resurrection of Christ, an association popular with Paul. Baptisms were performed at a cathedral but in a separate building called a baptistery, usually a round structure recalling the rotunda in Jerusalem's Church of the Holy Sepulcher, built over the traditional sites of Jesus' crucifixion, burial, and resurrection. There the candidate would customarily face west while renouncing the devil and his works (baptism is also a quasi-exorcism, a part of the ceremony that the Reformers eliminated), and east while reciting the Apostles' Creed. The candidate underwent a triple immersion, one for each member of the Trinity (or recalling Jesus' three days in the tomb), or else a sprinkling ("aspersion") while standing in the font, then was clothed in a white garment. But as the sacrament came to be administered privately to infants in local churches and by sprinkling instead of immersion (which the Baptist and Orthodox churches still retain), its location was moved inside to a special area supplied with a basin or font, and the basin was smaller and elevated.[2] Baptismal fonts were often richly decorated, usually with reliefs of the sacraments, and their shape reproduced baptism's death-and-rebirth meanings: four-sided, like a coffin; six-sided for Good Friday; or eight-sided for the Day of Resurrection (or the eight people saved in Noah's Ark, or the eight Beatitudes). Or the font could be round for the womb of rebirth, with the catechumen emerging from its waters as a child of God. Visitors to Ravenna in northern Italy can see the so-called Arian Baptistery, with its dome mosaic of Jesus' baptism, built in the fifth century and octagonal in shape.

Many of the first Christians seem to have waited as long as possible in order to avoid the harsh public penances levied on sins committed after they were baptized. So the first Christian emperor, Constantine, who was a great murderer of his enemies and had disposed of his son and wife, was baptized on his deathbed in 337 (Voltaire said the Christian emperors "had discovered the secret of living criminally and dying virtuously"); and St. Ambrose, then the governor of Northern Italy, was not baptized until he was about to be acclaimed bishop of Milan in 374.[3] As the medieval church established auricular confession and penance as the accepted ways to have personal sins forgiven, and as diseases were dooming many Christian children, the baptism of infants (pedobaptism) became the rule, intended, under the influence of Augustine, to remit the original sin incurred by the child's humanity within the family of Adam and to impart the grace and power of the Holy Spirit. Not to be baptized meant that an infant was consigned to the nonbiblical "limbo" (Latin: *in limbo,* "on the border"), a featureless annex of hell that entailed a loss of that heavenly union with God known as the Beatific Vision but not the hellish pains inflicted for personal mortal sins.

In subsequent tradition, baptismal "bathing" came to reproduce the first action whereby a convert is received into the life of the community, and the use of water as its visible sign involves one of the Bible's most suggestive symbols, implying both death and rebirth. In Genesis the waters meant the judgment and destruction of the Flood, but they also meant purity and refreshment and creation. In Exodus the Israelites pass through the waters of the "Red Sea," and in Joshua they enter the promised land through the waters of the Jordan River. Hence, new Christians, called "catechumens," were "reborn" from the "death" of their old lives, as they responded "I believe" to a series of questions about their new faith. They were then "sealed" with the sign of the cross, indicating, as Christ did by his death on the cross, a victory over the devil, and could "walk in newness of life" (Rom. 6:4) and be eligible to participate in the ceremony of the Eucharist, the truly distinctive Christian sacrament. The minister of baptism was normally a priest, though in emergencies it could be performed by laypeople. The Donatists, a powerful group of early

Christian heretics in North Africa, were the first to argue that the sinfulness or unworthiness of priests invalidated the sacraments they administered, but it has always been Christian teaching that Christ is the true minister of all the sacraments and that what mattered was the inherent efficacy of the sacrament and the intention, not the character, of the ministrant.[4]

The water of baptism was invoked in one version of the medieval "ordeal by water," whereby the accused was bound and lowered into water. If he—or, very often, she—did not sink, it was assumed the pure water had rejected him and he was guilty. Baptismal water also survives today in the "holy water" available in fonts to Roman Catholics to bless themselves with the sign of the cross as they enter and leave church, and in the *Asperges* ("You shall sprinkle") liturgy whereby the priest in procession sprinkles water over the faithful. Along with the cross, it has always been considered a potent safeguard against devils. On the other hand, the medieval Cathars ("Pure Ones," 11th–13th centuries), who were dualists and heretics, dispensed with water altogether in favor of an imposition of hands, arguing that water represented the material world from which the soul must be freed.

That no one seems surprised by John's baptizing suggests that baptism was an accepted if not standard ritual in the time of Jesus, deeply grounded in the Jewish equation of ritual purity with holiness, though it appears that whereas John can bring his followers to confession, repentance, and immersion (evidently without any probationary period), only Jesus will be able to forgive them their sins. Unfortunately, neither the Bible nor Christian churches today are clear or consistent on its sacramental status or the elements of its conferral or its theology, such as the difference between water-baptism and Spirit-baptism (the latter an experience of empowerment popular with Pentecostal Christians); the relative efficacy of immersion or submersion in water, pouring or sprinkling of water, anointing with the "oil of salvation," and laying on of hands (Acts 8:17); the use of salt on the tongue to symbolize the preservation of the faith; the priest's spittle on his hands as he touches the ear and nose to "open" them to God's word; the use of Latin or the vernacular; the exorcism-like renunciation of "Satan and all his works," whether by the candidate or the godparents; and, most importantly, its power to remit sins and "put on Christ" (Gal. 3:27). These multiple uncertainties have been a continuing source of division in Christian history, and they persist today, where baptism continues as the first Christian sacrament but is usually performed on children, traditionally eight days after birth, and represents God's first declaration of grace to the new Christian before he or she can commit actual sins.

The practice of baptizing infants who are innocent and can make no personal act of faith has always been a particular problem for theology, sometimes addressed by defining the rite as *ex opere operato*, that is, conferring grace simply "by the action performed," and an example of how God provides grace for those who have done nothing to merit it. Children can also be justified vicariously by the faith of the church (Aquinas) or of the child's sponsors (Luther and the Anglicans) or by their potential for faith (Calvin). Still, it did provide children with instant "salvation" at a time of widespread infant mortality; and although the NT evidence is distressingly scanty (it is assumed that when Lydia "and her household" were baptized at Acts 16:15, this included small children), it had an OT precedent in infant circumcision. It also publicly celebrates the child's entrance into the church and honors the families who will help to cultivate his faith. But questions were raised in the early church as to whether one can simply be made a Christian or must become one, and some denominations, known first in the sixteenth century as Anabaptists, or "rebaptizers," and now represented worldwide by Baptists, reserve it for young adults who have reached the "age of accountability"—"believer's baptism." The Mennonites in contemporary America follow the words of their founder, Menno Simons (1496–1561), who found it "an invented rite" and "a harmful superstition" without scriptural warrant: "It is not of God nor of His Word but of Antichrist and of the bottomless pit." Simons cited 19:14 ("Suffer little children . . . to come unto me.") to show that "Christ has promised the kingdom of heaven to small children without baptism."[5] They point out that Jesus was an adult when he was baptized and that he instructed his disciples at the end of Matthew (28:19) first to teach "all nations" and then to baptize them. The Anabaptists (for whom Matthew was the preferred gospel) suffered for this belief, as did the Baptists, who liked to use local rivers for the immersion rite they called "dipping." In 1526 a Zurich edict ruled that they be "drowned without mercy," this being considered an ironically appropriate punishment—the "dippers dipped"—for those who preached adult baptism.[6]

The Quakers, noting that Jesus did not baptize his disciples, and privileging the inner workings of the Holy Spirit over external rites, dispense with what William Penn called the "watery dispensation" altogether. Voltaire quoted a Quaker as saying: "We profess ourselves disciples of Christ, and not of John."[7] The Salvation Army does not baptize, whereas the Mormons perform proxy baptisms "for and on behalf of the dead" partly as a way to seal families together, partly to bring its spiritual benefits to those historical figures (Alexander the Great!) who did not know about Christianity.

During the Reformation, the Swiss Huldrych Zwingli (1484–1531) broke with Luther in regarding baptism, like the Eucharist, as no more than a spiritual aid, a ceremonial pledge to the community that the child will live a Christian life. Others regarded baptism, not as an efficacious instrument of grace, but as a purely external rite, not unlike circumcision, to be completed and confirmed (hence "confirmation") in adulthood by a baptism of belief, but important enough to be retained as a recollection of Jesus' own baptism and circumcision and as an exercise of faith for the child and its sponsors. Luther's position on infant baptism was conservative. Paradoxically, in the light of his elevation of Scripture over human traditions, he acknowledged that its biblical basis was weak (the same held for the Trinity), but in this case he appealed to "ecclesial infallibility," maintaining that it was validated by the practice of the universal church. He also saw it justified in Jesus' welcoming little children, and he argued that to do away with it in favor of a "believer's baptism" would emphasize individual works over sacramental grace as the condition of becoming a Christian.[8]

The Western church has sought to ratify infant baptism with the adult sacrament of confirmation. Designed to add strength to the graces of baptism, it is a kind of higher baptism, using consecrated oil on the forehead ("chrismation," as the sacrament is called in Orthodoxy), not water. It is usually administered with laying on of hands by a bishop to children old enough to understand their faith commitment. Originally, confirmation immediately followed baptism, and the Eastern church still administers the two sacraments together, regarding them as inseparable, with confirmation recalling the descent of the Holy Spirit in Matthew 3:16b. Confirmation was also a Reformation casualty. Calvin disapproved of this "gross and greasy liquid," for which he found no authorization in Scripture, and he argued that the laying on of hands was limited to the apostles. Better, he thought, that adolescent Christians be catechized, that is, "give an account of their faith before the church."[9]

The Kingdom of God

> Mine eyes have seen the glory
> of the coming of the Lord.
> —Julia Ward Howe

> Jesus foretold the kingdom, and
> it was the Church that came.
> —Alfred Loisy

John's message, that "the kingdom of heaven is at hand" (3:2), is the first of twenty-nine distinctly Matthean references to God's "kingdom," a concept almost completely absent from Hebrew scriptures, but one that adds a social, even cosmic dimension to Jesus' message, even though, oddly, God is never referred to as its king. Matthew, unlike Mark and Luke, usually calls it the kingdom "of heaven" rather than "of God," partly out of deference to an audience whose Jewish sensibilities made them reluctant to pronounce the divine name, partly to emphasize that the power of that kingdom, encompassing heaven and earth, also belongs to Jesus. What can puzzle readers is that the familiar words "at hand" generally refer, often bewilderingly, to a situation that is both spiritual and material, a new order of things that is local and universal, here on earth and there in heaven, now with Jesus and perfectly in the future.

Matthew records this ominous message at the very beginning of his gospel (also at 4:17) and will return to it fleetingly in the Beatitudes (5:10) and in the Lord's Prayer ("Thy kingdom come" [6:10]), more specifically in two verses of the Mission Charge ("The kingdom of heaven is at hand" [10:7] and "Ye shall not have gone over the cities of Israel, till the Son of man be come"[10:23]), and at length in the Olivet Discourse of chapters 24–25. The expectations aroused by these passages pervaded much of first-century Christianity.

Beginnings and endings have a fascination of their own, and Matthew's gospel that begins with a birth and ends with a death also tells of a God who created the world and will preside at its end, which it often suggests is alarmingly close. Thus, eschatology and apocalyptic take up some of the most vivid, if perplexing pages in all of Scripture. Although they are often used interchangeably, *eschatology* (a nineteenth-century coinage) refers to prophecies about what will happen in the end time, usually seen as the Four Last Things: death and judgment, heaven and hell; whereas *apocalyptic* refers to their revelation in literature and historical writings that are usually anonymous and always both imaginative and obscure. They both loom large in the intertestamental literature, the Apocrypha and the Pseudepigrapha, which are, for Protestants, noncanonical and hence often neglected. In the New Testament they are the great subject of Revelation, a book that brings the world—and the Bible narrative—to an end.

The problem is that nothing came of all these urgent and fearsome warnings, and the fact that the world did not end or significantly change has concerned Christians, for they are caught between the plain sense of Jesus' predictions and the historical fact that they did not materialize—which can make Jesus seem not only mistaken but like just another deluded doomsayer, not much different from those slightly ridiculous figures who are always heralding the world's end. Christianity's critics have regularly made the failure of the Parousia one of their main objections to the credibility of the gospels. "Unbelievers," said Voltaire, "want to make us blush for our faith, when we consider that the world is still in existence."[10] A classic of late-nineteenth-century Bible-bashing, George Foote's *Bible Handbook for Freethinkers and Inquiring Christians,* listed a number of end-time prophecies among what it called "Absurdities," "Contradictions," "Atrocities," and "Obscenities": "Either these prophecies were spoken by Christ, or they were not. If he uttered them, he stands ignominiously condemned as a false prophet. If he did not, the Evangelists have put them into his mouth without warrant, and the Gospels are 'unreliable fabrications.' In either case Christianity is based on falsehood."[11]

And the English editor and controversialist Robert Blatchford in *God and My Neighbour* (1903), a popular tirade against all things Christian, said of the prophecies, "They are distinct, and definite, and solemn, and—untrue."[12]

But the dissonance between Jesus' statements and the historical record is thus an argument for their scriptural authenticity, though some would attribute these predictions to the early church, not to Jesus, and would emphasize the presence of God's kingdom in Jesus—dramatically so in his miracles (12:28: "But if I cast out devils by the Spirit of God, then the kingdom of God is come unto you"). That this was also a problem for first-century missionaries is clear from a letter attributed to the Apostle Peter, in which he acknowledges that "scoffers" have mocked Christians for their unfulfilled expectations. But he reminds his readers that God's time is not theirs, since "one day is with the Lord as a thousand years, and a thousand years as one day," that the delay offers more time "that all should come to repentance," and that when the "day of the Lord" comes, it will be like "a thief in the night" (2 Pet. 3:8-10).

Others have seen Christianity's first great achievement in internalizing and allegorizing the "kingdom of God," based on such texts as Luke 17:21: "the kingdom of God is within [better: among] you"; John 18:36: "My kingdom is not of this world"; and various sayings attributed to Jesus in the noncanonical *Gospel of Thomas.* Similarly, Matthew 24:36 ("But of that day and hour knoweth no man") helped explain to disappointed apocalypticists why a kingdom of God was not established by Jesus on earth following his resurrection. And it is significant that with the exception of 5:28-29, John replaces the "coming kingdom" with "eternal life" (e.g., 11:25: "I am the resurrection and the life") and in 14:16 looks forward, not to the second coming of Jesus, but to the coming of the "Comforter" (Holy Spirit). There is little eschatology recorded in Luke's Acts of the Apostles, Paul preferred to emphasize Jesus' death and resurrection, and there is no evidence that these failed predictions caused widespread defections among first-century Christians. Finally, with the wild imaginings of Revelation in mind, to what extent should Matthew's readers allow for rhetorical exaggeration—what Matthew Arnold called "turbid Jewish fantasies" of "the grand consummation"?[13]

To rationalize this situation and give it contemporary relevance, there has been in Christian thought a progressive spiritualization (exegetical gymnastics?) of NT apocalyptic, so that its doomsday warnings and "adventist" message yielded to one of personal salvation. Origen (185–254) wrote: "It is clear that he who prays for the coming of the Kingdom of God rightly prays that the Kingdom of God might be established, and bear fruit, and be perfected in himself."[14] And Augustine claimed that Christ's coming "is happening all the time in his Church."[15] Continuing this process, modern critics have spiritualized these predictions—"The 'kingdom of heaven' is a state of the heart" (Nietzsche).[16] So the general understanding is "already, but not yet"—that if the world is not yet about to end ("imminent eschatology"), then the "kingdom" is somehow in Jesus already (for Matthew in the resurrected Jesus), or in the hearts of believers (all examples of "realized eschatology"), or in the visible church. Thomas Hobbes, arguing in his *Leviathan* (1651) for the absolute power of civil authority, would call this last identification "the greatest and main abuse of Scripture."[17] A proof text for this figurative interpretation is the Great Commission of 28:19-20, for why would Jesus instruct his disciples to "teach all nations" and promise to be "with you always, even unto the end of the world," if in fact he was about to return and establish his kingdom on earth?

For others in antiquity, eschatology seems to have been taken less as a timetable than as an expression of hope, an imaginative metaphor to account for present sufferings and to anticipate a future upheaval that would transform lives and alter the course of history in ways that could be left largely undefined. For Jews it had been Israel's hope that God would vindicate her in the face of her enemies, perhaps through the establishment of a messianic kingdom. But now in Matthew it takes the usual two forms: one in the present ministry of Jesus, which was a transforming experience and inaugurated a new age; the other in the anticipation of a second coming that was sometimes seen as near, at other times as distant. For if Jesus by his incarnation, death, and resurrection had not completely defeated Satan (since evil still flourished in the world), then it must have been only a provisional victory, and Christians must await his return—the Parousia—to see the final defeat of evil and the establishment of a new order on earth.

Readers have wondered why, if, as so often claimed, the events of Jesus' career were later formulated in such a way as to bring them into conformity with the early church's understanding of its faith, the gospel editors left untouched these predictions of events that they knew had not come to pass, at least not directly after the resurrection. Was the anticipation of the Parousia still so keen that toward the end of the first century it continued to preoccupy the evangelists and their communities? In the notorious chapter 15 of his *Decline and Fall of the Roman Empire,* Edward Gibbon (1737–94) summed up the evolving views and persistent appeal of an imminent end time from the viewpoint of the eighteenth-century Enlightenment: "Though it might not be universally received, it appears to have been the reigning sentiment of the orthodox believers; and it seems so well adapted to the desires and apprehensions of mankind that it must have contributed, in a very considerable degree, to the progress of the Christian faith. But, when the edifice of the church was almost completed, the temporary support was laid aside. The doctrine of Christ's reign upon earth was at first treated as a profound allegory, was considered by degrees as a doubtful and useless opinion, and was at length rejected as the absurd invention of heresy and fanaticism."[18] And the familiar words of Immanuel Kant (1724–1804) can summarize the Enlightenment view: "We have good reason to say that 'the kingdom of God is come upon us' once the principle of the gradual transition of ecclesiastical faith to the universal religion of reason . . . has become general and has gained somehow a universal foothold."[19]

Thus the kingdom of God is (somehow) both immanent and imminent, present and anticipated in the New Testament; and the same phrase is used to describe both God's redemptive sovereignty in Jesus, with its emphasis on individual salvation, and a future end time of justice and peace. The second understanding has recurred periodically in the crises of Western history, notably in the Reformation, where the instability of the times, the resurgence of biblicism, and the identification of the pope as the antichrist seemed to some radical Reformers to signal a purification of the church and society that would prepare for a second coming. On the continent it was the Anabaptists, particularly Thomas Müntzer (1489–1525), and in England the militant "Fifth Monarchy Men" among Cromwell's followers, who combined gospel passages such as these with the millenarian materials of *Daniel* (7) and *Revelation* (20) to imagine an earthly and, if necessary, violent transformation. But Article 17 of the *Augsburg Confession* (1530), the first creedal formulation of Lutheranism, condemned what came to be known as "Judaizing," abjuring "certain Jewish opinions which are even now making their appearance and which teach that, before the resurrection of the dead, saints and godly men will possess a worldly kingdom and annihilate all the godless."[20]

Nevertheless, many Christians have been obsessed with fixing the end time, and the "dating game" survived among Seventh-day Adventists and Jehovah's Witnesses. For the nineteenth-century followers of William Miller (1782–1849), an early progenitor of Seventh-day Adventism, the "advent" was to occur on October 22, 1844, a non-event later known to Millerites as the "Great Disappointment"; and the expectation of Jesus' early return is still an Adventist doctrine. Charles Taze Russell (1852–1916), the founder of Jehovah's Witnesses, favored 1914; and according to "Dispensationalism," popular in some fundamentalist groups and teaching that God has divided history into a series of periods, we are now in the "dispensation" that will precede the second coming. But for liberal Christians the whole subject remains something of an embarrassment, particularly since end-time preaching has so long been a staple of fundamentalism.

The great humanitarian Albert Schweitzer (1876–1965) was among those convinced that Jesus had meant these predictions seriously and that this expectation determined much of his preaching. So Schweitzer concluded that Jesus' moral teachings must have been an "interim ethic," their radical commands relevant only to the brief time before—or so his Jesus believed—the world would end. He theorized that Jesus was a Jewish apocalypticist who regarded himself as the messiah (but not divine) and who resolved to bring on the kingdom of God by personally enduring the traditional sufferings that had to precede its establishment, only to be disappointed when it did not happen. Jesus, "in the knowledge that He is the coming Son of Man lays hold of the wheel of the world to set it moving in that last revolution which is to bring all ordinary history to a close. It refuses to turn, and He throws Himself upon it. Then it does turn; and crushes Him."[21] But Schweitzer's approach tended to make Jesus eccentric in his own time and irrelevant in ours. It is hard to imagine that the full range of Jesus' teachings, which have enlightened and inspired for centuries, were meant as emergency regulations for only a restricted time; and Schweitzer's critics have shown that the "tradition" of messianic sufferings he invoked hardly existed. The Old Testament can speak eloquently of the suffering of the righteous (Christians especially favored Ps. 22), but there is no record of Jewish expectation that their messiah would die and be resurrected.

As anticipation of the end time weakened amid the realities of an industrializing world, many American Christians, mostly Protestants, sought to create at least a version of the "kingdom of God" on earth through the kinds of human efforts that they hoped would lead to social progress, moral improvement, and even material prosperity—a secular kingdom to match the spiritual kingdom preached by Jesus. One such effort was the creation of interdenominational agencies such as settlement houses, the YMCA, the WCTU, and campus organizations, which, along with evangelism, would provide worldly benefits. Another was the worldwide spread of missionary societies in the late nineteenth century, building schools and hospitals along with churches, particularly in the Far East and Africa.

The eventual establishment of God's "kingdom" was also the goal of a Baptist minister and seminary professor named Walter Rauschenbusch (1861–1918), who with like-minded colleagues preached a "Social Gospel" of public justice and reform to the rapidly developing America of the late nineteenth and early twentieth centuries. In a series of books, Rauschenbusch addressed and sought to empower Christians, not just as individuals, but as members of social institutions. Martin Luther King Jr. said that reading his *Christianity and the Social Crisis* (1907) left "an indelible imprint on my thinking."[22] Departing from traditional Protestant theories of human depravity and individual sanctification under the influence of Albert Ritschl (1822–89) and Adolf von Harnack (1856–1930), liberal Lutheran theologians, and drawing on his years of experience as an evangelical minister in New York's "Hell's Kitchen," Rauschenbusch offered a message of social betterment that he claimed was authentically biblical in that it considered Jesus not only as a divine individual but also as a historical figure in the context of his imperfect society.

For the proponents of the Social Gospel, original sin was greed and selfishness, not pride, and sin was an offense not only against God but against humanity. Hence faith was also a confidence in the "feasibility of a fairly right-eous and social order," and creating the "reign of God," not founding a church, was Jesus' true purpose during his ministry. His explicit message may have been of personal repentance and salvation, but implicit in his law of love was a criticism of society's injustices (why else would the Romans have crucified him?) and a vision of "humanity organized according to the will of God."[23] This was an exegetical position that was strong on principles—brotherhood of man, fatherhood of God—but weak on specifics, and one that required its proponents to urge reforms in, for example, labor relations, while maneuvering around passages indicating an imminent end time and without upsetting the capitalist system or alienating those Christians who supported it. It was not helped by the oft quoted "Ye have the poor always with you" (26:11; Mark 14:7; John 12:8), and its confidence in social progress was un-dermined by the catastrophe of two world wars. But its advocacy of a struggle for social justice, now militant and Marxist, was revived in the liberation the-ology popular in Latin America in the 1960s.

Jesus' baptism traditionally took place about five miles south of the Allenby Bridge, the location of the Greek Monastery of St. John. It is now in a mili-tary district inaccessible to visitors, but for those wishing to be baptized in the Jordan, the Israelis have built a facility where Lake Tiberias empties into the Jordan.

Jesus' baptism marks the first appearance of his (and probably Matthew's) opponents, "the Pharisees and Sadducees," an odd coupling that appears only in this gospel (also at 16:1, 6, 11, 12), and unexpectedly, since the two groups were opposed to one another. The historical record is meager, but *Pharisee* may mean "separatist." They were a close-knit group numbering about six thou-sand in a first-century population of some two million Jews and had been in existence for some two hundred years. The Pharisees taught that God had re-vealed two laws, written and oral. They were concerned to interpret them both, particularly purity regulations for fasting, dieting, and tithing, in ways that would enable observant Jews to sanctify their lives by observing (some would say "bending") the law, which was often vague and ambiguous in its in-junctions, especially in the difficult conditions of Greek and Roman rule. For the Pharisees, holiness was virtually synonymous with purity, and they taught that observant Jews would be rewarded by bodily resurrection and eternal life, while the faithless would find suffering in a lower world. The Pharisees were assisted by the "scribes," who were teachers of the law; however, their power was limited, since they did not control the temple, which was under the Sad-ducees and administered by priests and their assistants, the descendants of Jacob's son Levi, who were called "Levites." After the Romans conquered Jerusalem and destroyed the temple in AD 70, they conceded some power to the Pharisees, allowing them to open an academy in Jamnia on the Mediterranean, where they undertook to establish a rabbinic Judaism, that is, without sacrifices and temple cult but centering on the interpretation and application of the Torah, the first five books of the Bible. Their work eventually produced a collection of laws known as the Mishnah (Hebrew: "repeat and study") and the Mishnah commentary, the Talmud (Hebrew: "study, learn"). Unfortunately, their portrayal in the New Testament as advocates of an external purity seemingly contrasted with the interior holiness of Jesus, their exclusiveness opposing his inclusiveness, has made them into officious and sanctimonious legalists obsessed with formalistic details. Jesus openly and repeatedly denounces them, virulently in chapter 23 ("Woe unto you, scribes and Pharisees"); their name has become a synonym for bigoted hypocrites; and Protestants have often seen them as prototypes of the Catholic hierarchy. But all worship entails formalities, and hypocrisy and self-righteousness are not reserved to any one group. Thus, as fashions changed in biblical scholarship, the Pharisees have been rehabilitated to the extent that Jesus himself is associated with them at least in his concern to "fulfill the law."

As for the Sadducees, they were a smaller group of aristocratic Jews associated with the temple and concerned to maintain good relations with their Roman masters—they were, in effect, the Jerusalem Establishment. Since only priests could perform animal sacrifices, they were more involved with the temple's cult practices than with purity regulations, and they recognized only the Torah, the first five books of the Old Testament. It was they who provided the high priest and dominated the Sanhedrin, the Jewish governing body that met in the temple area, and they appear prominently in the Passion Narrative of chapters 26–27. Finally, there were the scribes (first mentioned at 5:20). So called because they had to copy the Torah by hand, they were also its interpreters. It is not clear from the Bible how much overlap there was among Pharisees, Sadducees, Sanhedrin members, scribes, and chief priests; or how their jurisdictions were defined, assigned, and administered; or how they normally interacted with the Roman authorities.

Here John addresses these "generations of vipers" by name, whereas Luke has him speak to "the multitude that came forth to be baptized" (3:7). In John Bunyan's *Pilgrim's Progress* (1678–79), John's warning, that they should "flee from the wrath to come," are put in the mouth of "a man named Evangelist" who starts the hero on his journey to Mt. Zion.[24] This warning was also cited in 1743 by John and Charles Wesley as the motive for the meetings, beginning in 1739, that were the origin of the societies that became Methodism.[25] John's cryptic command at 3:8 and his admonishment at 3:9 suggest that it is not enough for the Israelites to trust their status as Abraham's children; nor will the water of baptism save those who do not also perform good works. Since the Greek of verse 8 is as ambiguous as the literal KJV translation, this became an important proof text in Reformation controversies. For Catholics it meant that good works could contribute to contrition, could in fact earn remission of some of the temporal punishment due to sin; whereas for Protestants it meant that good works were the fruits, or results, of true contrition. Hence, the KJV's "*meet for* repentance" and the English translation of the "Repentance" entry in the Lutheran Augsburg Confession (1530) as "Bear fruit that *befits* repentance."[26]

Verses 11-12 are, with Luke 3:16, the source of the "baptism of fire," foreshadowing the appearance of the Holy Spirit to Jesus' apostles in tongues of fire at Pentecost, when the church is born (Acts 2:2-3). It can suggest warmth and light, but it also suggests access through suffering, perhaps with reference to the fire and flood tribulations of the end time. Later, martyrs were said to undergo a "baptism of blood," and for those unable to undergo the ordinary rite there was a "baptism of desire." "Baptism of fire" is now used to designate any initial exposure to danger and hostility. The motto of the Salvation Army is "Blood and Fire," with the fire of the Holy Spirit symbolized by the bright sun in the official crest.

In verses 14-15, Matthew wants to make it clear that Jesus, being without sin, did not require baptism. Commentators have suggested that he may have submitted to it in order to set an example for others and show them the way to "righteousness" (a favorite word for Matthew) or to show his solidarity with sinful mankind. Perhaps, too, it was a tribute to John and his ministry. Nevertheless, Jesus' baptism remains problematic: Mark has John baptize Jesus, but Matthew records a protest; Luke does not say who baptized Jesus; and John omits it entirely. Still, the account of Jesus undergoing a rite required of sinful converts is so incongruous that it meets historians' "criterion of dissimilarity," whereby the recording of events that apparently contradict an argument speaks for their authenticity.

Jesus' baptism is validated by the presence of the Holy Spirit, who is always associated with his baptism in the New Testament. Its descending "like a dove" on the water (16) recalls two other beginnings: the "spirit of God" that "moved upon the face of the waters" (Gen. 1:2), and the dove that Noah sent out to discover if the flood waters had abated (Gen. 8:8-12). So once again Matthew suggests that a new creation is at hand. The Holy Spirit is usually understood in terms of power, "tongues of fire," so the dove may seem an odd symbol, since in Greek paganism it was emblematic of the lustful Aphrodite. But its whiteness suggests purity, and it was also believed to be without bile and hence a symbol of gentle virtue. After first appearing carved on the famous sarcophagus of Junius Bassus (359; Vatican), it came to represent the Holy Spirit in medieval art; and it regularly appeared in the lives of saints, notably when it flew through a church window with a vial of holy and sweet-smelling oil for St. Remigius as he was baptizing Clovis, the first Christian king of France, on

Christmas Day 493.[27] The Holy Spirit is sometimes illustrated as a dove descending within a seven-pointed star, which represents its seven gifts: wisdom, understanding, counsel, strength, knowledge, godliness, and holy fear; and Calvin compared its manifestation of the Holy Spirit with the bread that manifests Jesus' body at the Last Supper.[28] Some have even seen the Holy Spirit in the animating finger of God that gives life to Adam in Michelangelo's celebrated painting on the Sistine Chapel ceiling. Its presence here along with Jesus and the voice of the Lord (often depicted in art by a hand appearing from above) makes this one of the New Testament's few Trinitarian proof texts, with the Father's "voice from heaven" making explicit the divine sonship of Jesus that was implied by "Emmanuel" ("God with us") at 1:23. Conversely, for some of those who claimed that Jesus was born and died a man, it was the Holy Spirit that here at his baptism filled him with the divine powers he exhibited in his ministry; and after his death and resurrection Jesus will in a sense "return" in Acts as the Holy Spirit. Early Christian representations of the baptism often added a river god personifying the Jordan, either in alarm or retreat, as befits a pagan counterpart of Satan.

Matthew's "This is my beloved Son" is a more public announcement than the "Thou art" versions recorded by Mark (1:11) and Luke (3:22), where the Holy Spirit speaks to Jesus—but neither John nor the crowds seem to hear it, and it is surprising that no one makes subsequent reference to this event. Though Jesus' divinity is also implied in the infancy narrative and elsewhere by his authority and powers, and his messianic status by the oft-repeated "Son of David," this expression of divine Sonship will recur explicitly at 8:29 (by devils), at 11:27 (by Jesus himself), at 14:33 (by his disciples), at 16:16 (by Peter), at 17:5 (by a voice from heaven), at 26:63 (by the high priest, accusingly), at 27:40 (by mocking passersby), and at 27:54 (by a Roman centurion). The significance of another title, "Son of Man," occurring some thirty times, is less certain, though it recalls the visionary "Son of man" who comes "with the clouds of heaven" at Daniel 7:13, a figure traditionally seen as a prototype of the returning Jesus.

The Temptation Narrative

> In those three questions the whole
> subsequent history of mankind is,
> as it were, brought together into one
> whole and foretold, and in them are
> united all the unsolved historical
> contradictions of human nature.
> —Dostoevsky

Chapter 4 presents one of Matthew's most dramatic episodes, a direct confrontation between Jesus and Satan that has come to be known as the Temptation of Jesus or the temptation narrative. "Temptation" is a traditional but misleading translation of the Greek *peirasmon,* since it suggests a kind of moralistic enticement. And though it persists in the familiar words from the Lord's Prayer, "Lead us not into temptation," it should rather be understood in the New Testament as a trial or a test or an ordeal—and that is how it is rendered in the *New Jerusalem Bible* (1985). Its first appearance is in Mark, where it was worth only two verses (1:12-13): "And immediately the spirit driveth him into the wilderness. And he was there in the wilderness forty days, tempted of Satan; and was with the wild beasts; and the angels ministered unto him." But even Mark's brief description, with the surprisingly forceful "driveth," provided the outline: Jesus in the wilderness for forty days; the attendant and presumably empowering "spirit"; the wild beasts, who perhaps were also harmless; the confrontation with Satan; the tempting; and, at its conclusion, the ministering angels (only the fasting is absent, and Mark does not make it clear when in the forty days the temptations occur). So it was in Q, the "Sayings Source," that both Matthew and Luke must have found the substance of the conflict between these mighty opposites, with Matthew influencing Luke as each evangelist shaped the story to fit his narrative and theological needs. A factual basis for this event is harder to determine, since there were no eyewitnesses, though Jesus might have described it to his disciples. Origen early noted its physical implausibilities, and some have thought that it might have originally been a parable that was subsequently dramatized. But many today prefer to regard it as an exclusively spiritual experience, a psychodrama of Jesus' preparation for the trials and vicissitudes of his ministry.[29]

The Sinai desert would have been an appropriate setting, but the traditional location of the wilderness is on Mt. Quarantina (Latin for "forty"), now Deir el-Quruntul, just outside Jericho and the site today of a Greek Orthodox monastery. The second temptation takes place atop the temple in Jerusalem. For the third trial there is no "exceeding high mountain" in Judea (Mt. Quarantina is only 1,200 feet), so Matthew's reference here may be to Mt. Pisgah, from which Moses was shown the Promised Land (Deut. 34:1), just as Jesus is shown—and offered—"all the kingdoms of the world." Voltaire wondered how this was possible, but the reference may be to the known world, for otherwise the fact that they could all be seen from this mountain might convince a literal reader that the earth was in fact a flat, round disk, which has made this the subject of many an ingenious speculation.[30] Did Satan do it with maps or mirrors? Or simply point in their general direction? Or, grotesque as it may seem, did he carry Jesus on a round-the-world flight? Or does the word "kingdoms" stand for worldly power? But it may be that Matthew intended this final "temptation" to be wholly visionary. In the *Geneva Bible* (1560), the Bible of Shakespeare and the Puritans, the marginal note was emphatic: "In a vision."[31] This was also Calvin's view, and he added, "In a doubtful matter like this, where ignorance does no harm, I prefer to pass no judgment, rather than to provide contentious people with something to quarrel about."[32]

The episode begins with Jesus being led into the wilderness by "the spirit," that is, the "Spirit of God" of 3:16, usually understood as the Holy Spirit, though nothing more of its activity or influence is reported. There, after forty days of fasting, the devil appears, here called the "tempter," although Matthew also calls him the "devil," as well as "Satan," the name used exclusively by Mark and Paul before him. His appearance here is unparalleled in Scripture, though Matthew makes no mention of his being a fallen angel, or coming from hell, or arriving with infernal attendants, or sporting a tail, horns, and pointed ears (borrowed from paganism's fauns and satyrs)—details that would later be added by the church's demonologists. But he at once subjects Jesus to three temptations, which are often classified as personal (food), religious (worship), and political (power), though it is well to remember—and often forgotten— that these are tests of Jesus' fitness for his mission, not of his resistance to "sin." So although he is being "tempted" by Satan, he is really being "tested" by God.[33]

Satan's motive is not specified, but most commentators tend to infer from "If thou be the Son of God" that he is using these tests to determine Jesus' status and test his obedience, especially now that he is alone and hungry, and, if possible, to subvert his ministry before it begins. In any case, the tests are not meant to evoke the Seven Deadly Sins, since few of God's creatures are ever tempted to change stones into bread, leap off temple roofs, or accept world rule from the hand of Satan. Nevertheless, they had to be made part of the Bible's moralizing tradition, so the earliest commentators saw them as replicating, and reversing, the temptations offered to Adam, in that he succumbed to Satan and ate the forbidden fruit so that he and Eve might "be as gods" (Gen. 3:1-6); and they saw Jesus' situation foreshadowed in Job, where another good man assailed by Satan (though not personally) would maintain his faith in God.

Satan directs his first temptation at Jesus' fasting, a physical ordeal that is usually interpreted as a sign of his human nature. He challenges him to appease his hunger by performing a magic feat, changing stones into bread. Jesus answers with Moses' words from Deuteronomy 8:3, where he reminded the Israelites that the Lord had provided manna when they hungered in the desert—and "man doth not live by bread alone" has become one of the Bible's best known citations. Later Jesus will, in fact, miraculously provide bread— but for others, not for himself (14:19, 15:36).

Then the scene changes to Jerusalem, the center of the world and the "holy city," a designation found only here and in Revelation 21:10. The "temptation" changes too, since now Jesus is asked to "test" his divine Father, unless, as some church fathers have held, he is actually referring to himself as Satan's "Lord" and "God." This test entails his leaping from a high part of the temple, and since it might have been precarious for them both to stand on a "pinnacle," this may refer to a parapet, probably on the southeastern corner of the Temple Mount, overlooking the Kidron Valley, the place from which St. James would later be thrown to his death. (One wonders in passing how what Milton called a "tottering and giddy act" might have played itself out before the crowds that daily thronged the temple courts, though the pinnacle may have been hidden from public view.)[34] The Lord will then be forced to interfere miraculously with the natural order and "bear up" the falling Jesus, probably by a flight of rescuing angels. Jesus' response is again from Deuteronomy, this time based on the passage (6:16) where Moses reminded the restive Israelites of how they had tempted the Lord at Massah (a word that itself means "test": Ex. 17:1-7) when they were thirsty, and how they had forced Moses to get water from a rock, a sign that would prove that God was with them. For Chrysostom, one of Matthew's first commentators, this was proof that in the face of temptation we should rely on our own faith; we must not presume upon God, test His providence, and hope to be rescued by a miracle from on high—which is coercion, not trust.[35] But in a ninth-century Muslim version of this temptation that denies his divinity, Jesus responds with "God ordered me not to put myself to the test, for I do not know whether he will save me or not."[36]

The final and climactic temptation (the third, Matthew being fond of groups of three and of seven), this time without the "Son of God" formula, is on a mountaintop, from where they can see "all the kingdoms of the world," which Satan offers to Jesus in return for his submission and worship. Longfellow wrote: "These kingdoms all are mine, and thine shall be, / If thou wilt worship me."[37] In the Salem witchcraft trials the same charge was brought against George Burroughs, formerly a Puritan pastor there, that among his other devilish offenses he had bewitched a woman by carrying her "into a very high mountain, where he show'd her mighty and glorious kingdoms, and said, He would give them all to her, if she would write in his Book." This contributed to his reputation as a "wizard"; and even though he recited the Lord's Prayer, a traditional antidote to the devil, he was hanged on August 19, 1692.[38] Of course, Satan may be lying, since he is after all the "Father of Lies" (John 8:44), but Jesus also calls him "the prince of this world" (John 12:31), so we may understand that at this point the power and the glory of this world, sometimes understood as the Roman Empire, belong to the devil and are his to give—a sobering consideration for those who seek worldly power. Interestingly, Jesus rejects Satan's demand for submission but not the power to rule the world. He will later claim his own kind of kingdom, but not before he has to wear a crown of thorns. This is a forceful reminder that Jesus' ministry is ultimately cosmic and redemptive, going beyond teaching, preaching, and healing to become a rescue operation, a story of human salvation from the powers of evil. Another attraction of this third offer is that Satan promises what many Jews must have yearned for, a messiah who would appear as a mighty warrior and world ruler. But Jesus' kingdom is not of this world; he is answerable to his Father; and again he cites Deuteronomy, this time a free version of 6:13, with "worship" replacing Moses' warning that the Israelites should "fear the Lord thy God."

There is no response from the devil, and he leaves him to the angels who "came and ministered unto him," which probably means no more than that they brought him food. This is the subject of Carracci's *Christ in the Desert, Served by Angels* (1608–10; Berlin). But even this detail is meaningful, for it is a way to show that the episode has ended happily (comedies, as opposed to tragedies, often end with a banquet, and a messianic banquet is part of some end-time scenarios). Jesus, successfully initiated into the power of evil and emerging unscathed from the wilderness, can now rejoin society and commence his ministry.

All three versions of the temptation narrative look before and after, back to the distant past of Israel and the immediate past of Jesus' baptism, and forward to Jesus' testing by his opponents—including Peter himself!—and ultimately to the final struggle with Satan that will mark the end time. Thus, they are rich in echoes, allusions, and associations, evoking in these few lines some of the most momentous events in Scripture. Like the Israelites in Exodus 14–16, Jesus passes from the water of baptism (Red Sea) to the desert of temptation (Sinai). And the motif of testing is in the Bible from its beginning: Adam and Eve by Satan in Eden (Gen. 3:1-6); Abraham ordered to sacrifice his son Isaac (Gen. 22:1-18); Jacob wrestling at night with a mysterious figure before he can enter Canaan and meet Esau (Gen. 32:24-32); Joseph questioning his brothers to find out if they have changed (Gen. 44:17-34); and Moses challenged again and again by the "murmuring" Israelites (e.g., Ex. 15:24, 16:2).

More specific is the mention of "forty days and forty nights," often indicating a period of hardship, such as fasting, which may have been required of candidates for baptism in the early church. Although forty can often stand for little more than a biblical designation of a large number, readers cannot help remembering that Moses was on Mt. Sinai for "forty days and forty nights" (Ex. 24:18) and that after breaking the tablets of the law he again fasted there with the Lord "forty days and forty nights" (Deut. 9:18), or that Yahweh made the Israelites "wander in the wilderness forty years" (Num. 14:33), or that Elijah would later fast on Mt. Horeb for "forty days and forty nights" (1 Kgs. 19:8). One might go further back and see in Jesus' fasting an indictment of Adam's eating, or associate this ordeal of forty days with the ordeal of the

Flood (Gen. 7:4). But the wild beasts of Mark 1:13 are something of a puzzle. Was there once a version in which Jesus, like some mythic hero alone in the forest, perhaps being prepared for kingship, had to prove his worth by overcoming them, too? Are we to recall Samson and the lion in Judges 14:5-6? Or are the wild beasts the servants of Satan (even the source of his horns), just as beasts, including a "great red dragon," accompany the antichrist in Revelation (12:3)? Or should we think of Isaiah 11:6-9, where in the messianic age the lion will lie down with the lamb (though if we are to believe Woody Allen, the lamb won't get much sleep) and imagine that Jesus' presence somehow tamed them? Or can this refer to Eden before the Fall, where Adam and Eve lived peacefully with animals, just as stories were told of certain early monks, anchorites who enjoyed power over the animals they encountered in their desert retreats? In the popular *Meditations,* Jesus is seen "humbly conversing" with them. In any case, wild beasts, like demons, belong to a wilderness, though this location rather belongs to the Israelites' wanderings as they slowly made their way from Egypt to the promised land, particularly since for them this was also a period of trial and temptation, one that even extended into their history in Canaan.

Reinforcing these references to Moses is the typology of the infancy narrative: both Jesus and Moses are leaders and liberators who survived an endangered birth and the threats of a hostile ruler, and both had to seek refuge in a foreign land. But a more immediate source is the preceding event: Jesus' baptism. In 3:17 "a voice from heaven" publicly proclaims, "This is my beloved Son, in whom I am well pleased," words overheard by Satan (according to Chrysostom) and repeated in 4:3 and 6, "If thou be the Son of God."[39] This is not the only instance of the devil quoting Scripture, for in verse 6 he quotes Psalm 91:11-12 in praise of the righteous believer: "For he shall give his angels charge over thee. . . . They shall bear thee up in their hands, lest thou dash thy foot against a stone" (though being the devil, he omits the reassurance of "to keep thee in all thy ways"). And in turn, Jesus' Deuteronomy citations witness his observance of the Mosaic law: the proverbial "Man doth not live by bread alone" is from 8:3; "Thou shalt not tempt the Lord thy God" is from 6:16; and "Thou shalt worship the Lord thy God" is from 6:13. All of this reminds Christians that, yes, the devil can quote Scripture, but, as Jesus shows, Scripture can also be used to defeat him. In fact, readers often fail to note that the only words Jesus speaks that are not scriptural are his final dismissal: "Get thee hence, Satan."

It is not surprising that the temptation narrative is laced with these references to the Hebrew Bible, and Matthew's fulfillment citations are regularly introduced by the formulaic "This was done that it might be fulfilled, which was spoken by the prophet" (e.g., 1:22, 2:15, 2:17, 2:23, 4:14, 8:17, 12:17, 13:35, 21:4, 26:56, 27:9). This formula, with slight variations, often specifies the prophet, usually Isaiah or Jeremiah, but there are many other instances, such as the Deuteronomy quotes here in 4:1-11, where the references are less explicit, even buried in minor or extraneous details of the narrative, and require secondary interpretation. However, in every instance Matthew wants to show that the Hebrew Bible also belongs to Christians and that its composers, particularly the prophets, gifted with a kind of divine clairvoyance, were preparing its readers for the ministry of Christ. The fulfillment citations may often be obscure and oblique and divorced from their context (as the Bible's critics never tire of insisting), but for Matthew and his readers they show that both Testaments offer a single, unified, and unfolding plan of salvation. Or, to paraphrase an old Latin jingle: What is "latent" in the OT is "patent" in the NT. The promises of the Old are fulfilled in the events of the New, an evolutionary process of revelation that for Matthew valorizes the writings of the Israelites, however much his critics may complain that it also undercuts the uniqueness and authority of the Hebrew Bible.

The temptation narrative also looks forward, foreshadowing subsequent events in Matthew's gospel and in the Christian Bible itself. The "exceeding high" mountain location of the third temptation is the first of a number of mountains that provide the setting for the "high points" of Jesus' ministry: the Sermon on the Mount (5:1), which Luke puts on a plain; the Feeding of the Four Thousand (15:29); the transfiguration (17:1); the eschatological discourse on the "mount of Olives" (24:3); and the Great Commission (28:19). Here Matthew deviates from Luke, who places the third and most spectacular temptation on the temple in Jerusalem (4:9), thus reflecting the latter's interest in Jerusalem and paralleling the sequence of temptations with the progress of his narrative, which will climax and conclude in Jerusalem—or, as John Lightfoot suggested in the seventeenth century, replicating the temptations to Eve: hunger; lust of the eyes (Gen. 3:6 "pleasant to the eyes"); and a "leap" (of pride).[40] By contrast, Matthew's sequence is symbolic, a progress of ascent, with the ascending scale of temptations matched geographically by a rise from the desert to the temple roof to a mountain. There Satan offers Jesus the highest temptation of all, universal power in exchange for submission and worship, and there Matthew can exploit the dramatic and authoritative effect of Jesus' final rebuke, "Get thee hence, Satan: for it is written, Thou shalt worship the Lord thy God, and him only shalt thou serve"—which later became a Reformation proof text against the veneration of saints. (A more familiar, almost proverbial, equivalent is the famous "Get thee behind me, Satan" from Mark 8:33.) This is the same rebuke that Jesus will later deliver to Peter, the "Prince of the Apostles," when even his faith falters and he will not believe Jesus' prediction of his passion (16:21-23). It is remarkable that this latter rebuke so closely follows Peter's "Confession" (16:16: "Thou art Christ, the Son of the living God") and his commissioning (16:19: "I will give unto thee the keys of the kingdom of heaven"), but it reinforces the message of the temptation narrative: Peter, like Jesus, must have the faith that will enable him to survive failed expectations, in his case that Jesus would be accepted as Israel's triumphant messiah.

The mountain setting of verses 1-11 also evokes the traditional image of "sacred mountains"—lofty, inaccessible, imposing—and their association with gods (Mt. Olympus is the most familiar example; even the pyramids in mountainless Egypt). So it is appropriate that here is where the evangelists oppose Savior and Destroyer, the Son of God with the Prince of Darkness, lords of their respective realms. Next, the "forty days" of 4:2 recur in Acts 1:3, where the apostles, like Jesus himself in the temptation narrative, are preparing for their ministry. And 4:1-11 also reaches to the very end of the New Testament, where, in the apocalyptic vision of Revelation, Jesus and Satan, represented by the forces of Good and Evil, meet in the final cosmic battle of the end time. Finally, the forty days of fasting remain a present reality for Christians, the season of Lent, when for more than five weeks of self-denial and penitence—the "fast before the feast"—they can prepare spiritually to celebrate the resurrection on Easter Sunday.

The tempting of Jesus by Satan also foreshadows the opposition his ministry will provoke as he is constantly challenged by the Jewish leaders. Here in the wilderness, the messianic vocation announced at Jesus' baptism (3:17: "This is my beloved Son") is being put to the test for the first time. It will not be the last, however, and four times Matthew records an explicit tempting. In 16:1 "The Pharisees also with the Sadducees came, and tempting him" wanted him to prove his divinity by "a sign from heaven"; in 19:3 the subject is divorce, and "The Pharisees also came unto him, tempting him"; in 22:18 it is the question of rendering tribute to Caesar, when Jesus said, "Why tempt ye me, ye hypocrites?"; and in 22:35 one of their number, a lawyer, "asked him a question, tempting him." Moreover, the words of divine Sonship that Satan uses to tempt Jesus will recur when he hangs on the cross and a passerby mockingly tempts him, "If thou be the Son of God, come down from the cross" (27:40).

If the infancy narrative brought Jesus onto the world scene, then the temptation narrative does the same for Satan. His prominence in the Synoptic Gospels (though he is allowed little to say in his own behalf), particularly in exorcisms, meant that his influence would not be limited to Scripture. It contributed to the establishment of the devil in Christianity as a personal and external force of evil with considerable autonomy, not just the "Accuser" of the prologue to Job (1:6-12, 2:2-7), or the folklore figure he became in normative Judaism, or the rebellious and fallen angel of Christian legends (described in

Milton's *Paradise Lost* and *Paradise Regained*), or the comic troublemaker of medieval drama, or the dark hero of Romanticism, or the vague personification of evil that he is for many modern believers.

Indeed, the devil comes into his own in the Christian Bible (in the Hebrew Bible it is the Lord who tests). The fact that the presence of the devil and demons is neither explained by Jesus nor doubted by his audience indicates their increasing acceptance in post-Exilic and Hellenistic Judaism as radical and objective agents of evil, responsible, if only temporarily and with God's implied consent, for the many sufferings of the Jewish people. Similarly, Scripture generally does not question its assumption that there exist intermediate spirits bridging the gap between God and man, from the benign angel-messengers of the Old Testament through the adversarial "Satan" of Job (and, retrospectively, of Genesis), to the fully-fledged demons of the Apocrypha and the New Testament (1 John 3:8: "For this purpose the Son of God was manifested, that he might destroy the works of the devil"). Later, in formulating a doctrine of the atonement, Christian theologians would see the ransoming of mankind from its bondage to the devil as one way of understanding Jesus' redemptive mission (cf. Matt. 20:28). One prominent theologian calls this temptation event "the dawning of the time of salvation," in that Jesus' victory here anticipates the resurrection.[41] As in the temptation narrative, Jesus is everywhere victorious in his encounters with Satan, although the historical—and sometimes pathological—obsession many Christians would have with the power of demons and witches has not been a very worthy demonstration of their faith in his "vanquishing" of the devil. But they could respond that what Matthew presents here is only a vanquishing, since the devil, inferior in status and limited in his power, can be defeated, but as an immortal—if fallen—angel, cannot be destroyed. He (and not even the most ardent feminists seem interested in questioning his gender) enjoys God's toleration if not His favor (they agree to disagree), and modern readers, more disposed to accept the universality of evil rather than its source, and perhaps reluctant to assert the existence of personal devils, must acknowledge the demonic element in human experience and so deal, as best they can, with "the wiles and wickedness of the devil."

The temptation narrative reappears throughout subsequent history, and Jesus' wilderness experience would be replicated in the lives of early Christian hermits who followed him there to serve God in solitude and detachment. But the desert is also the abode of evil spirits. Athanasius reports in his biography of Saint Anthony that the third-century founder of Western monasticism was assailed by demonic visitations that were not only frequent but often spectacular—with offers of wealth, glory, and carnal delights—and that fasting was one weapon that could be deployed against Satan.[42] The deceptive allurements the devils could offer made this event the first of those "pacts with the devil" that are familiar from the Faust legend. Furthermore, in the retelling of this event in the popular *Meditations on the Life of Christ* (late 13th century), readers are urged to imitate Jesus in four ways: "solitude, fasting, prayer, and corporeal suffering."[43] And it was during a forty-day fast on a high mountain that St. Francis received the stigmata, the wounds Jesus suffered on the cross. The value of Scripture was also enhanced when Jesus quoted Deuteronomy against the devil (Jesus' performance has been likened to a bar mitzvah, where a young Jew is tested on his ability to read from the Torah), so the need to read the Bible in order to combat Satan was cited by the Reformers as justification for a vernacular translation available to the laity.

That Jesus spurned an earthly kingdom offered a proof text for the papacy's superiority over secular rulers and was so used by the activist Gregory VII (1073–85), pope and saint, in his "Investiture Controversy" with the German emperor, Henry IV (1056–1106), ruler of the Holy Roman Empire, who had himself been crowned and anointed by the pope but whose authority depended on the allegiance of local bishops. This was a power struggle between popes and kings, and the question at issue was the right of lay rulers to make appointments to ecclesiastical offices (invest them "with ring and staff"), a question complicated by the fact that often the candidates were themselves royal officials. Gregory justified excommunication by citing 4:8-9 to Hermann, the Bishop of Metz, in a famous letter of 1081 that has become a classic statement of the popes' claim to universal jurisdiction ("Who can doubt that the priests of Christ are to be accounted the fathers and judges of kings and princes and of all the faithful?"), though his power to excommunicate kings did not include the means to depose them.[44] Eventually, Henry capitulated and stood barefoot in the snow at the gates of Canossa with his wife and child on three successive days in 1077 to receive the pope's absolution, although a final compromise was not reached until the Concordat of Worms in 1122.

But that is not all, for the three temptations have such a privileged place in the Synoptic Gospels that they were also, perhaps inevitably, applied to human experience—provided that hunger could be reinterpreted as gluttony, the testing of God as pride or presumption, and the rule of the world as vainglory or avarice. A scene of divine identity and preparation became a paradigm of worldly morality, and Jesus was seen as resisting the three great foes of humankind: the world, the flesh, and the devil. This was an interpretation slimly supported by the stories of Satan's two other testings—of Adam and Job—and tenuously linked to a dubious proof text from 1 John 2:16 ("For all that is in the world, the lust of the flesh, and the lust of the eyes, and the pride of life, is not of the Father, but is of the world"); but these three perils reverberated through patristic and medieval Christianity, even appearing in the baptism formula of the *Book of Common Prayer* (1559), where the candidate is called upon to "forsake the devil and all his works, the vain pomp, and glory of the world."[45] This might be seen as a homiletic understanding of 4:1-11, that Jesus' resistance was exemplary and didactic, an inspiration for individuals confronting life's temptations, though it took some hard interpreting to bring Satan's cosmic challenges into the orbit of common experience. Nonetheless, it is an understanding that can be found today in two of the most popular of Lenten hymns. One is attributed to St. Flavian: "Lord, who throughout these forty days, / For us did fast and pray, / Teach us with you to mourn our sins, / And close by you to stay" (Hernaman trans.). In the third stanza of the other hymn, "Forty Days and Forty Nights," even pleasure is perilous: "Shall we not thy sorrows share, / And from earthly joys abstain, / Fasting with unceasing prayer, / Glad with thee to suffer pain?" (Smyttan and Pott trans.). Praying was here added to fasting since it was assumed that Satan's visits left Jesus with a good deal of time on his hands that he undoubtedly spent in prayer. For whom? For sinners, that they might learn to repent their wrongdoings and amend their lives. Thus the forty days of Jesus' fasting became a period of prayerful intercession, and his time of preparation evolved into an opportunity for Christian penitence.

This curious interpretation of a gospel text that itself said nothing of prayer or repentance did not satisfy the Reformers. As for fasting, Augustine noted that Jesus celebrated the first Eucharist while he was eating with his apostles, though he also allowed for the custom of fasting before receiving the sacrament.[46] And in one of his few surviving sermons, John Knox, the founder of Presbyterianism, complained that "gluttony appears little to agree with the purpose of the Holy Ghost." He also argued that Christians should follow Christ's commandments, not imitate his actions, or else they would find themselves trying to walk on water, raise the dead, and go forty days without eating.[47] Calvin also objected to associating Jesus' hunger with gluttony, even with appetite, and he saw nothing meritorious in Lenten fasting, a practice dating from the fourth century and established by the Council of Orleans in 541.[48] It was yet another of the Roman practices that he deplored and was humanly impossible to imitate since no one but Jesus could last forty days without food (though Voltaire noted that the poor have to observe Lenten fasting all year).[49] Luther allowed for limited fasting as an "outward Christian discipline," since it seems to have been practiced by John the Baptist and his disciples, confirmed by Jesus' words at 6:16-18 ("when ye fast") and 9:15 ("then shall they fast"), and continued by his disciples (Acts 13:2, 14:23). Thomas More disagreed, pointing to 17:21 (a verse of doubtful authenticity), where Jesus connected fasting with prayer as weapons against the devil.[50] But for Luther, like Calvin, fasting smacked of "works-righteousness," and he cautioned that it not be done "for the purpose of making it an act of worship or a means of meriting something and reconciling God."[51] So while these Protestant leaders saw

Jesus' behavior as admirable and instructive, and acknowledged that his resistance offered a model for Christians facing less exalted temptations, they preferred to see his responses as representing, not the overcoming of temptations, but the victory of faith, a victory won through trust in God and His Scriptures.

Calvin's position was witnessed in literature, where John Milton's *Paradise Regained* (1671) is an extended version of the temptation, based on the Lukan sequence of tests, that plays down any exemplary role for Jesus.[52] Milton's version was preceded by a play, *The Temptation of our Lord* (1538), by a bishop named John Bale, and by a poem, *Christ's Victory and Triumph,* by Giles Fletcher (1549–1611). But it is *Paradise Regained,* with its emphasis on the power of faith (Jesus to Satan: "Why dost thou then suggest to me distrust?" [1.355]) that remains the classic Protestant treatment of the temptation narrative. Milton's "brief epic" also supplied a wealth of information that was missing from the gospels' severer accounts. Jesus and Satan engage in lengthy debates replete with biblical and classical references to geography, history, and philosophy; and Milton mined the tradition for poetic effects. The wilderness was "dusk with horrid shades" (1.296); the wild beasts confronting Jesus, including the "fiery Serpent" and the "noxious Worm," grow mild "at his sight" (1.310–312); Satan is first disguised as "an aged man in rural weeds" (1.314), later claiming that he too is a "Son of God" (4.518). The second temptation is preceded, somewhat unexpectedly, by an elaborate banquet scene (2.33–405); the third, by a storm (4.394–431); and the "kingdoms of the world" are a panorama of cities, kingdoms, and their peoples (3.267–385), culminating in Rome and Athens (4.25–284). The sight of Athens, the center of pagan learning, evokes another kind of temptation, a kingdom within: "Be famous then / By wisdom; as thy Empire must extend, / So let extend thy mind o'er all the world, / In knowledge, all things in it comprehend" (4.221–24). But Satan offers only learning, not divine wisdom, so Milton, who saw the temptations as largely a test of trust, has Jesus offer a good Protestant reply: "Alas, what can they teach, and not mislead; / Ignorant of themselves, of God much more, / And how the world began, and how men fell / Degraded by himself, on grace depending?" (4.309–12).

When T. S. Eliot later did his version of the temptation narrative in *Murder in the Cathedral* (1935), he too added a fourth temptation, the insinuation that Archbishop Thomas Becket's resolve was only a prideful desire for martyrdom ("But think, Thomas, think of glory after death").[53] But Becket's final tempter fails ("No! / Who are you, tempting with my own desires?"); and after the last temptation in Milton, on the temple's "highest Pinnacle" (4.549), it is Satan who "Fell whence he stood to see his Victor fall" (4.571), while angels provide Jesus with "A table of Celestial Food, Divine, / Ambrosial, Fruits fetcht from the tree of life, / . . . and as he fed, Angelic Choirs / Sung Heavenly Anthems of his victory / Over temptation and the Tempter proud" (4.588–95). Charles Dickens, in his retelling of the Gospels "written for his children," omits Satan and has Jesus "praying that He might be of use to men and women, and teach them to be better."[54] In a less reverential reference to the temptation narrative, the young Philip Carey, the protagonist of Somerset Maugham's *Of Human Bondage,* recalls Matthew's third temptation when he looks down from a hill in Heidelberg at "the whole world which was spread before him" and now divested of his religious faith accepts it as his to enjoy "free from degrading fears and free from prejudice."[55]

In his personal revision of Christ's life and teachings, *The Gospel in Brief,* the great Russian novelist Leo Tolstoy (1828–1910) reduced the temptation narrative to a contest of spirit (Jesus) and flesh (Satan), an interpretation that works only with the first temptation.[56] But it was Dostoevsky who in 1880 provided a darkly pessimistic interpretation of this event in the "Grand Inquisitor" section of his novel *The Brothers Karamazov,* in which, in a story told by the protagonist, Ivan Karamazov, Jesus makes a brief appearance on earth, in sixteenth-century Seville, only to be arrested, imprisoned, and condemned to be burned at the stake by the Inquisition. The Grand Inquisitor, a ninety-year-old cardinal, comes to his cell to explain why he must die. He accuses Jesus of having caused immeasurable unhappiness in the world by giving people a spiritual freedom they could not endure, and says that it is his church's mission to remedy the harm Jesus has done: "We have corrected Thy work and have founded it upon miracle, mystery, and authority." What Jesus has done, he says, is give "some promise of freedom which men in their simplicity and their natural unruliness cannot even understand, which they fear and dread—for nothing has ever been more insupportable for a man and a human society than freedom. But seest Thou these stones in this parched and barren wilderness? Turn them into bread, and mankind will run after thee like a flock of sheep, grateful and obedient, though for ever trembling lest Thou withdraw Thy hand and deny them Thy bread." It is the first temptation that interested Dostoevsky, so the Grand Inquisitor argues that in fact most people *do* live by bread alone, but that rather than having to earn it in the sweat of their faces (Gen. 3:19) their greatest hope is that someone will miraculously turn their stones into bread (and here readers will recognize Dostoevsky's usual complaints about the utopian promises of socialism). They do not want to follow Jesus in his faith, for faith entails anxieties and insecurities, so they prefer "mystery"—symbols and slogans, spectacles and superstition. They do not want freedom, they yearn for "authority," someone to guide them, to assume their responsibilities, make their decisions, guarantee their happiness.[57]

It would be easy to demonize the Grand Inquisitor, but given his premise, the weakness of human nature and its need for sustenance, his argument is sound and his actions benevolent and compassionate. He is in fact a tragic figure, caught between the spiritual inspiration of the temptation narrative and the nagging needs and discouraging debilities of his flock. He accuses Jesus of appealing to an elect, whereas he must deal with the frailties of real people, whom he characterizes as children and sheep. He insists that he loves his flock and that his church cares for its members, offering them bread and signs, forgiving their sins, punishing their enemies (he has just returned from torching a hundred heretics), and satisfying their worldly needs and ambitions—giving them the very rewards that Jesus had spurned. Some might want to point out that Christian freedom can be compatible with human happiness and that Dostoevsky's view of a spiritually elitist Jesus who makes impossible demands is too narrowly based on the special conditions of the temptation narrative, where Jesus is alone and subjected to tests that apply exclusively to his divinity. For all its drama and profundity, Ivan Karamazov's story does not account for the Jesus of the incarnation and the passion, and it ignores the kinds of "miracle, mystery, and authority" that are present elsewhere in the gospel, where Jesus ministers to the needs of his humblest followers. But Dostoevsky's Jesus seems to understand and forgive the Grand Inquisitor: "He suddenly approached the old man in silence and softly kissed him on his bloodless aged lips."

Despite its drama and importance, the temptation narrative has not left a distinguished record in art. For one thing, artists had the problem of simultaneously rendering three actions in three radically different locations, and for another there was the problem of representing Satan. Visitors to St. Mark's in Venice can see a mosaic with the three temptation scenes arranged in Matthew's order, as three dark and dwarfish Satans tempt three Jesus figures, the first seated, the next two on the temple and on a mountain, before Satan hurls himself down at the approach of angels. Another tradition, beginning with his appearance to St. Anthony (250–356), the first of the "Desert Fathers," had Satan disguised as a monk, which carried the absurd implication that he hoped to deceive Jesus, though artists could hardly be expected to dispense with his devilish features. In his version, Joachim Patnir (1485–1524) has a monk pointing at Jesus in the foreground, two tiny figures atop a steep crag instead of a mountain on the left, and in the background an undefined landscape representing the world's kingdoms. But some painters, like Juan des Flandes (fl. 1496–1519), combined both features: a web-footed "monk" with horns (1500; Washington, National Gallery). Botticelli did much the same in his version, which can be seen as a wall fresco (ca. 1482) by those visitors to the Sistine Chapel who are not preoccupied with Michelangelo's masterpieces. According to standard typology, whereby Moses foreshadows Jesus, it balances another fresco, *The Trials of Moses*. It is also a confused composition, with the three temptations in the middle distance and an apparently unrelated incident, the cleansing of a leper (8:2-4), in the foreground. As Satan falls off the mountain at the right, the wind blows open his habit and reveals the twisted body of a demon. Satan is an aged man, the wilderness a grove of leafy trees, and the blurry "kingdoms of the world" less than tempting in the twelve watercolors William Blake did for Milton's epic in 1817—not the poet/artist at his finest. But the picture that many readers know best is a dark engraving often included in illustrated Bibles, *Get thee hence, Satan* by Gustave Doré (1832–83), which shows Jesus standing on a dark and lonely cliff as a naked, horned, and winged Satan begins his flight into murky depths—another "Fall of Satan."

In film this episode seemed to Franco Zeffirelli to be a possible source of "dangerous confusion," and too "interior" to be included in his 1977 film *Jesus of Nazareth* (though he found room for the extra-evangelical betrothal ceremony of Mary and Joseph). But it indirectly inspired Martin Scorsese's *The Last Temptation of Christ* (1988), based on the novel of the same name by Nikos Kazantzakis (1883–1957). The temptation itself is in a deserted place and occurs before the entrance into Jerusalem. It shows a Jesus, confused and uncertain about his role in life, sitting in the middle of a circle he has drawn on the ground and enduring temptations, or rather, choices: sex from a devil in the guise of a serpent and with the voice of Mary Magdalene; revolutionary militancy from the voices of Judas and John the Baptist; and, finally, the voices Jesus heeds, that of a roaring lion within him and a fiery archangel without, both urging him to "enter your kingdom" and "become God." But the last temptation comes to him on the cross when a young girl, identified as his "guardian angel," appears in a fantasy sequence and leads him away to experience what might have been: a life of domestic tranquility and sexual fulfillment with Mary Magdalene ("God wants you to make children") and then with Lazarus's sister Mary, as the two women seem to compete at bearing him children. If this was his last temptation, then Judas offered him his first, since he is shown as a militant zealot, angrily—but vainly—urging Jesus to lead an uprising against the Romans (Jesus is first seen in the film as something of a collaborator, making crosses for Roman crucifixions). All of these temptations are designed to illustrate for Kazantzakis—and for Scorsese—the conflict of body and spirit, a theme they find embodied in the life of Jesus, caught, they claim, between the attractions of normalcy and the imperatives of a divine vocation.

The temptation narrative has not always been popular with those who look to the Gospels for Jesus the wise teacher or gentle Nazarene, and Thomas Jefferson chose to omit it from his deist version of the Bible.[58] But it has an assured place in the Synoptic Gospels, strategically positioned between baptism and ministry, and its range of affinities and resonances is astonishing. It is partly an initiation ritual, a confirmation following Jesus' baptism, or a kind of liminal experience whereby the young hero prepares himself spiritually for leadership by entering the wilderness alone, sustained only by his "spirit" and a knowledge of his tribal traditions, there to confront not only wild beasts but the reality of evil itself. It is partly an academic debate, with the disputants, like two rabbis, quoting Scripture at one another. It is partly a legend, a story bereft of any historical verification yet reproducing the motifs and themes that pervade both Testaments and have enjoyed a continuing influence. It is partly a drama, with towering antagonists, quotable dialogue, spectacular settings, sudden changes in scenery, mounting action, and victory for the main character. It is partly a mystery, since the presence of the Holy Spirit and the question of the "Son of God" lead directly to the Trinity, the presence of Satan raises the problem of evil, and Jesus' "victory" suggests the atonement. It is partly a lesson in doctrine, showing how the vagaries of interpretation could make it exemplify for Catholics an *Imitatio Christi,* while it demonstrates for Protestants the power of Scripture and the effectiveness of faith. But for all believers it remains one passage in Scripture that will be replayed in the lonely wilderness of their moral lives whenever the stakes are high, the temptations are powerful, and all choices are hard.

Meanwhile, Jesus hears of John's imprisonment, so for his own protection he goes home to Nazareth in Galilee, and from there to the nearby town of Capernaum (vv. 12-13). Again emphasizing the outreach of Jesus' ministry, Matthew notes that Capernaum (not mentioned in the OT) was a predominantly Gentile town. It is located on the northwest shore of the Sea—or Lake—of Galilee, which is now called Lake Gennesaret, suggesting the Hebrew word for harp, supposedly its shape. Capernaum was the home of Peter, Andrew, and Matthew; and "St. Peter's House," or what remains of it, is shown to visitors today. Buried under an octagonal Byzantine-style church (the first of its kind in the Holy Land), it is currently administered by Franciscans. Some claim that Jesus preached in a nearby synagogue that now lies beneath the imposing ruins of a much later synagogue. Most of Jesus' ministry was in villages like Capernaum, with almost no mention of the nearby Galilean towns such as Sepphoris, Scythopolis, or Tiberias (the last built over a cemetery and hence "impure" for pious Jews).

Jesus begins his preaching in 4:17, though "preach" is a lame translation for a Greek word that suggests a proclamation that is delivered with assurance and authority.[59] Here he begins with the apocalyptic message of John the Baptist, "Repent; for the kingdom of heaven is at hand." Verse 17, repeating 3:2, happens also to be the verse, in Latin, that on the Eve of All Saints' Day 1517 led off the *Ninety-five Theses* that Martin Luther was said to have nailed to the door of the Castle Church in Wittenberg (an event Luther never mentioned in his later life and that many believe was fabricated by his biographer, Philip Melanchthon). He was denouncing, as others had before him, the sale of papal indulgences providing for the remission in whole (plenary) or in part (partial) of the temporal punishment due to sins after the repentant sinner has had the guilt of sin removed by the grace of God and the act of confession. His denunciation eventually led to a frontal attack on the church's doctrines of penance and purgatory, a consequence Luther had not envisaged but one that made him famous—and that led to yet another division of Christendom.

Scripture has a good deal to say about sin, but only at 3:6 (also Mark 1:5) does it mention that sins are to be confessed, so it was the church, basing its authority on Matthew 16 and 18, that had to develop procedures of penance and reconciliation. The principle behind Catholic teaching on indulgences is that sin entails both guilt and punishment. The guilt is forgiven by God through a priest's absolution in the confessional, but the penalty, since justice demands that sin be punished, is assigned and administered by the church. This was called "temporal satisfaction," and in early times it imposed public and often lengthy acts of contrition, with heretics sometimes obliged to wear penitential garments for life. Serious sinners would be required to do penance throughout the Lenten season, a procedure they could undergo only once in their lifetime. They were barred from military service or ordination, and, if single, they could not marry. Naturally, sinners faced with such arduous penalties put off their acts of contrition as long as they could, often until their deathbeds. But if they could not complete this public contrition, or if the sin required extra contrition, then the remaining punishment would be inflicted in purgatory, with days and years specified. Since purgatory, that "halfway house on the highway to heaven," has no time, these specifics referred to the duration of penalties analogously, in terms of the sinner's lifetime.

As penance became a private sacrament, not a public demonstration, a practice first developed in sixth-century Irish monasteries between monks and their spiritual directors, the priest would normally levy a "fine," that is, assign a penalty in the confessional according to prescribed schedules. ("Anyone who gets so drunk as to vomit shall fast forty days if he is a priest or deacon; thirty days if he is a religious; twelve days if he is a lay person"—though later it became variations of the familiar "For your penance say five Our Fathers and five Hail Marys."[60]) But just as the church, acting for God on earth as Jesus directed (the "binding" and "loosing" of 18:18), could through the priest's mediation forgive the guilt of sin as Jesus had done, analogously it could also provide a "relaxation" (hence "indulgence") of the temporal penalty in return for good works of piety or charity performed by the offender. This it could do by drawing on the repository of spiritual merits earned by Christ, Mary, and the saints—that is, merits that were "works of supererogation," or in excess of what was required by divine law for their salvation. And since prayers for the dead in purgatory were—and still are—an important part of Catholic devotions, it seemed logical that these merits could, as indulgences, also be used to benefit the dead who had not yet attained eternal salvation (Luther's Thesis 27 as a jingle: "As soon as the coin in the coffer rings, / The soul from purgatory springs").

This custom of "time off for good behavior" was open to abuse, and it began at the top, as theological distinctions were ignored and noble intentions were betrayed by corrupt practices, first when it was expanded to offer "plenary" indulgences that would remit both guilt and punishment. In 1095 Pope Urban II, "through the power of God vested in me," granted full indulgences extending over "this life and the life to come" to participants who might perish in the First Crusade; and the Fourth Lateran Council (1215) extended them to "Catholics who assume the cross and devote themselves to the extermination of heretics."[61] What was actually being granted was only a remission of ecclesiastical penance, the "temporal satisfaction" that had already been assigned, and only for those who were "truly penitent and have confessed" (though these requirements, often evaded, were waived for those applying indulgences to the deceased); but it was widely understood that the Crusaders would automatically win forgiveness of their sins and salvation for their souls.

Next, indulgences were commercialized when Pope Julius II in 1510 and Leo X in 1515 offered them to "almsgivers"—contributors, that is, to papal projects (rebuilding St. Peter's Basilica was perhaps the worthiest, certainly more so than the indulgences granted to those contributing firewood for a heretic's pyre) via their local indulgence franchisers (Chaucer's "Pardoner" with his wallet full of pardons "hot from Rome").[62] This merchandising of a spiritual practice—sometimes called "commutation"—became one of the scandals that helped fuel the Protestant Reformation. Indulgences, said Erasmus in a letter, "were sold in every church (the red boxes, the crosses, the papal coat of arms were everywhere) and the people had no choice but to buy."[63] Luther's difficulties were both pastoral and theological: the false sense of security these purchased indulgences offered sinners when they should be performing genuine acts of contrition (he proclaimed, also in his first thesis, that Jesus "meant the whole life of the faithful to be an act of repentance"); the way they objectified sin and penance, putting salvation on sale and distracting the faithful from inner repentance; and the popes' extending them to souls in purgatory, whereas 16:19 specified that their powers were only "on earth." He later complained about Tetzel, the chief indulgence-peddler: "He even sold indulgences for future sins." The story was told of a nobleman who purchased an indulgence for a future sin from Tetzel and then beat him up, explaining that the beating was his future sin. Still, Luther never rejected indulgences altogether (so his Thesis 38), provided that they were kept a minor spiritual exercise, subordinate to sorrow, repentance, confession, and amendment.[64] And although the Catholic Church still endorses indulgences (if there is true contrition), it no longer assigns days and years to the purgatory time they are supposed to remit.

Repent in the Latin translation by St. Jerome (340–420) known as the "Vulgate" was "do penance" (*poenitentiam agite*), which seemed to confirm penance as a sacrament and to validate the church's penitential system. This misleading translation was first pointed out by Lorenzo Valla (1407–57) in his *Annotations to the New Testament,* published by Erasmus in 1505, one of the earliest philological commentaries on Scripture. Erasmus's revolutionary Greek text, published in 1516 with notes and a Latin translation, with one word, *metanoeite* ("be penitent"; literally: "change your mind"), established the present translation and profoundly influenced Luther ("My mind was quite in a fever with thinking of these things"), enabling him and other Reformers to drive a wedge between Jesus' words in Greek that suggested an inner contrition and change, and the church's practice of auricular confession and subsequent works of penance.[65] Luther accepted confession as the right of an individual, but he denied its sacramental character, since it was not divinely ordained. He dismissed any church-imposed obligation, and he emphasized personal contrition and faith in the promise that Christ has forgiven sinners (8:13: "As thou hast believed, so be it done unto thee"). For Calvin penance was "neither commanded by Christ, nor practiced by the ancient Church," and Zwingli rejected it completely.[66]

The next event (vv. 18-21) is the calling of the first four disciples. This is treated very summarily—there is no mention of their being baptized—and without any reason for their selection, except that it seems important for Matthew that Jesus be seen not as a lone charismatic figure but as the founder of a continuing community. Hence, it can be argued that Jesus does indeed found a church, though a counter-argument maintains that he assigns them no "priestly" duties, and his apocalyptic message would not allow time for any ecclesiastical functions. Certainly the original Twelve (whose names varied) had no visible organization and established no holy places or sites of worship to rival the temple or synagogues, but their number obviously recalls Israel's Twelve Tribes (and Mormonism is headed by a Quorum of the Twelve, also called Apostles). That they were all men has been a traditional argument that only men are eligible for the Catholic priesthood (an otherwise laudable preference for inclusive language is sorely tested when a translator for the NRSV chooses accuracy over familiarity in rendering verse 19 as "fishing for people"), and the Anglican-Episcopal ordination of women has become a serious obstacle to the union of the two communions. Their leaders were Peter, John, and James; and it is they whom Jesus took to witness his transfiguration (17:1). But apart from Peter and Paul, the "thirteenth Apostle," they left little record of achievement in the history of early Christianity; they are barely characterized, and only Judas affects the gospel story.

It is odd that among the disciples there are no shepherds, but Jesus, from a carpenter's family, seems to have been more familiar with fishermen working on the Sea of Galilee. So the fish acquired symbolic force in early Christian art, with water suggesting baptism and the Greek word for fish, *ichthys,* serving as an acrostic for "Jesus Christ, God's Son, Savior." On the other hand, the role of the shepherd, entailing care and concern for his charges, devolved symbolically on Jesus the Good Shepherd (26:31, regarding his crucifixion: "I will smite the shepherd, and the sheep of the flock shall be scattered abroad"). The title of apostle was also given to missionaries who first introduced the faith into pagan lands, such as St. Patrick in Ireland and SS. Cyril and Methodius, the "Apostles to the Slavs."

These verses also raise the question of how many Jameses there are in the New Testament. Traditionally, there are three. The first is James, "the brother of John," to be known as St. James the Greater because he is called before the second, St. James the Less (or Younger). He is present at the transfiguration (17:1) and in the Garden of Gethsemane (26:37), and in AD 43 was the first apostle to be put to death (Acts 12:2). He is said to have evangelized Spain, and after his martyrdom in Jerusalem his followers took his body back there and buried it in a Galician forest, where it was found in the ninth century. St. James was then adopted as the patron of Spain, and as "Santiago Matamoros" ("St. James the Moor-Killer") he appeared in full armor to save the country from the Moors at the Battle of Clavijo in 844. His burial site became the famous pilgrimage center of Compostela in northern Spain. The second James, "son of Alphaeus" and also an apostle, is something of a problem. Some would identify him with the James who is called the Lord's "brother" (or half-brother if he is the son of Joseph by a previous marriage, or cousin if he is the son of Mary's sister Salome), a somewhat elusive figure who is not an apostle but becomes the head of the Jerusalem church, which suggests a kind of family succession there. But the traditional, or Catholic view, dating from St. Jerome and maintaining the perpetual virginity of Mary, is that this was a third James, the son of the "other Mary," described as the wife of Cleophas (a husband other than Alphaeus, unless both names refer to the same man).

Important in the Orthodox Church is Andrew, superior even to Peter, his younger brother, in that in John's gospel (1:40) he was the first to be called and later he evangelized the Eastern world. He became the patron saint of Russia and of Scotland, where his relics were brought in the fourth century after he had been crucified by the Romans in AD 60. For this he chose his distinctively X-shaped cross, since he considered himself unworthy of a cross shaped like Jesus'. This cross appeared to the Scots in the shape of white clouds in the blue sky before a victorious battle against the Angles in East Lothian in 832, for many Scots the year their country was born. So the Scottish flag has a white St. Andrew's cross on a blue field, and it also appears together with the red cross of St. George on England's Union Jack. Legend had Andrew die a martyr, displaying the courage suggested by his name (Greek: "manly"), and the Vatican gives his statue pride of place next to the altar in St. Peter's Basilica. He was said to have been martyred at Patras, Greece, and in 1469 Pope Pius II received a reliquary containing his skull ("Here were the eyes that often beheld God in the flesh"). In 1965 Pope Paul VI returned his skull to Athenagoras, the Ecumenical Patriarch of Constantinople.

That the first apostles responded so directly (vv. 20, 22) inspired the young St. Anthony, the founder of Christian monasticism, as he was walking to church. He also thought of Acts 4:35, where Jesus' followers gave up their worldly goods, and once in church he heard 19:21, where Jesus says that "If thou wilt be perfect, go and sell that thou hast, and give to the poor, and thou shalt have treasure in heaven: and come and follow me." The next time he was in church it was 6:34, "Take therefore no thought for the morrow"; whereupon he gave up his property and embarked on a life of study, prayer, and self-mortification.[67] Subsequently, some monks took their poverty vow so literally that they even sold their Bibles and gave the money to the poor, depending thereafter only on the scripture texts they heard recited during readings and liturgies. But as this was an inspiration for those seeking spiritual perfection in this world, it was also a seedbed for heresy, since dissidents, such as the "Poor Men of Lyons" in twelfth-century France, contrasted this command with the church's worldly prosperity. This disjunction between the austerity of Jesus' message and the extravagances of his churchmen also contributed to the importance of the Bible, not the church, as the ultimate sanction of Christian behavior.

Jesus now begins his ministry of teaching and healing (vv. 23-25). Despite the New Testament's emphasis on private prayer and the prominence of the Sermon on the Mount, Jesus' visits to synagogues indicate that he was also a regular worshiper, knew Hebrew, and commanded enough respect to be allowed to read from the Law. The "Old Synagogue" in Nazareth is said to mark one place where Jesus taught, and in visiting it, the British writer Harriet Martineau (1802–76), an early and intrepid traveler to the Holy Land, remarked that it "interested me more than any place exhibited by the monks, in all Palestine." Like so many visitors, Martineau, a Unitarian, was often disappointed—and occasionally appalled—by the sacred sites she was shown in Jerusalem, and she deplored the sectarian wranglings of their current occupants. But this venue and the charitable purposes of verses 23-24 responded to her vision of Christianity and made her heart "beat with the true pilgrim emotion."[68]

3

The Sermon on the Mount

Chapters 5 to 7 are devoted to the Sermon on the Mount, and 1-17 of chapter 8 to miracles of exorcism and healing, notably the servant of a Roman centurion and the mother-in-law of Peter. The press of the crowds is such that Jesus leaves for the other side of the Sea of Galilee on a ship that is caught in a "great tempest." Jesus calms the tempest and then lands in "the country of the Gergesenes," but after driving demons into a herd of swine, he returns to Capernaum. There he recruits a tax collector named Matthew, disputes briefly with the Pharisees, consults with some of John's disciples, and performs miracles while preaching the "gospel of the kingdom" in the nearby "cities and villages."

> When the protest [in Montgomery]
> began, my mind, consciously or
> unconsciously, was driven back to the
> Sermon on the Mount, with its sublime
> teachings on love, and to the Gandhian
> method of nonviolent resistance.
> —Martin Luther King Jr.

If Matthew is both "the Jewish gospel" and "the church's gospel," it can also be "the Christians' gospel"—and nowhere more convincingly than in the Sermon on the Mount (5:1–7:29). These three chapters are sometimes called Christianity's "Constitution," or at least an early kind of catechism, being derived largely from the sayings of Q, and hence popular among those who prefer "Christianity Light," with a Jesus who was an itinerant teacher—a kind of first-century Jewish guru—and not the Savior and Redeemer of the Passion Narratives and Paul's Epistles. For many Christians the Sermon's apparent emphasis on good works, self-restraint, and personal perfection is preferable to the emphasis on faith, grace, and personal unworthiness in Paul's theology. As for its OT connection, we see again the "Moses motif," here a symmetry between Moses receiving the law on Mt. Sinai and Jesus ascending a mountain to preach a "Messianic Torah," a new law—or, better, a new and radical reorientation of values.

In Matthew the mountain is unnamed, but Luke puts his Sermon on a plain, since he is less concerned than Matthew with Jesus' role as the new Moses (in Luke, Jesus goes to mountains only to pray), and he includes just over half the verses found in Matthew. A traditional location for Matthew's "mountain" is a hillside near the Sea of Galilee, and this setting was the inspiration for the open-air preaching begun by the Methodist George Whitefield and brought to perfection by John Wesley in the mid-eighteenth century (the Sermon, said Wesley, was "one pretty remarkable precedent of field preaching").[1] Jesus is sitting, like a Jewish teacher or a Greco-Roman philosopher, as he addresses both his disciples (gathered in the front rows?) and "the multitudes" (Nicholas Ray assembled seven thousand extras for his 1961 *King of Kings* film), though it is often unclear which group is meant to be his primary audience. The former may stand for Matthew's own community; the latter for the wider world still to be evangelized.

It is odd that so large a block of discourse should appear so early in Matthew's narrative and at a time when Jesus has called only four disciples and has not performed any specified healings or miracles. Over the ages the sentiments of the Sermon have inspired, frustrated, and puzzled its readers; its sudden transitions can upset those who demand—and sometimes claim to discover— the kind of consistency and coherence that is not often found in ancient texts. In a catalogue of interpretations as bewildering as those visited on the "kingdom of God," Clarence Bauman notes that, among other readings, the Sermon has been dramatized, secularized, universalized, criticized, psychologized, politicized, and radicalized.[2] Its counsel of perfection may be elevating and challenging, yet it can also be subversive, since the impossibility of realizing it on earth can induce despair, persuading some—especially Martin Luther (who preferred the radically christological message of John)—that given the reality of human shortcomings, the Sermon is actually an argument for the necessity of divine grace. Albert Schweitzer could justify these radical demands by having his Jesus mandate them for only the few years before the world would end. But still some wonder how seriously Jesus meant what he said, since certain of his injunctions are obviously hyperbolic ("pluck out your eye"); while others seem inconsistent (what must be revealed at 5:15-16, like a light that shines, must be kept behind shut doors at 6:6); and some require an impossible, almost unimaginable effort ("resist not evil") or are tantalizingly vague (not to observe the law, but to "fulfill" it). Such absolute commands can be provocative, and they have had an irresistible appeal to religious rigorists as well as to extremists and fanatics who find them convenient in indicting the ways of ordinary Christians and their ecclesiastical establishments.

So how much is precept, how much are only "evangelical counsels"? Are they rules or principles? Confined to particular situations and spiritual athletes or universally applicable? And what allowance should be made for rhetorical exaggeration? Part of the problem may be compositional (it is both Mosaic and a mosaic), in that Matthew has here collected and juxtaposed various of Jesus' addresses and ad hoc comments that are now divorced from their clarifying contexts of setting, audience, occasion, and circumstances—and so the text deconstructs itself. Or, to put it more simply, Matthew tends to honor ideals and legislate goals that are, each in its own way, absolute—but that are ultimately irreconcilable in practice. Hence, marriage is indissoluble, but divorce is permitted; the dietary laws are valid, but may be modified; the Sabbath is holy, but may yield to emergencies; oaths are forbidden, but may be sworn under certain circumstances. And in most instances Jesus' counsels are personal and individual, not social; their focus is inward and spiritual, and doers of good deeds are often assured of rewards. "Jesus' concern is not so much the saving of society but a society of saviors."[3]

As with all things biblical, the Sermon has had its detractors. In antiquity, Celsus thought that Christianity's ethical teachings were neither original nor impressive. Savagely eloquent, and often as oracular and enigmatic as Jesus himself, was Friedrich Nietzsche (1844–1900), who admired Jesus but scorned his teachings. Although he rarely mentioned the Sermon by name, Nietzsche despised its "slave-morality," its ethic of nonresistance to evil, self-denial, pity, and neighborly love ("even God hath his hell: it is his love of man"). They were all sops to the weak and the weary, escapist counsels of submission and subjection, impediments to the human greatness aspired to by the exceptional individual, Nietzsche's *Übermensch*, who "says Amen to life, not to the words of a god." Christian faith instead is obsessed with guilt and sin; it sacrifices "all freedom, all pride, all self-confidence of spirit."[4] Many of these sentiments on the primacy of life experience were mediated to English readers through the works of D. H. Lawrence (1885–1930), though he chose to eliminate from the published novel *The Rainbow* (1915) his heroine's musings on the Sermon, where she refuses to be a city on a hill (5:14) or to take thought of the kingdom of God and his righteousness (6:33), imagining instead an affair with a fantasy Jesus who has chosen life over death, the world over heaven. And Somers, the hero of *Kangaroo* (1923), objects to the assurances of the Sermon's Beatitudes: "Life makes no absolute statement."[5]

The Sermon's interpretation has usually been marked by distinctions, which is probably appropriate for a section rich in antitheses. At the end of the fourth century, Augustine, who gave the Sermon its name, wrote a long commentary, *De Sermone Domini in Monte,* stressing the contrast between the Old and the New Laws.[6] Distinctions also figure in Aquinas's commentary, this time between the Sermon's binding "commandments," required of all Christians for their salvation, and its optional "counsels," which can only be achieved by those whose total commitment leads them to the religious life.[7] The Reformers also invoked the Sermon, the radicals among them, like the Anabaptists, often insisting on its literal application. Luther demurred, distinguishing between the spiritual commands, which required obedience from individuals, and the secular commands, which could be modified by worldly circumstances. Since the twentieth century there has been a new kind of distinction, between what in the Sermon came from the preaching of Jesus, what from the revisions of Matthew, or, with Albert Schweitzer, between what was valid for all time and what obtained only for the interval before the end time.

All of this is illustrated by the vexing question of Jesus' attitude toward the Mosaic law, which Matthew sees as combining both continuity and innovation. At 5:17-18 Jesus praises the law in all its details and asserts that he has come not to destroy but to fulfill it, with "verily I say unto you" stressing his personal—and messianic?—authority. And some have seen in Matthew's endorsement of the law a conservative response to Paul, who had preached in Antioch against justification "by the works of the law" (Gal. 2:11-21). Still, it should be noted that none of its injunctions, said to comprise 248 positive commandments and 365 prohibitions, are mentioned in the Sermon. This raises the problem of observing every "jot and tittle" of the law—such as circumcision, the Sabbath, and dietary regulations—and yet "fulfilling" it (completing? deepening? transcending? perfecting?), especially since Jesus himself freely abrogates its rules. Does the "fulfillment" of the law—generally understood as fulfilling its original intent—permit Gentile converts to abandon these practices? Should there be a distinction between moral and ceremonial laws? Are Jewish converts who still observe the old laws spiritually superior to their Gentile brethren? What is to be the relationship between those Christians who insist on observing the provisions of the law (given, after all, by God Himself) and those who feel that they have been transcended in Jesus' new and "fulfilled" law? Or is Jesus now the Lord's fulfillment, dispensing his followers from the law? Or replacing it with a new law of love?

After endorsing the law, a few lines later (vv. 31-42) we find Jesus abrogating it in incidental references to divorce, oaths, and retaliation. And further on in the gospel (ch. 23) he will denounce the Pharisees for their application of the law, but he will also instruct the crowds and his disciples to observe "whatsoever they bid you observe." It may be possible to reconcile these inconsistencies by distinguishing between the letter of the law, which can be variously interpreted and applied, and its spirit, which Jesus intends to fulfill, just as his ministry is fulfilling the words of the prophets. Or Matthew, for tactical reasons, may want to show Jesus defending the law's authority in the face of those "antinomians" in the evangelist's community who would abolish it altogether. Yet he may also want to concede that Jesus' messianic authority would inevitably alter the law, particularly by subordinating it to love of God and neighbor (22:37-40). These alterations and adjustments would continue after Jesus' ministry, fundamentally so as the church abandoned its Jewish past in the course of its subsequent mission to the wider Gentile world.

In terms of influence, the mixture of moral idealism and religious realism in these three chapters has probably generated more comment, particularly from those outside the Christian faith, than any other comparable section of the Gospels. Quotations from the Sermon appear in one of the earliest Christian writings, an anonymous second-century handbook called the *Didache* ("Teaching [of the Apostles]"), discovered in 1873 and comprising about ten pages in a modern text. It offers ethical and liturgical instructions, and in recommending what it calls the "way of life" over the "way of death," it refers eight times to chapter 5 in its opening section, mostly to the moral counsels of 39-48, and later includes the Lord's Prayer (6:9-13).[8] When the Latin apologist Justin Martyr wanted to impress the Roman emperor Antoninus Pius with the high morality of his fellow Christians, he filled two sections of his *First Apology* with quotations from the Sermon.[9] Later, the Sermon provided the Greek and Latin fathers with a treasure trove of Christian ideals divorced from dogma and doctrine. And in modern times Tolstoy wrote, "Of everything in the Gospels, the Sermon on the Mount always had for me an exceptional importance." Thus, he thought that all his doubts about Christianity could be resolved in what he saw as the Sermon's "clear and precise Christian principles."[10] Most of the Sermon is reproduced in the language of the KJV in *The Book of Mormon* (*3 Nephi:* 12–15), where Jesus delivers it to the apostles in the New World (!) after his crucifixion and institution of baptism.[11]

The Sermon begins, appropriately enough, with a blessing—the nine or, for most, eight Beatitudes (5:3-12; Luke has only four, at 6:20-22, and they tend to be less "spiritual" than Matthew's). Nine is an example of three Matthean triads; eight symbolizes rebirth, since the resurrection took place on the eighth day of the week and is recalled by the eight points of the Maltese cross. The Beatitudes offer reassurance and consolation, promising a share in the kingdom of heaven for those who know few rewards of this earthly kingdom. Their keynote is inner happiness—a vision of God in the sixth—available to the virtuous and the oppressed, particularly those who are personally depressed ("poor in spirit"), or of modest circumstances, or vulnerable to violence and injustice. For them there is the ultimate assurance of a divine reward: to be "blessed" and saved by God. In fact, the verb forms in 4, 5, 6, and 9 are examples of the "divine passive," with God understood as the agent, His divine action universal, not restricted to Jews. The "kingdom of heaven," already announced in 4:17 to be "at hand," seems to suggest by the present tense in the first and last Beatitudes that for some God's saving presence is already theirs, but for others the details of its time (how soon?), place (in Judea? in the world? in the human heart?), and entrance requirements (virtue? or virtue within humility and suffering?) are, as usual, uncertain.

The third Beatitude assures the meek, presumably those who are quiet, modest, and self-effacing, that they "shall inherit the earth" (5:5; also at Ps. 37:11, which foreshadows many Beatitude themes)—but not, so J. Paul Getty, the mineral rights—and G. K. Chesterton (1874–1936) suggested this happened only once in history, when the monasteries succeeded the Roman Empire in Europe.[12] On meekness, Baron d'Holbach (1723–1809), the French philosopher said to be Europe's first professed atheist, was cynical: Jesus recommended to his disciples a "pious docility" and urged "moderation and toleration as the means of insinuating themselves into people's minds," while the "peace and concord" he recommended were "necessary to a new born, weak, and persecuted sect, but . . . became superfluous when the sect had attained strength enough to dictate the law."[13] Perhaps, but meekness was not a virtue in a Mediterranean society traditionally obsessed with honor, status, and their public acknowledgement; so modern readers, more accustomed to professions of modesty and self-effacement, often fail to appreciate the subversiveness of the Beatitudes.

The sixth Beatitude praises the "pure in heart," and since "pure" is a rare adjective in the KJV's gospel translation, it offered a flattering honorific for English Puritans, their title being of uncertain origin and meaning. Next, and contrasting with the meekness of verse 5, are the three "activist" Beatitudes in 7-9. In fact, much of the Sermon tends to be activist, preaching a righteousness of works and culminating in an uncompromising, perhaps utopian demand for perfection (5:48). Little is said of faith or grace. Hence, it is easier for most Christians to regard its injunctions, not as radical rules of behavior (although most seem to be intended literally), but as a series of goals.

The Beatitude of the "peacemakers" (used in 1534 by Tyndale to replace his 1526 "maintainers of peace") provided the motto of James I of England, the "James" of the KJV, and for the twenty-two years of his reign, 1603–25, he did keep England free from foreign and domestic conflicts.[14] This Beatitude may, however, refer to peace within a community, possibly Matthew's, not among nations, since Judea was currently benefiting from the Pax Romana of the first century. Augustine noted that this is not an argument for pacifism, since it is the purpose of a just war to achieve peace.[15] "Placemakers" appeared instead of "peacemakers" in the second edition of the *Geneva Bible* (1562), and in *Monty Python's Life of Brian* (1979) someone at the edge of the multitude thinks he hears "Blessed are the Greeks." Another hears "cheesemakers," which a bystander explains is "not meant to be taken literally: it refers to any manufacturer of dairy products." The "Peacemaker" was also the name of the "Colt Single Action Army," the pistol of choice in settling the American West.

John Locke (1632–1704) recalled the "persecuted" of verse 10 when he argued for charity and restraint in his "Letter Concerning Toleration" (1685–86): "The Gospel frequently declares that the true disciples of Christ must suffer persecution; but that the Church of Christ should persecute others, and force others by fire and sword to embrace her faith and doctrine, I could never yet find in the books of the New Testament."[16] But others have pointed out that the phrase "for righteousness' sake" enabled believers to persecute those whose cause had—in the view of the persecutors—no righteousness at all. In this view heretics could not, or at least should not, invoke 11-12 in their own defense. Verse 11 was cited by John and Charles Wesley in 1743 in their rules for members of the United Societies as evidence of the hostility Methodists must be prepared to face whenever they implemented their "desire for salvation."[17] And verses 11-12 were proclaimed at the conclusion of an academic sermon that became a landmark in French Protestantism. The speaker was Nicholas Cop on November 1, 1533, the day when he was to be installed as the rector of the University of Paris. He followed their citation with the incendiary words, "Why, then, do we conceal the truth rather than speak it out boldly?" which for him was an evangelical interpretation of the "reward" of verse 12—that it was not a payment for human works but God's free gift. The result was that Cop and John Calvin, who may have had a hand in drafting the sermon, had to flee the city.[18]

"Salt of the earth" (v. 13), which first appeared in Tyndale's 1525 NT translation, is perhaps the most famous of more than fifty images in the Sermon, though it is something of a puzzle, since salt cannot lose its savor without ceasing to be salt, so it must mean that if salt is somehow adulterated it will be discarded as useless. But as a seasoning and a preservative it refers to the effect Jesus' teachings will have on the world—and "world," like "earth" in 14, already hints at the universality of Jesus' ministry. In some baptism ceremonies a pinch of salt is placed on the infant's tongue. Less edifyingly, Luther extended the usual meaning of this passage to include rubbing salt into the wounds of his opponents, usually monks and priests, as well as theologians at the University of Paris. Preachers, he said, must also practice this "ministry of salting" to convince their listeners of "their misery and incapacity."[19] In a 1937 sermon, Martin Niemöller (1892–1984), the Lutheran pastor whose heroic resistance to the Hitler regime condemned him to a concentration camp, noted how closely the salt and light images followed the blessing of the persecuted when he urged his listeners that their salt must not lose its savor nor their candle its light amid their current sufferings.[20] And in 1937, Pope Pius XI used the salt and light (and yeast) images in an encyclical letter to characterize the Mexican priests then being persecuted by that country's anticlerical regime.[21]

Next Jesus speaks of his disciples' exemplary roles. "Consider that wee shall be as a Citty upon a Hill; the eyes of all people are upon us" were words spoken by John Winthrop in a sermon, "A Modell of Christian Charity," that he delivered in 1630 while sailing to New England on the *Arabella*. This was Winthrop's prospect for the Puritans' Massachusetts Bay Colony, a sacred "community of saints" that was to be both a recollection of Jerusalem and a prefiguration of the New Jerusalem, and in modern times Presidents Kennedy and Reagan invoked it to characterize the exemplary role of America in the world.[22] Its image of an organized community has also served as a proof text for the establishment of an institutional church; and the light of 15-16, which should not be "put under a bushel [basket]," was cited by Charlemagne in 789 in urging the clergy to establish schools to teach boys to read and older men to copy manuscripts of sacred texts.[23] The same verse was later recalled by William Penn when he cited the words of his spiritual predecessor, George Fox, "Let your light shine among the Indians, and the Blacks and the Whites, that ye may answer the truth in them."[24] Penn proclaimed liberty of conscience among worshipers of all races in Pennsylvania, but unhappily these sentiments were easier to proclaim than enact, and the Quakers and Indians had their share of troubles throughout the eighteenth century. This verse was also the inspiration for "Jesus Bids Us Shine," a popular and sentimental Victorian children's hymn by Susan Warner (1819–95), and it is recalled in one of the verses of the Negro spiritual "This Little Light of Mine" ("Hide it under a bushel? No! / I'm gonna let it shine") and in the country song "You can't be a beacon (if your light don't shine)." Still, Calvinists would be more interested in the image of their community as a shining example of faith than as one producing good works.

The Sermon's central section (5:17–7:12) is enclosed by reference in both verses to the "law and the prophets," and Christians have long been preoccupied with the place of the Hebrew scriptures in their faith, its "fulfilled prophecies" ranking with miracles as confirmations of Christian truth. But one who early and radically rejected the Old Testament was Marcion (100–60), a gnostic Christian intent on "purifying" Scripture, whose heretical followers spurned the "God of the law and the prophets, declaring him to be the author of evils, a lover of war, inconstant in judgment, and contrary to himself."[25] The seeming incompatibility of law and gospel caused Marcion, a prosperous shipowner from the Black Sea who came to Rome in the mid-second century, even to reject most of the New Testament except for Paul and parts of Luke. He then created a version of Christianity that included gnostic asceticism (no use of wine at Eucharist and no bodily resurrection) and docetism (the divine Jesus only "seemed" to be human), and he had some success in founding "Marcionite" churches that used his anti-Judaic "scriptures." Marcionism has since been the term for the radical and invidious separation of law and gospel as practiced by those Christians who create a "canon within the canon" by ignoring or at least de-emphasizing vast stretches of the Old Testament in favor of those passages where they can find support for their own beliefs.

A modern Marcion was Leo Tolstoy, who learned Greek in his later years and produced his own version of the Bible. He rejected the Old Testament, and he ignored the miracles of the Gospels, especially the resurrection, in favor of a Scripture based largely on the Sermon on the Mount. His Christianity, inspired in part by the unaffected faith of Russian peasants, was simplified and eccentric: he humanized Jesus and divinized his laws, or at least some of them, particularly the nonresistance to evil, and he espoused an uncompromising if inconsistent morality (which he occasionally ignored) that drew heavily on the Sermon.

In the English Enlightenment, John Toland, author of the rationalizing classic *Christianity Not Mysterious* (1696), interpreted the "fulfill" of verse 17 to mean that Jesus intended to strip the truth "of all those infernal types and ceremonies which made it difficult before he rendered it easy and obvious to the meanest capacities."[26] But Toland had to regret that Gentile Christians corrupted the simple truths of their new faith with the "vain subtleties" of pagan philosophy; replaced Jewish rituals with their own, drawn from the mystery cults; and later, under the Christian emperors, adopted the pomp and ceremony of the Roman court. Later, Jesus' promise not to "destroy the law" was a boon for Christian missionaries who had to deal with the traditional social "laws" of the peoples they were evangelizing. In India, for example, they could preach the egalitarianism of 20:27 ("And whosoever will be chief among you, let him be your servant") and also use 17 to leave undisturbed the laws of caste distinctions.[27]

Jesus will now go on to specific cases (21-48), a set of "Ye have heard. . . . But I say unto you" statements that reflect Matthew's fondness for repetitions, as in the "blesseds" of the Beatitudes. Antithetical in form, if not always in substance, they are meant to extend, deepen, qualify, and abrogate—but not "oppose"—the law, since Matthew's Jesus is ostensibly concerned to preserve the law, even though this concern tends to create a new set of laws. His repeated distinction between the letter of the law and its spirit, between external behavior and internal disposition, does not solve all the practical problems raised by this spiritual dilemma, though he eloquently expresses his respect for the law by pledging to subtract from it not "one jot or one tittle." The "jot" is the smallest letter in the Hebrew alphabet; the "tittle" is a diacritical mark, a small stroke added to some letters (NRSV: "not one letter, not one stroke of a letter"). "Jot" found its way into the English expression "jot down" as well as "not one iota." That every jot and tittle of the law must be fulfilled reminded Luther of human powerlessness and consequent anxiety, which for him could only be overcome by God's grace.

The first antithesis (21), on killing and anger, was one that unfortunately the Anabaptist martyr Michael Sattler (1490–1527) applied to the Ottomans at his trial in the south German town of Rottenburg in 1527 ("We must not defend ourselves against the Turks"). He then went on to say that he "would rather take the field against so-called Christians who persecute, capture and kill pious Christians than against the Turks."[28] This extended his theological quarrels to the political arena at a time when the Ottoman Empire was threatening Europe, and it sealed his fate in the eyes of the Austrians. Accordingly, he had his tongue cut out (lest he utter any inspiring last words), his body was torn with red hot tongs as it was being chained to a wooden frame, and he was thrown into a fire with a sack of powder hung around his neck. His wife was then drowned in the Neckar River.

This antithesis raised the problem of distinguishing between anger and righteous indignation. Luther felt that Jesus' condemnation of anger did not apply to the "godly anger and vexation" of his attacks on monks, magistrates, opposing theologians, the pope, and, in one notorious instance, Jews; nor did verse 44 on loving one's enemies, and he cited Jesus' own asperity toward the scribes and Pharisees (23:13-33), where he himself uses the word "fools" (also at Luke 11:40 and 24:25).[29] Here Jesus' words culminate in the gospel's first mention of hell. "Hell fire" (v. 22, repeated at 29 and 30) is from the Greek for gehenna, the smoldering refuse dump in the Valley of Hinnom outside Jerusalem where the god Moloch was once worshiped with fire and human sacrifices. The name suggests a hell of eternal punishment, whereas "hades" can simply be a place for the dead who are not in paradise. The fires of hell are a peculiarly Matthean concern, particularly in chapter 25, which many modern readers find distinctly unappealing (Mark Twain: "Hell fire is gone, but the text remains").[30] It was not always so.

This passage (vv. 21-23) is also warrant for the "kiss of peace" exchanged between communicants before they approach the Eucharistic table. The conciliatory sentiments of 23-24 were cited in a joint declaration issued by Pope Paul VI and the Greek Orthodox Patriarch Athenagoras on December 7, 1965, when they sought to heal the centuries-old breach between the two Christian churches. They formally regretted the offensive words and acts, they repealed the mutual excommunications of 1054, and they deplored the subsequent mistrust and misunderstandings, although little progress was achieved in the following years.[31] The same verses were quoted by Fr. Camilo Torres to justify his abandoning his ministry to join a revolutionary movement in Latin America: "I have ceased to say Mass, but I will practice love for my fellow man in the temporal, economic, and social spheres. When my fellow man has nothing against me, when he has carried out the revolution, then I will return to offering Mass."[32] It is questionable how far the "revolution" could be "carried out," since the liberation theology he endorsed never formulated specific goals apart from a vaguely Christian—and utopian—socialism, and Fr. Torres was killed in a jungle firefight with Colombian soldiers in 1966. As to how quarreling brothers should be reconciled, Kant cited verse 25 in arguing that reparation be done personally and "quickly," and not simply disappear amid general regret and contrition.[33]

Notorious is verse 28, quoted by Athenagoras, a Christian apologist of the second century, who wrote an *Embassy* ("A Plea for the Christians") to the Emperor Marcus Aurelius and his son Commodus, in which he contrasted this rigorous morality, one that forbids even "wanton looks," with the endless couplings and incest practiced by the gods of paganism.[34] Matthew's Jesus would probably condone admiration and even what Augustine in his *Commentary* called "a sensation of carnal pleasure"[35] (and the "right eye," like the "right hand," intensifies the effect), but during his 1976 presidential campaign Jimmy Carter was ridiculed for admitting in a *Playboy* interview that "I have looked on a lot of women with lust. I've committed adultery in my heart many times." As usual, nothing is said about "lusting" women who "objectify" men. As for the "eye" in 29 (repeated at 18:9), Pope Gregory the Great (540–604), in his influential *Moralia in Job* (Morals on the Book of Job), saw the right eye as standing for the contemplative life, the left for the active, the latter life to be led by those "unfit or unable to behold the world above and spiritual things."[36] The English Reformer Thomas Cranmer (1489–1556), Archbishop of Canterbury under Henry VIII and sentenced to the stake under "Bloody Mary" Tudor, alluded to verse 30 ("this hand hath offended") when on the day of his death he renounced a statement of recantation he had signed. John Foxe, the historian of Protestant martyrs, reported "that stretching out his right, he held it unshrinkingly in the fire until it was burnt to a cinder . . . frequently exclaiming 'this unworthy right hand.'"[37]

Verses 31-32 turn suddenly and abruptly to the dissolution of marriage, though it is not always clear if the subject is divorce or separation, what the partners are free to do after their marriage ends, and how to understand the unique and controversial "Matthean Exception" ("saving for the cause of fornication"), which Jesus will repeat at 19:9. Does it reflect the teaching of Jesus, the practice of Matthew's community, or a concession to Gentile converts? Being both a social contract involving questions of property and inheritance, and a personal commitment involving choice and affection, marriage has had a problematic status in Christian theology; and it was not until the thirteenth century that it was established as one of the seven sacraments to be celebrated in church and in the presence of a priest. This then raises the vexed question of scriptural texts bearing on divorce and remarriage. Here the KJV specifies "fornication," though *porneia,* the Greek word used here, might include various sorts of immorality, including marriage with close kin, and *moicheia* was the technical word for adultery. It is assumed that adultery—a capital offense at Deuteronomy 22:22—is committed by the wife, who will then remarry; and nothing is said of adultery by the husband or by both spouses, presumably because the overriding concern is that a wife made pregnant thereby might bring back to the marriage an illegitimate child who would complicate matters of family property and inheritances. Also, it is the seriousness of adultery that, like desertion, it also offends against Genesis 2:24 ("they shall be one flesh"). Many, but not all, of the church fathers and councils maintained that the marriage remained valid and indissoluble, even after the offending wife had been dismissed, and that although divorce was permissible for just cause, neither spouse had the right to remarry (which could provide time for a reconciliation). As for the Church's ban on second marriages, Voltaire quoted a divorced man's complaint that "God permits me to marry again, but the bishop of Rome forbids me."[38] Those Protestant churches for whom marriage is not a sacrament but a voluntary contract and a civil institution have broadened the Matthean Exception to include almost any marriage failure, with a subsequent right to remarry in church. Orthodox churches have used it to permit divorce and remarriage, originally for the victims of adultery but now for other serious misbehaviors, though they regard only the first marriage as sacramental.

Oddly, nothing is said in the New Testament about polygamy, so in one of the most bizarre episodes in Christian history a radical Anabaptist "prophet" named Jan Bockelszoon (a.k.a. John of Leyden) had to appeal to the Old Testament to justify taking sixteen wives. The year was 1534 in Münster, Germany, where he appointed himself "king of the world" in preparation for what he proclaimed was an imminent end time, with only Münster to be spared. For a year he presided over a theocracy of compulsory polygamy, forcibly shared property, and general anarchy until a joint force of Catholics and Protestants recaptured the city and subjected him and his followers to barbarous tortures and execution.

Tertullian saw 5:36 as a warning to women who "stain" their hair, even trying to look blond and German; but the main subject in verses 34-37 is oaths.[39] According to Jesus, simple honesty, sincerity, and candor in making promises, and trust in those who promise obviate the need for elaborate oaths that demean God's dignity. The church, citing Paul in Romans 1:9, "For God is my witness," has traditionally interpreted this prohibition as referring to oaths sworn before men, not vows made in the name of God (who is not named); others, citing "communication" in verse 37, see it as a ban only on oaths in ordinary conversation; and Augustine understood it as forbidding Christians to perjure themselves.[40] Calvin, citing God's "throne" and "footstool," saw it as forbidding oaths "which by any abuse profane God's holy name"; and both Catholics and Protestants exempt the kinds of oaths required by civil authorities.[41] But it was taken seriously and literally by Anabaptists under Menno Simons, and in a sixteenth-century world where oaths routinely confirmed allegiances to the state as well as validating private and public transactions, their refusal to swear made them into subversives—while their nonresistance to evil made them victims of persecution. Later, a similar stance by the Society of Friends (Quakers) was one reason for their persecution by the governments of Old and New England, for they had made a ban on swearing oaths one of the principal public witnesses of their faith, along with their pacifism, their "thees" and "thous," their plain clothes, and their refusal to doff their hats. After citing these verses, they went on to argue that oaths were useless since they trivialized the hallowed name of God, they could not prevent lying, and they carried the offensive implication that someone not under oath could not be expected to speak the truth. Verse 37 was alluded to by the Quakers' early leader George Fox ("Our Yea is yea, and our Nay is nay") when he was imprisoned in 1664 in Lancashire, England, for not taking a loyalty oath. Fox wondered why the judge did not also imprison the Bible because of its prohibition of oaths.[42] He was confined under appalling conditions for a year in the Lancaster Castle dungeon and later in Scarborough Castle on the North Sea, then pardoned and released by order of the king. In 1689 Parliament passed an Act of Toleration that allowed Quakers to substitute "affirmations" for oaths, though they could not serve on juries or in public office. In 1718 they won approval from the government to substitute an affirmation for their oath of allegiance to the Crown, and in 1725 they were allowed to omit the crucial words "in the name of Almighty God." In America they governed their own state, Pennsylvania, without oaths, which immensely complicated their judicial system, since Quaker plaintiffs could not seek jury trials or swear in witnesses.

The Sermon's prohibition of oaths was cited in a famous "Memorandum" submitted by leaders of German's Lutheran Church to Adolph Hitler on June 4, 1936. They were objecting to the oath of allegiance to Hitler that was required of all German youths, one that could oblige them to engage in activities that are "contrary to God's commandments."[43] In general, the Nazis and their "German Christians," led by their chief ideologist, Alfred Rosenberg, who was later tried and hanged at Nuremberg, disapproved of the "Jewish gospel," especially Matthew's concern for Jesus as the fulfillment of Old Testament prophecies, the humility and nonresistance to evil preached in the Sermon, and the universality of Christianity called for in the Great Commission of 28:19-20. Rosenberg much preferred Mark's portrayal of what he took to be a "positive" Jesus, who delivered ringing speeches as well as disrupted the business of the Jewish temple.

This injunction, along with the ban on divorce, offers a good example of how subsequent "interpretations" and "understandings" by church and state sometimes absolutized but more often mitigated or abrogated provisions of the

Sermon. Or, as St. Thomas More observed in his *Utopia* (1516): "Priests . . . in finding that men grievously disliked to hear their morals adjusted to the rule of Christ . . . accommodated His teachings to men's morals."[44] What is remarkable about this precept is that, as Benjamin Jowett (1817–93) noted in a famous essay "The Interpretation of Scripture" (1860), it has been almost universally ignored although it is not "practically impossible of fulfillment or even difficult."[45] And before him, Kant (for whom the Sermon was a favored scripture) found it "hard to understand why this clear prohibition is held as so unimportant."[46]

The proverbial "eye for an eye" (v. 38; from Ex. 21:24 and Deut. 19:21) is not so vindictive or bloodthirsty an injunction as it seems, for it was intended to restrict disproportionate vengeance and to prevent the escalation of blood feuds, and there is no indication it was ever carried out. Its recommendation of a proportionate response can even be applied to hell, where an eternity of fiery torture is arguably appropriate for an offense against an infinite Being. The equally proverbial "turn the other cheek" (39) suggests a blow with the back of the hand (unless the striker is left-handed), more of an insult than an injury. But even if this command is restricted to Jesus' followers, it offers little evidence for Jesus as a social revolutionary and has long been invoked by pacifists ("An Eye for an Eye Leaves Both Blind!").

Next is the controversial "resist not evil" (v. 39), which has long preoccupied Matthew's readers, partly because Jesus does not comment on the consequences of nonresistance or on how it can be reconciled with the need for justice. Celsus early complained (7.58, 433) that Jesus had taken it from Plato's *Crito* (Socrates: "Then we ought neither to take revenge nor to do harm to any man, not even if we suffer anything from him"), and readers have often noted that it seems contradicted by Jesus' forcible exorcisms and his cleansing of the temple (21:12-13). Augustine, living in a Christian empire threatened by heretics from within and invaders from without, qualified the Sermon's pacifism with his "just war" theory, arguing that in this imperfect world a legitimately constituted government has the right to use armed force in maintaining peace, order, and justice.[47] Aquinas was in agreement, and with an eye to the Israelites' OT battles, he also allowed for the violent repression of disruptive heresies, but only "to prevent them from hindering the faith of Christ."[48] But Erasmus argued that "just war" was an ambivalent term, invariably invoked by all belligerents, particularly when they were Christians warring amongst themselves in the name of Jesus. It was then only a step from the just war to the holy war, and for the Crusaders this mandate could be extended to the armed protection of the Eastern church and the forcible liberation of the Holy Land, just as in Islam God promises an afterlife in paradise to those who die in a Holy War (Koran, 9.19). Later, the English Puritans felt no compunction about a Christian government's using coercive violence to impose its will, and when in 1649 an unplanned attack on the Irish town of Wexford proved successful ("an unexpected providence"), Oliver Cromwell concluded that in the ensuing massacre of soldiers, civilians, and religious, God "in His righteous justice, brought a just judgment upon them."[49]

Martin Luther, in the first lines of his essay "On Secular Authority" (1523), acknowledged that verses 39-40 seemed at odds with the acknowledgement elsewhere in Scripture that crimes deserve punishment (e.g., 26:52: "They that take the sword shall perish with the sword"). He dismissed one traditional explanation, that this was another of the "counsels of perfection" applicable to the spiritually enlightened, preferring instead to distinguish between "two kingdoms": the spiritual kingdom of God, present in the private lives of true Christians; and the secular—and overwhelmingly evil—kingdom of the world, where secular authorities have the responsibility to use coercion for the wellbeing of their citizens (which unfortunately leaves unresolved the problem of border conflicts between the two kingdoms). He also allowed for defensive wars and wars between equals, distinguishing between self-defense and defense of others. "Christians may seek retribution, justice, protection and help for others."[50] Thus evil may be resisted in the service of those who are unable to do so, such as parents' obligation to protect their children or the state's obligation to defend its citizens. Others have felt that to forbid self-defense is to collude with evil and perpetuate injustice, and Calvin distinguished between "vindictiveness" and "turning aside the force of an assault" without causing hurt or resorting to vengeful retaliation, noting too that Jesus' command, taken literally, might only provoke an attacker and aggravate the injury.[51] Thus, the debate continues, with the horror of atomic warfare galvanizing pacifists, and the horror of the Holocaust dramatizing the consequences of unresisted evil.

In the Reformation, the scriptural literalism of the Swiss Anabaptists' *Schleitheim Confession* (1527) was uncompromising: "There will also unquestionably fall from us the unchristian, devilish weapons of force—such as sword, armor, and the like, and all their use for friends or against one's enemies." And this verse was cited by Mennonites in their *Articles of Faith* (XIV), in which they pledged: "If necessity should require it, to flee, for the Lord's sake, from one city or country to another, and suffer the 'spoiling of our goods,' rather than give occasion of offense to anyone."[52] In modern times it was the verse that caused "the veil" to fall from Tolstoy's eyes and provided the key to his understanding of Christ's religion, his rather churchless mix of social anarchism, pacifism, and romanticism (following 7:1, he also rejected all oaths, for him the czarist legal system). It was for individuals to cultivate within themselves the love and truthfulness, the humility and forgiveness that was Jesus' teaching. But what particularly disturbed him was 5:22, "without a cause" (one word in the Greek), words "which destroy the whole meaning of Christ's teaching. . . . Christ did not utter, could not have uttered, this horrible word."[53] (He was delighted later to learn that there are manuscripts that omit them.) The founder of Mormonism, Joseph Smith, seems to have agreed, for he also omitted them from his "new translation" of the KJV. This was possible for Smith since he regarded his version as an interpretation assigned him by God (he transferred all the fulfillment passages from Matthew to Jesus); it was later published as a separate tract and then, along with the "Book of Moses," in *Pearl of Great Price* (1851; rev. 1878).[54] Verse 39 also evoked this response from Gandhi: "I was simply overjoyed and found my own opinion confirmed where I least expected it."[55]

Tolstoy was only the most notable of a number of socially conscious writers who have given the Sermon on the Mount—and, lately, the "sayings" document *Q* and the *Gospel of Thomas*—prominence in their own efforts to relieve the historical Jesus of what they took to be the dead weight of theology, dogma, and popular piety. All these encumbrances, they have contended, go back to the works of his followers (here Paul is regularly demonized), who began by fabricating the resurrection, turning Jesus into a god, making him the messiah of Jewish prophecy, and founding a church so that they could perpetuate his ministry and enjoy its prerogatives. In an "Enclosure" to his famous letter to Benjamin Rush, April 21, 1803, Thomas Jefferson, while president, lent his prestige to an early but typical view of this demystified Jesus and the fate of his moral doctrines: "They have been still more disfigured by the corruptions of schismatizing followers, who have found an interest in sophisticating and perverting the simple doctrines he taught, by engrafting in them the mysticisms of a Grecian Sophist, frittering them into subtleties, and obscuring them with jargon, until they have caused good men to reject the whole in disgust, and to view Jesus himself as an impostor."[56]

Having deplored the transformation of the Jesus of history into the Christ of faith, these writers felt it was now necessary for his modern and less gullible admirers to reverse the process and recover the human Jesus behind the ecclesiastical facade. Theirs was an effort that was initiated in the German Enlightenment of the eighteenth century by Hermann Samuel Reimarus (1694–1768), a professor of Oriental languages and the author of *On the Intentions of Jesus and His Disciples* (1778), and by his friend, the dramatist Gotthold Lessing (1729–81), who saw to its posthumous publication as the last of seven *Fragments of an Unknown Person,* also known as the *Wolfenbuettel Fragments* (1774–78; trans. 1879).[57] In scope it included all four gospels, and its effect, if not its purpose, was to present Jesus not only as Christ the Redeemer, the founder of a timeless religion, but as a Jewish nationalist from Nazareth, detached from the miracles and prophecies of the New Testament and concerned for individual betterment and social reform, but misguided into the political messianism that aborted his ministry and cost him his life.

This tragic event left it to his disciples to transform his gospel teachings into the new and non-Jewish religion of the Epistles. The publications of Reimarus and Lessing marked the modern beginning of the historical and critical study of Scripture, and though often their objections had been anticipated by Christianity's earliest critics and later by the English deists, they were popularized by Albert Schweitzer's *Quest of the Historical Jesus* (1906; trans. 1910) and remain a prevailing force in modern scholarship.

So pervasive is our historical consciousness that the "recovery" of the human Jesus and positioning of him in the context of first-century Judaism has been a flourishing enterprise for two centuries, especially among those who dissent from church dogma and authority. Early classics in the field were two unconventional biographies of Jesus. One in German by David Friedrich Strauss (1808–74) (*The Life of Jesus Critically Examined*, 1835; its two volumes subsequently revised, translated, and republished in 1864 as *The Life of Jesus for the German People*) emphasized what he called the "mythic" element in the Gospels (he accepted the priority of Matthew), those legendary accretions that attach themselves over time to the biographies of famous men.[58] Strauss objected to the rationalization of gospel miracles—that, for example, Jesus healed the sick with hidden drugs, or stood on a raft when he seemed to be walking on water, or was only resuscitated, not resurrected. For him, the lives of Jesus in the Synoptics were not the reliable accounts of eye-witnesses but a "sacred legend" produced out of the faith and the imaginations of Jesus' followers, who attributed to their departed leader the messianic convictions they borrowed from the Old Testament. The New Testament narratives are "mythic" in the sense that they are reports of events that did not happen in the way they have been told but were preserved because they convey truths more important than factual events. So the story of Jesus walking on the water at 14:22-33 is a dramatization of his ability to rise above life's stormy seas; his reviving the daughter at 9:25 is a reenactment of the life-giving miracles attributed to Elisha and Elijah; the temptation narrative tells of Jesus acting like Moses in an amalgam of Exodus episodes; and the "resurrected" Jesus was developed from the controversial Suffering Servant of Isaiah 53. Strauss's work, translated by the novelist George Eliot, was enormously influential in weakening the credibility of the Gospels in nineteenth-century England, with the poet Arthur Hugh Clough (1819–61) in his "Epi-strauss-ion" comparing it to a bright light that flooded through stained-glass windows.

The other, radically different biography, first written in French, was the *Life of Jesus* (1863) by Ernest Renan (1823–92), which emphasized the humanity of Jesus in a revision that was more a historical idyll than a retelling of the Gospels.[59] In America an analogous effort, though centered on Jesus' teachings and freed of "superstitions, fanaticisms, and fabrications," was made by Jefferson, whose rationalizing writings on Jesus' life, morals, and "philosophy" were finally published together in 1904 as *The Life and Morals of Jesus*. And in England, *Essays and Reviews* (1860), mostly by Anglican clergymen with Oxford connections, caused a public outcry when one of its contributors, Benjamin Jowett, claimed that the Bible should be interpreted "like any other book." Today this school of historical criticism is best represented by the "Jesus Seminar," where a group of liberal NT scholars regularly meet to discuss and judge the authenticity of Jesus' statements. They tend to be minimalists, having accepted only 16 percent of Jesus' recorded words. They have also been extraordinarily successful in using the media to attract popular attention, but the results are mixed, since practitioners of the historical quest stake out such varying and conflicting positions on the reliability of the Gospels and their relation to the Jesus of Christian theology and worship. And all of them must confront the fact that prior to the Gospels was the unrecoverable oral tradition as well as the writings of Paul, with their insistence on Jesus' incarnation and redemptive mission.

Unjust laws are a universal concern, and Aquinas cited verses 40-41 on those laws that "do not bind in conscience, except perhaps in order to avoid scandal or disturbance."[60] Hence it may be prudent to yield to illegitimate demands and "go that extra mile," such as in 41, which seems to refer to the Romans' forcing their subjects to give legionaries some assistance when they are on the march. As for giving "to him that asketh" (42), Luther responded yes, "but to the one who really needs it," not to those who want to live at the expense of others,[61] and Calvin distinguished between benevolent generosity and "a foolish prodigality."[62] Samuel Johnson noted that even ardent believers will not always take Scripture literally: "Let a man whose credit is bad, come to a Quaker and say, 'Well, Sir, lend me a hundred pounds'; he'll find him as unwilling as any other man."[63] Finally, the self-abnegation of 41-42 did not impress Elihu Palmer (1764–1806), an early American deist. It "solicits an accumulation of insults," he said, and "to comply with the spirit of this morality, we must invert the order of nature" and surrender our "natural dignity."[64]

In verses 43-44 Jesus is interpreting Hebrew scripture, since the text we have does not specifically order Jews to hate their enemies, and Proverbs 25:21 counsels: "If thine enemy be hungry, give him bread to eat; and if he be thirsty, give him water to drink." So harsh a command was probably directed more against enemies of their faith (Ps. 139:21-22: "Do not I hate them, O Lord, that hate thee?") than against personal enemies, since love might encourage enemies to convert, whereas retaliation would not; and some have seen here an allusion to the dissident Jewish sect the Essenes, whose members had no compunction about cursing their enemies. The most striking example of such a love is Jesus' prayer for his crucifiers, "Father, forgive them; for they know not what they do" (Luke 23:34), although in other situations, as with the Pharisees in chapter 23, he seems somewhat less benevolent.

Yet "Love your enemies" is probably the most famous injunction in the Sermon and has evoked a variety of responses. Tertullian cited it to show that Christians were benevolent citizens of the very state that persecuted them.[65] But Thomas Paine complained that it would turn the offended party into a "spaniel," and "to love in proportion to the injury, if it could be done, would be to offer a premium for crime."[66] Mark Twain (and others) have also wondered why God then does not forgive His other enemies and do away with the fires of hell. Reminded that love of neighbor undercut racial segregation, West Virginia's Senator Robert Byrd, in a last-ditch filibuster to oppose civil rights legislation, responded, "But the Scriptural admonition does not say that we may not *choose* our neighbor!"[67]

One high point of the Sermon is at 43-44 with the two great commandments of the Judeo-Christian tradition, love of God and neighbor (which here includes enemies). One is theological, the other ethical—though the actions, conditions, and circumstances of love are left unspecified. They are repeated in the Synoptics (Matt. 22:37-40; Mark 12:29-31; Luke 10:27); and the second appears twice in Paul (Rom. 13:9; Gal. 5:14) and once in James (2:8), with the ethical commandment favored by those who are indifferent or opposed to the "laws" of revelation, dogma, and liturgy. There are conflicting opinions about the role of preferences in love and about what Jesus meant by "as thyself," since a self-love that is egocentric or narcissistic opposes the charitable love (*agape* in Greek) that for Christians was exemplified by the incarnation and the cross and should be practiced by Jesus' followers. Hence, in John 15:9-12 Jesus emphasizes the responsiveness and reciprocity of love when he commands his followers to "love one another, as I have loved you."

For Kant, Jesus' principal "commandments" (as they are called in 22:40) were a version of his own "Categorical Imperative"—that they be performed "for no motive other than unconditioned esteem for duty itself." And "love every man as yourself," that is, further his welfare from good will that is immediate and not derived from motives of self-advantage: "These commands are not mere laws of virtue but precepts of *holiness* which we ought to pursue, and the very pursuit of them is called *virtue*." This, for Kant, is a pure form of faith, centered in the individual and divested of supernaturalism, though, like the deism it professes, it ignores "the law and the prophets," to say nothing of the workings of grace. So it is little wonder that in 1794 he was reproved by King Friedrich Wilhelm II and agreed not to publish anything critical of revealed religion.[68]

Since love is an emotion, an affection, a passion, "Love your enemies" is a proof text for the emotionalism of evangelical and revivalist Christianity. The competing roles of affection and reason were at the heart of an eighteenth-century controversy between two great New England preachers, Jonathan Edwards and Charles Chauncy. Although often portrayed as a grim Calvinist,

Edwards was an apologist for the "religion of the heart" and was a leader in the 1740 revival known as the "Great Awakening," while Chauncy, the liberal minister of Boston's First Church, opposed its emotionalism. Edwards saw the fire of the Holy Spirit as heat, Chauncy as light. Martin Luther King Jr., who had the opportunity to love more than his share of enemies during the civil rights struggle said: "We should be happy that he did not say, 'Like your enemies.' It is almost impossible to like some people. 'Like' is a sentimental and affectionate word." And in preaching—and practicing ("Throw us in jail, and we will still love you")—love in the sense of *agape,* "redemptive good will for all men," King drew attention to 45b, commenting, "We must love our enemies, because only by loving them can we know God and experience the beauty of his holiness."[69]

By the end of chapter 5 Jesus has progressed from the inner happiness and ultimate promise of the Beatitudes, through the "salt" and "light" injunctions whereby his message will be shared with the world, to the Sermon's goal, "perfection." Since divine perfection seems an unrealizable goal (though the Greek *teleios* can also mean "complete" or "unlimited"), some feel that, unlike the Ten Commandments and certain provisions of the Sermon, this simply restates an ideal aim, that Christians should seek to be as perfect as they can by means of prayer and fasting (inner perfection) and in their love of God and charity toward their neighbors (outer perfection). That despite human limitations perfection could be achieved in this world has inspired Christian Perfectionism, a periodically recurring phenomenon in church history whereby individuals strive for a personal holiness, often apart from their churches. At the end of the second century, Clement of Alexandria described this process of self-deification in terms of a quasi-Platonic ascent to divinity; and Pelagius (354–420) argued for a will that was not only free but strong enough to achieve a sinless life even without an infusion of divine grace. It later became a goal of monasticism; continued with medieval heretics like the Bogomils and the Cathars; appealed to deviant sects like the Adamites, who felt nudity would help them acquire an Edenic innocence; and, in the thirteenth century, inspired the members of the Free Spirit, who sought blessedness through a freedom from ecclesiastical obligations and conventional standards of behavior. More recently it has characterized such utopian movements as the nineteenth-century Oneida Community in upstate New York.

For some, true perfection could only be attained by mystics through a personal communion with God, but for the Reformers it was generally precluded by their rejection of monasticism and their insistence on original sin, human depravity, and the necessary operations of faith and grace (Calvin: "Whatever man has or does by himself we declare accursed"), for even the quest for personal perfection is corrupted by egocentricity.[70] But Christian perfection became a practical goal for John Wesley (1703–91), the founder of Methodism, for whom the imperative of verse 48 was, like all of Jesus' commands, also a promise. He redefined perfection as "only another term for holiness," that is, freedom from sin—though not, he cautioned, from ignorance, weakness, temptations, and mistakes, which can still coexist with pure love of God. "Entire sanctification" had been exemplified by Jesus and summarized in the Sermon's love of God and neighbor; it was achievable through faith; demonstrated by repentance, conversion, and sanctification; and productive of good deeds.[71] The Quakers broke with Calvinism's "total depravity" in believing that an individual who has fully taken in the spirit of Christ, the "inner light," could, without scriptural mediation and through the promptings of the Holy Spirit, "see into another or more steadfast state than Adam's in innocency, even into a state in Christ Jesus, that should never fall."[72] The liberal Boston clergyman William Ellery Channing (1780–1842) reflected the optimism of Unitarianism when he cited verse 48 in observing that in Christianity "I meet perpetual testimonies to the divinity of human nature."[73]

A colorful example is the story of the Oneida group, which sought to sanctify the world by achieving personal sinlessness. The idea of a perfectionist community began when its founder reported his reaction on reading Luke 1:35: "As I sat brooding over my difficulties and prospects, I listlessly opened my Bible and my eye fell upon these words: 'The Holy Ghost shall come upon thee.' The words seemed to glow upon the page, and my spirit heard a voice from heaven through them promising me the baptism of the Holy Spirit and the second birth."[74] These are the words of John Humphrey Noyes (1811–86) while a student at Yale Divinity School in 1833, who from that moment on became an apostle of Christian Perfectionism, founding the Oneida Community in 1848 to show that perfect holiness could be attained not only by individuals but by a social group. This experiment in Christian utopianism was abhorrent to orthodox Protestants, since its conviction that people could so totally commit themselves to God that they would achieve sinlessness in this life amounted to a denial of natural depravity. But for more than thirty years the charismatic Noyes guided his flock of two to three hundred believers, persuading them to practice a kind of biblical communism, including what he called "complex marriage," whereby they could overcome the selfishness and possessiveness of love and conventional marriage (which he characterized as "amative" and "idolatrous") by having husbands, wives, and children in common (he even coined the term "free love"). Noyes and his senior associates arranged these couplings, availing themselves of "Ascending Fellowship," which enabled young girls, usually around thirteen, to advance in spiritual perfection by first having sex with Noyes (their "first husband") and his inner circle of superior souls. These matings even included incest, which Noyes encouraged, labeling it "consanguineous stirpiculture." Here Matthew's gospel was pressed into service, since the community saw itself as a "branch of the kingdom of heaven." Jesus himself had said there is no marriage in heaven (22:30), so Noyes felt that there need be none in that part of heaven called Oneida. Still, by all accounts the members of the Oneida Community were happy with these arrangements, and differences were settled at regular sessions of mutual criticism conducted by Noyes, who considered himself God's representative on earth and the interpreter of His will. The community's neighbors in rural Madison County tolerated its existence and on weekends liked to visit its grounds for exhibitions and entertainments, generally regarding the Perfectionists as industrious, progressive, and a good source of jobs in their shops and businesses. But some local church people scoffed at their outward conventionality and fulminated against what they saw as the community's rampant concubinage and adultery. Their pressures, along with factional disputes, eventually fractured what was one of the most successful of the forty or so communes founded in the early nineteenth century by seekers after this-worldly perfection (two others were Brook Farm and New Harmony), and Noyes was forced to flee to Canada in 1879. The Oneida Community dissolved a year later, becoming a joint-stock company. But from its spoon factory Noyes's son and others created one of the world's largest and most respected producers of silverware, and tourists today can visit the community's Mansion House in Sherrill outside Syracuse, New York.

In chapter 6 Jesus speaks against ostentatious worship (vv. 1-8). Some find it hard to reconcile the private piety of this passage with the public witness recommended in 5:14-16 ("Let your light . . . shine before men"), though the earlier injunction seems aimed at encouraging his disciples to offer public evidence of their faith when they are being persecuted. In writing to his beloved Heloise, Abelard (1079–1142) saw this as an endorsement of monasticism, interpreting "closet" as "the seclusion of monastic solitude."[75] As for the promised "reward," Matthew uses forms of this word twelve times in his gospel, and the frequency of his references to rewards for good behavior and punishments for bad lend, for some, a depressing note of calculation and self-interest to actions that should be done or not for their own sake. On the other hand, the apparent activism of Matthew's Jesus is balanced by the Sermon's emphasis on attitudes and intentions.

Part of worship is prayer. The modern custom of holding palms together is derived from the medieval custom of a vassal's placing his hands, with palms joined, between the hands of his lord. But early Christians stood when praying, as did Jews, and they raised their hands, a quasi-pagan gesture that soon yielded to the stance of the *orans* (Latin: "praying") figure (English: "orant") seen in catacomb paintings—with bent elbows, raised forearms, and palms turned outward—a stance that for some Christians recalled the crucifixion. Erasmus quoted verse 7 in his *Enchiridion Militis Christiani* (1501) in advising the militant Christian to combat vice by using the weapons of prayer and knowledge—prayer to control the passions, knowledge to fortify the mind. But he condemned "vain repetition," as did the Reformers, who found them in recitations of the Catholic litanies and rosary.[76] Since the good Christian should pray everywhere, St. Ambrose interpreted "closet" as the inner spirit. "Even if you are in the midst of a crowd, you have within you your closet and secret room."[77] But Dietrich Bonhoeffer (1906–45), the modern Lutheran theologian, warned against exaggerating this public-private disjunction: "I can lay on a very nice show for myself even in the privacy of my own room."[78] As for God's response, Lily Tomlin quipped, "When we talk to God, we're praying. When God talks to us, we're schizophrenic."

The fundamental prayer of Christianity (Luther: "The best of prayers—superior even to the Psalms") is the Lord's Prayer (6:9-13; Luke 11:2-4). It is so named because it was taught by Jesus himself, though "after this manner" can also suggest that it is less an established text than an outline of *how* Christians should pray.[79] In its mixture of eschatology and "wisdom," it is an ecumenical, even Jewish prayer, since, like so much of the Sermon, it says nothing of the passion or resurrection. Its sentiments, which may derive from the ministry of John the Baptist, are communal and activist and might have been part of the earliest Christian devotions, since it is quoted in the second-century teaching manual, the *Didache.* If so, it is hard to know why a prayer expressly dictated by Jesus was not preserved in its exact words by all the evangelists.

Originally Aramaic and now located in the center of the Sermon, the Lord's Prayer is divided between heaven and earth, with three "thy" wishes followed by four "we/us" wishes, these seven equaling, in Augustine's count, the perfect number of the Beatitudes. But other commentators have noted that they also equaled the Seven Gifts of the Holy Spirit, the seven sacraments, the seven theological and cardinal virtues—and even the Seven Deadly Sins. Jesus supposedly taught it to his disciples in a cave on Mt. Olivet, the location now marked by the Church of the Paternoster, its interior decorated with plaques of the Lord's Prayer in one hundred languages. Later it was the only prayer allowed, and repeatedly recited, by the medieval Bogomils, a heretical sect from the Balkans; and their European counterparts, the Cathars, believed that pronouncing it over their food and drink would transform them into Christ's body and blood and that they would be damned if they failed to recite it at the point of death. It was considered a powerful defense against witches, and reciting it backward was a standard feature of Black Masses and other satanic rituals. It has also been repeatedly parodied, as when, on the eve of the French Revolution, royalists prayed: "Our Father, who art in Versailles, glorified be thy name, thy reign be eternal, thy will be done in the provinces as it is in Paris."[80] In 1848 the French revolutionaries who forced King Louis-Philippe (1773–1850) to abdicate responded with "Our Father, Louis-Philippe, who art in the Tuileries, cursed be thy name, thy kingdom cease."[81]

The Prayer's first word is *pater* ("father"), a term unique in the New Testament when referring to God. It is also interesting that Matthew does not record the more intimate word *abba,* which in Mark 14:36 is often taken as a sign of Jesus' personal relationship with God the Father. *Pater* also gives us "patter," in the sense of rapid speech, as when it was hurriedly recited by monks. Erasmus saw a call to Christian pacifism in the communal, even universal "our": "How can you call on a common father if you are drawing a sword to thrust in your brother's vitals?"[82]

"Hallowed be thy name" is the first of three parallel expressions (followed by, literally, "come be thy kingdom" and "done be thy will") that are obscured by the English translation. In 1525 Luther cited the last, along with "deliver us from evil," in vainly urging restive German peasants not to resort to violence during the Peasants' War. "That is the Christian way to get rid of misfortune and evil, namely, endure it and call upon God."[83] But it remains unclear what is entailed by God's "will," and how the faithful should "do" it. And since these words can be construed as counseling passive acceptance, they have irked social activists. Shaw, in a parody of the Lord's Prayer, rephrased them as "Get thy job done on earth which will then be heaven."[84]

"Thy kingdom come" is the most familiar evocation of Jesus' message, and similar references occur some 114 times in the Gospels; it is a concept elastic enough to be shared by both Jews and Christians and is often cited as a basis for interfaith understanding. Here its coming is to be anticipated by the doing of God's will here and now; and Luther, in his "Short Exposition" of the Lord's Prayer, has the kingdom of God beginning in individual souls to prepare them for the kingdom to come. This again raises the problems, already reviewed at our discussion of Jesus' baptism, of defining and situating the kingdom of God. Does its suggestion of a political institution such as the church and a defined location adequately represent the universality of Jesus' mission and God's sovereignty? How far are Roman Catholics justified in equating their church— or an idealized version thereof—with the kingdom of God? Or is it a prayer (so Calvin) "that the Lord may day by day add new believers"?[85] Or is it both an agenda and an imperative for Christian activists, to be realized in an ideal social order? There are tantalizing responses to all these questions scattered throughout the New Testament, and it is a pity that they do not cohere into a clear and consistent teaching.

"Our daily bread" (11), recalling the OT manna, may be a familiar phrase in English, but *epiousion,* the only adjective in the prayer and traditionally rendered as "daily," is rare and obscure (it could mean "tomorrow's" bread or, if the prayer is said in the morning, "this coming day's bread"), which is surprising if the Lord's Prayer was widely recited. Jerome's Latin Vulgate translates it here spiritually as *supersubstantialem,* suggesting Jesus as the bread of life, and at Luke 11:3 materially as *quotidianum* (Latin for "daily"). The Catholic

Church has inserted Jerome's Lukan word, *epiousion,* into the Matthean version. In 1905 Pope Pius X asserted that it was the "all but unanimous teaching of the holy Fathers of the Church" that this meant the Eucharistic bread; therefore, he took it as a proof text recommending the daily reception of Communion, and most Christian denominations do locate the Lord's Prayer in their Eucharistic liturgies.[86] But Voltaire invented a Dr. Tamponet of the Sorbonne, who claimed to find "a multitude of heresies in the Lord's Prayer," charging that this petition offended against verse 25, "take no thought for . . . what ye shall eat." Similarly, the petition "Thy will be done" overlooks the fact that nothing can be done unless God wills it; we dare not oblige God to forgive us our debts; and only the devil can lead us into temptation.[87]

The Reformers were at pains to point out that God's forgiveness of sin (v. 12), expressed here as moral "debts" owed to God, should not be seen as a reward for the good work of human forgiveness—though for many this petition is simply a restatement of the "works and rewards" system of popular Judaism. Translators have variously rendered Matthew's *opheilemata* as "debts," "wrongs," "shortcomings," "trespasses," or "sins," the last two closer to *hamartias* in Luke's version of the Lord's Prayer (Luke 11:4). Again, like Voltaire's Dr. Tamponet, Benjamin Franklin disapproved of the presumptuousness of "as we forgive . . . ," which "has the Air of proposing ourselves as an Example of Goodness fit for God to imitate," so he changed it to "and enable us likewise to forgive." He also disliked "our" daily bread, since it "seems to put us on a Claim of Right, and to contain too little of the grateful Acknowledgement and sense of Dependance that becomes Creatures who live on the daily Bounty of their Creator. Therefore it is changed to 'Provide for us this Day, as thou hast hitherto daily done.'"[88] The New English Bible (NEB) offers "wrong" in place of the misleading "debts" or "trespasses."

The Lord's Prayer was the first scriptural passage John Eliot (1604–90), the "Apostle to the Indians," used in an effort that would lead to the publication in 1663 of an 1,180-page Bible in Algonquian, a monumental achievement, considering the differences between Hebrew/Greek and the various Indian dialects. But the Massachusetts Indians whom Eliot instructed in Puritan Christianity found it difficult to understand why they should forgive (*nutaquontamounnonog* in Algonquian) the tribes with whom they had been feuding for generations.[89]

"Lead us not into temptation" (13) is a controversial petition, apparently contradicted by James 1:12-13 ("Blessed is the man that endureth temptation"). As Origen noted, "most people do not understand it," since they feel they cannot help but find their way into temptation without the Lord's leading them.[90] It is sometimes criticized as too "psychological," a translation of a line that should read, "Do not put us to the test" (New Jerusalem Bible), that is, to such terrible trials that our faith will be weakened; or it may be under-

stood as "Do not let us be led into temptation, where, given our human frailties, we might make the wrong choices." It recalls the temptation narrative,
though here it is most likely an allusion to a deliverance from the supreme trials before the apocalypse (Rev. 3:10: "I also will keep thee from the hour of
temptation"). But most Christians probably take it simply as "Do not let us
yield to temptation," or, with Luther in his "Short Exposition," more com-
prehensively as "Guard us from all afflictions and torments of the body"
(among them Luther listed syphilis).[91] Augustine in his *Commentary* distinguished being tried by fire and being consumed by it; and later, in arguing that
our wills, though free, are weak ("forgive us our debts" proved for him that no
one is without sin), he asked why Jesus included this request if we are able to
avoid temptations unaided.[92] Franklin, who preferred "keep us out of temptation," rejected the original concept that "God sometimes tempted, or directed
or permitted the Tempting of People" as a Jewish "Notion" and "unworthy of
God," since "we now suppose that Temptation, so far as it is supernatural,
comes from the Devil only."[93]

"Deliver us from evil" was for Augustine the comprehensive petition, the
one that includes all the others. The Greek reads: "from the evil" (neuter), but
the more generalized "from evil" is standard in the Western churches.
Nonetheless, with Luther and Wesley and in the Eastern churches, it may also
be understood as "the evil one" (masculine), the devil.[94] Calvin wrote: "There
is no need to make a controversy over the matter, for the sense stays practically
the same, that we are exposed to the devil and to sin, but God protects us and
snatches us away."[95] Possible also is an allusion here to the final conflict between God and Satan. For her Christian Science followers, Mary Baker Eddy
expanded "evil" to include "sin, disease, and death";[96] whereas the great proponent of the Social Gospel Walter Rauschenbusch insisted on the changing
face of evil, so that for him its current form was "the terrible power of organized covetousness and institutionalized oppression." In fact, he saw the Lord's
Prayer as "the great prayer of Social Christianity," since it addresses "our," not
"my" Father, calls for God's will to be done "on earth," asks only for as much
bread as is needed for the day, and pleads for brotherly love.[97]

"For thine is the kingdom." Although they are not in Luke, these beautiful
and familiar words—sometimes called the "Protestant ending"—are now in
the Roman Catholic mass but not directly added to the Prayer. Recalling the
"doxology," or words of praise, at 1 Chronicles 29:11 ("Thine, O Lord, is the
greatness, and the power, and the glory"), they mitigate the final allusion to
Satan and, for Calvin, remind us "that our prayers depend more on the power
and goodness of God than on any trust of ours." Apparently originating as a
solemn ending for the Prayer when it was recited in liturgies, it found its way
into some inferior Greek manuscripts and from them into the KJV's Matthew.
It was not in the Greek sources used by Jerome in his Latin Vulgate, but Eras-

mus included it in his Greek text (1516), noting that it was a later insertion. It is ironic that this addition to Scripture should be associated with the Protestant Reformers, who regularly decried "human additions" to Jesus' message. And surprisingly, this later insertion is retained in Mormonism's version of the Lord's Prayer (3 Nephi 13:13) as if it had been spoken by Jesus himself.[98]

The phrase "the power and the glory" is also the ironic title of Graham Greene's novel (*The Power and the Glory*, 1940) about an unnamed "whiskey priest" who, for all his human failings, courageously continues to minister to Mexican Catholics during the religious persecutions of the 1920s. A quasi-Christ figure, he is eventually betrayed by a local Judas and is executed. But the ultimate reduction of the Lord's Prayer appears in Ernest Hemingway's short story "A Clean, Well-Lighted Place," with "Our nada who art in nada, nada be thy name, thy kingdom nada, thy will be nada in nada."[99] This is the despairing prayer of an elderly waiter for whom only a "clean, well-lighted place" offers a refuge from the nothingness of existence.

The Sermon now turns to fasting, a religious practice recalling the temptation narrative but otherwise only occasionally mentioned in the New Testament. It may seem that verse 17 is an unexpected exception to the caution against external displays, but it probably means that they should do nothing more than their usual daily toilet. The next admonition, against the amassing of earthly treasures, culminates in the lapidary verse 21 (also at Luke 12:34). In his *Letter 22* ("To Eustochium"), Jerome reported that these were the words spoken to him in 374 by the "Judge" who appeared to him in a vision as he lay feverish and close to death and accused him of not being a Christian but a "Ciceronian," since he preferred the high style of the Latin classics to the crude rhetoric of the Hebrew prophets. "Thenceforth I read the books of God with a zeal greater than I had previously given to the books of men."[100] Some readers have noted that these world-denying sentiments were characteristic of the Cynic philosophers of Jesus' time, but he never advocated their personal autonomy or antisocial behavior, nor did he urge his followers to live "according to nature."

The Scottish Reformer John Knox (1513–72) quoted verse 22 (also at Luke 11:34) in his unfinished *Second Blast of the Trumpet* (1558), when he argued for the right of Christians to "punish and depose" even a lawfully appointed ruler—the "eye" of the kingdom—if he transgressed "God's Holy Precepts." The "he" might also be a "she," and Knox opposed women rulers, especially Mary Queen of Scots, in his *First Blast of the Trumpet Against the Monstrous Regiment of Women* (1558).[101]

Emerson imagined that while preaching the Sermon, Jesus "saw the lilies whitening the meadows, and the birds flying over his head," so in 24-34 he turned to his disciples to reassure them.[102] Verses 28-29 are often admired as one of Scripture's most beautiful passages, but they did not please one Edward

Harwood (1729–94), whose own translation substituted what he considered eighteenth-century elegance for the "barbarities" of the KJV: "Survey with attention the lilies of the field, and learn from them how unbecoming it is for rational creatures to cherish a solicitous passion for gaiety and dress—for they sustain no labour, they employ no cares to adorn themselves, and yet are clothed with such inimitable beauty as the richest monarch in the richest dress never equalled."[103]

The final words of verse 28 are the epigraph to Keats's "Ode on Indolence," but they are usually interpreted, not as a counsel against work, which monastics considered a duty and the Reformers, a vocation, but against the distractions and anxieties that work can often generate. Thomas Paine thought it the only passage in the New Testament that "has any reference to the works of God,"[104] and it is the one passage in Matthew that seems to reflect the personal freedom and self-sufficiency advocated by the Cynics. But Shaw wrote: "We have brought the necessity of taking thought for the morrow to such a pitch that very few of us are able to take thought for anything else."[105] And Elihu Palmer, a New England freethinker and Bible critic, argued that these counsels, "if reduced to practice, would bring upon the world universal starvation, and cause the human race to become extinct."[106]

The "fowls of the air" might be surprised to learn that God spares them the search for food. But Jesus' words are meant to throw into relief the point of the passage—the command at verse 33, "Seek ye first the kingdom of God, and his righteousness." Doing the will of God and trusting in divine providence will put worldly concerns into proper perspective. "Mammon" (v. 24; Luke 16:13) is an Aramaic word for wealth that became personified as an evil spirit of avarice, appearing as a devil in Spenser's *Faerie Queene* (2.7) and Milton's *Paradise Lost* (1.679), and as the greedy Sir Epicure Mammon in Ben Jonson's comedy *The Alchemist* (1610). It later became a pejorative term for corporate capitalism at its most unscrupulous.

There were various charges leveled against early Christians: that they were gullible fanatics since they relied on faith, not reason, and were too eager to martyr themselves; that they were immoral perverts since they held nocturnal orgies of incest and cannibalism; that they were not original in their ethical teachings since others before them had denounced violence and endorsed forgiveness; that they offered a doctrine that was deceptive since their leader was not God's son but a failed sorcerer and their Scriptures a tissue of contradictions and absurdities; that their claim to unity was false since they were rent by discord and factionalism; and that they were bad citizens since they did not acknowledge the gods of the state or participate in emperor worship. The last charge was repeated by Celsus, who cited verse 24 as proof that Christians were elitist and separatist and could not be loyal citizens of the Roman Empire—although they also contradicted themselves by worshiping "two masters," God and Christ. And he noted that the "Son of God" speaking here sounded quite different from the "Father God" of the Pentateuch, who promulgated laws and favored the prosperity of the Hebrews (7.18, 409). "Who is wrong? Moses or Jesus? Or when the Father sent Jesus, had he forgotten what commands he gave to Moses? Or did he condemn his own laws and change his mind, and send his messenger for quite the opposite purpose?" (8:2, 454).

Cyprian, the bishop of Cyprus (248–58), also quoted verse 24 in his attack on the *libellatici,* those Christians who had abandoned their faith during the persecutions (249–60) by the emperors Decius and Valerian and had obtained a *libellus,* a certificate attesting that they had sacrificed to the Roman gods in the presence of their local "Sacrifice Commission."[107] The persecutions caused so many varieties of apostasy, sometimes led by bishops, that after the persecutions subsided the church had to convene a synod at Rome to deal with the problem of meting out appropriate discipline and arranging subsequent rehabilitation. It was also cited by St. Ambrose in 384 in his famous dispute with Quintus Aurelius Symmachus (340–402), the prefect of Rome and a pagan, after the latter had sought the restoration of the Altar of Victory that the Emperor Gratian had ordered removed from the Senate House. Symmachus cited the altar's distinguished history as the protector of the emperors and guarantor of the empire's prosperity, and he appealed for tolerance of the ancient rites and traditional powers that had saved Rome from the Gauls in 390 BC and from Hannibal in the Second Punic War (218–202). But he was no match for Ambrose, then the bishop of Milan, who prevailed upon Valentinian II, quoting verse 24, to reject Symmachus's petition: "God wills not to be worshiped under the form of stones."[108]

In verses 25-27 the birds are the beneficiaries of the Lord's loving care, but in the "Parable of the Sower" (13:4) they devour the seeds that "fell by the wayside." As for adding cubits (about twenty inches), Tertullian quoted 27 (also at Luke 12:25) in charging that it was the devil's work that ancient actors wore high shoes; and he invoked the same verse against women who tried to increase their height with hair pieces.[109] Chapter 6 then ends with 34, a verse not likely to be the motto for an insurance company ("Be, therefore, not anxious about tomorrow . . ."), but a life led strictly according to the Gospels caused St. Francis to forbid one of his friars to prepare vegetables a day in advance or to accept alms for more than one day.

Chapter 7 begins with some familiar words ("Judge not . . ."), though not, said Bertrand Russell, "popular in the law courts of Christian countries."[110] Judgments have to be made, of course (among them Shaw counted letters to the *London Times*), and it is hard to see how Christianity could be propagated without at least implying judgments on the secular world. Furthermore, the Christian creeds all speak of Jesus returning "to judge the living and the dead," and judgments loom large in Jesus' own sayings. But in Greek, "judge" is closer to "condemn," and this prohibition seems directed against individuals prone to faultfinding and self-righteousness. Furthermore, those who judge maliciously in this world will have to face divine judgment in the next. This is one of the most often quoted verses in Scripture, but never so memorably as by Abraham Lincoln when talking of the North and South in his "Second Inaugural Address" on March 4, 1865: "Both read the same Bible, and pray to the same God; and each invokes His aid against the other. It may seem strange that any men should dare to ask a just God's assistance in wringing their bread from the sweat of other men's faces; but let us not judge that we be not judged."[111] And before Lincoln, Shakespeare found in verse 2 the title for one of his problem comedies (*Measure for Measure*, 1609?), in which the strict justice implied by the title is leavened by mercy and forgiveness.

The "mote" and "beam" in verses 3-5 are "speck" and "log" in the NRSV, hard though it may be to imagine a log in someone's eye. "Mote" and "beam" (as well as "strait is the gate and narrow is the way," v. 14), first appeared in the Wycliffe Bible (1382). Verse 6 can also puzzle modern readers. "That which is holy" refers to the meat from animal sacrifices, but it is "pearls before swine" that has become proverbial (the phrase, like much of this chapter, is from Tyndale). It is still an odd command, since Jesus himself associated with the "swine" of the earth, and yet here he appears to forbid the spreading of the gospel to Gentiles. It was sometimes interpreted as forbidding the Eucharist to the unbaptized or the unrepentant (*Didache* 2.5), or the "Good News" of the gospel on inappropriate occasions or to those who are spiritually unready or openly unreceptive; and it probably reflects a concern to maintain Christian identity in a pagan and hostile world. Later it was useful for heretical sects like the late medieval Cathars, who claimed secret rites and doctrines, particularly since a pearl can suggest something precious and beautiful that is also hidden. In the Middle Ages it also justified a ban on vernacular Bibles, not so much that powerful but fearful clerics could keep God's Word from the people (so some Protestant propaganda), as to guard against errant translations and interpretations that might have been based on inferior or unapproved manuscripts of the Vulgate. The injunction is obliquely recalled today in Catholic churches when catechumens, candidates receiving instruction, leave the church after the Scripture readings and before the Eucharist.

Verse 7 is Tyndale's rendering, repeated at Luke 11:9 and is a controversial verse, given its unconditional assurances along with its utter silence on what it is to be asked for. It could even be seen as encouraging dissidents to try to find support in the Bible without regard for church guidance. It has often been taken as a proof text for the traditional view that in terms of the covenant God has made with man, God has obliged Himself to respond to human initiatives. But the Reformers later came to the pessimistic view, influenced by Augustine, that individuals were so mired in sin that they could not even begin to make the effort required to merit a response, and hence they needed the gift of grace from God. We do not have the strength to knock, but God freely bestows it on us as long as we have the faith that is not just belief and assent but trust and commitment.

The "Golden Rule" (v. 12) appears in another version at 22:39, where "love" is added. It also appears in various forms in secular literature, such as the *Analects* of Confucius (551–479), though usually in its negative form (e.g., in the apocryphal *Book of Tobit:* "Do not do to anyone else what you would hate," 4:15). So it is significant that Jesus here enjoins, not the avoidance of harm, but the practice of virtue. The Golden Rule has had a persistent presence in Western thought and is ordinarily recommended.[112] But its prescriptive value as a seemingly self-evident principle of moral conduct has been questioned. The mutuality that it recommends can also seem to be a calculating reciprocity: it assumes that there is a social equality and a commonality of interests between agent and recipients; it is imprecise in that the undefined "doing" might well be harmful or immoral; and it can easily conflict with duty and responsibility, as when an employer must fire a worker or a judge sentence a criminal. Some cynics have revised it to "He who has the gold, rules." In 1791 Jonathan Edwards Jr. preached on this text to an Abolitionist group, applying it to the slave trade. "Should we be willing that the African or any other nation should purchase us, our wives and children, transport us into Africa and there sell us into perpetual slavery?"[113]

The reference to the "narrow gate" at 13-14 suggests the smaller city gate reserved for pedestrians and left open at night when the main city gate was closed, though here it leads in a direction opposite from the wide gate. Augustine interpreted this as the custom of serpents to force themselves through narrow openings and thereby slough off their old skins; that is, "Put off . . . the old man" (Eph. 4:22).[114] At the beginning of Bunyan's *Pilgrim's Progress* (1678), the words of 13-14 were inscribed over the Wicket-gate that Christian, as directed by Evangelist, must enter if he is to make his way from the City of Destruction to Mount Zion. Good-will opens the gate and directs him along the "straight and narrow" way.[115]

The "strait gate" is often confused with "straight" as referring to the direction of a path, as in "the straight and narrow," notably by Joseph Smith, when he included most of the KJV's version of chapters 5–7 in his *Book of Mormon*. For Kierkegaard (1813–55), the gate was widest and the way broadest in the worldly and complacent "Christendom" (his word) of his nineteenth-century Denmark. This was the impetus for his "crisis" theology, a personal and passionate appropriation of the Bible message.[116] These are, in any reading, unsettling words for those who believe that Jesus' mission was to save all the world's billions of peoples, including those who have never heard of him and who conduct their lives according to cultural and religious codes that Christians would find crude, benighted, and idolatrous.

Jesus' caution against "false prophets" made verse 15 a convenient verse in Reformation debates, since Christian clergymen on both sides could brand their opponents as "wolves in sheep's clothing." Although false prophecy is not limited to religion, this charge is almost always directed against clerics. Calvin said: "Christ had predicted not of strangers, but of men who should give themselves out for pastors, that they would be ravenous wolves."[117] But it was left to Churchill to vary the text in calling Clement Atlee "a sheep in sheep's clothing."

Again at 7:18-20 (and 12:33) Jesus speaks of the tree and its fruits, recalling John's words at 3:10. This verse was reported to be a proof text for the dualism of the medieval Cathars. "Since God is the highest good, evils are not from him; but since evils exist, and not from God himself, they come therefore from something other than God. Therefore, since God is the principle of good, there is another, the principle of evil."[118] In the Reformation the emphasis here on good works made Matthew seem an advocate for Catholicism, whereas Paul, with his theology of grace and faith, appeared to speak for Protestants—although the 542 references in Calvin's *Institutes,* placing Matthew just behind Psalms and Romans, witness to its abiding appeal to the Reformers. Since the apparent meaning is that as a tree is judged by its fruits, so will individuals be judged by their deeds, it is interesting that this meaning was reversed, and the passage became a critical proof text for Luther's conviction of the primacy and power of faith: that as the tree must be good before it can bear good fruits, so "good works follow and proceed from the good person." They are the Christian's grateful and almost spontaneous response to the grace freely bestowed by God; they cannot be offered, calculatedly, to God as a means of meriting salvation: "It is clear that the fruits do not bear the tree and that the tree does not grow on the fruits." This "fruit" might even include traditional acts of piety, which were useful in living the life of faith, but no pilgrimages or processions, no disciplines or devotions, no fasts or feast days—all human institutions—could justify sinners. As confirmation he cited 12:33, "make the tree good"; 12:34, "how can ye, being evil, speak good things?"; and John 15:5, "He that abideth in me, and I in him, the same bringeth forth much fruit." Also crucial for Luther was his understanding of 20, that by their good works "ye shall know" who are the good people. Yes, he argued, but this is only a superficial knowledge "in the sight of men" and has nothing to do with saving faith.[119] Appealing sentiments, though Erasmus (1466–1536), who had disputed with him on the freedom of the will and been the target of his abuse, later wondered why a Christian like Luther, who claimed to be filled with the "spirit of Christ," produced the fruits of "his foolish mocks, his vicious laughs, his slanders, threats, deceits."[120] Before he broke with Rome, England's Henry VIII also disputed with Luther, alluding to this image as well as to the "straight and narrow way that leadeth to heaven." Henry contrasted the "fruits" of the church fathers—their learning, faith, and holy lives—with what he saw as Luther's failings. "All your doing began of envy and presumption, proceedeth with anger and malice, blown forth with pride and vain glory, and endeth in lechery."[121]

None of this deterred Luther, and in his preoccupation with preaching the Word, he was less concerned with the institutional behavior of the believer transformed by faith and divine grace. So it was left to other Reformers, such as Melanchthon and Bugenhagen, to talk about church order and pastoral concerns—in short, to consider the quality of the fruits borne by the good trees. For Calvinists the bringing forth of good fruits was "sanctification" or "regeneration," the good and Christ-like works that supposedly followed— and validated—the grace of justification. Complications arose when considering biblical models of sanctification who nonetheless relapsed into sinfulness—such as David with his weaknesses, Solomon with his idolatry, and Peter with his three-fold denial of Christ—but none of their lapses was considered serious enough to outweigh or overpower their faith. Nietzsche was unconvinced: "Faith is a profound conviction on the part of Luther and his kind of their incapacity for Christian works."[122] Finally, this was a key text for Christian Scientists, since they regard the testimonies of those healed by their study of Mary Baker Eddy's *Science and Health* (1875) to be evidence for the fruitfulness of their beliefs.[123]

Forms of the word for "doing" (*poiein*) occur some twenty-two times in the Sermon, so it concludes here fittingly with Jesus' warning (21-27) that discipleship cannot be merely nominal; it carries with it obligations to act, just as Jesus does the will of his Father. John Locke noted the Sermon's emphasis on works: "But in this whole Sermon of his we do not find one word of Believing, and therefore no mention of the Messiah."[124] Benjamin Franklin cited verse 21 (repeated at 12:50) in asking, "What is Christ's Sermon on the Mount but an excellent moral Discourse?" As a Protestant, he allowed for the priority of faith, but as a deist committed to reason and conscience, he argued that faith is "a Means of producing Morality, and Morality of Salvation. But that from Faith alone Salvation may be expected appears to me not to be a Christian doctrine nor a reasonable one."[125] For Emerson, who warned against divorcing belief from behavior, "A man that uniformly does good works is good, and a man that uniformly does bad works is bad, let him say what he will, let him believe what he can."[126] And John Ruskin, who despite his evangelical upbringing sympathized with the Catholic theology of works-righteousness (he much admired Proverbs) wrote: "Read the Sermon on the Mount. It is work,

work, work, from beginning to end."[127] So faith alone is not enough; it entails obedience, a lesson that may have been directed at charismatics in Matthew's community.

Jesus also affirms himself here as king and judge, though Celsus wondered why Jesus denounced exorcists and miracle-workers when his followers claimed that these same wonders were evidence of his divinity. Origen responded that the circumstances would reveal the differences between Christ and the antichrists, just as there had been obvious differences in purpose between Moses and the Egyptian magicians when they competed as miracle-workers in Exodus 7–11 (2.49–50, 104–105). The Greek word for "iniquity" (v. 23) is *anomia,* and since it literally means "lawlessness" and is repeated at 13:41, 23:28, and 24:12, some feel it was directed at antinomians, perhaps even within Matthew's own community, that wanted to abolish the law altogether. Other such groups may be the "false prophets" of verse 15. The rock in verses 24-27 has usually been taken as Christ (and "these sayings of mine") or the church, the two houses as Christ (or the church) and Jerusalem; but the Reformers, concerned with "justification by faith," cautioned against the parable's emphasis on salvation earned by doing God's word. Edna St. Vincent Millay (1892–1950) wrote: "Safe upon the solid rock the ugly houses stand: / Come and see my shining palace built upon the sand!"[128] Matthew will offer a more famous "rock" image in 16:18.

Matthew's final words, that the scribes interpret the law, whereas Jesus imparts it autonomously and authoritatively as one who knows the will of God that lies behind the law, are ominous, since it is precisely this claim to divine authority that will alarm the Jewish authorities and lead to Jesus' passion. It was also this divinely sanctioning aspect of Jesus' teaching that for John Locke distinguished his teachings from those of the world's other wise men, since their followers could choose to heed them or not: "Or as it suited their interest, passions, principles or humours. They were under no Obligation: the Opinion of this or that Philosopher was of no Authority." In addition to authority, there was for Christians the "promise of assistance," for "if we do what we can, he will give us his Spirit to help us to do what, and how we should."[129] But that Jesus' authority has been challenged over the centuries by a competing authority was well expressed in an address composed in 1940 by the poet Robinson Jeffers for a meeting of the Phi Beta Kappa Scholarship Society: "We believe in the Christian values, universal love, self-abnegation, humility, nonresistance; but we believe also, as individuals and nations, in the pagan values of our ancestors; justice with its corollary vengeance, pride with personal honor, will to power, patriotic readiness to meet force with force."[130]

4

Miracles

In Chapters 8 and 9 we move from words to works, and the seated teacher becomes an itinerant exorcist and wonder-worker, displaying the authority attributed to him in 7:29. Here in the course of ten miracles, nine of them healings, Matthew is closely following Mark 5–7 but with some significant changes, and he may also want these acts to recall the ten miracles of Moses (Ex. 7–11), who is mentioned in 8:4.

> To pick Scripture miracles one by one
> to pieces is an odious and repulsive
> task; it is also an unprofitable one, for
> whatever we may think of the affirma-
> tive demonstrations of them, a negative
> demonstration of them is, from the
> circumstances of the case, impossible.
> —Matthew Arnold

For many modern readers, nervous about appearing gullible and uncomfortable with the unverified cures they witness on televised "healing" services, the accounts of miracles in the Gospels are something of an embarrassment. Like prophecy, visions, and speaking in tongues, they belong more to spiritual enthusiasm than to conventional belief. Nevertheless, the incomparable wonders of the virgin birth and the resurrection begin and end Jesus' earthly life, and miracles bulk large in the story of Jesus, at least before the Passion Narrative. They are usually understood as validating the revelations of Scripture and persuading witnesses to accept his divinity, although in 1778 Reimarus repeated the deist objection that Jesus' teaching should have been so persuasive that they needed no miraculous confirmation.[1] And Rousseau, among others, pointed out a vicious circle: "After the doctrine has been proved by the miracle, the miracle has to be proved by the doctrine." He also alluded to 4:17 ("Repent; for the kingdom . . . is at hand") in noting that Jesus preached before he performed miracles, and like others, he argued that the miracles, so easily confused with magic and fakery, can actually detract from the power of Jesus' teachings.[2] Be that as it may, their importance in Catholic tradition, where they are regularly found in the lives of saints, is undisputed. And in the great hymn "Praise to the Lord," God is seen as both "thy health and salvation."

In the Gospels miracles fall, in general, into two broad and overlapping categories: natural, that is, overriding the powers of nature, actions like walking on water and the multiplication of loaves and fishes; and therapeutic, that is, acts of healing and of reviving the dead and exorcising demons. Interestingly, there is no record of Jesus' restoring missing limbs, the one kind of miracle, according to the eighteenth-century English deist Thomas Woolston, that "no skepticism nor infidelity itself could have cavill'd at."[3] Apart from their literal occurrence, which can be affirmed or (more easily) denied but can be neither conclusively proved nor disproved, they have a theological dimension, with natural miracles overcoming the often chaotic or destructive powers of the world, and healing miracles overcoming the ruinous effects of sin and offering physical examples of the spiritual salvation that is Jesus' ultimate purpose.

It is not always clear how Jesus integrated specific miracles into his teachings and prophecies, apart from attracting crowds to hear him and rewarding those who had faith in him; and some miracles, like the drowning of the Gadarene swine (8:28-34) and the cursing of the fig tree (21:19), are simply bizarre. Of course, readers can know only about the effect of his miracles, not about his purposes, whether charitable or theological, in performing them. Curiously, Jesus himself does little to dramatize his powers. He never performs miracles for his own benefit, and in 24:24 he warns that in the end time "great signs and wonders" will be performed by false Christs. Furthermore, the gospel accounts are often perfunctory or inconclusive, and the rejections Jesus endures during his ministry suggest that many of his contemporaries must have been unimpressed even by these marvels. But his most frequent miracles, his healings, foreshadowing his own triumph over death, can also be seen as a visible sign of his claim to a greater and exclusively divine power—to forgive sins, or at least to pronounce, using the passive voice, that sins are forgiven (9:5-6). This power, which was intuitive, autonomous, and arguably blasphemous, since it bypassed the law's provisions for restitution and sacrifices as a show of repentance, amazed some and doubtless disturbed others. Yet the question still remains: Given their uncertain status (the Bible's accounts are only reports), how essential are they to the Christian faith?

The earliest Jewish charge against Jesus is that he was a sorcerer and, as the Pharisees complain to Pilate, a "deceiver" (27:63). Oddly, there seems to have been no contemporary effort to show that his miracles were hoaxes or to explain them away on naturalistic grounds ("This" said Dr. Johnson, "is a circumstance of great weight"[4]). Celsus saw them as products of Egyptian sorcery (1.68, 62–63); and the Roman emperor Julian the Apostate (331–63), the most notable example of a convert from Christianity to paganism, only complained that the miracles seemed to have conferred few benefits on Jesus' friends and relatives.[5] While pagan history is replete with wondrous occurrences, there is little evidence that the kinds of miracles performed by Jesus were common in Judea or anywhere else in the ancient world (apart from sorcery or shrines associated with healing divinities); thus, it may only be our cultural condescension that makes us believe that ancient witnesses were more credulous than modern ones. That one could work miracles was not necessarily defamatory, but it is clear that the Pharisees, though acknowledging Jesus' miracles, regarded them as aided by demons and as socially disruptive, designed to mislead and divide his fellow Jews.

The authenticity and verifiability of miracles has been a nagging problem since the seventeenth century, with the case against them most famously argued by David Hume (1711–76) in his essay "Of Miracles" in *An Enquiry Concerning Human Understanding* (1748). In this "insolent Book" (so John Wesley[6]) he contended that they violate the unalterable laws of nature and that testimony of their occurrence is not decisive, since they always seem to be performed in remote times and obscure places before witnesses who are simple and gullible. "No testimony is sufficient to establish a miracle unless the testing be of such a kind that its falsehood would be more miraculous than the fact which it endeavors to establish," according to Hume. The only miracle in Christianity, he argued, was in persuading reasonable people to accept it: "Whoever is moved by faith to assent to it [Christianity], is conscious of a continual miracle in his own person, which subverts all the principles of his understanding, and gives him a determination to believe what is most contrary to custom and experience."[7] Hume's was a view that would not persuade those who could accept the possibility of unique events as readily as they accepted the harmony of God's creation and the immutability of His natural laws (an immutability unknown in antiquity), or who were disposed to accept certain testimonies as credible and trustworthy, even if they offered second-hand descriptions of events contrary to common experience. Some have argued that miracles were not contrary to nature but only contrary to what we have learned to know and expect of nature; others have noted that what is disbelieved is not thereby disproved. Still, Hume's skeptical mistrust of the biblical record influenced all subsequent scholarship. A more eloquent rejection came from the youthful Shelley, who spoke for many skeptics when, in his "Notes on Queen Mab" (1812), he preferred to believe that the miracle stories were fabrications, since the lies of men are better attested in history than the violations of nature's laws.[8]

Hume's arguments were complicated in his own lifetime by a strange event that in 1731 testified both for and against the truth of biblical miracles. In the parish cemetery of Saint Medard at the tomb of one François de Paris, a deacon of the heretical sect of Jansenists, there occurred an array of apparent miracles, beginning with the cure of a paralytic. These "miracles" entailed violent convulsions and eccentric behaviors such as contortions, levitations, clairvoyance, speaking in tongues, and feats of superhuman strength. Thousands of people gathered at the cemetery to observe—and enjoy—the "dance of the convulsionaries" (many of them women), so there was no shortage of firsthand reports by credible witnesses. On the other hand, these wonders were performed in the name of a sect that had been condemned by the church in 1713, and subsequent investigations proved that many, if not all, were induced psychosomatically. So their probative value was mixed.

While accepting the miracles of Scripture and acknowledging a limited "age of miracles" in the early church, where they served to confirm revelation and persuade witnesses to accept it, the Reformers generally rejected Catholic claims to subsequent "ecclesiastical miracles," arguing that weeping statues and liquefying blood were, if not the work of the devil, then irrelevant to human need or Christian faith, and that the prodigies attributed to saints were the stuff of magic and legend. Catholics, in turn, generally felt that while the church validated miracles, they did not need miracles to validate the church. They also regarded the scarcity of Protestant miracles as evidence that theirs was not the one true church. Protestants generally preferred to see in strange and inexplicable events—what were once called miracles—evidence of God's providence whereby He temporarily alters the workings of nature often in response to prayers or as rewards of faith. It was divine providence, for example, that raised the storm disrupting the Spanish Armada on July 29, 1588, as testified by the inscription on a commemorative medal: "God blew with his winds, and they were scattered." And when marvels happened in the lives of individuals, it was a sign of God's "particular" or "special" providence. Skepticism increased in the nineteenth century with the growing consensus that the Gospels were composite documents of uncertain authorship and had been written without the eyewitness authority of their sainted composers. Some later skeptics were inclined to explain away miracles in naturalistic terms. Jesus' nineteenth-century biographer, Ernest Renan, regarded them as created by the crude expectations of his followers. They were "a violence done to him by his age, a concession forced from him by a passing necessity." As for the exorcisms, "a gentle word often suffices in such cases to drive away the demons."[9]

Islam does not acknowledge miracles, but the Koran has Jesus saying, "By God's leave I shall heal the blind man and the leper and raise the dead to life (3.48)," and in Matthew's gospel the beneficiary of Jesus' first miracle is a leper, who addresses him as "Lord" (8:2). Biblical "leprosy" is a generic term for a number of skin diseases that were seen not only as personal ailments but also as defilements entailing social exclusion. Such was their infectiousness that lepers were required to keep their distance, so it is significant that Jesus dares to touch him, and by both healing and cleansing he restores this outcast to society. (It was an encounter with a leper near Assisi, in which he kissed the man's hand and let himself be kissed in return, that began the religious career of St. Francis.) That the leper was to show himself "to the priest" (v. 4) has been made a proof text for private confession, though Calvin wondered where this verse said anything about absolving sins.[10]

The next miracle (5-13) is performed for a centurion's servant, and at a distance. It is remarkable for its involvement of a Roman soldier and for the "I am not worthy" in verse 8, which was taken over into the Eucharist celebration of the Catholic liturgy. Jesus, who spoke Aramaic, and the centurion, who spoke Latin (though he may have been a Syrian, not a Roman), probably had to use Greek to communicate—though Scripture has almost nothing to say about language problems. It is noteworthy that the miracle has to do with faith, but it is not said that the centurion was converted. Still, the receptivity of a Gentile is a harbinger of the future. The second indication of the centurion's faith ("thou has believed"), which is not in Luke (7:1-10), is consistent with Matthew's emphasis on the importance of belief and faith as well as on good works. It will often recur—next at 9:28, where "Believe ye that I am able to do this?" is added to the Markan account (8:22-26) of sight restored to a blind man.

Although the centurion was an army officer and his servant probably a slave, nothing is said here or elsewhere in the New Testament about the Roman occupation of Palestine, the service of Christians in the Roman army, or the legitimacy of slavery. One reason for the lack of political comment is that Judea was relatively peaceful in the 20s and 30s, and although Jesus "suffered under Pontius Pilate" (Nicene and Apostles' Creeds), there is no record of Romans systematically hunting down Jesus' disciples after the crucifixion. As for slavery, 9 is the only Matthean verse that might be cited in defense of slavery, as was done by John England (1786–1842), the Catholic bishop of Charleston, South Carolina—though he himself disapproved of the institution.[11] But it was so much a part of life that it hardly called for comment, and it is a remarkable fact that there was no "abolitionist" movement in antiquity. Jews had always treated their slaves comparatively well (the Essenes forbade slavery altogether); Christians were urged to be humane to their slaves; and after Constantine, the church held manumission ceremonies for wealthy families to liberate their slaves. Furthermore, ancient slavery was not burdened with the kind of racial differences that characterized the American experience, and slaves from Asia Minor, culturally superior to their Roman owners, often took on jobs entailing specialized talents and responsibilities and as freedmen sometimes achieved enormous wealth and influence. Slavery deprived its victims of their human rights, but it must be remembered that antiquity had no concept of inalienable rights. Indeed, it might even be argued that ancient slavery was a relatively humane practice in that it cut down on deaths in war, for victorious battles were the principal source of slaves.

Peter's mother-in-law is the subject of the next miracle (14-15), where, uniquely, Jesus takes the initiative. Apparently Peter—often called the first pope—was married; and 1 Corinthians 9:5 implies that his wife accompanied him on his missionary travels. In the healing of the demonically possessed (16-17), Matthew again puts out a lifeline to the Old Testament, this time to Isaiah 53:4 ("He hath borne our griefs, and carried our sorrows") in the "Suffering Servant" passage, as, unlike Mark, he emphasizes that Jesus' miracles and exorcisms are prophecy fulfillments.

In verse 18 Jesus prepares to move to the eastern side of the Sea of Galilee. But first, at 19-22 he returns to the cost of discipleship, repeated and expanded at Luke 9:59-62, where there is "no looking back." Verse 20 was cited in the Constitution (1536) of the Capuchins, Franciscans who wanted to recover the idealism of St. Francis by imitating their founder, "whose bed was often the bare ground," and of Jesus himself "in the desert." Thus, Capuchins were ordered to "sleep on a bare board, rush mat, or upon a little straw or hay."[12] The phrase "let the dead bury their dead" (also at Luke 9:60) has since turned into a proverb for those who wish to break with something in their past. Longfellow alludes to it in one of his most popular poems, "A Psalm of Life" (1838): "Trust no Future, howe'er pleasant! / Let the dead Past bury its dead! / Act, — in the living Present! / Heart within, and God o'erhead! / Lives of great men all remind us / We can make our own sublime, / And, departing, leave behind us / Footprints in the sands of Time."[13] Here it is ostensibly a shocking statement, one of the "hard sayings" of the Gospels. It violates the fourth/fifth commandment (unless the first "dead" be those who are spiritually dead and who put the affairs of the world before the Word), though it does lend great urgency to Jesus' call to discipleship. The humanized Jesus of George Moore's popular novel *The Brook Kerith* (1916), who survives the crucifixion, regrets it ("I fear to think of the things I said at that time").[14] At the end of *A Portrait of the Artist as a Young Man* (1916), James Joyce's Stephen Dedalus records this verse in his journal as he prepares to break with the "dead past" of Ireland and the Church and become "Soulfree and fancyfree."[15]

Jesus' next miracle exhibits his mastery of nature. Power over water or, more generally, spirit over matter, reaches back scripturally to Psalm 107:23-30 ("He maketh the storm a calm") and ultimately to God's original creative act in Genesis, just as Jesus' sleep, initially reminiscent of Jonah in a similar situation (Jonah 1:5), recalls God's rest after completing the acts of creation, the two actions suggesting Jesus as a new King of Creation. It also reminds Christians of their need of faith as they venture onto the stormy waters of an unbelieving world. Jesus' rebuke (26) notes that whereas Mark's disciples lack understanding, Matthew's lack trust; and four times Jesus will castigate them with the now proverbial "O ye of little faith" (6:30, 8:26, 16:8, 14:31 for Peter alone). The boat they board was later seen as a symbol of the church, but the hull of an actual boat, the "Kinneret boat," approximately 26.5 feet long, 7.5 wide, and 4.5 deep, and dated to this time, was recovered from the Sea of Galilee when its level fell during a drought in 1986.

In the light of modern psychiatry's achievements—and limitations—Christian churches are uncomfortable with demon-possession and exorcisms, often preferring to think that it was an aspect of Jesus' healing ministry, bordering on magic and superstition, that has been largely superseded and might be better left to the entertainment industry. Or are some irreducible and unexplainable forms of human pathology beyond the reach of medication and therapy? Much depends, of course, on how seriously one takes the devil and his powers, and the first century seems to have taken them seriously indeed. So Jesus was an exorcist, though unlike others he used no material aids or magic formulas, and he never invoked supernatural powers. Of the Synoptics, Matthew is least interested in exorcism (there are none in John), and in his reporting of the Gadarene swine episode (28-34), he reduces Mark's version (5:1-19) from nineteen to seven lines and omits the vivid details of a single demoniac who breaks his chains and bruises himself on the tombstones.

Since there are two thousand pigs in Mark's herd, Baron d'Holbach noted that the distribution of three devils to each pig might well "induce them to commit suicide."[16] This episode, often applied to those who are hell-bent on self-destruction, is beset with difficulties; and, like the cursing of the fig tree (21:19-20), it has also been a favorite of those who deny the authenticity and relevance of scriptural miracles. It tells of a bizarre and violent exorcism in a location that is uncertain, since Gadara is some six miles from the Sea of Galilee, and an alternative, Gerasa or Gergesa (KJV: "the country of the Gergesenes"), is more than thirty miles away. Furthermore, it is unclear if the pigs belonged to a Jew or a Gentile, and it is odd that Jesus, of all people, should be instrumental in their wanton destruction. Porphyry, who thought the story was "nonsense," wondered what sort of savior Jesus could be if, instead of overcoming evil, he only relocated it, first into the pigs, who died, while the devils simply returned to the water, one of their traditional habitats.[17] The incident later preoccupied Voltaire, who protested the injustice done the hapless owner of the swine, who he thought lived in a pagan area and must have been a Gentile.[18] And in the late nineteenth century it became a kind of test case for the scientist (and agnostic, he having coined the term) Thomas Huxley (1825–95) in his debates with the Anglicans Henry Wace and William Gladstone. It recurs throughout the essays in his book *Science and Christian Tradition* (1897) as the prime example of a scriptural miracle claiming to command belief but that rested on discrepant sources, was inherently improbable, and had no obvious relation to religious faith. For if, he argued, the Gadarene miracle did not happen as reported (and for Huxley it did not), then its spuriousness subverted not only belief in demonology but in the whole spiritual world of the New Testament. And John Colenso (1814–83), the Anglican bishop of Natal, whose OT criticism was a *cause célèbre* in his day, noted the problems these stories raised for missionaries: "And how will we teach the Zulus to get rid of superstitions if we teach them stories of demonology?"[19]

But others do not take so literally or so seriously an episode—the "deviled ham" miracle—that has some folktale features (and the destruction of an unclean animal would not have bothered a Jewish audience), but that dramatizes Jesus' power over demons. As for Gadara, Mark Twain, disappointed by the bleakness of the area (he compared it unfavorably to the Lake Tahoe region), felt the swine "doubtless thought it was better to swallow a devil or two and get drowned into the bargain than have to live longer in such a place."[20]

Asked to leave, Jesus returns to Nazareth at the beginning of chapter 9, where he cures a man "sick of the palsy." This episode (vv. 2-7) was a conversion experience ("As I read, the healing Truth dawned upon my sense . . . ") for Mary Baker Eddy (1821–1910), the founder of Christian Science, who recalled reading this episode and being unexpectedly healed after she had suffered a fall in Lynn, Massachusetts, in February 1866. "The result was that I rose, dressed myself, and ever after was in better health than I had before enjoyed," she continued. "That short experience included a glimpse of the great fact that I have since tried to make plain to others, namely Life in and of Spirit."[21] It is uncertain how severe her injuries were, but she compared the "fall at Lynn" with the fall of the apple that inspired Newton; and it became one of the foundation narratives of Christian Science. Among modern denominations Christian Science is alone in paying more attention to Jesus' therapeutic miracles than to his ethical teachings (though "healings" are a large part of Pentecostal revivals), and Mary Baker Eddy lamented that Christianity had lost its healing mission. But sickness, which includes blindness, and death have persisted in Christian thought as metaphors for sinfulness, a figure enriched by the paradox that it was Christ's death that delivered humanity from its spiritual "death." Thus, theologically this event is important, since by claiming to forgive sin Jesus is implying his divinity or at least claiming one prerogative of divinity. Such a claim, along with the "authority" of 7:29 and the "fulfillment" of the Mosaic law at 5:17, provides a Matthean proof text for the incarnation, for the definition of Jesus' "two natures," first formulated at the Council of Chalcedon in 451, and for the high Christology of orthodox Christianity.

The next episode (v. 9) is of particular interest to readers of this gospel, since it is the calling of Matthew, a "publican," or collector of taxes and tolls (he is called Levi in Mark and Luke and may have belonged to the priestly tribe of the Levites). In art, Caravaggio's *The Calling of Saint Matthew* (1597–98; Rome) shows the future apostle in a contemporary setting, sitting at a table in a darkened room with fashionably dressed Roman *bravi* and gesturing questioningly at himself. This is in response to the pointed finger of Jesus, who is identified by a nearly invisible halo but illuminated by a shaft of light. There is a similar exchange of pointed fingers in *The Calling of Saint Matthew* (1621; Utrecht) by the Dutch painter Hendrick Terbrugghen. This, like the conversion of Paul, was also a favorite subject for Protestant artists, since it illustrated the mysterious workings of divine grace in that Jesus chose a man who had not only done nothing to merit his selection but was a tax collector, hated for his collaboration with Gentiles as he exacted—and probably extorted—money in service to the Roman authorities. The point is underlined three verses later when Jesus offers another Reformation proof text (taken from Hos. 6:6 and repeated at 12:7—a "Matthean doublet"): "I will have mercy, and not sacrifice." It is worth noting that no connection is made here between this Matthew and the author of the gospel.

In literature Matthew appears in Mikhail Bulgakov's novel *The Master and Margarita* (1939) as a recorder of Jesus' life and deeds, and in accusing Jesus of intending to destroy the temple, Pontius Pilate reads from Matthew's parchment record. Jesus protests: "I never said a word of what was written there." At first Pilate is inclined to sentence this "mentally deranged" vagrant to exile, but when he hears from him that he is predicting a future age with no need of (Roman) authority, he accedes to the wishes of the Jews and orders his crucifixion. Bulgakov's Matthew is the only disciple who remains with Jesus, where he plays the part of Joseph of Arimathea, taking his body down from the cross and seeing to its burial.[22] (Tradition has it that Matthew's remains are in a sarcophagus in the cathedral dedicated to him in Salerno, Italy.)

Jesus' ability to enlist and inspire talented followers was yet another sign of his business genius, according to Bruce Barton (1886–1967), a pioneer in American advertising and the man who created "Betty Crocker." In 1925 Barton published a hugely best-selling book, *The Man Nobody Knows,* in which he protested against what he felt was the standard Protestant portrayal of Jesus as a weak and slightly effeminate sermonizer. For Barton, Jesus was a skilled carpenter, a good mixer, and such a gifted executive that he managed to establish the Christian Church, the world's greatest organization. And in the spirit of the "muscular Christianity" so popular in the late nineteenth century and concerned to banish the image of Christ as "baby Jesus" or as a pale and long-haired philosopher, Barton's Jesus was extremely fit, with "muscles hard as iron," as witnessed by his ability at overthrowing the tables outside the temple (21:12). Barton imagined that if there had been a *Capernaum News,* the next day's headline might have read, "Prominent Tax Collector Joins Nazareth Forces. Matthew Abandons Business to Promote New Cult. Gives Large Luncheon."[23]

At verse 10 we see Jesus at table with "publicans and sinners." Already Jesus' table habits are acquiring messianic significance and are anticipating the "Messianic Banquet," one of the images of end-time blissfulness. Since eating together in antiquity entailed a kind of fellowship, even implicit approval of one's table mates, the Pharisees are shocked. It can be difficult for modern readers to appreciate how deeply Jewish sensibilities were offended by Jesus' table fellowship with tax collectors, who were ritually "unclean" because they were in the service of pagan Rome, and with those called "sinners"—not for their human weaknesses, but because they could not observe all the purity laws or, like usurers and prostitutes, chose to live in open defiance of the Torah. Celsus noted that pagan mysteries specified that participants be pure, whereas Christianity seemed to make sinfulness a membership requirement ("Why on earth this preference for sinners?" [3.64, 171]); while Voltaire once said that the only thing he had in common with Jesus is that they both dined with sinners.

Jesus replies that his mission is not "to call the righteous, but sinners to repentance" (13). This is a dramatic definition of his ministry, and St. Benedict quoted it in his *Rule* in urging his followers to show compassion if one of their number should fall into mortal sin.[24] Luther also cited it in defining his "Theology of the Cross," the divine love that does not enjoy the virtuous but turns to "where it may confer good upon the bad and needy person."[25] Oddly, though, the Gospels offer little evidence of sinners actually expressing regret or doing penance for their sins in response to the forgiveness offered them. Nor do we usually hear of specific sins or the names of sinners. Verse 13 was named as "scripture" in the so-called Second Letter of Clement, a sermon from the beginning of the second century, an early indication that a quote from Jesus (and Matthew) enjoyed the same prestige as a quote from the Old Testament.[26]

Jesus is next visited by some of John's people (14-17), who wonder why his disciples do not fast. His reply, illustrated by images of a bridegroom, a garment, and a bottle, is that there will be time and opportunity for them to fast when he is no longer with them. In his *Holy Scriptures* (1867), based on the KJV and better known as the "Inspired Version," the Mormons' Joseph Smith added four verses here, with a surprisingly assertive Jesus rebuking the Pharisees: "If ye had kept the law, ye would have received me, for I am he who gave the law" (3 Nephi 15:5). Smith's justification: "From sundry revelations which have been received, it was apparent that many important points touching the salvation of men had been taken from the Bible, or lost before it was compiled."[27]

Jesus is then interrupted by the appearance of a father seeking the resuscitation of his dead daughter, whom he will revive from her "sleep" (18-19). Matthew identifies him as a "ruler," but significantly chooses to omit a detail that Mark mentions four times, that the father "ruled" a synagogue. As Jesus is about to visit the ruler's daughter, he heals a woman suffering from a hemorrhage, though he specifies that it is her faith that has healed her, not her touching "the hem of his garment," a gesture Calvin characterized as "thoughtless zeal" that "pushed her somewhat off the right way."[28] According to the Venerable Bede (673–735) in his *Ecclesiastical History of the English People,* Pope Gregory the Great cited this episode in 597 when advising St. Augustine of Canterbury, the missionary to the Anglo-Saxons, that menstruating women should be allowed to enter churches. Menstruation, he explained, though a human infirmity like hunger and thirst, is not personally sinful.[29] This scene is also recalled in stanza 5 of the hymn "Immortal Love, Forever Full": "The healing of his seamless dress / is by our beds of pain; / we touch him in life's throng and press, / and we are whole again." The touching of the hem was recalled in the Catholic mass at the elevation when the altar boy, representing the congregation, lifted the border of the priest's chasuble as he was lifting the host, thus providing a continuum of grace from man to priest to God.[30] It has now been discontinued.

When Jesus enters the ruler's house (23), he tells him that his daughter is not dead, only sleeping (24). There is no indication that this suffering woman was a sinner, but that Jesus' words included "thy faith hath made thee whole" turned this healing miracle into a proof text in the Reformation debates over faith and good works. The chapter then continues with the healing of two blind men, a miracle that once again depends on their faith. It will be repeated with two other blind men at 20:30-34, another example of "Matthean doubling." Reimarus wondered if Jesus' instruction ("See that no man know it") was not intended to have the opposite effect, which in fact it did (31), as, according to Reimarus, he acceded to his disciples' expectations that he move from being a spiritual teacher to becoming Israel's messiah and worldly liberator.[31]

The last miracle (32-34) is an exorcism, acceptable to the Pharisees, but for them Jesus can perform it, not as the "Son of David," but only with the aid of the devil. This charge will be repeated at 12:24, again an instance of "doubling." The chapter then ends with a connection that has inspired social activists, in that Jesus combines his preaching of the kingdom with teaching and healing. And verse 37 is one of the few utterances of Jesus that appear in the gnostic *Gospel of Thomas,* the collection of 114 sayings found in Egypt in 1945 that has since acquired some notoriety as a "secret" gospel.

5

Disciples

Chapter 10 begins with a list of the twelve apostles, whom Jesus commissions to extend to other Jewish areas his work of preaching (that "the kingdom of heaven is at hand"), healing, and exorcism. After he has advised them on how they are to conduct their missions, he leaves Capernaum at the beginning of chapter 11 to preach in other cities, two of which, Chorazin and Bethsaida, are named and denounced. He also receives two disciples from John, who is in prison and wants to know if Jesus is indeed the Messiah. In chapter 12 narrative yields to preaching and healing; in chapter 13, to parables.

> Luther had said that grace alone could
> save; his followers took up his doctrine
> and repeated it word for word. But they
> left out its invariable corollary, the
> obligation of discipleship.
> —Dietrich Bonhoeffer

Chapters 10 and 11, studied while he was in military service and on maneuvers in Lower Alsace in the summer of 1894, were crucial for the development of Albert Schweitzer's "eschatological" theology. It puzzled Schweitzer that nothing came of Jesus' two predictions: that his disciples would be persecuted on their journey, and that the Son of Man would appear before their mission was completed (10:23). He rejected two current explanations, that this was a later addition to the text (for why would anyone attribute to Jesus events that had not taken place?), or that these predictions should be "spiritualized," in the sense that Jesus was actually speaking, not about the end of the world, but about his own death and resurrection, and that he was inaugurating not a real but an "ethical" kingdom of God. So for Schweitzer the persecution of chapter 23 referred to the "tribulation," the traditional period of suffering that would immediately precede the coming of the messiah; and here Jesus must have felt it was about to happen and that then his messiahship would be recognized and acknowledged. But it did not happen at once (the disciples are back with him in chapter 12). So according to Schweitzer, Jesus took it upon himself to make it happen through the tribulation of his passion, leaving be-

hind the Sermon on the Mount as a moral instruction to help his disciples prepare for the coming kingdom. He could counsel them not to be anxious about
their earthly condition, for it was soon to end.[1]

Chapter 10 is Jesus' "Mission Charge" to the twelve disciples, although
readers know of only five by name. Only here (v. 2) are they called "apostles,"
since Matthew prefers the more inclusive "disciples," which can also be understood as extending to his own followers. (Ironically, "Apostles" was also the
name of a Cambridge University society, founded in 1820, that was often
highly critical of Christianity, counting among its members, always twelve in
number, the philosophers G. E. Moore and Bertrand Russell.) The listing of
the apostles by twos is more "Matthean doubling," and the number twelve is
meant to symbolize the twelve tribes of Israel (19:28: "ye also shall sit upon
twelve thrones, judging the twelve tribes of Israel").

It is odd that Jesus says so much about his disciples' conduct and activities,
so little about the content of their preaching. How did they present and develop their message of the approaching kingdom to those they were proselytizing? Did they try to organize proto-Christian groups in the villages they
visited? It is odd, too, that nothing more is said about the progress or success
of their mission after they return at 12:1. In any case, their evangelizing must
have produced the first transmission of "gospel" materials to prospective converts, and some have thought that their preaching of Jesus' words was the basis
of the "Sayings Source" known as *Q.*

For now the disciples' mission is limited to other Jews (v. 5), not to "all nations" (28:19), and the only Gentiles they will meet are the officials at verse
18, though even before (not "against," as in the KJV) them they can bear witness to Jesus. In a 1522 sermon, Zwingli saw this as evidence that Jesus, who
most often moved among the humblest, "does not overlook anyone, and least
of all the greatest."[2] And missionaries often found that first converting local
rulers was a convenient way to bring their subjects into the church—a Christian version of the "trickle-down" effect.[3] At verse 11 Jesus mentions "city or
town," so it is strange that neither he nor his disciples seem to visit the nearby
city of Tiberias. Verse 23 suggests that the troubles of the end time are imminent (there is no talk here of forgiving enemies) and that the Parousia will arrive before a mission to the Gentiles can be undertaken. As often remarked,
this notion stands in stark contrast to the gospel's final words, where the resurrected Jesus speaks of what will certainly be a long and arduous mission to
the Gentiles. It is also ironic that despite the many disparaging references to
Gentiles in Matthew (although almost no notice is taken of the gods of Greek
religion), it was they who soon outnumbered Jews among Christian converts.

The last words of verse 8 ("freely ye have received, freely give") were twice
cited by John Hus (1369–1415) in his tract *On Simony:* "Since now the clergy
do not receive freely, they likewise do not give freely, neither absolution, nor

ordination, nor extreme unction [last rites], nor other spiritual things."[4] Hus's views on clerical avarice—a greedy pope he called "the vicar of Judas Iscariot"—helped earn him official condemnation at the Council of Constance in 1415. On July 6 of the following year he was burned at the stake as a heretic, and his ashes were thrown into the Rhine. Later the Quakers' William Penn (1644–1718) cited this as a proof text against compulsory tithing: "The maintenance of gospel ministers should be free and not forced."[5] Verse 8 also appears at the beginning of the *Consilium de Emendanda Ecclesia* (1537; "Advice on Reforming the Church"), an important Counter-Reformation document, whose authors considered that there was no "greater and higher ordinance" than "that it not be permitted even for the Vicar of Christ to obtain any profit from using the power of the keys conferred on him by Christ."[6]

As for their expenses (v. 9), it seems unlikely that fishermen had, in the best of times, gold or silver coins, and the other evangelists speak only of money. So some have speculated that a passage like this—along with Matthew's change of Luke's "Blessed be ye poor" (6:20) to "Blessed are the poor in spirit" (5:3) for his first Beatitude, and his parables of a wealthy "householder" (21:33-41), a king's wedding (22:2-14), and an affluent investor (25:14-30)— indicates that Matthew's audience was relatively well off. His may have been a largely urban community, since he has twenty-six mentions of "city," whereas Luke has fifteen, Mark only nine—although, ironically, Matthew's gospel's hero remains a man of the village. So these instructions have become something of an embarrassment for Christian ecclesiastics who have chosen a more comfortable lifestyle, and their rationalizing interpretation is that this injunction applied only to the time of Jesus, or that the order to take nothing with them implies that normally they would own all the things they now temporarily relinquished. Dante cites it in his *De Monarchia* (3.10, 14) as a proof text against the church's acquiring temporal possessions that rightly belong to the state.

As a sermon text, verse 9 so impressed the future St. Francis as he was hearing mass at Santa Maria degli Angeli in Assisi on February 24, 1209, that he at once determined to adopt a life of poverty and penitence: "This is what I wish; this is what I seek; this is what I long to do with all my heart."[7] He subsequently went to St. Nicholas's church for further inspiration, and, opening the Gospels at random (the widespread practice of biblical divination), he happened upon two other Matthean texts, 19:21 on seeking perfection through poverty, and 16:24 on taking up his cross and following Jesus. Soon he attracted followers ("little brothers," all laymen), and within a year he had organized the Franciscan order of "Friars Minor."

That the disciples should "shake off the dust of your feet" (v. 14) was cited in describing the departure in 1054 of Cardinal Humbert and the papal legates from the Cathedral of Hagia Sophia in Constantinople after they had deposited a bill of excommunication on the high altar ("[Patriarch] Michael [Cerularius] and his followers, unless they repent, we declare to be anathematized"). This was the single most dramatic act in the estrangement between Western and Eastern Christianity that became known as the Great Schism. In his reply, dated July 7, 1054, the patriarch referred to the bill as an "impious, distasteful document," noting that the Roman delegates came from the West, "out of the darkness"; and he ordered that it be preserved "to the perpetual dishonor of those who have committed such blasphemies against us."[8]

Finally, the combination of simplicity and prudence enjoined in verse 16 is unique to Matthew and surprising in its apparent allusion to the serpent of Eden and the dove of the Holy Spirit. This has made the verse almost proverbial, and it seems to have a parallel in Paul's advice to the Romans (16:19) to be both wise and simple. This was the counsel given to Christian missionaries in an anonymous letter from the middle of the third century in which they were also warned not to "cast your pearls before swine" (7:6), that is, sing psalms or read Scripture in the presence of disruptive or disrespectful pagans.[9] The same advice had a special appeal for St. Thomas More as he made his way to martyrdom through the religious and political troubles of early-Reformation England.[10] In his drama *The Jew of Malta* (1588), Christopher Marlowe (1564–93) put a negative version in an aside by his protagonist, Barabas: "Now will I show myself to have more of the Serpent than the Dove; that is, more knave than fool" (2.2). But there was a more favorable understanding of the serpent: that as it sloughed off its old skin amid briars and rocks, so too must Christians put off their old selves amid the world's obstacles and emerge into a new life. And as it was believed the serpent would sacrifice its body to save its head, so Christians must be prepared to sacrifice their mortal selves to preserve their faith.

In one of the church's first—and most questionable—demonstrations of its power over the state, St. Ambrose cited verses 19-20 in asserting his right, as bishop, to reprimand the Emperor Theodosius for rebuilding a synagogue destroyed by a Christian mob in 388.[11] Moreover, two unexpected references emerge from Jesus' instructions. At 20 he alludes, surprisingly, to the Holy Spirit, who will not be formally available to the disciples until Pentecost (Acts 2:4). And at 23 he offers another apparent—and unfulfilled—prediction of an imminent Parousia, similar to Mark 9:1, again raising the question why the evangelists would preserve and report sayings of Jesus that were evidently erroneous. To account for the delay, the "coming" of the Son of man could also be interpreted here to mean Jesus' death and resurrection or the establishment of the new Christian faith. Since "Son of man" is a mysterious honorific, with suggested meanings ranging from simply "mankind" to someone imbued with the spirit of God or to the Messiah himself (26:64), some would deny that here the Son of man was Jesus, and would make the "cities of Israel" refer to wherever Jews happened to be living. Similarly, the "end" of 22 (repeated at 24:13) came to be understood as the end of each individual's life, not the end of the world; and in his monastic *Rule*, St. Benedict quoted it in recommending to his monks that they humbly endure the hardships of their cloistered lives.[12] But some denominations, such as Jehovah's Witnesses and the various Adventist (Latin for "coming") and end-of-the-world-is-nigh groups still maintain their faith in an imminent—if delayed—apocalypse and second coming. As for its location, Mark Twain wondered why Jesus, having once been to Jerusalem, would want to return there.[13]

Verse 26 of Jesus' instructions was quoted in 1974 by Senator Sam J. Ervin Jr. (1896–1985), in his "Meditations" on the Watergate affair. He added Galatians 6:7 ("for whatsoever a man soweth, that shall he also reap").[14] Verse 28, with John 12:25 ("life eternal"), was a proof text for the immortality of the soul and was so cited by Pope Leo X at the Eighth Session of the Fifth Lateran Council (1512–17), though generally Scripture sees souls as inseparable from bodies. But the suggestion that the soul can be destroyed in hell was also a proof text for annihilationists, who believed that God will eventually terminate hell's punishments and the souls of the wicked will simply cease to exist. Verse 29 is recalled in Hamlet's words, "There's a special providence in the fall of a sparrow" (5.2.232), expressing his hard-won faith in a providential direction of his actions; and 29-30 have traditionally been cited as a proof text for divine providence, Christianity's response to the waywardness of chance and fortune—God not just as Creator but as "everlasting Governor and Preserver"—that preoccupied late antiquity.[15] And addressing George Washington at the Constitutional Convention in Philadelphia on June 28, 1787, Benjamin Franklin alluded to the sparrow in arguing (surprisingly) that each session be opened with a prayer: "God governs in the affairs of men. And if a sparrow cannot fall to the ground without His notice, is it probable that an empire can rise without His aid?"[16] No action was taken, and Franklin did not get into the problem of how God governs through secondary causes or how divine providence can be reconciled with humanity's free will and nature's haphazardness. Finally, verse 33 is interesting since in fact Jesus did not deny Peter for his threefold denial (27:69-75).

Probably the most shocking sentiments in Jesus' address are at 34-36 ("I am come not to send peace, but a sword"), words that seem to contradict the peacemaking commended by the Beatitudes (they are also at Luke 12:51, where "sword" is softened to "division"), but they have been of great usefulness for Christian militants of all denominations. They were cited by the English bishops in their "Reply of the Ordinaries" (1532) to justify the church's initial determination to oppose Henry VIII's decision to seek an annulment of his marriage to Catherine of Aragon; a year later they capitulated, and in 1534 papal supremacy was ended.[17] They are also important for those who want to see Jesus as a political activist, even a revolutionary in the Zealot tradition; and militant Christians could combine them with OT evocations of God as the "Lord of hosts" (cf. Ps. 148:2) or with His instruction to the Israelites on how they are to treat the original inhabitants of the Promised Land: "Thou shalt smite them, and utterly destroy them" (Deut. 7:2). But they are outweighed by Jesus' concern for spiritual change and personal salvation unrelated to social conditions, by his preaching of nonresistance to evil, and by his own surrender to the Jewish and Roman authorities. Nevertheless, variants of this militant interpretation appear in the American "Social Gospel" theories, in the Christian Socialism of Europe and England, and in the liberation theology of Latin America—all attempts to realize some version of the kingdom of heaven on earth.

For most Christians, verses 34-37 are hard words (and a great favorite of Bible-bashers), and Celsus was scathing in his account of how Christian missionaries would turn children against their fathers (3.55, 165–66). Still, this is a key text for a church that has often required its adherents to break off family ties and longstanding friendships, and it is even employed by quasi-Christian cults determined to isolate adherents from their families. The mention of a sword would not reassure an administrator concerned to maintain the Pax Romana (if these sentiments happened to be reported to him) in first-century Judea, and Augustine preferred to interpret the sword as Jesus' words.[18] But its plain sense can seem to justify violence, and in the Middle Ages pilgrims to the Holy Land became Crusaders, carrying a sword in addition to the traditional staff and purse. There are similar sentiments at Luke 19.27 ("those mine enemies . . . slay them before me") and John 18.36 ("then would my servants fight"), though here the context indicates domestic discord, not military bloodshed. Martin Luther cited these words on April 18, 1521, in defending himself before the Reichstag in Worms against the charge of fomenting trouble within the church. This was the occasion on which he was reported to have uttered his famous words, "*Ich kann nicht anders, hier stehe ich*" ("I cannot do otherwise; here I take my stand"). The fiery Thomas Müntzer, in his "Sermon Before the Princes" (July 13, 1524), invoked these words to justify violence against his opponents (including Luther): "Get them out of the way and eliminate them."[19] They were also cited by John Knox in a 1588 letter to Mary, Queen of Scots, in defense of his uncompromising opposition to the "damnable idolatry" of her Roman Catholicism.[20]

These verses appalled Voltaire ("These terrible words . . . have caused more Christians to die than ambition ever did"),[21] and for one anonymous nineteenth-century freethinker, "We can hardly imagine any calamity greater than a sword without, and families all enemies to one another within. . . . Is this the peace of God which passeth all understanding?"[22] Shelley called it the "one prediction of Jesus Christ" that "has been indisputably fulfilled" in subsequent history.[23] Hence, they provide a convenient proof text for those deploring the violence perpetrated in the name of Christianity. In modern times they were cited by Bertrand Russell: "All this means the breakup of the biological family ties for the sake of creed—an attitude which had a great deal to do with the intolerance that came into the world with the spread of Christianity."[24] He went on to argue that this kind of Christian individualism, along with the doctrine of the immortal soul and its salvation, made Christians both intolerant and uninterested in social betterment. But for some fundamentalist Christians, anticipating the chaos that will precipitate the second coming, they are words of reassurance. Evangelicals contend that Christianity's purpose is not to better the world but to save individuals from the world; hence, conflicts are inevitable and anti-war efforts are futile, since only the presence of Christ can bring true peace to the world. Jesus' words also undercut the common charge that it was the Christian establishment that transformed the "Prince of Peace," the "gentle Jesus, meek and mild," of the Gospels into a figure of dogma and oppression. Chesterton argued that in fact it was the church that used a selection of texts to turn the scriptural Jesus, who is often enigmatic, impatient, or irritated, into the sentimental Jesus of "love."[25] Significantly, there are no hymns based on this text, and no church has a statue of an angry Jesus.

Verses 35-36 are the epigraph for chapter 12 of the novel *In His Steps* (1897) by a Congregationalist minister, Charles M. Sheldon (1857–1946) of Topeka, Kansas. In this chapter a grandmother refuses to stay in the house of her granddaughter, who has brought home a "fallen woman," a girl whom she found drunk and homeless in a slum area known as "The Rectangle." This is but one inspiring event in the most famous of the American Christian social novels and one of the most-read books—or tracts—of all time, having sold, by one report, more than eight million hardcover copies. The narrative tells how a Protestant minister named Henry Maxwell enlists volunteers from his congregation, all fairly well off, "who will pledge themselves earnestly and honestly for an entire year not to do anything without first asking the question, 'What would Jesus do?'" And after asking that question, each one will follow Jesus as exactly as he knows how, "no matter what the result may be."[26] A newspaper editor decides to eliminate sensational news stories and discontinue his Sunday edition (fortunately, he finds a wealthy society lady to finance his new Christian-oriented paper; she also uses her inheritance for a slum-clearance project); a railroad superintendent resigns after inadvertently discovering and promptly disclosing that his company has been violating an interstate commerce regulation; a businessman creates cooperative relations with his employees; a singer volunteers her talents in the service of the church instead of accepting money from a theater company; and a scholarly college president enters politics in a noble but losing temperance campaign against "the saloon." The movement spreads from

"Raymond" (a town conveniently free of Catholics, Jews, and racial minorities) to Chicago, where a minister and his bishop resign their comfortable positions to toil in inner-city missions. Not all of Sheldon's people are totally successful, but they all benefit from the spiritual rewards of forsaking nominal Christianity for the higher satisfaction of practicing their faith in the everyday world. And over a half century later his book inspired the "What Would Jesus Do?" movement, and millions of bracelets have been sold with the initials WWJD. It has even been parodied ("What Would Martha Stewart Do?").

It was verses 34-39 that inspired Pier Paolo Pasolini to make his 1964 film *The Gospel According to St. Matthew,* a version notable for its exclusive use of Matthew's words. For Pasolini Mark was too crude, Luke too sentimental, and John too mystical; whereas Matthew captured the revolutionary power of Jesus' ministry. Hence, he filmed it in the poorest areas of southern Italy, employed nonprofessionals (he cast his mother as Mary), and used the simplest of local settings and costumes. His Jesus is an often angry and impatient activist, restlessly roaming the hills and villages, and with little time for the major miracles, the parables, or Mary Magdalene (usually a staple of "Jesus" films), or for experiences like the transfiguration that would emphasize his divinity. Verse 38, with its "cross" and call to discipleship, was not included in the interesting Hebrew Gospel of Matthew, a fairly close version of the canonical Matthew attributed to Shem-Tob ben-Isaac, a Jew practicing medicine in fourteenth-century Spain. Part of a medieval corpus of anti-Christian writings designed to refute church claims and to prepare Jews for their debates with churchmen, it avoids identifying Jesus as "the Christ," or the Messiah, although it acknowledges him as the "Son of God."

Verse 39 ("he that loseth his life for my sake shall find it") was important in Albert Schweitzer's decision to become a doctor in French Equatorial Africa (now Gabon): "I had already tried many times to find the meaning that lay hidden in [that] saying . . . Now I had found the answer, I could now add outward to inward happiness."[27] But in his *Dialogue Concerning Heresies* (1531), Thomas More followed a church tradition in interpreting these words as a proof text for the veneration of saints, who by their prayers could then intercede with God.[28] The intercessory role of saints was enhanced by churches' statues and paintings, particularly by the medieval rood screen that separated the altar from the congregation and that, with its illustrations of Mary and the saints, suggested that they stood between the faithful and God. Since the Reformers considered individual salvation as the work of God's grace, they abolished rood screens and rejected any mediating or intercessory role for the saints. Finally, verse 42 (Mark 9:41) is a striking formulation of what the Reformers considered the ultimate misinterpretation: that salvation could be a "reward" for good works ("a cup of cold water") irrespective of God's grace. But this has always been Catholic teaching, summarized by Augustine: "Those good works of ours, which are recompensed with eternal life, are occasioned by the grace of God."[29]

Chapter 11 is difficult since so little is known of the lines of communication between Jesus and John, and no mention is made here of the messiah. For example, John's question (v. 3; repeated at Luke 7:19) is surprising, since he had apparently predicted the coming of Jesus as the messiah and had baptized him, but he may have subsequently wondered when Jesus would begin to meet his messianic expectations (passing the fiery judgment predicted at 3:12?) and there is no record that Elias (Elijah) was to be the forerunner of the messiah. Jesus' answer to John's disciples has its obscurities.

Verse 11 probably contrasts the coming kingdom of heaven with the present world, and 12 seems to refer to Jesus' opponents and the violence already done to John and soon to be done to Jesus, which will later afflict the generation preceding the messianic age. But it remains one of Matthew's most opaque verses. The verse's second half was to appear at the beginning of a book by Galileo (1564–1642), *Letters on Sunspots* (1662), but censors objected to the notion of violence, and "the violent" was softened to "men of valiant minds."[30] It reappeared in the title of Flannery O'Connor's novel *The Violent Bear It Away* (1960). She thought it "the best thing about the book," but regretted not making "the title's significance clear," explaining that for her it was "the violence of love, of giving more than the law demands, of an asceticism like John the Baptist's, but in the face of which even John is less than the least in the kingdom."[31]

Next (vv. 18-19), Jesus dissociates himself from John's Nazirite lifestyle (represented in the OT by Samson), but although Matthew was a "publican," there is little evidence in the Gospels for the charge that Jesus was "gluttonous" and a "winebibber." Later, a literal understanding of the common phrase "hath a devil" (v. 18) helped Christianity's witch-hunters impute demonic influences to what may have been only odd or antisocial behavior. "But wisdom [Jesus, as the 'wisdom of God'] is justified [vindicated] by her children [Jesus' followers]." Jesus then concludes (20-24) with a denunciation of unrepentant cities that is reminiscent of the OT prophets' attacks on cities hostile to Israel. Tyre and Sidon, Phoenician coastal cities, survived, while the three lake towns were in fact destroyed. This became a proof text for the workings of divine grace: all may receive the same gift, but not all will respond equally. Capernaum seems an odd choice for destruction (and for comparison to Sodom!), since "great multitudes" (8:1, 18) from Jesus' "own city" (9:1) had followed him—but apparently few became his disciples.

That God offers revelations to "babes" (the simple and the humble) that he withholds from "the wise and prudent" (v. 25) shows that faith is in some measure a gift from God, though it did not commend itself to those Christians who maintained that their faith was fully compatible with reason. Verses 25-30 were the text for Luther's last sermon, in Eisleben on February 15, 1546, three days before his death. Once again he distinguished between what he considered Jesus' genuine revelations to the simple readers of Scripture and their revisions by kings, bishops, and that "decoy duck in Rome."[32] Deists later cited this verse (repeated at Luke 10:21) to show that deceiving the unwary was one of the techniques of Christian priestcraft. (This is also a convenient proof text for those readers who feel justified in interpreting Scripture without regard for either wisdom or prudence.) The pithy verse 26 was also evidence for predestination: that it was determined in God's sovereign "sight" who would be elected and who would be condemned. That "all things are delivered" by the Father to Jesus, and that he can claim after his resurrection that "all power is given unto me in heaven and in earth" (28:18) made these convenient proof texts for the popes' claims to universal power as Jesus' successors and vicars on earth. Finally, the messianic consciousness suggested by the "Father-Son" exchange at 27 is typical of John's gospel and is often called the "Johannine Thunderbolt" (also at Luke 10:22), since it appears to be a theological discourse here attributed, unexpectedly, to Jesus.

Arianism

> There's no Son up in the sky,
> Stormy weather.
> —Koehler/Hollister

There are a number of verses throughout the Gospels that suggest a radical disjunction between Father and Son, and 28:18 ("All power is given to me") implies that Jesus' power was not his but was bestowed on him. Verse 27 was also an important proof text for the Arians as they conflicted with orthodox Christians in the first of two great christological problems that had to be debated and somehow resolved if the early church was to have a distinctive doctrine of God. The first centered on the relation of the historical incarnation to traditional monotheism, and the second on the relation of divinity to humanity in the historical Jesus. The first dispute was named after Arius (255–335), an ordained church elder ("presbyter") at Alexandria who theorized that since the Father "begot" the Son, there must have been "a time when he was not"; thus, the Son must be created by, derivative from, and subordinate to the Father, particularly since properties distinctive of God—He was unbegotten and unbegettable—simply could not be shared or imparted. Moreover, the unchangeableness of divinity could not be attributed to one who had lived as a man. Arius affirmed that Jesus could be called God and was worthy of prayer and worship but believed that, since he had been created by God and only participated in divinity, he was not co-eternal with the Father. Since such speculations, emphasizing Jesus' human affiliations, seemed to dilute his divinity, diminish his atoning and salvific power (since no figure less than God could forgive sins committed against God), and undermine the emerging doctrine of the Trinity, the Emperor Constantine, aware of the political value of a peaceful and united church, convened a Council in 325 at Nicaea ("Victory City") in Bithynia near his capital at Constantinople. There, with more than two hundred bishops in attendance, almost all from the Eastern church, the lines were drawn between two Alexandrians, Arius and Athanasius, the latter a deacon and the secretary of that city's bishop. But it was Constantine himself, impatient with theological squabbles and barely able to follow the Greek discussions, who endorsed a compromise formula to define the relation of the Father and the Son—"consubstantiality," or "of the same essence," using the Greek word *homoousios,* as contrasted with *homoiousios,* "of similar substance/essence" (the fifth letter of the Greek word became another example of the "one iota" people don't care about). The word is nonscriptural, though John 10:30 ("I and my Father are one") approximates its meaning. To Arius it suggested that Jesus was God's brother, not his son, but it came to be inserted in the "Nicene Creed," which, when it was finally formulated at the Council of Constantinople in 381, read, "begotten [that is, with subsistence imparted by the Father], not made [that is, not created, like the world, from nothing], of one substance with the Father by whom all things were made." This is a difficult concept, since it depended on a distinction between generation and creation, and "one substance" also had to allow for separate and distinct identities in a Godhead that was supposed to be indivisible. But the *homoiousios* faction could be conciliated by interpreting "like" as "equal," not as "similar," and *homoousios* as "same," not as "identical." And "same substance" was distinguished from "different persons." Again, analogies were pressed into service when terminology faltered, and Athanasius liked to see God as the sun, with the Father its light, the Son its brightness. And the theology of the Holy Spirit—later said to be divine and to "proceed" from the Father—was still largely unformulated.

But the importance of Nicaea is that there Christianity became not only scriptural but also creedal, that is, with defined dogmas to be explained, preached, and now defended—and backed—by imperial authority. So Arius was appropriately pilloried: "Examination was made into impiety and lawlessness of Arius and his followers, in the presence of our most God-beloved sovereign Constantine, and it was unanimously decided that his impious opinion should be anathematized."[33] And the victorious Athanasius, who later became bishop of Alexandria, went on to write the hugely popular *Life of Antony,* a biography of the ascetic founder of monasticism. In the fourth century three intellectuals known as the "Cappadocian Fathers"—Basil of Caesarea, his brother Gregory of Nyssa, and Gregory of Nazianzus, who was briefly bishop of Constantinople—championed Nicaean orthodoxy in the East, while Ambrose, the bishop of Milan, and the Emperor Theodosius did the same for the West.

Although Arius himself confessed his faith in the new formula, his "subordinationist" and "adoptionist" teachings spread rapidly through the empire in the fourth century, when most of the emperors were pro-Arian (including Constantine's son Constantius, who ruled its eastern half), and they engendered a number of competing creeds that omitted or bypassed *homoousios*. Arius's version of a human Christ heroically and triumphantly overcoming suffering and death appealed to Germanic tribes, and the Goths who sacked Rome in 410 had been converted to Arian Christianity, notably by the missionary Bishop Ulfila, who had translated most of the Bible into Gothic. So Arianism became the first and most serious of the great christological controversies that have periodically vexed the orthodox church as it tried to harmonize its monotheism with its mysteriously triune God, its human Jesus who suffered and died with its divine Christ who atoned and redeemed, and its theological interpretation of Father and Son with those words' usual suggestions of pluralism and subordination. And "Arianism" was to acquire a high place in orthodoxy's vocabulary of abuse against those who questioned the doctrine of the Trinity.

Two modern variations of Arianism have been Socinianism (named after its founder, Faustus Socinus, or Fausto Sozzini [1539–1604]), which, though limited in number of adherents, preoccupied orthodox theologians and polemicists throughout the seventeenth and eighteenth centuries; and later, deism, with its rejection of religious revelation and mysteries such as the incarnation and the Trinity and its exaltation of human reason as the access to divinity, its adherents committed to rationality in matters of religion and to conscience in matters of morality. Since Socinus also rejected baptism and disavowed theories of original sin, predestination, and the atonement, its contemporary equivalent is Unitarianism, which developed from liberal Congregationalism in late-eighteenth-century America. Modern views of Jesus as a moral leader, a wholly human expositor of God's will and guarantor of His promises, are a radical advance on Arianism's acceptance of the divinity and worship of Jesus and the Holy Spirit, so Unitarians claim a position not very distant from that of Jews and Muslims, though based, they claim, on a rational and critical reading of Scripture.

More ominous was the presence of Constantine at Nicaea. His intervention initiated within Christendom a long and fateful tradition of "Caesaropapism," amalgamating church and state, with the church calling on civil authority to protect its faith, and the state using the church's ecclesiastical network to further its interests. Augustine and others cited Luke 14:23 ("compel them to come in") as scriptural warrant for coercion and punishment; and in 383, two years after Emperor Theodosius had made Christianity Rome's official religion, a Spanish bishop named Priscillian, apparently a gnostic and a Manichaean, was the first heretic to be officially executed. In 438 the Theodosian Code enjoined all unorthodox groups from assembling, proselytizing, or otherwise practicing anything "publicly or privately which may be detrimental to Catholic sanctity." And forever after both Eastern and Western Christianity became, for better or worse, a part of the political process and the public culture, with the cross that still appears in the flags of many European nations a lingering symbol of Caesaropapism.

Chapter 11 ends with the "Call of the Savior" (28-30), found only in Matthew (though a version of it exists in the "sayings" *Gospel of Thomas* [90]) and endlessly cited. Its most striking appearance was during Augustine's conversion experience (*Confessions* 7.21), where he recognized in these words sentiments of love and compassion he had never found in the books of the Platonists. The early "Semi-Pelagian" theologian John Cassian (360–435) interpreted the verse to mean that God wills the salvation of all, since, given the fact of original sin and actual sin, there is no one on earth who is not "heavy laden."[34] It later became an important Reformation text, much favored by Luther. Zwingli put it on the title pages of his publications and added it to the Communion liturgy in 1523; and it appears as "comfortable words" in the "Holy Communion" service of the Anglican *Book of Common Prayer,* having been inserted there by Thomas Cranmer in 1549. What had traditionally been interpreted as referring to the heavy burden of the Mosaic law (though Tertullian invoked it against women's pearl and diamond necklaces), Erasmus and the Protestants could now attribute to the accumulation of Catholic laws, rituals, practices, and doctrines. They complained that in the interests of Roman uniformity and discipline, canon law had replaced the Mosaic law, and church legislation had gradually "sacralized" all areas of life, regimenting everything from ceremony to matrimony, from calendars of feast days to the eating of foods. Bells and beads, bowing and kneeling, holy days and holy water—little was exempted from papal, episcopal, or clerical regulation. Customs became commands, each command imposed an obligation, and together with their sanctions, they weighed heavily on Christian consciences. The scrupulous found no "rest." What had happened to the Christian "freedom" proclaimed by St. Paul?

One Reformation response was to internalize spirituality through their doctrines of faith and grace "alone," and to revive the ancient philosophical notion of "indifference": that there are certain externals that are not ends in themselves and so neither good nor bad, neither prohibited nor commanded. For Christians these externals are not required by God, nor are they necessary for salvation. Laws of some sort are, of course, unavoidable, but they could be reduced in number and scope, renamed "precepts" or "exhortations," and located in Scripture. This was cause for much discussion among the Reformers, for it raised unsettling questions: Are all externals equally indifferent? Ceremonial vestments and ecclesiastical regulations, for example, about which Scripture is silent? Is everything permitted that the Bible does not expressly forbid? But this would lead to licentiousness and anarchy. Or is nothing allowed that the Bible does not expressly command? But this, Luther noted, would lead to privation, since then the Eucharist could be celebrated only in Jerusalem. So even the most spiritual of doctrines entails practice, and practice embraces worship and liturgy, and all of this must be regularized. Moreover, there were pastoral concerns with the stubborn devotion of "weaker brethren" to the very externals, many of them cherished customs, ceremonies, and traditions that the Reformers had branded as papist, idolatrous, and superstitious. So rites and regulations have continued, as they must, still a continuing source of division, though not dispute, among the various denominations.

The Reformers could also use Jesus' invitation to "Come unto me" to discredit the intercessory function of the Virgin Mary and the saints, just as Jesus does not say that burdened souls need earn their way to him by good works. It appears that only reliance on Jesus is required—another statement of the Reformers' doctrine of "faith alone"—and the Geneva Bible glossed verse 28 "with sinnes [*sic*]" to make it clear that Jesus was not there simply to lighten the burdens of daily life.[35] John Wesley cited it in his "Free Grace" sermon (1739) as a proof text against advocates of predestination: "You represent him as mocking his helpless creatures, by offering what he never intends to give."[36] And the Anglican theologian Gilbert Burnet (1643–1715) quoted verse 30 as proof of Christianity's "easiness": "Wherein we are freed from all the barbarous and cruel rites of Gentilism, and from the oppressive bondage of Judaism."[37]

A study of Puritan conversion experiences notes that, along with Isaiah 55:1 ("Come ye to the waters") and 6 ("Seek ye the Lord") and John 6:37 ("Him that cometh to me I will in no wise cast out"), this was one of the verses most often quoted in spiritual testimonies.[38] And in the popular piety of Catholicism, the Vulgate's *ego reficiam vos* ("I will refresh you") has been associated with the power of the host to effect physical healing, especially when it is elevated during the mass. This passage was also the inspiration for some favored hymns: "Come, Ye Sinners, Poor and Needy" ("Come, ye weary, heavy laden, lost and ruined by the Fall; / If you tarry till you're better, you will never come at all"); "Are You Weary, Heavy Laden?" ("Are you weary, heavy laden, are you sore distressed? / 'Come to me,' says One, 'and, coming, be at rest'."); and "What a Friend We Have in Jesus" ("Are we weak and heavy laden, cumbered with a load of care? / Precious Savior, still our refuge—take it to the Lord in prayer!").

In Catholic tradition, Jesus' yoke (vv. 29-30) is represented liturgically by the stole, a long and lightweight strip of material worn round the neck of a priest or deacon, and monastically by the scapular, the long cloth garment, rectangular in shape, worn over the shoulders, and with an opening for the head, hanging down in front and behind almost to the feet. It is worn by monks over their habits, while laypersons can wear a smaller version, two square pieces of cloth at the ends of two ribbons and worn next to the chest and back. Popular piety has it that the Virgin Mary promised salvation to anyone who dies while wearing a scapular. When Thomas Becket gave up his chancellorship and became Archbishop of Canterbury in 1162, he put on a hair shirt. "But the stole, the emblem of the sweet yoke of Christ, was every day and night around his neck."[39] Finally, the animal suggested by 29-30 is the ox, which became a symbol of Christian strength, endurance, and service.

Chapter 12 begins with a sudden and unlikely (in a wheat field!) appearance of the Pharisees, who criticized Jesus for letting his disciples pluck corn (grain) on the Sabbath. They might have responded to Jesus that David did not eat the bread of the Presence (twelve cakes that could be eaten only by the priestly sons of Aaron) on the Sabbath (1 Sam. 21:1-6). The question of Sabbath observance is also at Mark 2:23-28 and Luke 6:1-5. Baron d'Holbach saw this "theft" of corn as a precedent for Christian behavior: "Apparently on this principle, moreover, several Christian doctors have claimed that all things belonged to the righteous," including "the property of infidels and the unholy," land in the Americas, and the right of the pope "to dispose of crowns at his pleasure."[40]

Verse 8 sees the third appearance of the mysterious and authoritative title, "Son of man" (which only Jesus uses) as he again claims divine lordship, this time over the Sabbath. It is odd that none of his auditors are reported to have been surprised or puzzled by this elusive title, Aramaic in origin, which appears some eighty-six times in the New Testament, usually in the Gospels. It has never been used by the church in liturgies, and its ambiguous usages in Scripture (God, man, angel?) continue to evoke a wide range of modern opinions, with one extreme taking it as a definitive expression of Jesus' divinity and messianic mission, equal to the heavenly figure of Daniel 7:13-14, and the other simply as an honorific title meaning little more than "human being." So readers can easily sympathize with the question at John 12:34: "Who is this Son of man?" On the subject of Jesus' divinity, Benjamin Franklin wrote a month before his death (1790) that it was "needless to busy myself with it now, when I expect soon an opportunity of knowing the truth with less trouble."[41]

Jesus next enters "their synagogue" (v. 9), and these words or their equivalent, occurring six times in Matthew but not in the parallel passages, Mark 3:1 or Luke 6:6, betray the growing estrangement between Matthew's community and its Jewish opponents. There Jesus gives examples of what it is lawful to do on the Sabbath, and his question at 12a was recalled by Walter Rauschenbusch, America's most vigorous proponent of the Social Gospel: "Jesus asked, 'Is not a man more than a sheep?' Our industry says 'no.' It is careful of its livestock and its machinery, and careless of its working force. It keeps its electrical engines immaculate in burnished cleanliness and lets its human dynamo sicken in dirt."[42]

Verse 14 suddenly strikes an ominous note, as the Pharisees consult about Jesus and "how they might destroy him." He departs—and for Ulrich Luz these repeated "withdrawals" (12:15, 14:13, 15:21, 16:4) are symbolic of Matthew's community itself withdrawing from the synagogue in the face of its leaders' hostility.[43] It is typical of Matthew that a "withdrawal" be followed by an OT citation (e.g., 2:13, 22; 4:12). Verses 18-21 comprise the longest OT quotation in Matthew, and, as is often the case, it is a free adaptation, now of Isaiah 42:1-4, the first of the four "Servant Songs," here emphasizing Jesus' gentleness and his mission to the Gentiles. Verses 19-20 were cited by Tolstoy as "prophetic words" that supported his Christian pacifism.[44] The poor in spirit are "bruised reeds," not mighty trees, and the "smoking flax" are those for whom the flame of faith, about to go out, needs to be fed and fanned. The two images provide the title for *The Bruised Reed and Smoking Flax,* a spiritual classic by Richard Sibbes (1577–1635), a preacher who was popular and influential among Puritans. These images derive from Isaiah 42, and here they suggest that Jesus will not coerce anyone into conversion. Next Matthew's words on faith (21) are recalled in the hymn, "'Tis so sweet to trust in Jesus" ("O how sweet to trust in Jesus, just to trust his cleansing blood").

The Pharisees are back at verse 24, accusing Jesus of employing demons to perform exorcisms. Part of Jesus' response is of a "house divided against itself," a phrase that will often be repeated to describe everything from domestic disputes to civil wars. That such a "kingdom" is "brought to desolation" became for Jacques-Benigne Bossuet (1627–1704), the great French orator and controversialist, a proof text for the unity and paternal authority that only a hereditary monarchy can provide, since it reflects God's absolute rule in the universe. Most of Bossuet's examples come from the Old Testament, particularly from the reigns of Solomon and David, but he saw in Jesus' compliance with Roman authority a divine sanction for an imperial regime.[45]

The Pharisees do not deny that Jesus performs wonders, which they regard not as miracles but as demonic acts, and they call him a demon himself. Jesus responds that they are contradicting themselves: If he is a demon, how can he be said to cast out demons? He points out that the Pharisees' students ("your children") also perform exorcisms, and were they to tell their own students that they are doing this by the power of the devil, then the students would judge them harshly. So Jesus was not the only exorcist at work in Palestine, although he seems to have operated on his own authority and without the use of props or magic. "Beelzebub" may refer to the Canaanite god Baal, but his name was etymologized derogatorily as "Lord of the flies," the insects attracted to garbage, dung, or Baal's impure sacrifices, so it could have been an abusive nickname directed by his enemies at Jesus himself (10:25). His name variously spelled, Beelzebub appears often throughout literature as one of Satan's chief associates. In Marlowe's *Dr. Faustus* (1604), he is invoked by the tragic hero as he is about to sign a pact with the devil ("There is no chief but only Beelzebub / To whom Faustus doth dedicate himself" [1.3]). William Golding chose the derogatory epithet "lord of the flies" as the title of his immensely popular 1954 novel to represent the force of ugly and anarchic evil that turns a group of boys into savages when they are shipwrecked on a deserted island.

Here at verse 28, when he is speaking against the kingdom of Satan, Matthew specifies the kingdom of God, not his usual kingdom of heaven. This parallels "Spirit of God," an allusion both to Jesus' divine power and, indirectly, to the working of the Holy Spirit. That "the kingdom of God is come unto you" (also at Luke 17:20-21, where the kingdom of God is "within you") is a proof text that it is a present reality ("realized eschatology"), embodied in the power of Jesus' ministry, not a future event ("imminent" or "consistent" eschatology). Although he saw religion mainly in terms of morality, the "kingdom of God on earth" was a concern for Kant, and he cited this verse in arguing that the "kingdom" would not be upon us until "ecclesiastical faith" had been transformed into the "universal religion of reason" and individuals were bound by conscience and duty.[46] That Jesus performs exorcisms "by the Spirit of God" is also taken as a proof text for his divinity, in that as victories over demons they anticipate the end time and God's final vanquishing of Satan.

This passage appealed to Phineas Parkhurst Quimby (1802–66), who inspired Christian Science's Mary Baker Eddy. He construed the "Spirit of God" as "science or law," this being a kind of mental power "of harmony" that could control the body's afflictions. Its universal reception, he claimed, would "free man from disease and error" and lead to "a new heaven and a new earth." Quimby was the first of the "Christian physiologists," who equated virtue with health, sin with disease, and who sought to achieve the millennium through the mind's ability to master and apply the "laws" of our "being."[47] Later, Mary Baker Eddy alluded to Matthew (16:18) when she claimed that she had turned from Quimbyism to the Bible: "I have built Christian Science upon the Petra of the Scriptures."[48]

Verse 30 ("He that is not with me is against me") has achieved almost proverbial status, and John Henry Cardinal Newman (1801–90) quoted it at the end of his "Tract No. 1," published in his *Tracts for the Times* (1833–40).[49] Thus began the Oxford or Tractarian Movement, initially a protest against the government's plan in 1832 to reform the national Church of Ireland and use the savings for secular projects, but one that developed into an effort by An-glican conservatives to renew the Church of England spiritually and restore its traditional customs and ceremonies. In "Tract No. 1," Newman invoked the apostolic succession in exhorting his fellow clerics to defend the church's in-dependence, but his "Low Church" opponents feared the Tractarians were pro-moting "Romanism" through such practices as the honoring of saints, the sign of the cross, and auricular confession.

Verses 31-32 comprise one of Jesus' "hard sayings." Traditionally, the sins against the Holy Spirit are presumption and despair. These the church cannot forgive, for by their nature they betray a hardness of heart that precludes re-pentance. Examples in literature are at the end of Marlowe's *Dr. Faustus,* where the hero laments that he has lost all hope of forgiveness ("Faustus' offense can ne'er be pardoned; the Serpent that tempted Eve may be saved, but not Faus-tus," 5.2.42), and in the doomed heroes of Romanticism such as Byron's Man-fred, Hawthorne's Chillingworth (*The Scarlet Letter*), and Melville's Ahab (*Moby Dick*). But that sins could be forgiven "in the world to come" (missing from the parallel passages in Mark and Luke) suggested to some that there had to be a purgatory, since sin could not be forgiven in heaven.

Verse 31 was also a proof text for Hosea Ballou, an early Universalist, who taught that there are different gradations of sin and that all mortal sins do not deserve an infinite and irreversible punishment.[50] But earlier this verse was cited by Gregory of Nazianzus (328–90), bishop of Constantinople, as a proof text for the divinity of the Holy Spirit, though there is only fragile evidence in the Gospels for the dogma and mystery of the Holy Spirit and its place in the Trinity as God the Sanctifier together with God the Creator and God the Re-deemer.[51] The Western church insisted that as the Son "proceeds" from the Fa-ther, the Holy Spirit proceeds from both the Father "and the Son" (*filioque*), not from the Father "through the Son." The word *filioque* was inserted into the Nicene Creed at a Toledo synod in sixth-century Spain to impress the equality of the Son upon the Visigoths, recently converted to Western ortho-doxy from Arianism, where the Son was subordinated to the Father. This "double procession," accepted by Charlemagne for inclusion in the creed re-cited during mass but unauthorized by either pope or council, contributed to Orthodoxy's break with Rome, since the Eastern church regarded it as a uni-lateral addition to the faith and a reduction of the Holy Spirit, whereas the Western church saw it as another example of the consubstantiality of Father and Son.

Next, in verses 38-41, the Scribes and the Pharisees ask Jesus for a "sign." (Muhammad was equally reluctant to provide "a sign": "Signs are in the hands of God. My mission is only to give plain warning," 29.49.) But Jesus does not produce prodigies on demand, so instead he responds with a prediction that invokes the OT prophet Jonas, whose message was heeded by the Ninevites.

The story of Jonas, with its message of deliverance, was the most popular subject in the catacomb art of early Christianity; and his three-day death and resurrection, which is only in Matthew, made him a prototype of Jesus himself —though the literally minded might object that Jesus was in the tomb for only two nights. Since the Jonas reference comes directly from Jesus, he seems to be validating the controversial practice of typology and the authority of Jonah (of all people!) as a "prophet." As for the Queen of Sheba, she traveled a great distance to hear the wisdom of Solomon, he tells them; whereas the scribes and Pharisees have a wiser man than Solomon in their very presence, and his message they refuse to heed. Jesus then continues with the image of the unclean spirit (43-45). Allegorized historically, it refers to the Jews freed of one demon by the law and then repossessed by it and seven others after rejecting Jesus; spiritually, it refers to the initially liberating benefit of baptism and then the relapse into the seven deadly sins by the negligent Christian. It is repeated at Luke 11:24-26. But Luther, noting that Zwingli had been a priest before becoming his bitter opponent, remarked that his last state was worse than his first.[52]

Jesus' talk is interrupted at verse 46 by the appearance—and problem—of his "brethren," with four being named at 13:55. Traditionally, Protestants have held that Mary had more children, so these were true siblings (although both Luther and Calvin accepted her perpetual virginity), whereas the Orthodox Churches have accepted the solution of the *Infancy Gospel of James* (150), that they were the children of the widowed Joseph by a previous marriage. Catholics have considered them to be Jesus' first cousins, the children of the Mary who is the wife of Cleophas (John 19:25), a position weakened by the publication in 2002 of an inscription identifying James as the "son of Joseph." The biblical evidence is sparse and inconclusive, and some are surprised that more is not said of his close relatives or how they interacted with the apostles. On the other hand, Jesus' "brother" James did head the Jerusalem church, and upon his martyrdom in 62, pushed off a temple parapet after preaching on 26:64, he was said to have been succeeded by another "brother," Simeon. Interestingly, there are no traditions, not even legends, about Jesus' sisters.

Chapter 13 is devoted to a series of "kingdom parables" in which the kingdom of heaven is said to be like a seed, a treasure, a "pearl of great price," and a catch of fish. Some might wonder why a sower would waste seed on places where it could not germinate, but the image seems to be that of a farmer sowing seed all around his property, with some blown by the wind and falling on paths, others where the topsoil was thin, and still others among the hedgerows. Then, in the midst of the "seed" parable, we have another "hard saying" (12-13): "For whosoever hath, to him shall be given . . . but whosoever hath not, from him shall be taken." It is softer than its counterpart in Mark 4:12 ("lest at any time they should be converted"), which seems to rule out conversion and the forgiveness of sins. Here Matthew corrects Mark's misunderstanding of Isaiah 6:9-10 ("Hear ye indeed, but understand not"), verses that explained to early Christians why the Jews had rejected Jesus. For Matthew, some can see Jesus and hear his words but not grasp their meaning. Similarly, God's graces will be given more abundantly to those who act on them; they will diminish for those who neglect them. Unfortunately, the parable is often taken to mean only that the rich get richer, the poor get poorer.

The "mysteries" of verse 11 seem to be that the kingdom of God is present in Jesus. But the mention of mysteries has suggested to some that Christianity was just another of the "mystery cults" that characterized the religious life of late antiquity, particularly since these cults had a number of features in common with the new faith. Thus, their mother-goddess seemed a version of the Virgin Mary; their annual dying-and-rising gods, such as Attis, Adonis, Osiris, and Tammuz, seemed a counterpart to Jesus crucified and resurrected; the banquet of the Mithraeans seemed to be a kind of Eucharistic meal; and the cult of the sun shared its solar symbolism with "the true Light" (John 1:9). But like rites of initiation, purification, and salvation, these are features of all religions, and the seasonal fertility rites that underlay these mystery cults had little to do with the historical realities of Judaism and Christianity. Only Christianity had a leader who had lived and died in historical time; only Christianity preached a faith that was open and accessible to all; only Christianity generated a written literature to explain and defend its teachings; only Christianity institutionalized its beliefs. And yet a chance remark by an atheist friend about the cults' "dying god," that it "almost looks as if it had really happened once," had a "shattering impact" on C. S. Lewis and contributed to his passage from theism to Anglican Christianity.[53]

The sowing parable continues (18-23) as Jesus describes varying degrees of receptiveness and commitment to the "seed." In these remarkably high yields, medieval numerologists saw (among other correspondences) the Trinity in 30, the days of Creation in 60, and perfection in 100.[54] But it is the parable of the tares that has evoked a long discussion on church conduct and discipline in matters of heresy, with Matthew here providing the liberal response to Luke's uncompromising "compel them to come in" (14:23). As is customary with most things biblical, this parable yields diverse meanings. Are the "tares," understood as weeds, heretical persons, or doctrines? Or simply immoral members of a church that, like Noah's ark, must accommodate both clean and unclean animals? Does rooting them up imply admonishing, disciplining, or killing deviant church members? And who should do this? Ministers of the church or magistrates of the state? In modern times this parable was cited by Pope Pius XII in his 1953 discourse on "The World Community," when he noted that the common good can require the acceptance of diverse moral and religious convictions.[55] But in 1518 his predecessor, Leo X, was less tolerant of Luther when he wrote to Duke George of Saxony to "extirpate this tare and cockle from the fertile field of the Lord."[56] In attacking the heretical Donatists and their exclusivity, Augustine had used it to recommend that for prudential reasons the church could allow heterodox doctrines to coexist with orthodox, heretics with the faithful. The Donatists also contended that the efficacy of sacraments depends on the worthiness of their ministers, a regular complaint of Christian dissidents who are appalled that evil men should have privileged access to God's mysteries and sacraments. Augustine responded that tares could take the form of bad priests and bishops, but as long as their intentions were good, the sacraments they administered were valid.[57] Aquinas contended that such is the contagiousness of heresies that its propagators, after due warning, should not only be separated from the church but should be delivered to the secular authorities for execution.[58] Thomas More alluded to 13:7 in proclaiming religious peace and toleration for his *Utopia* (1516; Eng. trans. 1566): "But if the struggle were decided by arms and riots, since the worst men are always the most unyielding, the best and holiest religion would be overwhelmed because of the conflicting false religions, like grain choked by thorns and underbrush."[59]

St. Paul was the best example of a "tare" turned "wheat," and in a work, *De Haereticis* ("Concerning Heretics"), written in 1554 to protest the execution for heresy of the anti-Trinitarian Michael Servetus a year before in Geneva, its presumed author, the Reformer Sebastian Castellio, remarked that "Christ and his disciples were put to death as heretics."[60] The same image was used by conservative Reformers in a vain attempt to preserve Christian unity amid the proliferation of radically reformist doctrines, and it was often noted that in the Gospels Jesus advised the admonishment and restoration of dissidents, and that his followers put no one to death for unbelief. Hence, Luther saw the doctrine of purgatory as an example of "tares" that were sown "while the bishops slept" and listed it as number 11 of his *Ninety-five Theses*. But until his final years and the Peasants' War, he had no interest in taking his enemies' lives— all the more so since he had himself been a victim of persecution. Although Milton rejected the toleration of "popery and open superstition," he conceded that "it is not possible for man to sever the wheat from the tares, the good fish from the other fry; that must be the angels' ministry at the end of mortal things."[61] And this parable was such a favorite of Roger Williams (1600–83), the pioneer settler of Rhode Island, founder of Providence, and early champion of religious toleration, that he devoted ten chapters to it in his classic *The Bloudy Tenent of Persecution for Cause of Conscience* (1644).

But advocates of tolerance, such as Erasmus and Castellio, had to meet the counterargument that religious heresy was subversive of social order, that heretics, if not forever silenced, endangered not only their own souls but those of their followers, and that some radical Reformers, like Thomas Müntzer, believed in spreading their versions of the gospel with fire and sword. John Hus insisted that just because tares are mixed with wheat does not mean that tares are wheat; analogously, reprobate clergy may be in the church, but they are not of it; and "bind them in bundles to burn them" was scriptural warrant for the binding and burning of heretics.[62] Furthermore, the argument for tolerating tares until the end-time's "harvest" was difficult to reconcile with the call for immediate church discipline at 18:17.

The parable of the mustard seed (31-32) is puzzling, since mustard seeds are not "the least of all seeds" and grow into plants, not into trees where birds can nest. But the hyperbole conveys the contrast between the modest beginnings of Jesus' ministry and the immensity of the kingdom it promises. It was quoted by John Wesley in a sermon to describe the Order of Salvation: "how it begins in faith through grace, which is available to all, and then proceeds from Justification, whereby we are saved from the guilt of sin, and restored to the favour of God," to sanctification, whereby "we are saved from the power and root of sin, and restored to the image of God."[63] The grain of mustard seed will recur at 17:20 as an example of the growth of faith, so powerful that "nothing shall be impossible unto you." This message is so uplifting that it has been traditionally engraved in lockets that also hold a single grain (preferably from the Holy Land).

The next parable, of leaven (v. 33), with its suggestion of the transforming effect of Jesus' message, has endured a number of interpretations: that, for example, the three measures are Europe, Asia, and Africa; or body, soul, and spirit. But it has also had historical associations, since in the Great Schism between the Eastern and Western churches, the use of leaven in the Communion bread was a central issue. The Passover tradition of unleavened bread was cited by a spokesman for the Greek Orthodox patriarch Michael Cerularius in reminding his Roman Catholic counterparts that the Jewish law had ceased, so they should give up their "Judaizing" use of bread without the yeast that was for Orthodoxy a palpable sign of the New Dispensation. In recent times this parable received some notoriety from the "Jesus Seminar," where it received a 90 percent vote (meaning "Jesus said it" or "Jesus probably said something like it"), since its comparison of the "kingdom of heaven" to leaven, which the Jews regarded as "a symbol of corruption," was "unexpected" and "provocative."

At 13:36 we are halfway through the gospel. Jesus sends away "the multitude," who have not accepted him, and henceforth speaks only to his disciples.

The fate of the tares, to be "burned in the fire" (40), is, like the inedible fish (48), another reminder that the Christian doctrine of hell with its eternal fires and awful punishments derives largely from Matthew. Mark mentions it only once, at 9:43; Luke only occasionally, with "weeping" borrowed from 8:12 for the familiar "weeping and wailing and gnashing of teeth"; and when this parable later appears in the gnostic *Gospel of Thomas* (8), there is no reference to any "furnace of fire." These dolorous activities were also an indirect proof for bodily resurrection, since there can be no gnashing without teeth. Mark Twain, noting that eternal damnation is largely a NT doctrine said: "The first time the Deity came down to earth he brought life and death; when he came the second time, he brought hell."[64] And in his 1915 "Preface" to *Androcles and the Lion,* Shaw was confident that "belief in that hell is fast vanishing. All the leaders of thought have lost it; and even for the rank and file it has fled to those parts of Ireland and Scotland which are still in the XVII century. Even there, it is tacitly reserved for the other fellow."[65] But it was chapter 25 (see below) that provided the classic texts for the traditional hell-fire sermons.

The parable of the buried treasure (v. 44) was cited by Origen in defense of allegory as a device to reveal the "dark and invisible and buried treasures" hidden in the fields of Scripture, though the hidden treasure can refer to many aspects of the kingdom first revealed by Jesus.[66] And the short pearl parable (45-46), which is unique to Matthew, reappears in Hawthorne's *The Scarlet Letter* (1850), where Pearl is the name of Hester Prynne's illegitimate daughter. "But she named the infant 'Pearl,' as being of great price—purchased with all she had—her mother's only treasure!"[67] It also provided the title of the anonymous medieval poem "Pearl," where it refers to a lost child, though it is sometimes taken as representing the soul. In modern literature it came to stand for virginity or sexual purity. Both the hidden "treasure" and the "pearl of great price" were cited by the Lutheran theologian Dietrich Bonhoeffer (1906–45) to describe "costly grace," the "gift which must be *asked* for, the door at which a man must *knock*." For him it was the opposite of "cheap grace," which is "the preaching of forgiveness without requiring repentance, baptism without church discipline, Communion without confession, absolution without personal confession." Costly grace, said Bonhoeffer, "costs a man his life," as it did for him when he was hanged by the Nazis for his role in the German resistance.[68]

That there is but "one pearl of great price" (46) as well as only one "grain of mustard seed" (31) showed Luther that "Christ is not divided."[69] Analogously, Scripture is one and harmonious, and he believed that what appeared to be inconsistencies and contradictions would ultimately be resolved. *Pearl of Great Price* is also the name of one of Mormonism's fundamental scriptures, said to contain selected revelations to Joseph Smith from Abraham and Moses that expand the biblical accounts. Reportedly translated by him from Egyptian papyri, they were published in 1842 and have been revised several times since. Matthew was Smith's favorite gospel; and in *Pearl,* along with alleged revelations from God, Jesus, the angel Moroni, and John the Baptist, he also included his rearrangement of the contents of Matthew 24 "in accord with the revelation of the Holy Ghost."[70]

At verse 54, Jesus is in "his own country." It is odd that his countrymen seem to know nothing of the extraordinary events surrounding Jesus' birth (55-57), and one can only wonder how much of Jesus' childhood the apostles heard from Mary. The most familiar representation of Jesus as a "carpenter's son" is a genre painting by John Millais, *Christ in the House of his Parents,* or *The Carpenter's Shop* (1849–50; London). It combines sentimental realism with a prefiguration of the crucifixion, since the boy Jesus seems to have just suffered a cut in his palm. The painting appalled Charles Dickens, and the *London Times* was "disgusted" by Millais's attention to "loathesome minuteness."[71] In his encyclical *Divini Redemptoris* (March 19, 1937) directed against Communism, Pope Pius XI cited this verse as an example of how, through Jesus as "the carpenter's son," human labor "was elevated to its true dignity" in contrast with the classical world's disparagement of physical work.[72] The Greek word for Joseph's trade can indicate a woodworker, though in a relatively treeless country he must have worked in other building materials too, and some would make him a stonemason. Still, Woody Allen has a character in his film *Love and Death* (1975) wonder what he might have charged for bookshelves; and at the beginning of Martin Scorsese's film *The Last Temptation of Christ* (1988), Jesus is shown making crosses for Roman crucifixions.

In narrating the fate of John the Baptist in chapter 14, Matthew generally follows Mark 6:14-29, although what Mark had related as a past event is related illogically by Matthew as if it were current, with Jesus hearing about his execution at 14:13. This episode also presents problems with names. "Herod the tetrarch" ("leader of a fourth," not the "king" of v. 9) is Herod Antipas, the son of Herod the Great, and now ruling Galilee and Perea (Transjordan). Herodias had actually been the wife of Herod Antipas's half-brother, who was also named Herod but may have been called Philip. The scandal arose when she agreed to marry Antipas only if he removed his current wife. Philip was also the name of the husband of Salome, the daughter of Herodias by her previous marriage; Salome thus became Herod's stepdaughter. Mark gave a very dramatic and personal interpretation to Herod's hatred of John the Baptist (6:18: "For John had said unto Herod, It is not lawful for thee to have thy brother's wife"); but in *The Woman's Bible* (1895–98) Elizabeth Cady Stanton defends Herodias, pointing out that according to Josephus the only villain was Herod, who feared John's popularity and influence.[73] There was probably a mixture of personal and political motives: Herod urged by his wife to do away with a man whose message of repentance and prophecy that sinners were to be punished in an imminent end time (3:7: "the wrath to come") must have seemed to threaten the royal family. Interestingly, more is known from extra-biblical sources about John than about Jesus, since Josephus admired John and ranked his execution among the worst of Herod Antipas's crimes. He praised John's revivalist message but said nothing of any messianic predictions.

Salome's mother, Herodias, is the villain here (though less openly than at Mark 6:19, 24); and legend had her receiving John's head from Salome, pulling out his tongue, and repeatedly stabbing it. But it is the dancing Salome, un-named in Scripture, and her veils (also missing) that have interested artists from Giotto to Moreau and writers from Heinrich Heine to Oscar Wilde—though it is unlikely that a princess of Herod's court would dance for his birth-day-party guests. She joins the ranks of the Bible's "bad women"—Eve, Job's wife, and especially Jezebel, since with Ahab she persecuted Elijah, the OT pro-totype of John (1 Kgs. 19). It was Josephus who first reported her name; and although Matthew's narrative presents her as a young girl manipulated by a vengeful mother, Salome became a symbol of lust and murder in late-nineteenth-century music and literature, and her "Dance of the Seven Veils" in Richard Strauss's *Salome* (1905), based on the one-act play by Wilde, is one of the great show-stoppers in opera. In Heine's long poem, *Atta Troll* (1847), Herodias has John beheaded because he spurned her love, and she carries his head with her, throwing it in the air and catching it "as if she were playing with a ball" (ch. 19). Flaubert follows Renan's romanticized *Life of Jesus* and restores Salome in his carefully researched *Hérodias* (1877), giving a richly sensuous de-scription of her dance ("She twisted from side to side like a flower shaken by the wind").[74] The symbolist painter Gustave Moreau (1826–98) exhibited two paintings at the Paris Spring Salon in 1876, *Salome* and *The Apparition,* in which Salome interrupts her dance to point at John's severed head that appears suspended in an aureole of light. Both paintings were described in Huysman's novel *Against the Grain* (1903), whose "decadent" hero Des Esseintes repeat-edly reads and ponders verses 6-11, endowing Salome with an erotic and Sa-tanic destructiveness ("the symbolic deity of indestructible Lechery, the goddess of immortal Hysteria, the accursed Beauty . . . the monstrous, indis-criminate, irresponsible, unfeeling Beast").[75] In the best-known version, Wilde's *Salome* (French, 1893; English, 1894), it is the young princess herself who is enraptured by John ("Let me kiss thy mouth"). But when he spurns her advances, she uses her gyrations to beguile Herod into fulfilling his promise by presenting her with John's severed head. She kisses its lips, and as the play ends, a shocked Herod orders his soldiers to crush Salome beneath their shields.[76] But it was left to Hollywood to show that Salome was not all bad, so in a 1953 film of the same name, Rita Hayworth was converted by John and danced for Herod in a vain attempt to save his life.

Unfortunately, Salome's notoriety has also contributed to a reluctance to in-clude dancing, especially mixed dancing, in religious ceremonies; and the aid of St. Vitus, a fourth-century saint, was invoked to cure those who were swept up in the quasi-pagan dancing mania of fifteenth-century Germany, a craze considered the work of the devil, though the dancing more usually ended in exhaustion than in exorcism. A recent and relevant Vatican document, *Dance in the Liturgy* (1975), while acknowledging that in certain cultures dance has a ritual legitimacy (2 Sam. 6:14: "David danced before the Lord"), ruled that in the West it is most often associated with entertainment and sensuality and hence impermissible in Catholic liturgies. Even less hospitable are those Baptist denominations that frown on social dancing. Nonetheless, a kind of simple folk dancing was always part of Quaker and Shaker services; rhythmical movements have characterized Pentecostal services, particularly in black churches; and a number of liturgical dance groups have made their dance performances part of Christian worship. Since church pews would obstruct the participation of congregations, the usual practice is for professional dancers, appropriately attired, to represent the congregation through a kind of bodily prayer or gestures of praise and adoration that are compatible with the liturgy.

Herod Antipas had John put to death in his fortress-palace at Machaerus, in the hills east of the Dead Sea (10), but Christian tradition located his birthday party in Samaria, which was in the jurisdiction of Pontius Pilate. Herod the Great had renamed it Sebaste ("Augustus" in Greek) in honor of the Roman emperor who had given him the city. Near the modern city of Nablus (ancient Shechem), the spiritual center of the Samaritans, this was the ancient capital of Omri, who had ruled the Northern Kingdom (1 Kgs. 16:24). It flourished under Jeroboam II (784–48 BC), much to the displeasure of the Prophet Amos; it enjoyed a splendid rebuilding program under Herod the Great; and it later boasted a Byzantine basilica said to contain the tomb of John the Baptist. But according to the *Golden Legend* (2.138), John's head was not buried with his body but kept at first in a grotto as an object of veneration and a cause of various wonders, then taken to Constantinople, and finally to Poitiers, where the fourth-century Baptistery of St. John is one of the oldest Christian monuments in France. Other sites claimed it too, though most had to settle for teeth. Legend has it that Normandy also received the finger used by John to point at Jesus (John 1:29-30) and that the sword of the beheading was later acquired by King Arthur of England.

When Jesus hears of John's fate, he departs by boat for a "desert place" (v. 13). Recalling the desert of the Exodus, it became in Christianity—literally so in the monastic tradition—a place for prayer and contemplation, where God can be most intimately apprehended. But it is not so remote that people can not come to him "out of the cities" (13), so a great crowd follows him, and he provides them miraculously with food. The feeding of the five thousand (21) is recorded by all four evangelists (the four thousand are fed at 15:38), though the people seem oddly unaware that they are the beneficiaries of a miracle. It recalls the manna of the Exodus (Exod. 16) as well as Elisha's feeding the people of Gilgal at 2 Kings 4:42-44, and it anticipates the Eucharist and the Last Supper, with drawings of the "loaves and fishes" often used to symbolize the Eucharist in catacomb art. Deriving details from the other gospel accounts, the allegorists imagined the five loaves as the Pentateuch: they are of barley because barley grains, like the hidden truths of the Old Testament, are covered with chaff; the boy who brings them is Israel, its people reclining on the grass, which is the carnal world (Isa. 40:6: "All flesh is grass"); the two fishes are the OT prophets and kings, their two functions now united in Jesus; and the twelve baskets of fragments are the higher truths reserved for the twelve apostles.

Voltaire thought this only a Christian version of the ancient myth of the cornucopia.[77] Later, the modern German dramatist Bertolt Brecht, who claimed that the Bible (of all books!) was his main literary influence, has his Catholic chaplain recall this episode in *Mother Courage and Her Children* (1939), adding cynically that Jesus could preach love of neighbor only to a crowd that was fed.[78] Lloyd C. Douglas (1877–1951), in his best-selling novel *The Robe* (1942), adopted a traditional interpretation: the "miracle" is that Jesus' words persuade his listeners to share their food with others.[79] In Pasolini's Matthew film, where there are so few actors that this scene is more like the "Feeding of Fifty," he plays down the gospel's miracles in favor of Jesus' social teachings, as one might expect from a film produced by a Marxist intellectual. The Last Supper hardly looks like a meal, and the resurrection is mostly the Great Commission of 28:19-20. And since the film reduces Matthew's "multitudes" and leaves Jesus alone with his disciples on deserted hillsides, it is hard to imagine that Pasolini's Jesus could have had the kind of impact that would warrant his crucifixion.

After feeding the five thousand, Jesus bids his disciples sail to the other side of the Sea of Galilee while he ascends a mountain to pray (22-23). The ship is caught in a storm, and Jesus rejoins his disciples, wondrously, if unexpectedly, walking on the waves, his feat recalling the Israelites' passage through the Red Sea (Exod. 14:21-22) and the River Jordan (Josh. 3:14-17). Erasmus, reflecting on the stormy controversies of his time, noted that the church is always in the dark and in trouble "whenever the spirit of Christ is absent."[80] When Mark Twain asked to cross the Sea of Galilee, the Arab boatman wanted to charge him so much that he remarked "Do you wonder now that Jesus walked?"[81] This episode is recalled in the first stanza of a well-known hymn by William Cowper (1731–1800): "God works in a mysterious way, / His wonders to perform; / He plants his footsteps in the sea, / And rides upon the storm."[82]

The story also shows Matthew's special interest in Peter, the first-called disciple, and looks forward to the commissioning scene of 16:17-19. Matthew's portrayal is not always positive, for although Peter walks on the water here, he begins to sink when his fear overcomes his faith, as will happen during the Passion Narrative (26:69-75). And only here does a miracle evoke a "son of God" response, though, as usual, it is hard to know what those in the ship meant by this title. But it is, with 16:16 ("Thou art the Christ, the Son of the living God"), Matthew's contribution to the Christology that will be further developed in John's gospel.

In the ninth-century *Heliand,* a fascinating Old Saxon epic in alliterative verse that adapts the Gospels to the sensibilities of a heroic German audience living in a perilous world, this event is lengthened and undergoes some typical revisions. The apostles are warriors and Jesus' retainers, while their leader, Peter, is his "sword-thane." The "earls" are sailing over the sea in their "high-horned" Viking ship when they find themselves caught in fog. It is the power of Jesus, their "chief," that enables him to walk on water, just as it is not so much a lack of faith as a lack of courage and persistence that causes Peter to sink. And it is also Jesus' obligation, as lord to vassal, to save his second-in-command. After warning him to be firm in his faith, "Together they made land, coming through the water's onslaught. They thanked the Ruler, they praised their Chieftain in words and in deeds, they fell at His feet and spoke many words of wisdom. They said that they knew that he was the son of the Chieftain and that he had authority over the middle world and that he was able to be of help to every human being's life-spirit."[83]

The anonymous author's attempt to cope with Christian theology, the Bible's Near Eastern culture, and the Latin language produced a number of other adjustments in the *Heliand*'s nearly six thousand lines: Scripture consists of secret runes; Bethlehem, like other towns, is a "fort"; the magi are "foreign heroes"; the massacre of the innocents is described in some detail; the temptation takes place in a forest, not a desert; the disciples seem to live by the shores of the North Sea; the peacemakers of the seventh Beatitude are those who do not start fights; Jesus has the power to transfigure himself; the money-changers in the temple ("shrine") become usurious money-lenders; the scribes and Pharisees are simply Jesus' warrior enemies; the Last Supper takes place in a handsomely decorated mead-hall; the cross of the crucifixion resembles a tree from which Jesus is hanged; and, after the resurrection, Jesus ascends to heaven where, like Wotan, he is able to observe everything that is happening on earth.

At the end of chapter 14, Jesus' fame attracts the sick for a display of mass healing. The "hem of his garment" (36) that cures them became a proof text for the veneration and efficacy of relics, though not as impressive as Paul's "handkerchiefs or aprons" in Acts 19:12, which could heal the sick and effect exorcisms even if Paul were not present. The theological rationale for turning such materials into relics is that the superabundant divine grace that pervaded the bodies of saints while they were alive and performing miracles continues to linger in their remains and in objects associated with them, thereby sanctifying and protecting their owners. Collecting relics reaches back to the earliest days of the church when, in the mid-second century, Christians exhumed and honored the bones of the martyr St. Polycarp; and the current interest in the Shroud of Turin shows that it is unlikely to abate very soon despite fears that this kind of devotion—sometimes called the "theology of the poor"—borders on superstition.

The Middle Ages was the great time for relics, particularly after their traffic was endorsed by a decree of the Second Council of Nicaea in 787 that required the presence of a saint's relic in each new church that was consecrated; and the Vatican has long had a service providing relics to be enclosed in church altars. This practice derives from the ancient custom of celebrating the anniversaries of martyrs' deaths by holding a Eucharist liturgy at their tombs, and it has contributed to the idea that the Roman Catholic altar is not only the table of the Last Supper but also the tomb of one who lived for the faith. The accumulation and distribution of relics has always been a going concern, though more popular in the Western than in the Eastern church, which was preoccupied instead with creating and defending its holy icons. It flourished again when the Crusaders returning from the Holy Land brought back relics in abundance, especially such quality items as fragments of the True Cross and a white limestone dust known as the Milk of the Virgin from a Bethlehem grotto. Churches then vied with one another to expand their collections of such memorabilia as straws from Jesus' crib and nails from the cross. Helena gave two nails to her son Constantine, one for his crown, the other for his horse's bridle ("A crown made from the Cross, that faith may shine forth; reins likewise from the Cross, that power may rule, and that there may be just moderation," St. Ambrose explained).[84] Unfortunately, nails from the cross were few in number, but they were said magically to reproduce themselves and to give off no end of iron shavings; and there were always bits and pieces of saints, especially their bones. Objects only associated with saints were of somewhat less worth, though here too there was a scale of values. In the "General Prologue" to his *Canterbury Tales,* Chaucer's Pardoner (a minor churchman who collected alms in return for indulgences) claims among his relics a piece of the sail from Peter's ship. When he died in 1274, Aquinas's fellow Dominicans boiled up his corpulent body to supply the relics trade; whereas St. Francis's followers stored his coffin in a rock vault in a "Lower" church in Assisi to keep the relics-seekers from his remains, and it was not found again until 1818. Such relics were usually preserved for exhibition in reliquaries that were elaborately constructed and ornately decorated, and the churches and monasteries that possessed important relics then became pilgrimage goals, though they suffered terribly in the fury of Reformation iconoclasm.

Needless to say, the Reformers, with the intellectuals' characteristic revulsion against popular pastimes, unanimously and vehemently denounced the church's veneration and merchandising of relics. Celsus joked that if Jesus had been hanged, it would have been called the "rope of immortality" (6.37, 352); and Calvin has some entertaining pages on the cult of passion relics, counting fourteen nails, four spears, so many crown thorns that "it would seem that its twigs had been planted that they might grow again," and the seamless robe that "from inconsiderate zeal" and "purposes of adoration" Christians had torn to pieces.[85] But they also recognized their popular appeal, and the marginal note to verses 35-36 in the Geneva Bible (1560) was conciliatory: "It seemeth they were led with a certain superstition; notwithstanding, our Saviour would not quench the smoking flax and therefore did bear with their small beginnings" (p. 9, spelling modernized). Catholics pointed out that the Reformers' rejection of relics did not keep them from fetishizing the Bible, and in many a Protestant home its mere presence, though unopened and covered with dust, was believed to ward off evil spirits.

6

Jesus and the Pharisees

Jesus' ministry is interrupted by the appearance from Jerusalem of "scribes and Phar-
isees," with whom he contends in 15:1-20. He then departs for the "coasts of Tyre and
Sidon," there meeting a Canaanite woman and healing her daughter. Next he returns to
the Sea of Galilee and on a mountain continues his healing, again feeding a multitude,
this time four thousand, with seven loaves and "a few little fishes." At the end of chapter
15 he comes to "the coasts of Magdala," and at the beginning of 16 he denounces the Phar-
isees and the Sadducees. In the middle of the same chapter, he is at the northernmost point
in the gospel, Caesarea Philippi, where Peter makes his confession of faith and is in turn
commissioned (according to some) to head the church of Christ.

Here in chapter 15, the scribes and Pharisees accuse Jesus' disciples of con-
travening tradition by not washing their hands before eating, an act entailing
ritual purification as much as personal hygiene. Jesus trumps their objection
by charging that they do worse: they break the commandments to preserve
their traditions. He offers the example of a son's vowing to present to the temple resources he should have used to support his parents, an odd practice but
one sanctioned by tradition and the oral law, although it contravened the more
serious Torah commandment to honor one's father and mother. The *American Folk Gospel* (1999) supplies this interpretive translation: "Now it's like you
might say to a father or mother, 'I will be benevolent, but you got to pay me
for it!'"[1]

In his *De Monarchia* (3.3.15) Dante uses this incident to question the
church's appeal to tradition in its claims of papal authority, and Catholicism
has always, perhaps excessively, nourished its traditions. Hence this episode,
along with verses 9 and 13, were premium Reformation proof texts for the
abolition of longstanding Catholic dogmas and practices, particularly the
traditional mass, monastic vows, and clerical celibacy (*Augsburg Confession*,
XXVII), which the Reformers regarded as customs innovated by the church
without sanction in Scripture. Zwingli was explicit: "One sees here that God
does not desire our decree and doctrine when they do not originate with Him,
that He despises them, and says we serve Him in vain."[2] Next Matthew has

Jesus speak to "the multitude," touching on the sensitive issue of dietary laws, though Matthew typically does not include Mark's more conclusive comment, "He thus declared all foods clean" (7:19, not in the KJV). Hence the implication is that although inner purity is superior, the dietary laws remain valid, as Matthew once again allows for both the claims of the ideal and the necessities of the practical.

The sometimes appalling ignorance of many parish priests was a concern for the medieval church, and verse 14 ("blind leaders of the blind"; also at Luke 6:39 and "saying" 34 in the *Gospel of Thomas*) was cited in Canon 27 of the Fourth Lateran Council (1215), which provided for the adequate preparation of the clergy. Pieter Bruegel the Elder illustrated verse 14 in his painting *The Blind Leading the Blind* (1568; Naples). Falling "into the ditch" may have been a commentary on the religious disputes of his time, and both Luther and Calvin used it to describe the pope's leadership. For Roger Williams, arguing for religious toleration in Puritan New England, it showed that the state need not persecute religious heretics for their blindness to the "truth," since left alone, they would be led to self-destruction by their equally blind leaders.[3]

Jesus' next journey (21-28) is reminiscent of 10:5 ("Go not into the way of the Gentiles"), since for now Jesus' own mission is to Israelites and the Jewish villages—but not cities—of Galilee. Here, however, he travels near Tyre and Sidon, formerly Phoenician cities on the Mediterranean coast. It is not clear why Jesus went there, though it is generally interpreted as an indication of his mission to the pagan world, for which there is little evidence in the Gospels, considering the missionary command that concludes Matthew (28:19: "Go ye therefore, and teach all nations") and the fact that Christianity would soon prosper among Gentiles. In this odd and abrupt miracle story, where a "foreign" woman, who appears to be unaccompanied, not only dares to accost Jesus publicly but even shouts at him (the centurion was more respectful at 8:5-13). The woman is an example of perfect faith, the "children's bread" is Jesus' teaching addressed to the Israelites (but the woman had asked for healing, not instruction), and the "dogs" are Gentiles (a rather harsh comparison). The woman's response resembles Jesus' own technique of turning his interlocutors' words against them, but her faith is persistent, even in the face of her treatment at 23-26, and it may be seen as foreshadowing the Gentiles' eventual acceptance of Christianity. Verse 24, taken out of context, was a proof text for the heretical Cathars, medieval dualists who interpreted it to mean that their "good" God saves only certain souls.

Here Jesus ascends a mountain, and again he is visited by crowds whom he will feed (29-39). The repeated feeding is problematic, and the eccentric English deist Thomas Woolston was surprised that so great a crowd was not followed by "retailers of cakes and gingerbread."[4] But the "miracle of the loaves and the fishes" appears in all four gospels, so it must have been especially meaningful to the early church, whose members, like everyone else in the ancient world, lived perilously close to famine. Jesus had promised he would share a "Messianic Banquet" with his apostles in the kingdom of heaven (26:29), and feasting scenes, deriving in part from the pagan custom of funerary meals, are a recurring subject of catacomb art. It may be that these four thousand are Gentiles, since "they glorified the God of Israel." Augustine interpreted the feeding as "the preaching of the New Testament," and the "few little fishes" as Jesus' first believers who proclaimed the gospel in "the stormy sea of the world."[5] Furthermore, seven is a "Gentile number" (Acts 6:3), and the four has been taken as the four corners of the earth that will eventually be evangelized. After the second multiplication of the loaves and fishes, Jesus leaves for Magdala.

At the beginning of chapter 16, the Pharisees and Sadducees anger Jesus with their request for "a sign from heaven." The only sign that will be given to them is the "sign of the prophet Jonas" of death and resurrection (here, he repeats 12:39). The connection Jesus makes between the feedings and the "leaven of the Pharisees and of the Sadducees" (v. 11) is unclear, but their "leaven" evidently refers to the effects produced by their teachings as contrasted with the power of Jesus. The familiar phrase "signs of the times" (from Tyndale) was cited at the Second Vatican Council (1965) near the beginning of its most radical statement, *Gaudium et Spes* ("Joy and Hope"): "The Church has always had the duty of scrutinizing the signs of the times and of interpreting them in the light of the gospel."[6] It saw its task as entering into dialogue within the human family to promote the common good of individual dignity, human equality, social justice, and the avoidance of atomic and chemical warfare.

Jesus and his disciples then move on to what is the principle event in chapter 16, the Petrine Confession. Matthew 16:13-19 was the first Bible passage translated by Luther: it was from the Latin Vulgate, for a sermon on June 29, 1519, when he was in Leipzig for a "Disputation" with the Vatican's Johannes Eck. It appears only in Matthew and comes at 16 in response to Jesus' question at 13 (which should read, "Who do people say that the Son of man is?"). Since in the Synoptic tradition Jesus seems mostly concerned to communicate what he is not, it is tempting to speculate that more than one of Jesus' followers must have directly asked him who he was and how he understood his ministry and that information on this point may have entered the nonscriptural tradition and reinforced the early church's conviction of his divinity. Peter's "Thou art the Christ" (NRSV: "You are the Messiah") was a 1762 change in the KJV from "Thou art Christ." This follows the Greek; Latin lacks a definite article.

The setting is Caesarea Philippi, a heavily Gentile area in rural upper Galilee, where Herod's son Philip rebuilt the town of Panarea and named it "Caesarea of Philip" in honor of the Roman emperor (and himself) and to distinguish it from Caesarea Maritima on the coast. There is still great uncertainty on how Peter understood Jesus' messianic role, and it was not until Nicaea in 325 that Jesus was dogmatically identified as "true God of true God." Later, for Calvin, "the confession is short, but it embraces all that is contained in our salvation,"[7] and for many these words, not the incarnation, mark the true beginning of Christianity. Not so the Koran, which says: "The Messiah, the son of Mary, is only a prophet, prophets before him have passed away" (5.75).

Jesus' response to Peter's "confession," which appears only in Matthew, is one of the most contested passages in the Bible, both as to its authenticity—Is it a Matthean fabrication? A post-resurrection interpolation? If so, why here and not in the other gospels?—and as to its meaning—What does "this rock" refer to? How much is directed personally to Peter? Or to all the apostles in his name? What is entailed by "whatsoever"? How is this ecclesiastical authority to be exercised and transmitted? Who, in case of disputes, is to be the final authority? And what is meant by "the gates of hell"? Moreover, it is complicated by varying interpretations and competing denominational claims. What is uncontested is that Simon is given a new name—a nickname, actually—that in both Aramaic and Greek also means "rock," although it works better in Aramaic (*kepha*) than in Greek, where Peter is *petros* and rock is *petram*. Protestants have long noted the oddity that the papacy's powers should derive from a pun, but that someone embarking on a new phase of life receives a new name is familiar from Abram/Abraham and Sarai/Sarah (Gen. 17:5, 15) and, later, Saul/Paul (Acts 13:9). This custom was followed by subsequent popes—though none has chosen "Peter."

The mention of "church" (Tyndale: "congregation," suggesting a gathering rather than an institution) at verse 18 is rare and probably reflects not Jesus' words but Matthew's interest in Christianity as a community that must somehow organize itself in defense against its opponents and in expectation of the Parousia. (There is even a tradition that when the apostles were in hiding after the ascension and formulated their "Apostles' Creed," it was Matthew who introduced the words *sanctam ecclesiam catholicam* [Latin for "holy Catholic Church"]). The special commissioning of Peter, the leader and spokesman among the disciples and a link between its Jewish past and its missionary future, has been taken by the Roman Catholic Church as the foundation of the papacy, with some understanding the plurality of "keys" as additionally sanctioning the pope's civil authority—an interpretation much argued during the rivalries between Christianity's Eastern and Western churches and during the Reformers' attacks on the popes. Furthermore, some Catholics have darkly suspected that more recent scholarly arguments against the priority and Matthean authorship of the "first" gospel were yet another Protestant attempt to discredit the papacy.

Thus, this text has generated a long tradition of disagreement among commentators. Earlier Erasmus, following Origen and Ambrose, had considered the "rock" to be the faith of the church, and the Geneva Bible concurred in its notes (p. 9). Others, noting that this passage appears only in Matthew, have taken "rock" as referring to Jesus (1 Cor. 3:11), and John Wesley in his 1754 "Explanatory Notes" suggests that "perhaps, when Our Lord uttered these words, He pointed to Himself."[8] Or it may refer to Peter's confession of faith that Jesus is the Messiah, and "church" may refer to Jesus' contemporary community, with Peter named only as a representative or exemplary disciple, one who will share authority with the other eleven but only for his lifetime. In arguing against papal authority over Henry VIII, Thomas Cranmer, the king's Archbishop of Canterbury, contended that these words "were not spoken nor meant to Peter's person, but all bishops and priests and to the whole Church."[9] Other Reformers pointed out that his fellow apostles do not defer to him as their leader; that he is not singled out in the Great Commission of 28:19-20; that it was James, not Peter, who became the head of the Jerusalem church; and that the very connection of Peter with Rome is based on tradition, not on Scripture or history. They also argued that at 18:18 the powers of "binding and loosing" are given to all the disciples, and though it is unclear what exactly is to be bound or loosed (perhaps provisions of the law to be strictly or liberally applied), the implication is of a collegial sharing of power, and that Peter's role was to be representative, not authoritative. For Luther, the keys were given to the "whole Christian community,"[10] not just to Peter, and they "have no reference to doctrine or policy, but only to refusing or being willing to forgive sin. Whatever else the Romanists claim in virtue of the keys is an idle invention."[11] Still others have distinguished between the faith and the institutional church, with Jesus the cornerstone of Christianity but Peter here designated as the foundation of the ecclesiastical establishment. And all note that in 23:8-12 Jesus reminds his disciples that they are all "brethren" and only Christ is their master.

After the loss of Jerusalem, where James, not Peter, led the local community, the early church gradually divided into four great patriarchates, Rome, Alexandria, Antioch, and Constantinople, with Rome enjoying pride of place as St. Peter's church and, until 330, the imperial capital—though it remained unclear if its primacy was divinely ordained, if its authority was final, or if it could impose its will on other jurisdictions. The other patriarchates thought not, and they resisted its influence, though they naturally deferred to the imperial metropolis, the only "apostolic" city in the Western empire, the place where tradition had Peter serving as "bishop" and where he was martyred with Paul some time around 67. In his essay "On the Unity of the Catholic Church," Cyprian, a third-century bishop of Carthage and the first great theorist of church organization, maintained that these verses established a necessary unity amid Christian diversity (the church a single sun with many rays, a single tree with many branches, a single spring with many streams) as well as an apostolic succession (Islam recognizes a succession of prophets), with the implication that authority, at least in the West, would reside with the bishops of Rome.[12] Still, Peter's earliest successors were never designated as "popes" and had little effect on church history. But when Christianity was first permitted by Constantine in 313 and then officially established by Theodosius I in 391, the Roman church enjoyed imperial favors, including the Empress Fausta's Lateran Palace for its bishop and for its principal church a basilica built over the shrine to Peter's martyrdom in the Vatican. Prestige became power, a development that Roger Williams regretted. For "then began the great Mysterie of the Churches Sleepe, the Gardens of Christs Church turned into the Wilderness of Nationall Religion." For Williams this acquisition of power fatally compromised the purity of the faith, turning Christianity into militant "Christendome."[13]

The bishops of Rome gradually developed the mandate implied in these verses, though it was often disputed, as in 424 when North African bishops meeting in Carthage protested that they should conduct their own affairs "unless it be supposed that God can inspire one individual with justice and withhold it from a multitude of bishops in council."[14] So it was not until centuries later that Rome fully asserted its sovereignty as the "Holy" See (Latin *sedes,* "seat"; also *cathedra,* "chair," as in "cathedral"), claiming an unbroken and "apostolic" succession of popes and insisting on a preeminence of spiritual authority. Damasus (366–84), who commissioned Jerome's Latin translation of the Bible, was the first to speak of an "apostolic see" and to call his fellow bishops "sons," not "brothers." Supported by St. Ambrose, bishop of Milan and an ardent advocate of *Romanitas,* his successor Siricus (384–99) was the first to issue "decretals," letters resembling the communications that relayed imperial decrees to Rome's provincial governors. Next, Leo the Great, Rome's bishop from 440 to 461, a time when the city was no longer the capital of the empire, having lost that eminence to Milan in the West and Constantinople in the East (though neither could claim an apostolic connection), insisted that as Jesus had singled out one apostle, so must one individual—the bishop of Rome—inherit and exercise the powers entrusted to Peter. When he was faced with an independence movement by Gallic bishops, he persuaded Emperor Valentinian III to "decree by a perpetual edict [July 17, 445] that nothing shall be attempted by the Gallic bishops, or by those of any other province, without the authority of the venerable Pope of the Eternal City."[15] In 494 Pope Gelasius (492–96) reminded the Eastern emperor Anastasius that priestly power, entrusted with the care of immortal souls, including those of rulers, and answerable to God, is necessarily superior to royal power.[16]

The ninth century saw the forgery of the so-called Pseudo-Isidorian Decretals, a collection that exploited the name of the great Spanish saint and scholar Isidore of Seville (560–636) and purported to offer a series of earlier papal decrees as historical precedents for papal sovereignty. These were cited as authoritative in a succession of papal "Dictates" (1020–85) that were uncompromising, for example, "that it may be permitted to him to depose emperors"—a policy Pope Gregory VII (1073–85) carried out in deposing Henry IV during the Investiture Controversy.[17] Their use by Gratian, the "father of canon law," in his *Decretum* (1151) further justified papal absolutism, and they retained their authority until the Reformation. The primacy assured by these documents applied only to the Western empire, but it was enhanced when the title *Papa* ("Father") began to be reserved for the bishop of Rome, who also took over the old pagan and imperial title *Pontifex Maximus;* and it was buttressed by appeal to a number of other scriptural texts, particularly the "Feed my lambs . . . feed my sheep" instructions Jesus gives to Peter at John 21:15-18.

Pope Innocent III (1198-1216) is credited with promulgating the theory of the papal "plenitude of power," a power that is unshared, when he reiterated the eccentric tradition that the Aramaic *kephas* ("rock") in John 1:42 was, in part, "head" in Greek (*kephale*), and that although the church's body derives strength from its limbs (i.e., the faithful), the fullness of its power lies in its head, Peter and his papal successors: "I have received from Peter the mitre for my priesthood and the crown for my royal state."[18] So as God's earthly vice regent, the pope is above the law (who can judge him?) and enjoys unrestricted powers (who can resist him?). According to Boniface VII (1294–1303) in his decree *Unam Sanctam* (1302), the pope is preeminently the "spiritual" man of whom Paul said, "He that is spiritual judgeth all things, yet he himself is judged of no man" (1 Cor. 2:15). This accumulation of powers persisted throughout the Middle Ages, when Europe became a virtual theocracy, and it remains essentially intact today, though in practice much curtailed. It was forcefully reiterated at the Vatican Council on July 18, 1870, when, over strong protests, papal infallibility in matters of faith and morals was made church dogma. It asserts that the pope is not only the "vicar" of Peter but also the vicar of Christ—and indeed of God himself, since Jesus had given him, as the successor of Peter, the powers of "binding and loosing" that were the prerogatives of divinity.[19]

Challenging the "plenitude of power" was one of the Middle Ages' greatest philosophers, William of Ockham (1285–1347), an English Franciscan, who argued that such power was incompatible with the freedom of Jesus' New Law and effectively reduced Christians to slaves of the papacy. He interpreted Matthew's "servant" texts (20:25-27, 24:45-47) as showing that the pope's role in feeding his sheep is to provide spiritual nourishment, not to exercise political control, and that such control did not in any case extend to nonbelievers.[20] And John of Paris (1241–1306), a French Dominican, maintained that authority flowed up from the faith of the whole community and could only be defined by a general council. In addition to these theoretical objections were the competing political claims of Constantinople, Rome's great rival to the East and the emperors' capital, still flourishing after Rome's "decline and fall" had reduced the once powerful imperial city to a beleaguered provincial outpost. And just as Constantine had had to impose his will on quarreling churchmen at Nicaea in 325, his imperial successors in Constantinople were determined to "defend the faith," that is, to use the church as a unifying and supportive force within their own regimes. All power is from God, said Paul, and the rights of temporal rulers also had a firm base in scriptural history, for had not Jesus implied by his command to "render unto Caesar" that there was in fact a division of powers? And were not Melchizedek and Solomon and David both kings and priests? And though the bishop of Rome might claim that he had his power from God, had not Jesus said that his kingdom was not of this world? Yes, and successive popes were prepared to acknowledge the rights of rulers to administer their territories, particularly when it came to defending the rights of the church. St. Ambrose, while bishop of Milan, seems to have been the first major churchman to influence his emperor, interfering with Theodosius's attempt to punish Christian mobs in Thessalonica in 388 and 390, and pressuring Valentinian II not to permit the return of the pagan Altar of Victory to the Roman Senate. But popes also cooperated with Western rulers in defending Rome against barbarian incursions: in 452 Leo the Great journeyed to Mantua to persuade Attila and his Huns to spare the city (illustrated by a spectacular Raphael fresco [1512–14] in the Vatican), and at the end of the sixth century Pope Gregory (the first monk to become a pope) personally saved Rome from the Arian Lombards.

Nonetheless, since the spiritual is always superior to the material, at least theoretically, and the pope is directly answerable to God for all his flock, including his sovereign, he could always claim a final and universal authority. In the East the emperor crowned the patriarch of Constantinople, but in the West the pope's ultimate supremacy over the Holy Roman Emperor was confirmed by the *Translatio Imperii* ("Transfer of Power") when Pope Leo III crowned Charlemagne "Emperor of the Romans" on Christmas Day 800, giving him theoretical sovereignty over Byzantium (Luther: "In so doing, the Romanists wished to make the power of the Roman empire subject to themselves").[21] He was the "father," the rulers, like the other bishops, were his "sons"; he was the sun, they were the moon; he was the soul, they were the body; and, as Pope Leo IX reminded Michael Cerularius, the Orthodox Patriarch whom he excommunicated during the Great Schism of 1054, he was the hinge that "remaining unmoved, opens and shuts a door."[22]

Still, despite their theoretical superiority, the popes needed the secular powers to help them survive the upheavals of the next few centuries. And unfortunately, the authority they also claimed over the Eastern church was weakened by their isolation in Italy after losing Spain and Africa to Islam, and by doctrinal disputes such as iconoclasm and jurisdictional rivalries in Sicily and Bulgaria that contributed to their break with Constantinople in the eleventh century. A further problem was a succession of unworthy popes and the scandal of three rival claimants during what Petrarch called the "Babylonian Captivity" (1378–1417), when seven popes lived in Avignon, France. So it was not until the fall of the Eastern empire and its patriarchates to invading Turks in the fifteenth century that the papacy recovered some prestige as the center of Christendom. Meanwhile, the efforts of monastic reformers in the eleventh century at Cluny and elsewhere in northern Europe, for example, were giving the church new spiritual impulses; and by the late thirteenth century, the pope's authority in faith and morals came to be called infallible, much to the consternation of those who noted that it was the pope himself who would decide what constituted "faith and morals." This dogma was rejected by the Orthodox Churches, whose patriarchs claim only an authority of honor under the supreme authority of Christ.

Matthew 16:18-19 also inspired the notorious and fraudulent "Donation of Constantine," a late-eighth-century document supposedly dated March 30, 315, and said to have been deposited by the emperor on the tomb of St. Peter in Rome. In it Constantine, in return for a miraculous recovery from leprosy and permission to move his capital to Constantinople, purported to grant to Pope Sylvester I (314–35) and his successors temporal jurisdiction over the Western empire as well as the right to name its emperors, while handing over his Lateran palace and surrendering his royal standards, insignia, and clothing—even ordaining that clerics could wear white linen socks. It read in part: "We therefore ordain and decree that he shall have rule as well over the four principal sees, Antioch, Alexandria, Constantinople, and Jerusalem, as also over all the churches of God in all the world. And the Pontiff who for the time being presides over that most holy Roman Church shall be the highest and chief of all priests in the whole world, and according to his decision shall all matters be settled which shall be taken in hand for the service of God or the confirmation of the faith of Christians."[23] Though its authenticity was sometimes questioned, the "Donation" was long understood to justify the popes' creation and control of their own "papal states." (There is an irony in the popes' claiming powers from a Roman emperor that they felt they had already received from God.) In 1440 Lorenzo Valla (1405–57) proved it a forgery by showing that its terms were unhistorical and its Latinity was medieval. But visitors to the Vatican's "Sala di Constantino" (1519–25) can see the "Donation" taking place in a large painting, along with illustrations of Constantine's victory over Maxentius at the Milvian Bridge, his vision of the cross, and his baptism by Pope Sylvester in the Lateran basilica.

These papal states remained embroiled in a thousand years of European power politics and conflicts until 1861, when they became part of Italy and the pope was limited to control of Vatican City, a sovereign state under the terms of a 1929 Concordat with the Fascist regime of Benito Mussolini. For many Reformers this gradual acquisition of temporal power by the popes had compromised the "pure" Christianity of the early church, but it was also a warrant for Luther's conceding secular authority to civil rulers (who he assumed would be Christians). The abuses of papal power also offered arguments for those who would insist on the inwardness and spirituality of religion and would radically separate it from power politics. But "I came not to send peace, but a sword" (10:34) suggests a militancy that does not accord well with Scripture's more irenic texts.

The Reformers and their followers reinterpreted the "Petrine Commission," insisting that the church consists of a spiritual communion of the faithful and that its head is not the pope but Jesus Christ alone, as in the well-known hymn "The Church's One Foundation [is Jesus Christ her Lord]." Already in 1384 John Wycliffe wrote, "If you say that Christ's Church must have a head here on earth, you say truly; for Christ is the head. . . . And if you say that Christ must needs have such a vicar on earth, you deny Christ's power and place this devil [the pope] above Christ."[24] In 1415 one reason to burn John Hus at the stake was that in his book *On the Church* he claimed that the pope and the cardinals were only a part of the church. And with the defection of the Eastern church and the loss of Africa, Egypt, and much of Asia Minor to Islam, it did seem as if the gates of hell had begun to prevail against the Roman church.

In the Reformation, the Petrine Commission was central to the Leipzig Disputation of 1519, on Christian authority and the legitimacy of the papacy, between Luther and Johannes Eck. The outcome was inconclusive, but for Luther, who contended that the head of the church "can be none other than Christ," it was a critical step toward a break with Rome. Calvin thought the name Peter also belongs to all the faithful, and for about half of Book 4 of his *Institutes* he rails against the primacy of Peter, the usurpation of church authority by the popes (collectively called "the Antichrist"), and the privileging of Rome as the church's center of universal authority—"as if Rome, by the detestable murder of the Apostle, had procured for herself the primacy."[25] Others have found Jesus' choice of the often-unworthy Peter an intriguing parallel to God's choice of the often faithless Israelites in the Old Testament. As for the apostolic succession, the Catholic claim that its bishops enjoy a continuous ministry deriving from the apostles, even when the Reformers conceded an "episcopal" succession, they insisted that the true succession was one of Word and doctrine, not of particular persons, with honor and adherence reserved for whoever best preached the Scriptures.

Nevertheless, Catholicism's understanding of 16:18 is evident to visitors to Rome when they see it in Latin in gilded letters, each six feet high, under Michelangelo's dome within St. Peter's Basilica, itself built over a cemetery thought to contain the remains of Peter himself. Also in the Vatican is the magnificent fourth-century sarcophagus of Junius Bassus, which pictures the *Traditio Legis* ("Delegation of the Law"), a popular episode—though unrecorded in Scripture—in which Christ hands over the "New Law," often figured as a scroll, to Peter, much like a Roman emperor delegating authority. Going back to medieval drama is the representation of Peter, keys in hand, as heaven's doorkeeper, which has provided the first line for all the jokes about those arriving at heaven's "pearly gates" and being given or refused entrance.

Finally, the last words of verse 18 appear in the fourth stanza of the familiar hymn "Onward, Christian Soldiers" by Sabine Baring-Gould (1834–1924): "Gates of hell can never / 'Gainst the Church prevail, / We have Christ's own promise, / And that cannot fail."

The binding and loosing in verse 19 may be post-resurrection, since it so closely resembles John 20:23 on remitting and retaining sins. It is a Matthean proof text, along with the same words in 18:18, for the Catholic sacrament of penance, which came to be understood as vocal confession to a priest, since only he could decide whether the sins should be retained or loosed, and only after he had heard them. What Chaucer correctly calls "Confession of Mouth" (*Parson's Tale*) was approved by Luther despite its weak scriptural basis but was rejected by Calvin, who interpreted this provision as Jesus' assurance to the apostles that he would be with them in their preaching. It was not until 1215 and the Fourth Lateran Council that annual confession became a requirement (now obligatory only for mortal sins) under pain of excommunication.

Crossed keys are the symbol for St. Peter (crossed swords for St. Paul) and often appear on Catholic and Episcopalian seals. Besides representing position, privilege, and authority, the key suggests the presence of an institution, access to its interior, and the opening to a new life. Hence, it may recall the key of Isaiah 22:22, used to open and close the king's palace. For Aquinas it opened the way to salvation via the church and her sacraments.[26] But for the Reformers the keys belonged to the whole church, and their power resided in the preaching of the gospel, since it was preaching that unlocked the doors of Scripture (always provided, of course, that such preaching conformed to the Reformers' understanding of Scripture). For Milton in his "Lycidas," Peter was "the Pilot of the Galilean Lake," and "two massy keys he bore of metals twain

/ (the Golden opes, the Iron shuts amain)," presumably referring to salvation and damnation. If the "metals twain" are thought of as gold and silver, then for Catholics they could also represent the pope's spiritual and secular sovereignty, most famously evoked in Perugino's fresco, *The Delivery of the Keys* (1482), in the Sistine Chapel, with a background that suggests both spiritual and secular power, a domed church between two triumphal arches.

Verse 21 initiates a new division of the gospel, signaled, as in 4:17, by "from that time forth." Jesus is no longer the "Son of man" (except at 17:22 and 26:64) but is now called "the Christ," the "Anointed One," and here he announces to his disciples the journey south to Jerusalem and the events of his passion. This is the first of three such predictions (also at 17:23 and 20:19), and it is odd that after the crucifixion Jesus' disciples do not seem to recall them. But this messiah will not be a triumphant liberator as Peter and others hope, but a Suffering Servant; and those who follow him can also expect sufferings (v. 24). The rock has become a stumbling block, and Jesus calls Peter "Satan" (in the sense of "tempter"), since Peter wants him to fulfill human hopes for a national and political messiah. The unexpected harshness of the rebuke offers such a striking contrast with the commissioning of Peter in 17-19 that in antiquity it shocked Porphyry, and in recent times H. L. Mencken found it "a curious irony but not without its consolations to Protestants."[27]

Jesus then speaks to his other disciples, and the command to follow Jesus has been taken as a sign of his messianic self-awareness and authority. The other command, to take up their cross (also at Mark 8:34, 10:21; Luke 9:23), here meant as a call to assume the burdens of discipleship, is a foundation text for monasticism. It was also the call by Pope Urban at the Council of Clermont on November 27, 1095, to the men who joined the Crusades and pinned colored crosses on their clothes, thus creating the first military uniforms in post-classical Europe. "Girding" oneself "with the cross" was also invoked in Canon 3 of the Fourth Lateran Council (1215) in approving the extermination of heretics, with a promise of the same "indulgences and privileges granted to those who go in defense of the Holy Land."[28] But biblical swords tend to cut in many ways, so this could also be interpreted as a command to avoid public actions. The Radical Reformer and Anabaptist martyr Michael Sattler (1490–1527), in the sixth of the "Seven Articles" of the *Schleitheim Confession* (1527), maintained that just as Jesus refused to be a king, Christ's disciples should deny themselves public service once they take up his cross.[29]

The idea of the cross as weapon derives theologically from its role in Christ's victory over sin and death, and historically from its legendary appearance to the Roman emperor Constantine before the Battle of the Milvian Bridge in 312 with the words, "In this sign thou shalt conquer." The Christian apologist Lactantius, who was a tutor to Constantine's son Crispus, reported that the emperor was also instructed in a dream to have his soldiers make a version of the cross on their shields before that battle.[30] In 326 the True Cross was supposedly discovered in a cave under Jerusalem's Church of the Holy Sepulcher by Mark Twain's "good old enthusiast," Constantine's mother, Helena, who, as he noted, invariably found whatever she was looking for.[31] It was said to have been carried by Byzantine armies against their pagan foes, finally disappearing when Saladin took it to Damascus after defeating the Crusaders on July 4, 1187, at the Horns of Hattin outside Tiberias. Of course, fragments were among the medieval world's most popular relics, and in Rome the curious can visit the Chapel of the Relics in the (much-restored) church of Santa Croce in Gerusalemme, said to have been built by Constantine to preserve fragments of the True Cross that his mother had brought back from the Holy Land.

Although it came relatively late to Christian art and is rarely found in the catacombs, the cross is represented architecturally in the central nave and crossing transept of Christian churches. Protestants have traditionally preferred the empty cross as a sign of Jesus' victory over death, and for the same reason the Eastern churches usually replace the figure with precious stones. The Puritans tried to eliminate the cross from churches, but in "The Crosse" by John Donne it is everywhere: "Who can deny me power and liberty / To stretch mine arms, and mine own Cross to be? / Swim, and at every stroke, thou art thy Cross, / The mast and yard make one, where seas do toss. / Look down, thou spiest out Crosses in small things; / Look up, thou seest birds rais'd on crossed wings. / All the globe's frame, and spheres, is nothing else / But the meridians crossing parallels."[32]

Justin Martyr saw the cross's shape as symbolic of humanity: "The human figure differs from the irrational animals precisely in this, that man stands erect and can stretch out his hands, and has on his face, stretched down from the forehead, what is called the nose, through which goes breath for the living creature—and this exhibits precisely the figure of the cross."[33] For Athanasius the crucifixion had a symbolic fitness, for only on a cross could Jesus spread out his arms, so "that with one He might draw the [Jews], and with the other the Gentiles, and unite both in Himself."[34] This welcoming gesture can best be seen today in the Christ the Redeemer statue that rises high above Rio de Janeiro. Its counterpart in Christian symbolism is the circle, and the globe often seen in art at the foot of the cross images Jesus as the king of the world. The obvious contrast with the cross is the Communion host that in its composition recalls the bread of the Last Supper but in its roundness symbolizes perfection. This is the visual message of Raphael's great fresco *Disputation over the Sacrament* (1509–10; Vatican), where the circle of the host is repeated in the monstrance that holds it, in a roundel containing the dove of the Holy Spirit, in Christ's halo, and in the painting's semicircular frame. In the West the transition from a bare but ornamented cross to a crucifix, that is, with Christ crucified, not a triumphant victor but a suffering victim, took place in the ninth century; and in 1754 Pope Benedict XIV ordered that a crucifix be displayed on all church altars.

Today the cross remains Christianity's most potent symbol. It is mounted on churches, carried in processions, worn round their necks by ranking clergy as pectoral crosses, brandished against demons in popular culture, and regularly trivialized in costume jewelry; and it has generally been exempted from the OT law against graven images. The "sign of the cross" is a fundamental Christian gesture (Tertullian: "We make the sign of the cross on our forehead at every turn").[35] It is characteristic of Catholicism and Orthodoxy but also finding increasing acceptance among Protestants, particularly Lutherans. Its origins were in the earliest churches, whether marked on external objects or on the body, either on the forehead alone ("believing"), usually with the right thumb, then repeated on the lips ("preaching") and breast ("loving"). More common is the "large" sign, from forehead to breast and from shoulder to shoulder (left to right in the West, right to left in the East), either with the fingertips of the right hand or, symbolizing the Trinity, with the thumb and first two fingers, the other two folded in honor of Christ's two natures. There is a great variety in the words uttered during the sign of the cross, though they most often recall the baptism formula of the Trinity. The Reformers, however, rejected the traditional practice of making the "sign of the cross" before and after prayers and when entering or leaving a church.

Still, the veneration of the cross also had its opponents, and Claudius, a ninth-century bishop of Turin known for his opposition to relics, complained that "Christ ordered [his disciples] to bear the cross, not to adore it."[36] Bernard Gui, a fourteenth-century Inquisitor, noted that contemporary heretics, particularly the Manichaeans, resent any veneration of the cross, arguing: "No one adores or venerates the gallows on which his father or some relative or friend has been hanged."[37] Others complained that if the cross is to be glorified, so too should the crown of thorns and the lance that pierced Christ's side. But it could also be a mark of shame, with heretics sometimes obliged to wear double crosses, and dissenters brought before the Inquisition were fortunate if their repentance could win them the mildest sentence, the wearing of a large yellow cross on their clothing. John Adams (1735–1826) took a less-than-reverential view of the cross, writing to Jefferson: "I almost shudder at the thought of alluding to the most fatal example of the abuses of grief which the history of mankind has preserved—the Cross. Consider what calamities that engine of grief has produced."[38] Nietzsche objected to cross typology, part of what he called "the attempt to pull the Old Testament from under the feet of the Jews." "Whenever a piece of wood, a rod, a ladder, a twig, a tree, a willow, a staff is mentioned, it is supposed to be a prophetic allusion to the wood of the Cross."[39] Shaw, remarking how much he disliked the popular hymn "When I Behold that Wondrous Cross," saw it "not as an emblem of Christianity but as an emblem of what the Romans called justice, a very cruel, unchristian, and horrible thing."[40] And today some feel that its visual message of submission and suffering is an implicit argument for the acceptance of injustice and oppression.

The familiar words of verse 25 ("whosoever will lose his life for my sake shall find it"; also at Mark 8:35; Luke 9:24, 17:33) interested Albert Schweitzer when he read them as he was lying in bed on a summer morning in 1896: "I settled with myself before I got up that I would consider myself justified in living till I was thirty for science and art, in order to devote myself from that time forward to the direct service of humanity. Many a time already had I tried to settle what meaning lay hidden for me in the saying of Jesus! . . . Now the answer was found."[41] In 1905 he began the medical studies that would take him in 1913 to equatorial Africa. The equally familiar words of 26 appeared early in Christian literature when they were quoted by St. Ignatius of Antioch (d.117) in one of the seven letters he wrote while being escorted to Rome to be punished in the arena for not participating in the cult of emperor worship. This was a martyrdom he eagerly anticipated ("I am the wheat of God, and let me be ground up by the teeth of the wild beasts, that I may be found the pure bread of Christ").[42] They are also recalled in Robert Bolt's *A Man for All Seasons* (1960), when Thomas More learns that England's solicitor general has betrayed him in return for an appointment as attorney-general for Wales. "For Wales? Why, Richard, it profits a man nothing to give his soul for the whole world. . . . But for Wales?"[43]

The often-discussed "Son of man" here suggests the God who will judge man at the end time "according to his works." This was again a Matthean "rewards" sentiment that the Reformers carefully qualified in preserving the primacy of faith. These are rewards, Calvin warned, "which only those who have been adopted as sons by the Lord will obtain; and for no other reason than this adoption."[44] But in his *Life of Johnson,* Boswell cites this praise of works in objecting to the faith-righteousness of the Methodists: "The principal argument in reason and good sense against methodism, is, that it tends to debase human nature, and prevent the generous exertions of goodness, by an unworthy supposition that God will pay no regard to them."[45] Chapter 16 then concludes with another reference to the imminent Parousia, though at the time Matthew wrote there must have been few survivors from Jesus' lifetime. Moreover, the imminence of the end time is undercut by the parables of the leaven, the mustard seed, and the tares (ch. 13), which suggest a passage of time, and by the

Great Commission (28:18-20), which envisions an extended period of missionary authority.

Chapter 17 begins with the transfiguration, a kind of epiphany that concludes Jesus' Galilean ministry and proclaims his divine Sonship. Its likely location is Mt. Hermon on Israel's northern border, but one tradition puts it on Mt. Tabor, southwest of the Sea of Galilee and more accessible to pilgrims. However, it is not near Caesarea Philippi, and at about two thousand feet it is only relatively a "high mountain." The "voice out of the cloud" in this event looks back to the words spoken at Jesus' baptism, which it repeats, and looks forward to his ascension, though some prefer to see it as a visionary experience of the apostles (Jesus himself calls it a vision at v. 9) or as a transposed resurrection appearance. Its occurrence directly after Peter's confession, "Thou art the Christ," makes it appear as a validation of Jesus' messiahship, just as "hear ye him" underscores his authority. Since Matthew sees Jesus as the new Moses, his shining face (v. 2) recalls a similar description of Moses as he came down from Mt. Sinai (Exod. 34:29-30), a recollection that for David Friedrich Strauss was another example of how the evangelists used the Old Testament to mythologize Jesus.[46] The words of the heavenly voice were often invoked in the early church's christological controversies against, for example, the "adoptionists," who claimed that Jesus was only the adopted son of God. John Damascene (675–749), the last of the Eastern church fathers, offered a Neoplatonic reading in which the mountaintop represents perfection: "For the person who has arrived at the summit of love, in a certain sense, having gone out of himself, understands the invisible."[47]

But the episode was also a problem for the Bible's critics, and the making of the three "tabernacles" is still obscure. Thomas Woolston, commonsensical but captious, wondered about the conversation alluded to in verse 3: "The three greatest Prophets and Philosophers of the Universe could not possibly meet and confer together, but on the most sublime, useful and edifying Subject. It's strange that the Apostles, who overheard their Confabulation, did not make a report of it and transmit it to Posterity for our Edification and Instruction."[48]

At verse 10 his disciples question Jesus, and it is tempting to speculate how well these unschooled Galileans understood their own Scriptures (which they never quote) and how often they recognized these fulfillments that were so important for Matthew. Here Jesus explains that Elijah ("Elias") represents the Prophets (as Moses represents the Law), so he has already come in the person of John the Baptist. And just as Elijah and John suffered, so too must the "Son of man." Jesus' qualified allusion to Malachi 4:5-6 ("I will send you Elijah the prophet") is one of the texts that seemed to prove to Christians, on divine authority, that OT prophets did on occasion foretell the future. The "tabernacles" of verse 4 are tents where God "dwelt" with His people in the wilderness (Exod. 25:9) and where Peter vainly hopes that Moses and "Elias" will now remain with Jesus.

A nimbus of light, the traditional symbol of divine glory and often in the shape of an oval mandorla, became conventional in artistic representations of the transfiguration. In the Eastern church the transfiguration is an important feast day and is the subject of a great sixth-century mosaic in the apse of St. Catherine's monastery at Mt. Sinai. It is often represented on icons, since Orthodoxy sees as its mission the spiritual transfiguration of its members and their world. There it is the divine and uncreated light that also appears to the mystic who achieves a vision of God; and it will shine from Christ at his second coming. The physical experience of this light was the goal of the Hesychast (Greek for "quietness") movement developed among medieval Greek monks and combining meditation and the repetition of simple prayers with fixed posture and controlled breathing. It was the most important mystical exercise in Orthodoxy, and its claim to recover the light of Tabor caused great controversy within the church and in its relations with Western Christianity, where the mystical tradition is more spiritual than physical and tends to center on the events of the passion. The whiteness of Jesus' clothing is the only significant use of color in the Gospels, and the abundance of symbolic colors—red, green, black, rose, violet—in liturgical vestments is entirely a creation of the church. In the lower half of his *Transfiguration* (1517; Vatican), Raphael adds the story of the boy, probably an epileptic, whose demons Jesus' disciples could not exorcise (vv. 14-21). He is called a "lunatick" in the KJV, since such people were regarded as "moonstruck," or affected by the moon's changes.

The last episode in the chapter concerns taxes (24-27), presumably the temple tax. This is a uniquely Matthean event, with the evangelist featuring Peter, since it is he, not Jesus, who speaks to the tax collectors. Matthew then has Jesus explain that just as the Romans exacted tribute, often excessively and brutally, from their subject peoples but not from their own citizens, Jesus, as Son of the King, does not have to pay the annual temple tax, "half a shekel" (Exod. 30:13), but as a good Jew he is willing to do so, if only to avoid giving offense (though it is never reported that he brought offerings to the temple). Analogously, Jesus' followers do not have to pay Roman taxes, but it is better if they do. The question of tax obligations is not settled, but the episode ends wondrously when the shekel—about a two-day wage—appears in the mouth of a fish, a mysterious event with readers left wondering if indeed Peter found the coin. Although Origen allegorized this incident as Peter's "catching" a convert,[49] it was one example for David Strauss of how a folkloristic motif—a fish that swallows valuables—has infected the biblical narrative. Since it appears only here, many scholars regard it as, well, a fish story. To paraphrase Sportin'

Life in Gershwin's *Porgy and Bess* (1935), this may be one example of how "the things that you're liable / to read in the Bible, / They ain't necessarily so."

That the "children are free" was cited by Aquinas in arguing that Christians, as children of God, though subject to secular rulers, are not obliged to obey tyrants.[50] It was also a proof text exempting clergy from taxes, and in 1327 Pope John XXII argued that Jesus' willingness to pay the tribute must not be seen as implying the subordination of the church to the emperor. Luther later cited Jesus' voluntary payment as a notable example of the free and disinterested service that Christians should perform for their neighbors, but out of duty or kindness, not with an eye to gaining heavenly merit.[51] This event appears in a narrative fresco by Massaccio (1401–28) in the Brancacci Chapel in Florence, where side panels of the temptation of Adam and Eve and their expulsion from paradise suggest the atonement, and the fish that providentially supplies the coin foreshadows the resurrection. Visitors to the Sea of Galilee can dine on what is called "St. Peter's fish," but it is actually tilapia, caught in nets, not by hook and line.

Chapter 18 begins with the "church discipline" discourse delivered to the disciples and emphasizing humility and obedience (3-14, with children seen as models of meekness and submissiveness, not necessarily innocence or simplicity), fraternity (15-20), and forgiveness (21-35). This seems to be a collection of scattered comments (sometimes called the Little Sermon on the Mount) that Matthew has assembled here to instruct church members on how they should behave toward each other, and it again reminds readers of Matthew's interest in continuing Jesus' ministry as an organized community. It appears in the final chapter of Tolstoy's novel *Resurrection* (1860), when Nekhlyudov (a mouthpiece for Tolstoy) is overwhelmed by its message of forgiveness, an experience that causes him to read Matthew from the beginning until the Sermon on the Mount.

The reference in verse 3 to "little children" may not be as sentimental as it seems, since Jesus was probably alluding to the humility (v. 4) entailed by children's—or anyone's—lack of rights, privileges, or social standing. Celsus saw the allusion to children as yet another sign that Christianity appealed to the uneducated (3.44). The child here was said to be the later St. Ignatius of Antioch. Verses 1-6 were a proof text both for and against infant baptism, with the Anabaptists citing it as proof that even without baptism children "are surely saved by the suffering of Christ, the new Adam," and that "infant baptism is a senseless, blasphemous abomination, contrary to all Scripture."[52] But along with the "babes and sucklings" of 21:16, these were important verses for those Reformers who wanted to demystify and deprofessionalize Christianity by removing it from the anointed priests and academic theologians into the hands of laypeople guided by their preachers and inspired by what they took to be the plain and transparent sense of Scripture. Tolstoy's understanding of verse 3 assured him that he could read Scripture without regard for "all the interpretations of the wise critics and theologians."[53] The words about children were later quoted by Pope Pius XI in his encyclical *Non abbiamo bisogno* (1931) against the campaign by Italy's Fascist regime to suppress Catholic youth organizations.[54]

The next two verses appeared in two prominent historical contexts: Jesus' expostulation in 7 was cited by Abraham Lincoln in his Second Inaugural Address on March 4, 1865, with reference to the "offense" of slavery and the "woe" of the Civil War; and 8 was cited by the Radical Reformer Andreas Karlstadt to justify (against Luther's advice) the relentlessness of his attacks on the traditional mass and what he called "the idolatrous filth" of saints' images: "Christ never said that we should proceed slowly with offenses."[55] It was also recalled by Thomas Cranmer, the Archbishop of Canterbury, on March 21, 1556, as he thrust his offending right hand into the flames that were consuming him, for it was with this hand that he had signed a series of recantations pledging his return to Catholicism. When they failed to prevent his death sentence during the persecutions under Queen Mary Tudor ("Bloody Mary"), he recanted his recantations at the stake and perished as an Anglican martyr.[56]

Jesus next speaks of the "Son of man" coming "to save that which was lost" (v. 11), using a striking image for a Palestinian audience, since one of their shepherds would be sure to secure his flock before abandoning it to go off and search for a sheep that had strayed. But it is one source of the popular representation of Jesus as the "Good Shepherd" (more familiar from John 10) concerned to recover lost souls.

In complaining that the Bible is "one of the most miscellaneous books in the world," Edmund Burke argued in 1772 that "if we would preserve in the Church any order, any decorum, any peace, we must have some criterion of faith more brief, more precise and definite than the scripture."[57] Here at 18:15-20, Matthew's Jesus provides one scriptural basis for the sensitive subject of church discipline; and the passage is distinctively Matthean in its emphasis on community. It was also Luther's justification for claiming that even the pope was subject to the judgment of the church when, in his opinion, he was acting "contrary to the Scriptures."[58] Verse 17 also proved to Luther that any Christian, not just the pope, had the right to convoke a council, and Zwingli cited this passage to argue that the mandate of the church is organizational and jurisdictional, not educational and sacramental.

The same verse was scriptural authorization for "banning," "shunning," or "disfellowshipping" unworthy church members, although it exists in some tension with the "judge not" of 7:5 and the "tares" parable of 13:24-30, which advise tolerance. Since its usual consequence was loss of status and social ostracism, it was a powerful weapon against community dissidents. It was cited in the Anabaptists' *Schleitheim Confession of Faith* (1527), with the provision that offenders be "admonished twice in secret" and that the ban take effect "before the breaking of the bread, so that we may break and eat one bread, with one mind and in one love, and may drink of one cup."[59] Banning is still practiced by the Amish; a milder form is Quaker "disownment." Other Reformers used this passage to argue against secret confessions made to a priest, since it suggests that only the offended party can forgive an offense. Hence, it offered them a clear example of a procedure commanded by Jesus and scripturally attested that had been superseded by an ecclesiastical institution and enforced by manmade rules. Luther approved of secret confession to "any brother or sister," though he railed against what he called the "pestilential doctrines" of the "Romanists," whereby absolution and the assignment of penance were reserved to the clergy: "I refuse to go to confession because the pope has commanded it."[60]

"Tell it unto the church" (v. 17) has been a controversial injunction in church history (modern Christians often seem more interested in telling it to the media). For one thing, it offers the second and last appearance of *ekklesia* (Greek for "church") in the Gospels, here referring to a specific congregation, not the ideal institution of 16:18, with Matthew suggesting a relation between Jesus and his followers that is analogous to the covenant between Yahweh and Israel. Names matter, but in both cases its use by Jesus seems premature and hence doubtfully authentic, since it was not until the late first century that this became the name for Christian communities. It is also unclear if "church" here refers to its leaders or to the whole congregation, and it is surprising that Jesus should be so hard on heathens and publicans.

The English word *church,* like Scottish *kirk* and German *Kirche,* comes from the Greek *kyriakon* ("Lord's [house]"). Its first official use, referring to Christian houses of worship, was in 313 when the dying Roman emperor Maximin granted permission for their construction, and it was later brought to Europe and England by missionaries. "Catholic," in the sense of "universal," appears for the first time in an epistle of St. Ignatius, "To the People of Smyrna," toward the end of the first century ("Protestants" was the name given to those Reformers who protested against the Catholic authorities at the Diet of Speyer in 1529). Since the Quakers' founder, George Fox, regarded churches as meetings of the faithful, he referred throughout his *Journal* to the buildings as "steeple-houses."

Matthew's value as a resource is such that he has supplied proof texts to authenticate the claims of both church and state, papal supremacy and conciliar authority, absolutism and constitutionalism. In writing to the bishops of France in 1204, Pope Innocent III (1198–1216) cited "tell it unto the church" as a proof text for popes, "who have been called to the rule of the universal

church by divine providence," to make final decisions in whatever secular matters involve morality.[61] Hence, he could intervene in hostilities between England's King John Lackland (of Magna Carta fame) and King Philip-Augustus
of France (1165–1223) on the grounds that their treaties had been sealed by
religious oaths and hence came under church jurisdiction; and he could refuse
Philip when he petitioned for a divorce from his wife, Ingeborg of Denmark.
In arguing for a separation of church and state and for the privacy of religious
beliefs, Joseph Priestley, in 1791 one of the founders of Unitarianism, noted
that Jesus said nothing here of civil punishments for "trespasses." Priestley also
observed that when Jesus sent out his disciples in chapter 10, he did not send
them to the Jewish and Roman leaders so that, persuaded, they might impose
Christianity on their subjects. "On the contrary, their whole conduct shows
that they considered religion as the proper and immediate concern of every single person, and that there was no occasion whatever to consult or advise with
any earthly superior in a case of this nature." Finally, with reference to 28:20,
he observed that Christians, in seeking civil protection for their faith, "must
have forgotten that Christ himself had promised to protect his church."[62]

So "tell it unto the church" was central to the dispute between popes and
prelates: Is final authority vested in the papacy or in a council of bishops and
cardinals? Partisans of the pope based their position on the Petrine commission of 16:18; while their opponents noted that the College of Cardinals
elected the pope and that they were the "church" here in 17, with the power
to bind and loose proclaimed in 18. And they insisted that when Jesus at
28:20 promised to be "with you always," it was with the whole church, not the
popes. But the reference in 18 to binding and loosing, repeated from 16:19,
has often been cited in defense of papal authority, most notably by Pope Pius
II in his bull *Execrabilis* (1460), in which he sternly forbade, under penalty of
excommunication, any appeal from a papal decision to a future council.[63] Paradoxically, verse 18 also became the medieval world's strongest endorsement of
secular authority. John of Paris noted in his *Tractate on Royal and Papal Power*
(1302–1303) that there were kings before there were popes, that kings are also
concerned for their subjects' spiritual welfare, so there are, indeed, areas of
temporal welfare in which royal authority, itself derived from God, is autonomous and absolute.[64] It was also cited by Marsilius of Padua (1275–1342)
in his *Defensor Pacis* (1324). His argument was that the authority to indict,
judge, acquit, or condemn belongs not to any of the clergy but to the whole
community of believers, and that the authority of the pope was limited to assembling a General Council. Hence the state, comprising the whole body of
citizens, is the supreme legislative institution in society and has the right to
control the church, just as Jesus subjected himself to the authorities of his
world. In 1327 Pope John XXII condemned Marsilius's arguments for popular sovereignty as contrary to Scripture and hostile to the faith and excommu-

nicated their author. But his work had great currency among the advisors of Henry VIII in his break with Rome and in Parliament's passing the Act of Supremacy (1534) that made him head of the Church of England. Finally, "hear the church" (v. 17) was quoted by Pope Pius XI in his encyclical *Mit brennender Sorge* (1937) directed against the Nazi regime's campaign to suppress Catholic freedom and activities in Germany—"the divine mission of the Church, whose work lies among men and operates through men."[65]

Verse 20 (again from Tyndale) was generally cited in the early church to show the divine presence in liturgical assemblies, but it was also important for the Reformers, since it could warrant the transfer of worship from priests (Calvin: "a paltry few tonsured, shaven, linen-wearers"[66]) to all believers, and it also seems to rule out the custom of "corner masses," the private masses said each day by priests, often in cathedral chapels. It is a foundation verse for Congregationalists and is also invoked by those believers, such as Quakers, who prefer to dispense with churches and clergy, or Baptists, for whom the gathered congregation is the true church. John Locke (1632–1704) cited these verses in his "Letter Concerning Toleration" (1689) to argue against the necessity of ecclesiastical establishments for the "salvation of souls." It is quoted in Whittier's "The Meeting": "God should be most where man is least: / So, where there is neither church nor priest . . . / 'Where, in my name, meet two or three,' / Our Lord hath said, 'I there shall be.'"[67] It is also a proof text for Catholic advocates of "conciliarism," which would give primacy in church government to councils of bishops, not the pope. But Joseph DeMaistre (1753–1821), a notoriously conservative defender of papal (and monarchical) authority, denied its relevance since in his view such councils, assembled with difficulty and meeting only occasionally, could not provide consistent leadership.[68]

This passage must be supplemented by others—and there are not many—that suggest the degree of involvement by participants in the gathering, from silent spectators to active celebrants, as well as the use of prescribed ceremonies, set prayers and hymns, and the reading of scriptural texts. It is also recalled in a memorable speech by Tom Joad, the hero of John Steinbeck's *The Grapes of Wrath* (1939), movingly delivered by Henry Fonda in the 1940 film: "Wherever there's a fight so hungry people can eat, I'll be there."

Jesus' order to pardon "seventy times seven" (v. 22) was cited by Sebastian Castellio, whose 1554 book *Concerning Heretics* protested the torture and burning of Michael Servetus at Geneva the year before for denying the Trinity. Castellio was one of the few Reformers to plead for the toleration of dissenting voices, finding it shocking that Jesus, who in his lifetime was so "patient of injury," should now have followers who lash, burn, and drown those who do not understand Jesus' precepts "as the mighty demand."[69] Finally, the parable of the Wicked Servant illustrates the almost—but not totally—limitless forgiveness recommended in verse 22. This is a restatement of the Lord's Prayer's "Forgive us our debts as we forgive our debtors," teaching that people should treat one another with the same love, mercy, and forgiveness they receive from God. In this case the "debt," ten thousand talents, is so wildly exaggerated that numerologists have tended to allegorize it. Rabanus Maurus (780–856) saw them as the Ten Commandments that the Israelites had broken, and so God "sold" them into Babylonian Captivity. But when they were released and forgiven, they treated their Christian "fellow servants" so badly that they were delivered to the "tormentors," the Romans, who seized their land and destroyed their temple.[70]

7

Jerusalem

In chapters 19–25 Jesus leaves Galilee and moves south toward Jerusalem. Attended by his disciples and on occasion confronted by the Pharisees, he continues to teach, usually by parables. After entering Jerusalem amid cries of "Hosanna," he drives the moneychangers out of the temple. In chapters 24 and 25 parables yield to apocalyptic in his preaching on "the Mount of Olives," as he describes the tribulation of the end time, the Last Judgment, and the fires of hell that are awaiting those who refuse to do God's will.

> Both read the Bible day and night—
> But thou readest black when I read white.
> —William Blake

In chapter 19 Matthew presents two texts (12, 13-15) that have had significant human consequences, since they relate to marriage and celibacy. They are regularly cited in Catholic defenses of clerical celibacy, notably by Pope Paul in his 1967 encyclical *Sacerdotalis Caelibatus* (though without mention of the "eunuchs" of v. 12). Voluntary celibacy is a gift, and its special advantage is that it is both an "imitation" of Jesus and a renunciation of those human relationships that might impede Christian commitment. Important among the "eunuchs" are those who remain celibate in order better to serve the Lord, particularly in preparation for the tribulations that will precede his early coming. (Jesus may also be alluding to the celibate Essenes.) In the third century, Origen took this injunction (and 5:29: "It is profitable for thee that one of thy members should perish") so literally that he castrated himself while still a young man, an experience that may have later helped him see the advantage of allegorical and figurative interpretations. And for Peter Abelard, who was castrated at the order of the uncle of his lover, Heloise, these words, along with "cut them off, and cast them from thee" (18:8), had a special poignancy. His consolation was that, unlike Origen, he had suffered this mutilation at the hands of others; but like him, this awful fate had at least freed him from the forces of lust. "Only thus could I become more fit to approach the holy altars, now that no contagion of carnal impurity would ever again call me from them."[1]

While virginity and celibacy have a respectable place in Christian service, it was only one Kondraty Selivanov who, in late-eighteenth-century Russia, took these verses so literally that he founded a sect of eunuchs ("Skoptsy"), hoping to increase their number to the 144,000 souls who would be saved in the end time (Rev. 7.4). Also encouraged by 18:8, the Skoptsy saw their self-mutilation as a kind of radical circumcision and an act of spiritual transcendence. Boys as young as ten or twelve were ritually castrated, while a less drastic procedure was available to women.[2]

Other sayings of Jesus that seem to devalue marriage and family ties—or at least subordinate them to the ideal of ascetic celibacy—are 22:30 ("For in the resurrection they neither marry, nor are given in marriage") and Luke 21:23 ("But woe unto them that are with child"); to which can be added St. Paul's familiar endorsement of celibacy (1 Cor. 7:32: "He that is unmarried careth for the things that belong to the Lord"). These sayings, however, may also be interpreted as signs that in the kingdom of heaven these human ties will be transformed or transcended. And in his argument against the church's institution of marriage, Tolstoy noted that Jesus promised "everlasting life" to those who forsake wives and children "for my sake."[3]

The next paragraph (13-15) is one of a number of texts that associate children with the kingdom of heaven and was a Reformation proof text for the availability of God's grace, freely given, to those who could not possibly have done anything to merit it. Although Jesus does not baptize children—as was often pointed out by the opponents of infant baptism—Luther, Calvin, and other Reformers also saw this as a proof text for the practice, especially since in Luke 18:15 they are called "infants." Luther cited it in his dispute with the Anabaptists, and it was a favorite subject of the artist Lucas Cranach the Elder. Later it proved to those who reject original sin, like the Unitarians, that human nature is not innately and inherently depraved. Henry Ware (1764–1848) asked: "But if they were depraved, destitute of holiness, averse from all good, inclined to all evil, enemies of God, subject to his wrath, justly liable to all punishments, could our Saviour declare respecting them 'of such is the kingdom of God'?"[4] Similarly, in James Joyce's *Portrait of the Artist as a Young Man*, Temple asks, "If Jesus suffered the children to come, why does the church send them all to hell if they die unbaptized?"[5] But most will recognize this sentiment in the hymn "Jesus Loves Me, This I Know": "Little ones to him belong: they are weak, but he is strong."

The following section (16-22) deals with the biggest question of them all: How is one to gain "eternal life"? Jesus' response, with its allusion to the Ten Commandments and the Sermon on the Mount, has served as a proof text for the freedom of the will and the necessity of good deeds for salvation. But Chaucer's lusty Wife of Bath, while acknowledging that "Verginitee is greet perfeccioun," felt that Jesus' message here (v. 21) was for a young man "that wolde live parfitly— / And lordynges, by your leve, that am not I" (111, 117–18). Verse 17 was a favorite proof text for Catholics in their disputes with Lutherans and Calvinists, though even Aquinas had conditioned it with "The will of man should be prepared with grace by God."[6] The Reformers had to "qualify" and "interpret" the final injunction, since for them it was scripturally witnessed that no one could satisfy the law, and justification by faith took precedence over good works. Hence, Calvin devoted a section of his *Institutes* (4.13.13) to this passage, arguing that Jesus said this so that the young man might acknowledge his vanity and weakness and turn to faith for help.[7]

This passage also served as a proof for the freedom of the will, and it was argued by the Anabaptist theologian and martyr Balthasar Hubmaier that "willing and keeping must have always been in the power of the young man."[8] As a standard proof text for Arians, its mention of God alone provided a warrant for Unitarians arguing that theirs is the "original" Christianity, since there is no hint here of the Trinity, and the divinity of Jesus is not made explicit until John's gospel. William Ware (1797–1852) wrote in 1831, "In these and a multitude of similar expressions and declarations do we trace the origin of Unitarian Christianity, to the highest antiquity, to the words of our Lord himself. We think the gospels, when judged by the same rules, and read in the same impartial spirit as other books, are plain books on this subject, and would never suggest to a mind which approached them wholly unprejudiced such a doctrine as that of the Trinity or the deity of Jesus Christ."[9]

The problem of personal wealth caused Clement of Alexandria to deliver a sermon at the end of the second century, "The Rich Man's Salvation," that softened this injunction, partly by spiritualizing it ("It is the soul and the disposition which are to be stripped of the passions"), but mostly by distinguishing between the proper and improper uses of wealth, for if there were no wealth, there would be no almsgiving.[10] And in distinguishing "evangelical poverty" from the "vulgar mendicancy" of Catholic monks, Melanchthon claimed that Jesus wanted this man to be poor only so that he might give his wealth to others.[11] Hence, its official status is as a pious counsel, not an absolute command. But it continued to be taken literally by others, notably St. Anthony, who was said to have been fortuitously inspired by this verse to rid himself of his worldly possessions, give the profits to the poor, and retire to a desert hermitage.[12] This verse also recurs in the garden scene of Augustine's conversion in 386. When next in church, he had his decision confirmed by 6:34 ("Take therefore no thought for the morrow"). Remembering that Anthony began a new life when he happened to hear these verses, Augustine opened his copy of Paul's Epistle to the Romans, happened to read 13:13-14, and knew that his life had changed forever.

St. Anthony is credited with founding monasticism, the first organized attempt by Christians to follow Jesus' command literally and by poverty, chastity, and obedience to achieve spiritual perfection or completeness. He would be followed by St. Pachomius (286–346), the founder of community monasticism. The withdrawal, solitariness, and asceticism practiced by the monks found little favor among the Protestant Reformers, and history shows that the ideal of monasticism, to achieve the kingdom of God within oneself and to fulfill the command of neighborly love by constant prayer for others, was often betrayed by its imperfect realization. Nevertheless, the quest for spiritual perfection in an imperfect world (5:48: "Be ye therefore perfect, even as your Father which is in heaven is perfect") has been a persistent challenge to Christians.

No one responded to this challenge more literally than a prosperous merchant and moneylender from Lyons in southeastern France named Valdes (also Waldo and Waldes), who heard it preached one day in 1173 (so the legend) and, in the spirit of apostolic poverty and perfection, organized the "Poor Men of Lyons" (poor also in the sense of 5:3, "poor in spirit"), a reform movement better known in the annals of Christian heresy as the Waldensians. What is reported about them comes mostly from their adversaries within the church, but apparently they rejected oaths and judges, indulgences and intercessory prayers for the dead; they demanded a vernacular Bible since most did not know Latin; they scorned the priesthood and the hierarchy since they considered themselves, like the apostles, directly empowered by God; and they demanded the right—even for women—to preach, a privilege restricted by canon law to the ordained clergy under episcopal supervision and hence a critical issue. Peter Waldo (d.1205), as he was more commonly known ("Waldo" was Italian, and the "Peter" perhaps borrowed from St. Peter), gave up his wife and family, sold his worldly possessions, and, publicly invoking 6:24 ("Ye cannot serve God and mammon"), became a beggar and public preacher. Together with his like-minded followers, he embarked on a quest for spiritual sanctification. But his calls for radical ecclesiastical reforms—he was doctrinally orthodox—saw him excommunicated in 1184 and his followers hunted down. Eventually, he recanted, but his followers persisted, dividing into a number of sects that rejected masses, pious practices, and all sacraments except baptism and the Eucharist. Christianity's first "Protestants," the Waldensians were one of orthodoxy's most persistent dissenters (some communities still survive in northern Italy today) and were among the first victims of the Inquisition. Their persecution was immortalized by Milton in his Sonnet XVIII, "On the Late Massacre in Piemont."

An orthodox version of the Waldensians' asceticism and idealism was created by the new mendicant orders of Dominicans (O.P. for "Order of Preachers," but popularly known as *Domini-canes*, "Watchdogs of the Lord") and Franciscans, whose founder, another wealthy young man, was born in 1182 and converted to poverty in 1206. Francis's "little brothers" (*Fratres minores*, or "Friars minor") were at first an order pledged to evangelize while working and begging, living as itinerants without a Rule and without the security of local monasteries. In 1209 Francis met with Pope Innocent III and received grudging permission to organize his followers but on the condition that they restrict their preaching to morality, not complicated matters of theology. Unlike the Waldensians, the Franciscans accepted the institutional church, though they soon divided into two groups: the radical "Spirituals," who insisted that all the clergy should imitate Christ by giving up their personal property, and the "Conventuals," who resembled a traditional order. The monastic vow of poverty was rejected by the Reformers, with Melanchthon distinguishing between good poverty, which results from giving to others, and bad poverty, when monks expect to receive from others.

Jesus' illustration (v. 24) of the spiritual burdens imposed by wealth has continued to impress readers—though there is nothing here about how to bridge society's gap between the rich and the poor. In his encyclical *Rerum Novarum* (1891), the first to deal with industrialized society, Pope Leo XIII cited verses 23-24 in reminding Catholics of the right use of the wealth generated by capitalism, adding that one day the "King" will want to know what they did for "the least of these, my brethren" (25:40).[13] In the early church, Celsus's claim that Jesus took this idea from Plato, who had once written that it was impossible for a good man to be rich (*Laws* 743A), caused Origen to scoff at the notion of a Jewish carpenter's son reading Platonic dialogues (6.16, 329). But more to the point, Porphyry wondered what Jesus would say of the wealthy who are virtuous and the poor who are wicked.[14] Later, moralizing preachers liked to imagine that there was a particularly small gate in the Jerusalem wall called "Eye of the Needle," to be used by pedestrians when the main gate was closed, and for which camels had to have their baggage unloaded before passing through; hence the lesson that the burden of our worldly possessions may keep us out of heaven. In 1925 Aimee Semple McPherson (1890–1944), the notorious Californian evangelist, used a live camel when preaching on this text in one of her "illustrated sermons."

Some forty-five states refer to a divine power in their mottoes or constitutions. For example, "With God all things are possible" (v. 26b) is the state motto of Ohio. These words, reportedly suggested by a Cincinnati schoolboy, were adopted by the Ohio legislature in 1959, but in 2000–2001 they had to survive a lawsuit by a Presbyterian minister who claimed that the motto "trivialized" his faith and by the American Civil Liberties Union, which argued that it favored Christianity and hence violated the Establishment Clause of the First Amendment. But the Sixth Circuit Court of Appeals eventually ruled that its words were generic and decontextualized and that it was a symbol of "a common identity," much like "In God We Trust" on American currency. A dissenting opinion found that Ohio's motto "conveys a sectarian view of God as interventionist, active and omnipotent," and it is true that this verse has often been cited in defense of such marvels as the incarnation and the resurrection.[15]

Peter protests (v. 27), and his words were repeated to Erasmus by a monk who then claimed that "in this is perfection." Erasmus disagreed, arguing that "true religion consisted in the offices of charity."[16] The Latin Vulgate rendering has also been wittily applied to Catholicism's four major orders: "Behold [us]" to the Benedictines for their splendid liturgies; "we have forsaken all, and followed thee" to the mendicant Franciscans; "what therefore?" to the philosophizing Dominicans; and "[it] will be ours" to the aggrandizing Jesuits. Jesus then responds (v. 28) with another eschatological "prediction" that did not come to pass. But it has become an important text in millennium scenarios that call for the conversion of the Jews—to their consternation—before Christ's thousand-year reign, with "judging" understood as "ruling." Most millenarians tend to find this item in the end time agenda even more embarrassing than the need to rebuild the temple on the present site of Islam's Dome of the Rock. But it made a notable appearance in "To His Coy Mistress" by Andrew Marvell (1621–78), where the impatient lover thinks that if they had "but world enough, and time," his lady could "refuse / Till the conversion of the Jews." Still, the biblical evidence for the precise roles and relationships of Jesus, the Son of man, and the disciples in the kingdom of God is incomplete, inconsistent, and inconclusive.

According to one version, verse 29 was cited by Pope Urban II in the notorious "Crusade Sermon" he preached at the Council of Clermont on November 27, 1095. This was the sermon in which he promised salvation—or so his words were understood—to those who might die en route or in battle. At its conclusion, his audience rose to its feet shouting *Deus lo volt!* ("God wills it!"), which became the battle-cry of the Crusaders. It was also cited by Luther in asserting that subjects may renounce their allegiance to a ruler whose policies are evil. Earlier he had cited the final verse of chapter 19 in 63 and 64 of his *Ninety-five Theses* (1517), contrasting the "holy Gospel" with the "treasure of indulgences," which makes the "last to be first." On the other hand, Voltaire wondered why, if the "first shall be last," he was so much poorer than the Archbishop of Toledo.[17]

Chapter 20 begins with the uniquely Matthean parable of the Vineyard Laborers (the source of the expressions "the chosen few" and "at the eleventh hour"), illustrating how the generous availability of God's grace may exceed human notions of proportional justice and social equity. Like Jesus' law of love and the stress on inner virtue in the Sermon on the Mount, this parable is an eloquent response to those who find in Matthew's Jesus an excessive emphasis on external works and their rewards and punishments. Hence, in 1525 Luther found a good Protestant message in the parable, specifically in verse 15: salvation depends on God's mercy, not on works, as the first laborers discovered to their dissatisfaction. The last laborers have generally been identified with Christians, who came late to faith and caused the Jews to murmur "against the goodman of the house"; and the "penny" has been identified as representing eternal life. Early exegetes liked to correlate the hours of the day with periods of biblical history from Adam to Jesus; or with the succession of patriarchs, prophets, and apostles; or Jews, Christians, and Gentiles. Muslims see morning, noon, and evening corresponding to Judaism, Christianity, and Islam. Or the hours could refer to the ages of an individual's life, with the last laborers representing those who converted late in life. In a retelling of the parable in *Pearl*, a fourteenth-century poem about the death of a young girl, even her two years of life qualify her for the joys of salvation. But Senator Robert Byrd, in his famous 1964 argument against the Civil Rights bill, cited 15a to justify a property owner's right to discriminate (he also used the story of the wise and foolish virgins [25:1-13] as a proof text for social differences: "If all men are created equal, how could five of the virgins have been wise and five foolish?").[18]

Matthew is not a gospel for sentimentalists, and that only a few will be "chosen" or saved (16; repeated at 22:14) has been a rich source of Christian pessimism, even despair, since it seems to suggest that God's justice requires almost all Christians (assuming Jews, heretics, and pagans are already condemned) to suffer the fires of hell. (Its grim counterpart in the Old Testament is the many who perished, the few who were spared, in the Flood.) Later, Augustine tried to redress the imbalance between the few who are saved and the many who are condemned by adding unbaptized infants to the latter total. For some these familiar words can encourage a spiritual smugness: "We are God's chosen few, / All others will de damned; / There is no room in heaven for you; / We can't have heaven crammed."[19] But many have found this difficult to reconcile with God's infinite benevolence, the purpose and effectiveness of Christ's redemptive ministry, other biblical texts promising universal salvation (such as 1 Tim. 2:3-4: "God . . . will have all men to be saved"), and the demonstrable virtue of so many non-Christians. For example, a popular medieval legend, often represented in art and recorded by Dante in his *Divine Comedy* (*Purgatory* 10, 73–93), held that the Roman emperor Trajan was so just and charitable that through the intercession of St. Gregory he was removed from limbo and restored to earth so that he could become a Christian and be saved. But Trajan could hardly make up for the countless peoples who have lived in "invincible ignorance" of Christianity, and it is regrettable that the New Testament says nothing of their place in the scheme of redemption. Again, the Bible may be religiously authoritative, but it is not exhaustive.

Although Paul provided the basic text: "For whom he did foreknow, he also did predestinate" (Rom. 8:29), and Augustine the theological rationale, these words, along with verse 23, that say that places at the messianic banquet have been "prepared of [by] my Father," have also been cited in the Western church's discussions of predestination, that long debate between partisans of free will and those of divine election and condemnation ("reprobation"). Pitting divine justice against divine love, logical speculation against available evidence, it was a problem that for Milton even devils could not resolve, as they talked "Of Providence, Foreknowledge, Will, and Fate, / Fixt Fate, Free Will, Foreknowledge absolute, / And found no end, in wand'ring mazes lost" (*Paradise Lost*, 2.557–61). The orthodox view is that election and reprobation lie remotely in God's eternal and inscrutable will (Hamlet: "There's a divinity that shapes our ends") and proximately in the cooperation of human freedom with enabling grace ("Rough hew them how we will"). But that God's decision to save or to condemn simply confirms an individual's moral choices seemed to Calvin (and others) to be a version of Pelagianism, the fifth-century heresy that salvation depended largely on human effort, with divine grace serving as an aid to individual initiative. To this the orthodox had responded that Pelagianism denied original sin and subverted divine sovereignty. Man, they argued, was dependent on God, not God on man. Calvin quoted the uncompromising words of 15:13: "Every plant, which my heavenly Father hath not planted, shall be rooted up."[20] One traditional "explanation," as in the Lutheran "Formula of Concord" (1577), distinguishes between fore-knowledge and fore-ordination: that God foresees but does not cause those actions that will lead to damnation, though to orthodox Calvinists this has the unacceptable implication that God's decrees are partially determined by human choices. For many of the faithful it is a source of great comfort and assurance to feel that through predestination they are the object of a divine initiative, that God will not forsake them, and that their personal piety and virtue are "signs of election." In fact, far from inducing complacency, these "signs" can operate as a stimulus to further sanctity.

Predestination was first qualified by the Dutch theologian Jacob Arminius (1560–1609), who saw human weakness as an inclination to sin but not a propensity. He invoked God's foreknowledge and respect for human effort. But the traditional view—"unconditional election" and "irresistible grace"—was confirmed at the Synod of Dort (1618–19), and "Arminianism" became something of a Calvinist heresy. For other Protestants, the classic break with what Luther called "that hidden and fearsome will of God" and even Calvin called a "dreadful decree" came with the Anglican revivalism that led to Methodism. Specifically, it came with John Wesley's 1739 sermon "Free Grace," in which he argued that predestination violated the spirit of the Bible, which is God's love ("This doctrine not only tends to destroy Christian holiness, happiness, and good works, but hath also a direct and manifest tendency to overthrow the whole Christian revelation").[21] Here Wesley applied the Reformers' famous—and, for some, notorious—"analogy of faith," whereby isolated passages of Scripture are to be "referred to Christ," that is, understood in the light of faith and in accordance with what they took to be the whole tenor and message of the Bible. (This was the hermeneutical principle that enabled the Reformers to qualify Matthew's apparent endorsement of meritorious works, usually by privileging Paul's theology of faith and grace.) Wesley went on to base salvation or damnation on the individual's voluntary response to the "prevenient" grace of God, which is available to all, and the workings of the Holy Spirit. The Quakers, following Robert Barclay's authoritative *An Apology for the True Christian Religion* (1678), reject double predestination, labeling it "horrid and blasphemous." But still the logic—and mystery—of predestination remains and must be acknowledged as such by most Christians, though it seems to have had little effect on moral conduct in that anyone's sense of election led to complacency or of reprobation led to despair.

In debating with Shaw, Chesterton looked at predestination from the viewpoint of a Catholic polemicist: "To the Catholic every other daily act is a dramatic dedication to the service of good or evil. To the Calvinist no act can have that sort of solemnity, because the person doing it has been dedicated from eternity, and is merely filling up his time until the crack of doom. The difference is something subtler than plum-puddings or private theatricals; the difference is that to a Christian of any kind this short earthly life is intensely thrilling and precious; to a Calvinist like Mr. Shaw it is confessedly automatic and uninteresting. To me these three score years and ten are the battle. To the Fabian Calvinist they are only a long procession of the victors in laurels and the vanquished in chains. To me earthly life is the drama; to him it is the epilogue."[22]

The rest of this chapter (17-34) and the next, which begins Jesus' Jerusalem ministry, follow Mark (10:32–11:14). For the third time, Jesus prophesies his passion, death, and resurrection (19), and then has to remind the mother of James and John, who has ambitions for her sons and wants them to have places of honor at the messianic banquet, that the "cup" Jesus specifies is one of suffering, not of drinking. Since a different sort of hierarchy will prevail in his kingdom, he expects his disciples to be servants, not masters. Ironically, it will not be her sons but two thieves who will be at Jesus' right and left and will share his cup of suffering. So their selfish hopes will be unfulfilled, since they play no important role in the early church (though in AD 44 James was the first of the Twelve to be martyred, and John was sometimes taken as the author of the Fourth Gospel). Mark has the two brothers address Jesus directly, but Matthew shifts the burden to their pushy mother. Jesus' words, that honored places in heaven are "not mine to give," imply his subordination to the Father and hence served as an Arian proof text and was cited by John Milton in arguing against the Trinity in Book I.5 of his *Christian Doctrine* (1652–74).[23]

Pope Gregory the Great (540–604) used verse 27 to coin the papal title *Servus servorum Dei* ("Servant of the servants of God"). Later, in responding to his condemnation by the pope, John Wycliffe cited this incident in insisting that "the Pope leave his worldly lordship to worldly lords." Verse 25 was cited in Article 4 of the *Barmen Declaration* (1934), in which Germany's "Confessing Church" stated the Lutheran opposition to the "German Christian" movement sponsored by the Nazis. With this verse they rejected the regime's appointment and imposition of "special 'leaders' equipped with power to rule."[24] This leader was "Reichsbishop" Ludwig Müller (1883–1945), a close friend of Hitler's, whose followers sought to rid Scripture of its Jewish presence by eliminating the Old Testament and the epistles of "Rabbi" Paul.

Atonement

> For unless you know why Christ put
> on flesh and was nailed to the cross,
> what good will it do you to know
> merely the history about him?
> —Melanchthon

Jesus' announcement here that he will give his life as a "ransom for many" (v. 28; also at Mark 10:45) and later "for the remission of sins" (26:28) reminds readers that one of the oddities of Christian theology is that its central concern, Jesus' redemptive work (if that is what it was) to repair the damage caused by human sin, has been much discussed but never formally defined and proclaimed. It was not part of the evangelists' teaching; it was not treated in depth by the early church fathers; it was not on the agenda of any councils; and there is no "Feast of the Atonement." Though generally understood as beginning with the incarnation and aiming at the restoration of a right relationship between man and God, it lacks a firm scriptural and patristic basis, perhaps because the early church looked forward to a second coming (the New Testament ends effectively with Rev. 22:20, "Come, Lord Jesus"), not backward to what Jesus might have accomplished in his first coming. Even the Nicene Creed, basic and authoritative for all Christian denominations, is vague, speaking only of Jesus becoming incarnate "for us and for our salvation." And since secular ethicists have never agreed on questions of human crime and punishment; of innocence, guilt, and judgment; and of retribution, retaliation, and expiation, these problems become infinitely more complicated when they involve God's sovereign powers, divine justice, and inscrutable will. So what was God's purpose in ordaining Jesus' earthly mission? What was the "Divine Plan"? Did "redemption" reside in Jesus' incarnation, in his ministry, or in the self-sacrifice of his suffering and death? Or did it reside in his resurrection and ascension? What did his "victory over Satan" entail? How and when was it achieved? For whom was it intended? Was it a "ransom for many" as here, or "for all," as in 1 Timothy 2:6? To whom was it paid? Why did it not appear to lighten the world's burden of sin, evil, and suffering? Was the fact that God became man enough to divinize humanity, raise it up from its fallen state ("God became man so that man might become God [i.e., enjoy fellowship with God]")? Or was it the purpose of his ministry to bring mankind knowledge of God, to reveal God's love through himself, and to help mankind become pleasing to God? Or was his defeat of the devil—as in the temptation narrative and the many exorcisms—a saving example for his followers? Or were his suffering and death necessary to make up for what was lost by Adam's sin? To placate an offended God? And was his resurrection, his victory over death, intended to overcome the mortal death that was Adam's penalty? Was Jesus the paschal lamb whose sacrificial blood, shed at Passover, cleansed mankind of sin? Or was his death an expiatory and substitutionary sacrifice on the model of Isaiah's "Suffering Servant" (53:11), with Jesus as the good shepherd who "giveth his life for the sheep" (John 10:11), accepting the punishment owed by sinners and by his blood blotting out the sins of mankind? Why could not all of this have been effected by God alone? And how were the benefits of Jesus' passion to be passed along to humanity, both believers and nonbelievers? Through the preaching of Scripture? Or through the church's sacraments? Or in each individual's act of faith? Or is the redemption in the future, to be accomplished at the second coming?

These are all important questions, and the Gospels' responses are only marginally useful in helping Christians understand and formulate the doctrine— or, better, the mystery—of the atonement. In this passage, Jesus' redemptive mission is seen, analogously or metaphorically, as a "ransom," the paying of money to free—or "redeem"—a slave or captive. (It appears in the familiar Christmas hymn: "O Come, O Come, Emmanuel / And ransom captive Israel.") The theology developed from these references—and there are not many—sees mankind as victimized through Adam, and slaves and captives of sin who must be bought back "from the power of Satan unto God" (Acts 26:18) by the payment of Christ's blood. Unfortunately, neither Mark nor Matthew expands on this "ransom" term, which they may have derived from Paul (1 Cor. 6:20: "Ye are bought with a price"), and Adam is not mentioned in the Gospels.

Ransom has been just one of the metaphorical ways of understanding and formulating the Christian doctrine of the atonement (Tyndale's translation of the Greek *katallage*—and one theological term that does not come from an ancient language). Other terms for atonement, most of which are used by St. Paul, are sacrifice, deliverance, martyrdom, expiation, satisfaction, justification, propitiation, transformation, restoration, redemption, and, in the Eastern church, deification or divinization. A multiplicity of terms, each supportable by scriptural citations, none dogmatically defined—together they contribute to that branch of Christianity known as "soteriology," the theories regarding Jesus' salvific mission. Some early theologians, such as Irenaeus, Tertullian, and Origen, understood atonement rather crudely as Christ's victory (as foreshadowed in the temptation narrative) over Satan, who through the Fall had acquired power over humankind. God, who had been offended by Adam's sin, could not forgive man, so instead He sent His Son to free Adam's guilty race with the ransom of his own blood. The devil accepted Jesus as ransom for mankind, only to be deceived by the human appearance that concealed Jesus' divinity, and was finally overcome when Jesus escaped his power and rose from the dead—thus delivering mankind from Satan's dominion. For Augustine in a striking, if homely, formulation, "The cross of the Lord was the devil's mousetrap; the bait by which he was caught was the Lord's death."[25] For Gregory of Nyssa (330–95) the bait was Jesus' human flesh, the hook his hidden divinity, with the devil, like a fish, forced to regurgitate Jesus along with everyone else he had swallowed since the Fall. Jesus, victorious in battle, frees the prisoners whom Satan had captured.[26]

The rough justice of this exchange was refined in a later formulation, one that bypassed the military imagery and the devil and eliminated the rather tawdry notion of God's dealing successfully, if deceptively, with Satan. It was still an objective model, but one based instead on satisfaction done vicariously by Jesus to God's offended honor, and it was provided by St. Anselm of Canterbury (1033–1109) in Book 2 of his *Cur Deus Homo?* ("Why Did God Become Man?"), in 1098 the first book-length study of the subject. "It is necessary that God should fulfil His purpose respecting human nature," Anselm wrote. "And this cannot be except there be a complete satisfaction made for sin, and this no sinner can make. . . . None therefore can make this satisfaction except God. And none ought to make it except man. . . . One must make it who is both God and man."[27] It is through their faith in Jesus, who is both man and God, that Christians can appropriate for themselves the merits of the atonement (Jesus' self-sacrifice being excessively meritorious), and it is through the church and its sacraments that sinners come to know Jesus in a faith relationship. A brilliant formulation, it is sometimes described as "penal substitution," though it is unclear how this "appropriation" operates in individual lives, and some might object to the conception of God as an angry judge requiring compensation—the bloody sacrifice of His divine son—for sins He could also forgive. On the other hand, too easy a forgiveness could offend against justice and trivialize the seriousness of human sin and the damage it does to the world. But did Jesus not twice say, "I will have mercy, and not sacrifice" (9:13, 12:7)?

Other problems with Anselm's theory are that it favors the passion over the resurrection; that it seems to entail an even greater evil than it seeks to remedy, the suffering and death of God in the person of the innocent Jesus at the hands of men; and that it fails to allow for Jews and pagans in God's saving action. It also tends to make atonement a matter of divine justice without human involvement. Still, it was taken over by Aquinas in Part III of his *Summa Theologica,* where he discusses the incarnation and goes on to argue that Jesus in his passion pays—indeed, overpays—the debt of punishment incurred by sinful humanity. This debt might have been forgiven by God, but it was His will that just as individuals can demonstrate love and charity in helping each other, so only Jesus' sufferings could make the sort of satisfaction that is acceptable to God: "For by suffering out of love and obedience, Christ gave more to God than was required to compensate for the whole human race."[28] This satisfaction, however, is not automatically effective; it must be appropriated by individuals through the church's sacraments, with non-Christians sharing in the benefits on the basis of their life and merits.

Anselm's younger contemporary, Peter Abelard (1079–1142), generally accepted these "objective" theories, though he was not edified by the thought of God's requiring, or at least accepting, the blood of His innocent son as the price of reconciliation. So he suggested a subjective model, with an emphasis on love, not justice, on Christ's inspiring words and exemplary life rather than his sacrificial death. For Abelard the incarnation was an act of divine love ("So our redemption is that supreme love inspired in us by the passion of Christ"), and Jesus' humanity was God's gift to mankind, inspiring in humans a corresponding love for Him and for their neighbors (1 John 4:11: "Beloved, if God so loved us, we ought also to love one another").[29] This was indeed an inspiring theory (and it had been discussed by the early church fathers), shifting the emphasis from Jesus the lamb to Jesus the man. It is widely current today, though his critics have noted that it seemed to allow too much to free will and not enough to divine grace. It led to a secular and demystified version of the atonement, a redemption without the devil and without the cross, as the dying savior turned into a sublime and inspiring teacher, his life a lesson in virtue. William Ellery Channing, writing in "Unitarian Christianity" in 1819 said: "We regard him as a Saviour, chiefly as he is the light, physician, and guide of the dark, diseased, and wandering mind."[30]

Atonement was not an issue in the Reformation, and God's forgiving love remained its basis for Luther, a blend of satisfaction and transference, which he took from Anselm and Aquinas. With Calvin and the other Reformers, he saw Jesus voluntarily enduring the punishments owed by sinful man, the benefits then acquired through the sinner's faith in Christ and the workings of the Holy Spirit. Scripture, according to Calvin, teaches that man was "estranged from God through sin, is an heir of wrath, subject to the curse of eternal death, excluded from all hope of salvation, beyond every blessing of God, the slave to Satan . . . at this point Christ interceded as his advocate; took upon himself and suffered the punishment that, from God's righteous judgment, threatened all sinners; that he purged with his blood those evils which had rendered sinners hateful to God; that by this expiation he made satisfaction and sacrifice duly to God the Father; that as intercessor he has appeased God's wrath; that on this foundation rests the peace of God with men."[31] Bach gave voice to this vicarious and "substitutionary" satisfaction in his *St. Matthew Passion:* "The master pays the penalty for his servants" (Chorale 55), and "He bore for us the heavy burden of our sins" (Double Chorus 35). And it is reflected in words from the popular hymn "Rock of Ages": "Nothing in my hands I bring. / Simply to thy Cross I cling." John Wesley and the Methodists were more optimistic, arguing that the atonement relieved sinners of their helplessness and their inherent depravity; it was a divine initiative to which one could respond or not through the church.

As usual, not all have been persuaded, much less edified, by juridical or penal interpretations. Although we speak of bearing one another's burdens (so Gal. 6:2), and the innocent must often endure and try to right the wrongs of the guilty, for Jews, Muslims, and those Christians who insist on personal autonomy, it is the individual who must work out his or her own atonement. Early on, Celsus wondered why God could not have saved humanity Himself, or why He waited so long and then had it happen among a people of no prominence or significance (4.3, 185–86). Others deny or attenuate original sin, arguing that while we may have to live with the consequences of Adam's misdeed, our sins are our own and our guilt is personal, not inherited. They point out that in the Gospels Jesus freely forgave sinners without demanding propitiation and satisfaction, and they also note that all these theories leave unexplained how the atoning effects of Jesus' death made any visible change in the world. They wonder, too, how the benefits of Jesus can be applied to the millions who have never heard of Christianity and must live by their consciences and the dictates of their religions. Faustus Socinus, called "the first Unitarian," rejected all theories of satisfaction or vicarious punishment as incompatible with God's mercy; while for John Locke in his *Reasonableness of Christianity* (1695), Jesus was a revealer, not a savior (though he often referred to him as "our Saviour"). His mission on earth was to provide mankind with the doctrine of "the One Invisible True God," with the laws of morality and their heavenly rewards and hellish punishments, and with the assurance of assistance by the Holy Spirit. None of this had been formulated in the "airy commendations" of pagan philosophers or provided by the rituals of their priests, and Jews were too weak and unpopular to be able to propagate them throughout the world.[32] Kant had little sympathy with Christ-centered devotions, so he rejected vicarious satisfaction, arguing that the burden of sin, the "most personal of all debts," is the result of human freedom, which is absolute; it is not transferable or transmissible (a murderer's father cannot serve his son's life sentence), and faith in another's assuming that burden is not enough to assure a future of good conduct. For him Christ's atonement was a moral example of the Christian's experience of the passage from sin to virtue.[33] The Socinian Joseph Priestley devoted well over a hundred pages of his *History of the Corruptions of Christianity* (1782) to attacking the doctrine as "a gross misrepresentation of the character and moral government of God" with "no countenance whatever in reason or the scriptures."[34]

Thomas Paine also spoke for the Enlightenment in calling the atonement "a strange affair." He recalled hearing a sermon on the subject when he was "about seven or eight," which led to his own "garden experience": "After the sermon was ended, I went into the garden, and as I was going down the garden steps (for I perfectly recollect the spot) I revolted at the recollection of what I had heard, and thought to myself that it was making God Almighty act like a passionate man who killed His son when He could not revenge Himself in any other way, and, as I was sure a man would be hanged who did such a thing, I could not see for what purpose they preached such sermons."[35] And Baron d'Holbach (1727–89), on what he called "the inconceivable principles" which serve as the basis of Christian theology, wrote: "They [theologians] maintain that a just God, wishing to appease himself, from the beginning destined his innocent son to sufferings, in order to have a motive for pardoning the guilty human race, which had become hateful to him through the transgression of Adam, in which, however, his descendants had no share. By an act of justice, whereof the mind of man can form no idea, a God, whose essence renders him incapable of committing sin, is loaded with the iniquities of man, and must expiate them in order to disarm the indignation of a father he has not offended."[36] It was also rejected by the Unitarians: "It is Scripture, reason and good law never to condemn the innocent to exculpate the delinquent."[37] Similarly, under "Bible Atrocities" the iconoclastic *Bible Handbook* said: "A father requires the agonising death of an only Son as a victim before he can relinquish his vengeance on sinners whom he made imperfect."[38] And since his denial of Jesus' divinity precluded his accepting the atonement, Shaw objected to what he called "Crosstianity" or "Salvationism," Christians' use of vicarious satisfaction to relieve their consciences and evade their responsibilities by laying their sins off "on a scapegoat or on the Cross."[39] Finally, there was Robert Ingersoll: "The idea that man made salvation possible by murdering God is infinitely absurd. This makes salvation the blossom of crime—the blessed fruit of murder. According to this the joys of heaven are born of the agonies of innocence."[40] Nietzsche wrote in his *Antichrist:* "The 'bearer of glad tidings' dies as he lived and *taught*—*not* to 'save' mankind, but to show mankind how to live."[41] And more recently René Girard has observed in *Things Hidden Since the Foundation of the World* (a book deriving its title from 13:35) that the theology of the atonement, with its slighted honor and blood sacrifice "has done more than anything else to discredit Christianity in the eyes of people of good will."[42]

From victory to ransom to dishonor to exemplary love: over the centuries—and over objections—the theology of the atonement, beginning with an objective scene of divine combat, has moved then to human indebtedness, and finally to a subjective experience of individual conversion and reform. But it remains a mystery—or, with Cardinal Newman, a doctrine to be "reserved until Christians feel the need of it." In an 1867 letter he admitted, "But *how* these sufferings affected reconciliation and *why* they were necessary this certainly I did not know then, nor do I know now, and never shall know in this world."[43]

Chapter 20 concludes with another healing of two blind men, as at 9:27-31, though this time without mention of their enabling faith. It is the last such miracle in Matthew, and one of only three healings in the second half of the gospel.

Chapter 21 begins with Jesus and his disciples approaching Jerusalem, with Jesus not walking as a pilgrim but riding as a king—though on a lowly ass. This event is celebrated by Palm Sunday processions in some Christian churches, with the singing of hymns and the distribution of palm fronds; and in the subsequent service, the passion story of choice is usually from Matthew. Here the fulfillment verses come from Zechariah (14:4: "And his feet shall stand in that day upon the Mount of Olives"; and especially 9:9: "Behold, thy King cometh unto thee: he is just and having salvation; lowly, and riding upon an ass, and upon a colt the foal of an ass"). The KJV, misunderstanding the Hebrew parallelism, has Jesus riding on two animals, not one. Origen accepted the two, allegorizing the ass as the Old Testament, its foal as the New Testament, both bearing the Word of God into the soul (Jerusalem);[44] and asses are said to have been honored by a cross mark on their shoulders. In the Middle Ages these biblical associations made the donkey the transportation of choice for wandering preachers. G. K. Chesterton honored this humble animal in his poem "The Donkey." After three stanzas describing how the donkey has always been ridiculed and mistreated, he concludes: "Fools! For I also had my hour; / One far fierce hour and sweet: / There was a shout about my ears, / And palms before my feet."[45] But some have wondered if the reason for not walking the short distance was only to fulfill the prophecy of Zechariah 9:9.

Mark has no great throngs welcoming and praising Jesus, since such a reception might well have alarmed the Roman authorities. But in 21:8-11 Matthew wants to make of Jesus' entry a kind of majestic and triumphant—for some, messianic—procession, so he reports a greater acclamation than does

Mark. But there remains a startling contrast between the crowds (rent-a-mobs?) that welcome Jesus on Palm Sunday and those—the same?—that condemn him on Good Friday. Still, the glad hosannas of the crowd made verse 9 the source of the great Palm Sunday hymn by St. Theodulph of Orleans (750–821), rendered as "All glory, laud, and honor / To Thee, Redeemer, King."

A similar acclamation greeted the renegade Quaker James Nayler (1618–60; also Naylor) when he and a few rain-soaked associates rode into the city of Bristol on October 24, 1656. Nayler, a retired quartermaster from Oliver Cromwell's army, had heard the "call of Abram" (Gen. 12:1) while at his plough and had gone on to become a preacher and, reluctantly, a messiah ("the Quakers' Jesus"). Though he may not have believed that he was Christ incarnate, his followers, mostly women, seemed certain that he had the spirit of Christ within him (he even resembled popular pictures of Jesus), and many Quakers regarded his arrival as ushering in the end of the world. He and his followers were arrested and interrogated, then his case was forwarded to the Puritan-controlled House of Commons. After a long debate marked by his evasive and enigmatic testimony (legend has it that he repeated Jesus' responses to Pilate, "Thou sayest"), Nayler was convicted of blasphemy and barely escaped the death penalty. Instead, he was publicly whipped, had his tongue bored and his forehead branded with a "B," was forced to ride backward through Bristol, and was imprisoned at hard labor. After repenting, he was released in 1659 and died a year later.

Jesus' arrival in Jerusalem reenacts the elaborate arrival ceremonies staged for ancient rulers when entering the cities of their realms (the familiar triumphal arches recall the city gates where these ceremonies were held), with all the pageantry that Jesus' arrival recalls and reverses. When the German Kaiser Wilhelm II, who harbored some messianic delusions of his own, visited Jerusalem in 1898, he wore a gold crown and a white mantle and rode into the city on a horse. The city moat was filled in, and part of the wall at the Jaffa Gate had to be torn down to accommodate his entourage. The entry procession was also a favorite subject for decorating the long sides of Roman sarcophagi, with the beardless Jesus of early Christian art. It is symbolized in the Orthodox liturgy by the "Great Entrance," when the clergy bring the bread and wine to the altar, just as the "Little Entrance," a procession with the Gospels at the beginning of the liturgy, symbolizes the beginning of Jesus' public ministry. The liturgies of Eastern Christianity more closely reenact the life of Christ than do their Western counterparts, just as Eastern churches, with their gilded domes and their icons of the holy family and pictured ranks of apostles, martyrs, and saints recreate for worshipers a sanctified world.

That in verse 11 Jesus is called a prophet—or teacher—as well as a king and priest made the schoolhouse, the town hall, and the church the Puritans' three most important institutions, usually positioned around the center green of New England towns.

The next episode is the "Cleansing of the Temple (Precinct)," or, less reverently, Jesus' "Temple Tantrum," fulfilling Isaiah 56:7 ("Mine house shall be called an house of prayer for all people"). For some typologists it is foreshadowed by the expulsion of Adam and Eve from Eden (included in a cameo in the Frick version of El Greco's painting [ca. 1600; New York]) and prefigures the destruction of the temple in AD 70 or even the apocalypse itself. It is reported by all four evangelists, and since it is an unexpected, even implausible incident, and hardly complimentary much less messianic, it meets critics' "criterion of dissimilarity" and is probably authentic. That Matthew omitted in verse 13 the words "of all nations" that are in Mark suggests that he was writing after the temple's destruction in 70.

That God's "house of prayer" had been turned into "a den of thieves" made verse 13 a convenient text for those Reformers denouncing the practice of Catholic priests accepting money to say private masses for the benefit of individual souls. The Council of Trent, in Session 22, likewise quoted 13 in condemning the avarice, irreverence, and superstition that had corrupted the mass, and the "cleansing" was interpreted in the Counter-Reformation as Jesus' driving heretics from the Roman Church. It is also popular with those who would make Jesus a revolutionary activist, the Galilean peasant attacking the clerical establishment, and it provides a spectacular scene in filmed versions of the Gospels (Scorsese's Jesus goes berserk). In the rock musical *Jesus Christ Superstar* (1973), it is a bazaar that Jesus proceeds to wreck.

Tolstoy in chapter 2 of his moralizing version of the four gospels, *The Gospel in Brief,* chose to omit the overturning of the tables. Instead, Jesus drives out the cattle, frees the doves, and delivers a short homily on the superiority of love to animal sacrifices.[46] For Christians the symbolism is that the temple—here linked with a barren fig tree—and the allegedly corrupt priesthood are at an end and must give way to a new faith, whether it be Christianity or a new and restored Judaism. The time of atonement by animal sacrifices is past, and for Christians the Eucharist would supersede all such rituals. Sacrifices were in fact forbidden by the Romans after they captured Jerusalem in 70. Their restoration was to become one of the signs of the messianic age at the end of time, and there are orthodox groups in Israel today already preparing for that eventuality, even to the extent of breeding the "red heifer, without spot, wherein is no blemish, and upon which never came yoke" called for in Numbers 19:2.

The moneychangers were positioned in Herod's royal stoa (portico), where they changed visitors' currency into the Tyrian coins or "temple shekels" that, because of their high silver content and absence of human images, were acceptable for temple charges and taxes; the doves and other small animals were sold for sacrifice. It is not made clear how these activities, conducted only in the outer court where Gentiles could worship, became blameworthy, or how the temple cult could function without the changing of money needed to buy the unblemished animals required for sacrifices. Similarly, both Jesus' motives and the extent of his disruption are uncertain (could some overturned tables be construed as an attack on the temple itself?), and the reaction—if any—of the temple guards or the Roman soldiers stationed in the nearby Antonia tower is unreported. But it is evident that Jesus' action—and this is the only violent act of his public ministry—constituted a blasphemous outrage, since for Jews the temple was not just a sacred building but a visible symbol of God's presence among them. So it is understandable that this incident fueled the animosity of the temple establishment, particularly since it happened so close to Passover. Combined with the apocalyptic sentiments of the next few chapters, it offers compelling motivation for his arrest, trial, conviction, and execution. But it should also be noted that for all the commotion he causes, Jesus never explicitly denounces temple worship.

John moved the "temple cleansing" to the beginning of the ministry (2:13-17), and he specifies that Jesus used a whip, a sign to Origen of lawlessness and an indication that the incident had to be spiritualized and allegorized, with the whip representing the power of Jesus' words.[47] Since it is difficult to demonize the moneychangers (and did none of them resist?), some commentators have chosen to read it as an attack on simoniacs, those who trade in ecclesiastical offices. In his polemical tract "On Simony" (1413), John Hus noted the presence of doves: "And what can be signified by doves but the Holy Spirit, who appeared above the Lord [at his baptism in the Jordan] in the likeness of a dove? And who are the dove sellers but those who, by the laying on of hands, sell the Holy Spirit for a consideration?"[48] Voltaire, who sometimes regarded Jesus as a Socrates gone bad, deplored the uncharacteristic violence of his action, finding it more quixotic than messianic and comparing it to an attack on a bookseller at St. Paul's Cathedral in London for displaying the *Book of Common Prayer*.[49] The episode ends with a nice contrast between the acclamations of the children and the displeasure of the "chief priests and scribes." The authors of the Oberammergau Passion Play went beyond Scripture when they had temple merchants collaborate with Judas in the plot to betray Jesus. Since this addition tended to reinforce the negative stereotype of the dishonest Jewish merchant, it was eliminated in 1984.

Jesus next leaves Jerusalem, spends the night in Bethany, and the next morning pronounces a "curse" that is as controversial as the temple cleansing. Matthew's version of the cursing of the fig tree demonstrates the power of faith (he adds the moving of mountains), whereas for Mark (11:20-26) it was a judgment on the faithlessness of Israel. Luke omits the episode altogether, perhaps because he was bothered by the tree's seeming inoffensiveness. That Jesus' curse is both miraculous and destructive has made it a favorite target of Bible-bashers. The deist Thomas Woolston called Jesus "peevish and impatient," since this was not yet the season for figs. "What if a yeoman of Kent should go to look for Pipins in his orchard at Easter . . . and because of a disappointment, cut down all his trees?"[50] It has usually been taken as a judgment on Israel, historically fulfilled with the destruction of the temple in 70.

Verse 22, known familiarly as "Ask, and ye shall receive," is an endorsement of petitionary prayer (e.g., "Give us this day our daily bread"), the one religious practice accepted and encouraged by all religious faiths, and it has been said that more such prayers are offered each day in Las Vegas than in Vatican City. One little boy, tired of praying for a bike and not getting it, decided to steal one and then pray for forgiveness. In Maugham's *Of Human Bondage*, verses 21 and 22 inspire young Philip Carey to pray for a cure to his clubfoot. When his prayers are not answered, he consoles himself: "He had learned already that in the Bible things that said one thing quite clearly often mysteriously meant another."[51] But prayer still leaves to theologians the problem of how they can influence a deity who is by nature unchanging. One rationale is to locate the power of prayer not in favors granted but in the spiritual experience of believing and asking, of pious submission when the favor does not materialize, of joy and gratitude when it does; whatever the outcome, prayer unites the individual with God. This verse served as a proof text against quietism, which prescribed the futility of moral effort, the annihilation of self, and total surrender to the divine will. Since this is also the way of the Christian mystic, not all the quietists' practices were condemned as heretical, some being branded only as rash or scandalous.

Later, in the temple (vv. 23-37), the chief priests and elders question Jesus' authority, but he turns their questions against them, observing that unlike "the people" they are supposed to lead, they were deaf to the prophetic authority of John the Baptist. He then relates two parables (28-31, 33-41). The first contrasts deeds with words and has long been understood to imply that the "publicans and the harlots," for all their failings, will sooner come to God's law through John's ministry than their spiritual leaders, whose actions belie their professions. The second is a quasi-allegory suggesting that the "householder" is God, the vineyard is Israel (or Jerusalem), the husbandmen are Jews, the servants are the OT prophets, and "his son" is Jesus. Or possibly the vineyard is the temple after its destruction in 70, one of "his servants" is John the Baptist, and "other husbandmen" are the Romans. The same parable is at Mark 12:1-12 and Luke 20:9-16, but only Matthew adds verse 43, that the kingdom of God will be taken from Israel and given to "a nation bringing forth the fruits of it" (the church?), another indication of his community's situation in the late first century, and a standard proof text for "supersession," the idea that in the evolving history of salvation Christianity would succeed and replace Judaism.

The violent husbandmen supplied the title for Roger Williams's classic, *The Bloudy Tenent of Persecution* (1644), in which he argued for religious toleration through a separation of church and state.

"This is the Lord's doing, and it is marvelous in our eyes" (Ps. 118:23), quoted in verse 42, were the words of Elizabeth I, in Latin ("*A Domino factum est . . .* "), when she fell to her knees on hearing of the death of Queen Mary ("Bloody Mary") in 1558.[52] The verse was later printed on gold coins.

Chapter 22 begins with a Matthean parable as curious as 21:33-41 (Luke has a variant at 14:15-24, in which the invited guests offer excuses). Here a king responds to his rejected wedding invitations by sending armies to kill the people who were to be his guests and to destroy their city, a surprising reaction that is not in the Lukan version (14:21) and must have shocked their fellow citizens. Since so violent a response is missing from Luke and also seems implausible, these verses may have been inserted as another reference to the Romans' destruction of Jerusalem. One of the oddities of the Gospels is their authors' silence about that event, even though it does fall outside their narrative frames. It was a catastrophe for the Jews, and some Christian apologists, such as Justin, Tertullian, and Origen, saw the city's fall as God's punishing them for the crucifixion of Jesus. Furthermore, the Romans' "punishment" was the destruction of Pompeii and Herculaneum in 79, and the Orthodox "suffered" for their schism by the loss of Constantinople to the Turks in 1453.

The allegorized meaning of both parables is clear, with God as the king and the second group of invited guests as Gentiles, who accept the invitation to the heavenly banquet that is refused by the Jews (the slayings of 6 can refer to the prophets and Jesus) or by Christians who resist God's grace. But the situations they present are bizarre. The oddities continue in 11-14, where it is hardly imaginable that someone who has been summarily forced to attend a wedding would be cast "into outer darkness" because he had no "wedding garment" (appropriate clothes). Voltaire wondered why the king did not give him one.[53] But perhaps the "wedding garment" refers to the repentance, belief, and good works Gentiles should bring to the faith. The "servants" of 3, 4, 6, 8, and 10 are slaves, while the "servants" of 13 are attendants (*diakonois;* Tyndale: "ministers"), another example of how the KJV translators often used one English word for different Greek and Hebrew words, just as they, like other translators, often introduced variations that were not present in their sources.

Jesus' next exchange with his adversaries (vv. 15-22) involves taxes and the respective jurisdictions of church and state. The "penny" was a silver denarius with the image of the Emperor Tiberius; it was the daily wage for an agricultural worker and the currency of taxes. Jesus is asked a leading question, designed to trap him between religious compromise, which would anger Jewish nationalists, and political dissent, which would make him a seditionist. But in view of the power imbalance between Romans and Jews in first-century Palestine, the famous phrase probably meant "render unto Caesar the things which are Caesar's so that his officials will allow you to render unto God the things you believe are God's—which should, in any event, include prayers and sacrifices for the emperor's welfare." It was also a distinction that became blurred when the monarch was not Caesar but a Christian; and it leaves unanswered the terrible question of what to do in those many areas that belong to both Caesar and God. John Stuart Mill (1806–73) was not the first to notice the New Testament's deficiencies in prescribing civic responsibilities: "And, while in the morality of the best Pagan nations, duty to the State holds even a disproportionate place, infringing on the just liberty of the individual; in purely Christian ethics, that grand department of duty is scarcely noticed or acknowledged."[54]

This passage has become a key text in the history of political thought and action, though it is a good question whether these famous words solve the problem or simply restate it. Its disjunction of Caesar and God has enabled both sides to invoke them as a proof text throughout history's long and occasionally bloody conflict between church and state, priest and king. Certainly the Roman emperors, absolute rulers and heirs to a tradition that had them descended from gods and accustomed to receiving divine worship, harbored few doubts about the extent of their authority. Constantine received his own vision from God and went on to preside over the Council of Nicaea in 325—in fact, he eventually made it from being a pagan god to being a Christian saint.

But Christianity introduced a new hierarchy of values and claimed a spiritual transcendence and an institutional autonomy that had to infringe eventually on the prerogatives of civil rulers. So already in 356 Bishop Ossius (a.k.a. Hosius) of Cordova, who had been Constantine's advisor at Nicaea, cited this verse in urging his son, Constantius II, now the ruler of the Eastern empire, not to "interfere in matters ecclesiastical" (Constantius was sympathetic to Arian heretics): "We are not permitted to exercise an earthly rule, and you, Sire, are not authorized to burn incense."[55] Pope Gelasius in 494 was more assertive, distinguishing between authority, which was legislative and belonged to the church, and power, which was executive and left to rulers. In a letter to Emperor Anastasius in Constantinople, he insisted that "of the two [powers ruling the world] the priestly power is much more important because it has to render account for the kings themselves at the Divine Tribunal. For you know, our very clement son, that although you have the chief place in dignity over the human race, yet you must submit yourself faithfully to those who have charge of Divine things, and look to them for the means of your salvation."[56] Nevertheless, this verse seemed to allow an autonomous area to rulers, and they could supplement it with other texts—a favorite was John 21:15-17 ("Feed my lambs"). In the Middle Ages rulers could turn to the Old Testament for examples of military men who were also religious leaders, whereas the popes favored the New Testament and its texts that seemed to establish them as Christ's vicars on earth. It is ironic that Christianity, which Constantine had once envisioned as a unifying force, not only spawned its own competing factions but often saw its civil masters as its natural adversaries.

The early church's attitude toward Rome, which had been both its persecutor ("Antichrist") and protector, was correspondingly ambivalent. It could claim that Christianity and the empire had been born at about the same time and had enjoyed a common growth and prosperity. And though Tertullian rejected emperor worship, he recognized that authority is God-given, so he could reassure his pagan readers in his *Apology* 30 that "we offer prayers unceasingly for all our emperors." Later the church grew to appreciate Roman sovereignty, particularly when Christianity became the empire's official religion in the late fourth century and the church could wield in its own behalf some of the power it had so long resisted. What had been a sin would now become a crime, and heresy could be construed as treason. Even before then, Celsus, the church's second-century critic, had warned Christians who defied their pagan emperors that by undermining Roman authority they would expose themselves to infinitely worse treatment by the barbarians threatening the empire's borders.[57] And Tertullian would later say (*Apology* 31): "We know that the great upheaval which hangs over the whole earth, threatening terrible woes, is only delayed by the respite granted to the Roman Empire."[58] St. Jerome, who experienced the fall of Rome in 410, also thought the end of the empire portended the end of the world ("The bright light of all the world was put out . . . the whole world perished in one city").[59] Not really, since it was the papacy that lived on, in Hobbes's words, as "no other than the ghost of the deceased Roman Empire, sitting crowned upon the grave thereof."[60]

The church found a special convenience in the doctrine of "two swords" (Luke 22:38), which was cited by the militant Pope Gregory VII in the "Investiture Controversy" with the German King Henry IV (1056–1106) of the Holy Roman Empire, as they quarreled over the right of secular rulers to appoint church officials. It was also cited by Pope Boniface VIII in his bull *Unam Sanctam* (1302) as the basis for church-state relations, with the church wielding the spiritual sword, the state the temporal, in its own behalf but also in the interest of the church. In 1198 Pope Innocent III had compared the interdependence of pontifical and royal power to the sun and the moon, both created by God but the latter receiving its light from the former and therefore "inferior to the sun in both size and quality, in position and effect."[61] He also appealed to Jeremiah 1:10: "I have this day set thee over the nations." All such totalizing claims must, however, deal with Jesus' more explicit statement "My kingdom is not of this world" (John 18:36) and his record of generally conforming with civil laws.

For John of Paris, writing in the early fourteenth century on the powers of church and state, they are separate and independent, neither deriving authority from the other, but such theoretical distinctions are not helpful in disputes that involve both jurisdictions.[62] Dante, in his *De Monarchia* (3.15.18), agreed, though he acknowledged the prerogatives of the papacy: "Let Caesar use that reverence towards Peter, therefore, that a son ought to use towards his father." Later, Luther radically separated the "two kingdoms," one the public and secular realm—the "Sword"—based on reason, history, and law and devoted to justice and the preservation of peace; the other the private and spiritual realm, God's kingdom—the "Word"—based on Scripture and devoted to grace and mercy. He accepted civil authority as sanctified by natural law, so he saw both as manifestations of God's will (along with the third "estate," the organized church), with the spiritual in practice influencing the secular, the secular providing freedom and order for the preaching of the gospel. The relative autonomy this left to the state (at least in theory) has caused Luther to be charged with quietism, or even attacked as a precursor of totalitarianism, but unfairly, since his intention was to give civil society and its restraints on human lawlessness its own sanctifying role in the scheme of salvation.

Matthew 22:21 was twice cited by Luther in 1525 regarding the Peasants' War. After first justifying his neutrality with 7:1, "Christ's command . . . that we are not to judge," and then citing Romans 13:1 (that favorite of the powers that be), "Let every soul be subject unto the higher powers," he encouraged the Princes: "Smite, slay and stab, secretly or openly, remember that nothing can be more poisonous, hurtful or devilish than a rebel."[63] There was a cruel irony in these words from traditional Christianity's greatest rebel, but the princes were more than willing to do his bidding, and they slaughtered some five thousand peasants in a final battle at Frankenburg in Thuringia. Moreover, King James I of England, defending the hereditary rights of monarchs ("God's lieutenants on earth") in his *True Law of Free Monarchies* (1598), noted that the "spirit of God" recommended tax-paying even though the Roman emperors were notorious for "idolatry and defection from God, tyranny over their people, and persecution of the saints."[64] Similarly, Jacques-Benigne Bossuet (1627–1704), the eloquent defender of French royalty, argued that Jesus' submission to Tiberius, even though he was a pagan, showed his endorsement of hereditary monarchy. Jesus "did not examine how the power of the Caesars had been established: it was sufficient that he found them established and reigning, and he intended that the divine order and the foundation of public peace should be respected in the form of their authority." A further proof for Bossuet was Jesus' silence before Pilate (27:14); and he saw his counterpart in Socrates, who in Plato's *Crito* is offered a chance to escape but instead chooses to accept the death penalty.[65]

Jesus is next approached by some Sadducees (23-33), with Matthew noting that they, unlike the Pharisees, rejected any idea of resurrection. The Sadducees seek to trap Jesus with a tricky—but reasonable—question about married life in the hereafter for someone who has had a number of spouses in this life. One implication in Jesus' reply is that life in God's kingdom does not include marriage, and that virginity and celibacy are higher vocations. But for the Reformers, men and women are "called" to a variety of stations in life, so they rejected the quest for spiritual perfection that seemed reserved only for celibate religious. The idea of immortality is then underscored by Jesus' quotation of Exodus 3:6, God's words to Moses, which Matthew understands as attributing some sort of continued existence to the deceased patriarchs; and he repeats that the Christians' God is also the God of the Jews. This passage is often taken as a proof text for eternal life.

But the most quotable verse in chapter 22 is the Great Commandment (37), often cited as a summary of the Ten Commandments. It appears in the three Synoptics, but only Matthew has the question posed by a Pharisee, and only he mentions "all the law and the prophets." None of Matthew's adversaries would dispute it, since its God-neighbor division summarizes the two halves of the Decalogue. But it does raise questions, and in his *Analects* (14.34), Confucius wondered if one repaid evil with good, how should one repay good? Better, he thought, to repay good with good, evil with justice. The mention of self-love (from Lev. 19:18) contrasts oddly with the more usual Matthean emphasis on self-denial and "losing" one's life (10:39), but presumably we are to see God in our neighbor. The primacy of love makes this one of the Bible's most inspiring messages, and, as often with "favorite" passages, no one questions its authenticity. Jesus, as usual, does not go into the specific applications and complications of this elusive emotion, nor does he suggest that the Great Commandment invalidates lesser commandments.

As "great" as the commandment of verse 37 is the question of 42: "Whose son is he?" To the answer, "the son of David," Jesus cites Psalm 110:1, explaining that the messiah cannot be David's son alone, since David has acknowledged him as "my Lord," that is, as someone greater than he. Psalm 110 became very important for early Christian apologists, with "my Lord" understood as Jesus, and it is the OT passage most often alluded to in the New Testament. It was also a Trinitarian proof text, since it suggests that the "Lords" are equal. Finally, it was an important passage in discussions of biblical infallibility, since Jesus' authority seems to validate the authority of the Old Testament by certifying David as the author of the Psalms. Biblical scholars would disagree with this ascription, though some might respond that Jesus was simply reflecting a common assumption.

Chapter 23 is a catalogue of seven denunciatory "woes," balancing the blessings of the Beatitudes. Its abusive rhetoric is directed against the "scribes and the Pharisees," although it begins, paradoxically, with an endorsement of the Pharisees' teachings (3), which they delivered from the mysterious "Moses' seat" (2). This may have been a chair in the synagogue reserved for the Torah scroll or the place where the Pharisees sat when reading out the Torah (as Jesus sat when delivering the Sermon on the Mount), and Jesus may be distinguishing between the sanctity of the Law as they recited it and the hypocrisy with which they practiced it.[66] Surprisingly, provision is made for "good" scribes in verse 34. This chapter should perhaps be included with the eschatology of 24–25, the gloom of those two chapters reflecting the bitterness of 23. Readers have long noted that here there is no talk of loving, blessing, caring, and praying for one's enemies as in 5:43-48. Some might wish today that chapter 23 were a later addition, but woe oracles are prominent in the OT prophets (e.g., Hab. 2:9-20). Its intemperate language recalls the prophets' tirades and is standard for sectarian disputes (here still a family quarrel), where both sides make claims that are absolute and exclusive and where each feels mortally threatened by the other. Bitter quarrels within Judaism were not infrequent, and a story is told of a pious Jew stranded on a desert island who built himself two synagogues so that there would always be one he wouldn't be caught dead in. Readers who are uncomfortable with Jesus' attack and the subsequent reaction of the Jewish leaders should read these verses in conjunction with Jeremiah 26:8, where an OT prophet, speaking with the authority of the Lord, evokes a similar reaction: "Thou shalt surely die." It is also important to note that Jesus attacks no one personally, and, in fairness, we do not know what his opponents were saying about Matthew and his community.

The polemics of chapter 23 reinforce the view that Matthew was composed at the time when Jewish rabbis, consolidating their faith after the fall of the temple, were explicitly condemning the new sect of Christianity and when Christians, in turn, were frustrated by Jewish opposition and rejection. Nevertheless, the authority of Scripture, readily available and easily misapplied, and the terrible history of anti-Semitism within Christian societies have given these verses frightful repercussions, and Matthew's attack on certain Jewish leaders at a specific point in time was transformed into a generalized condemnation of all Jews. Since the Pharisees are caricatured as the villains of the Gospels, these verses could be cited in Article VIII of the Lutheran *Augsburg Confession* (1530) as a proof text that "the sacraments are efficacious even if the priests who administer them are wicked men."[67]

The charge of pharisaism, that the behavior of religious people does not always match their principles, is universal; it was noted in the Talmud and in the Dead Sea Scrolls and would resonate through Western history. So there is nothing in these complaints that could not be equally applied to Christian hypocrites, some of whom might have been in Matthew's own community. It is also well to remember, though it is often forgotten, that although the Pharisees offer convenient examples of ostentation, hypocrisy, and self-righteousness, they seem to have been popular with their fellow Jews. Furthermore, Jesus offers no evidence of their wickedness, and he points out in verse 3 that the selfish behavior of religious teachers does not invalidate their teachings ("whatsoever they bid you observe, that observe and do").

The adversarial rhetoric of chapter 23 has made it a ready source for polemicists. In 1845 verses 4 and 23 were quoted by the black Abolitionist Frederick Douglass as he recalled his experiences with "Christian" slaveholders in the South: "Dark and terrible as is this picture, I hold it to be strictly true of the overwhelming mass of professed Christians of America."[68] Verses 8-10 ("call no man your father upon the earth") were a proof text for Reformers rejecting that "imperious and pompous domain," the Catholic hierarchy of offices, titles, and jurisdictions, while conceding that "we must take heed that we spoil not the ministers of the church of all their lawful authority."[69] They cited verse 9 as sanction for the elimination of monastic orders altogether, though "father" and its equivalents—pope/papa, priest/father, church fathers, patristics—are a fixture of church tradition, and titles are simply a practical necessity. The Quakers, however, argued against flattering titles and for the plain language of "thou" and "thee." In replying in 1901 to the Russian church's edict of excommunication, Tolstoy admitted that he rejected all the sacraments, citing 8-10 against ordination. He also cited 6:6 ("When thou prayest, enter into thy closet") in claiming that the church's public prayer was "plainly forbidden by Jesus."[70] Moreover, one Christian feminist has noted that "the church has not obeyed the command of Jesus to 'call no one father, for you have one father,'" and this "has resulted in legitimizing ecclesial and societal patriarchy."[71] Finally, in a letter (1520) to Pope Leo X, "the most holy father in God," that master polemicist, Martin Luther, cited verse 33 in justifying the abusiveness of his attacks on the "pestilential" Roman See, saying, "I have Christ's example."[72]

In the course of his tirade, Jesus again refers to the swearing of oaths (16-17), an important but complicated affair, since here there is no absolute prohibition as in 5:33-37. Jesus seems to want oaths sworn only by whatever is greater than the one swearing, that is, by temple and altar, not by the gold in the temple or the gift on the altar. The gold of the temple was taken to Rome by the Emperor Titus (39-81) after his victory in the Jewish War (66-70), then lost to Gaiseric and the Vandals in their sack of Rome in 455.

Three other verses are interesting. For "strain at" (v. 24), read "strain out a gnat" (Rieu: "You filter your wine to get rid of a gnat"), an early KJV misprint that has never been amended.[73] Luther cited this verse when he wrote in 1517 to Archbishop Albert of Mainz, including a copy of his *Ninety-five Theses,* as the words Christ will eventually direct at bishops who allowed "the Gospel to be silenced" but permitted "the pompous proclamation of indulgences."[74] The "whited sepulchres" (27) were tombs that the Jews whitewashed before Passover to make them visible, especially at night, so that passersby would not be inadvertently tainted by contact with the dead. This verse was cited by the Roman emperor Julian the Apostate in denouncing the cult of martyrs after he had heard that Christians were worshiping at the tombs of Peter and Paul: "Jesus says the sepulchres are full of uncleanness. How is it then that you invoke God upon them?"[75] Finally, some Muslims have seen in the "prophets" of verse 34 an allusion to the coming of Muhammad.

The lament over Jerusalem (37-39) obliquely alludes to the destruction of the city and the temple (also referred to at 24:2), and its charming image of a hen and her chickens is repeated four times in an analogous passage in *The Book of Mormon* (3 Nephi 10:4-6). For some Jews these cataclysmic events must have been signals of the end time, and the visions of the apocryphal 2 Esdras and the pseudepigraphical *2 Baruch,* two books of the first and second centuries, record apocalyptic responses to the desolation of their "house." Many Christians must have interpreted it as a sign of God's judgment on the Jews, who had not only crucified their "savior" but had remained stubbornly resistant to this new version of their old faith. Still, one of Scripture's puzzles is its paucity of direct references to this disaster, even though its writings date from the years soon after the temple's fall. Later, the French writer François-René de Chateaubriand (1768–1848) in his Romantic defense of Catholic Christianity—"not beautiful because it's true, but true because it's beautiful"—cited Jesus' concern for Jerusalem as an example of his "love of country."[76]

In his debate with Luther in 1524–25, Erasmus placed verse 37 first on his list of NT passages that proved for him the freedom of the will, with particular emphasis on "you refused" (KJV: "ye would not!"). He has Jerusalem respond to Jesus, "Why do you torment yourself with vain tears? If you did not wish us to listen to the prophets, why did you send them? Why impute to us what has been done by your will?" In arguing for good works and against necessity, he also brought up all the ethical exhortations from the Sermon on the Mount, and especially 7:20, "By their fruits ye shall know them." Luther, who regarded the will as free in things beneath man but not above him, read Erasmus' arguments with "disgust, indignation, contempt," because for him their moralism failed to acknowledge that such commandments could only remind Christians of their depravity and dependence, while they circumvented the spirit and grace of God as well as His secret, immutable, and eternal will. So they talked past one another, since Erasmus regarded Scripture as enlightening and guiding, Luther as moving and transforming; analogously, Erasmus thought of freedom in relation to responsibility, Luther in relation to salvation. Without the enabling presence of grace, the will remains "in bondage," and Christians are bereft of the comfortable assurance that their salvation depends on God's bountiful mercy, not their inadequate works.[77] Erasmus's arguments would be raised again in the eighteenth century by John Wesley ("God helps those who help themselves"), who in his celebrated "Free Grace" sermon twice paraphrased verse 37 ("How often would I have gathered you together, and ye would not!") to show that it is human obduracy, not the divine will, that condemns and that predestination is a "doctrine full of blasphemy."[78]

Chapters 24–25 deal with the apocalypse. Some sort of apocalypticism seems to belong to first-century Christianity, as an apocalyptic mood appears typical of small religious sects seeking to survive and prevail in a hostile environment. Here the "Olivet Discourse" is Matthew's version of Mark's "Little Apocalypse" (ch. 13), though both lack the complicated symbolism characteristic of such writings. Its inclusion in Matthew is somewhat surprising, since he is so concerned to provide for a missionary enterprise that would continue Jesus' ministry into the future and to "all nations" (24:14, 28:19)—which reassured seventeenth-century Christians that the world would not end before the American Indians were converted. But verse 14 also reminds readers that it may be some time before these dread events come to pass, and in verses 36 and 42 as well as in the parables of the "goodman" (43-51), the "ten virgins" (25:1-13), and the traveler (25:14-30), we are warned against predicting the time of their arrival.

The apocalypse provided the subject for one of America's earliest poets, the Puritan Michael Wigglesworth (1631–1705), whose ballad-like *Day of Doom: or a Poetical Description of the Great and Last Judgment* (1662) was a huge bestseller, last printed in 1929. Much of its popularity was due to its singsong style, which was at odds with the grim details Wigglesworth drew from these two chapters (with additions from Revelation): the foolish maids, who "Virgins unwise . . . Had closed their eyes"; those feckless souls who cared only about eating and drinking; the sudden appearance of the Son of man as "The Judge draws nigh, exalted high"; the separation of the sheep from the goats, when "At Christ's right hand the Sheep do stand." Wigglesworth then departed from Matthew for a long catalogue of sinners and unredeemed heathens, whom the saved will judge along with Jesus. For them "there's no excuse for their abuse," their "filthy facts and secret acts." The poem then concludes with contrasting pictures of the miseries of hell, where "The pain of loss their Souls doth toss," and the joys of heaven, that "glorious place, where face to face / Jehovah may be seen."[79]

Nevertheless, given the generality of these conditions and their applicability to almost any era in human history, the world always being in some sort of "great tribulation," these chapters have been a great and continuing inspiration for millenarians. For example, the calamities of 24:7 sounded enough like the conditions of World War I to Jehovah's Witnesses, who strongly opposed American participation, that they announced that the world would end in 1914. When the ordinary world did not end, they made it the beginning of Christ's active rulership—through the agency of the Witnesses. Others have argued that a rise above 6.0 in Richter scale readings since 1940 is evidence for the earthquakes of the same verse. All have had to take their place in a long line of doomsayers, including a popular Victorian astronomer and evangelist, Henry Grattan Guinness (1835–1910), who was convinced that missionary activities "in all the world" (14) and the translation of the Bible into hundreds of languages showed that "we are living in the very last days."[80] More recently, David Koresh, leader of the Branch Davidian group that died in Waco, Texas, on April 19, 1993, took chapter 24 as a crucial text, imagining himself to be the "lightning" and, as martyr, the "carcass" of 27-28. Fortunately, the doomsayers do have one thing in common: they have all been proved wrong. But since one of them was Jesus himself, Christians have had some difficulty in harmonizing these dread predictions with the facts of history. One consolation is the escape clause of 24:36 ("of that day and hour knoweth no man"); another is their insistence that an apocalyptic context does not invalidate the urgency and authority of Jesus' positive teachings.

Christopher Columbus cited 24:14 (and 34) in his unfinished *Book of Prophecies* (1501), a collection of eschatological citations (with his commentary) from the Bible and the church fathers, in arguing that his expedition to the "Indies" would secure the resources for a campaign to recover the Holy Land and bring about the universal conversion that would usher in the end time. He quoted other Matthean passages—on the importance of faith (17:20) and the special revelation he had that was hidden from "the wise and prudent" (11:25)—to offset his uncertainty as to how this would be accomplished. His book was intended for Isabel and Ferdinand but was never sent; and although he made a fourth voyage to the New World, he died in 1506 without achieving his grand vision.[81]

The resounding "abomination of desolation" (v. 15) is an allusion to Daniel 9:27, often taken with verses 1-2 as predictive of the destruction of the temple by Titus's Romans in 70, but it is as oddly oblique and enigmatic as are most NT references to this catastrophic event. After the suppression of another Jewish revolt, led in 130 by Bar-Kochba in protest against the building of a shrine to Jupiter on the Temple Mount, the Emperor Hadrian drove the remaining Jews out of Palestine and renamed the city Aelia Capitolina (his family name was Aelius). Later, Christians were enraged when, after they had attempted to Christianize the city, Emperor Julian the Apostate announced that he would refute Jesus' words by rebuilding the temple and letting the Jews return and renew their animal sacrifices (human sacrifices, said his Christian opponents), a part of religion that appealed to him. Christians saw the truth of this prophecy confirmed when his death in battle in 363 ended his attempt to restore the temple. The foundation had been laid, but a mysterious fire broke out and prevented the continuation of work. Legend has it that Julian's dying gesture was to throw drops of his blood at heaven while conceding, "*Vicisti, Galilaee,*" which Swinburne, in his "Hymn to Proserpine" (1862), expanded to "Thou hast conquered, O pale Galilean; the world has grown grey from thy breath."

Erasmus quoted verse 23 to make fun of the ambitions of competing religious orders: "The Observantines say, *Christ is here,* not with the Coletines or the Conventuals. The Jacobines say, *Here is Christ,* not with the Augustinians. Again, the Benedictines clamor, *Here is Christ,* not with the Mendicants. Finally, the whole tribe clamor, *Here is Christ. Christ is not with the secular clergy who wear no cowl.*"[82] And 24 was cited by Luther against the miraculous "signs and wonders" ("The Evil Spirit can also work miracles") attributed to Catholic images, shrines, chapels, and pilgrimage sites ("These extra-parochial chapels and churches . . . should be pulled down.").[83] Protestant iconoclasts took most of their scriptural arguments from the Old Testament's ban on "graven images" in the Decalogue, a part of the old law that for them had not been abrogated by Jesus. But Luther always urged restraint on the wreckers, whose destructive rage was one of the tragedies of the Reformation. He was really more concerned about those who thought they could earn spiritual merits by the creation or financing of artworks, and he exempted crucifixes from any ban on "graven images" and allowed his own Bible translations to be illustrated.

Verse 27 is the warrant for those Christian churches built on an east-west orientation, with the sanctuary usually toward the east, but Scripture was never as compelling a warrant as considerations of terrain and convenience.[84] Further evidence of the east as the direction of faith was Luke 1:78, identifying God as "the dayspring from on high," and John 8:12, "I am the light of the world" (with the caution that this should not imply sun worship). Helping to strengthen this scriptural symbolism was the traditional location of Eden in the east, the paradise that is the goal of all Christians and the place from which Christ, the Second Adam, would return. The west, on the other hand, was the land of darkness and the devil, and even the Greeks located one of hades' entrances in the far western Mediterranean. Accordingly, Christians face east when they pray, as Jews turn toward Jerusalem, and Muslims toward Mecca (for Muslims this has been a proof text for the coming of Muhammad from the Arabic world). This was also the reason for the placement in many Gothic churches, such as Notre Dame in Paris, of the Last Judgment over the western portal, at the "beginning" of the church, just as mass began with a confession of sinfulness. It reminded arriving worshipers that their actions had eternal consequences and that they should continue their progress toward the table of the Lord. Verses 30-31 also offered the typical arrangement for such sculptural representations, with the addition of St. Michael the Archangel and some details borrowed from Revelation 4.

The remainder of chapter 24 deals with the ever-popular "tribulation of those days." Because the fig tree Jesus cursed at 21:19 might refer to Israel, its blossoming here has been construed by some evangelical Christians as the "rebirth" of Israel on May 14, 1948; and since a generation can last forty years, this meant that the world would end in 1988. When it did not, an alternative was 2007, forty years after the Israelis' capture of Jerusalem in 1967. Further evidence was the reference to Noah, which suggests that the people who perish in "those days" will equal the number who drowned in the Great Flood of Genesis, itself precipitated by human corruption. This made 37-38 a popular subject of sermons preached during the plagues that began in 1347 to devastate Europe. This whole passage has also provided the initial scenario for premillennialism: the belief that Christ's return will be preceded by various social and natural cataclysms and followed by a thousand-year period of peace and righteousness before evil forces led by the antichrist erupt against the rule of Christ and his elect, only to be defeated in preparation for the resurrection of the dead, the Last Judgment, and the eternal establishment of heaven and hell. It has also evoked considerable comment both for what it promises (the dramatic appearance of the Son of man) and what it overlooks (God's participation, the resurrection of the dead, and the Last Judgment). The "sign of the Son" (30) is usually understood as a cross, which will precede the appearance of Jesus, who is often shown in art with a scroll in his hand. Speculations also include a total eclipse of all heavenly lights, followed by a blinding brightness and the coming of Christ in the clouds with his angels.

Voltaire took personally the prediction of verse 34: "Generations passed, and if none of these things took place, it is not my fault."[85] Later Shelley was more assertive, arguing that this apparently "plain prophecy" of Jesus' early return (34), which is also at Mark 13:30 and Luke 21:32, "thus conspicuously false, may serve as a criterion of those which are more vague and indirect, and which apply in an hundred senses to an hundred things."[86] But it was another key text for Jehovah's Witnesses, who long maintained that it was the "generation" of 1914 that would see the "Great Tribulation" and the establishment on earth of the kingdom of God. But as members of that generation died off, Witnesses quietly dropped the date (as they had previously dropped 1925 and 1975) and began to refer only to a new and peaceful world that they would help to establish in place of the wickedness of modern society. Still, despite the cautionary verse 36, which, like Acts 1:7, is a discouraging text for those who like to set dates for the end of the world, "this generation" has long attracted millennialists. Hal Lindsey, whose books sell millions of copies, predicted that by 1988 the end time would begin with a joint Russian-Arab (led by Egypt)-African attack on Israel. Since there was no obvious reason for such an invasion, one had to be invented: vast and immensely valuable mineral deposits, such as potash, and geo-thermal energy sources presumed to be somewhere under the Dead Sea.[87]

A different problem is also raised by verse 36, where "nor the son" should be added after "heaven" from early Greek manuscripts unavailable to the KJV translators, whose manuscripts and the Latin Vulgate omitted "the son" on the assumption that Jesus, as the divine Son, should know the time of the end. Unfortunately, adding "the son" raises the question of Jesus' ignorance, which must then be resolved by attributing it to his human nature. This is the theological doctrine of the *communicatio idiomatun,* or "interchange of properties," whereby Jesus' divine and human natures were shared.

Four end-time parables conclude the chapter, as Matthew distinguishes between the meekness of Jesus' first coming and the glory of his second coming as the "Son of man." Augustine was among the first to formulate the full scenario: "Elijah the Tishbite will come; the Jews will believe; Antichrist will persecute; Christ will judge; the dead will rise; the good will be separated from the wicked; the world will be destroyed by fire and renewed."[88] The "thief in the night" image (43) also appears in Paul (1 Thess. 5:2). Matthew probably knew at least some of Paul's letters, and they seem to have agreed on matters of Christology, church organization, and the need to evangelize the Gentile world before the approaching end time, though Matthew's emphasis is as much on works as on faith and grace. And verse 48 ("My lord delayeth his coming"), repeated at Luke 12:45, is an important text for those who were vainly awaiting the second coming or who have so often been proved wrong after specifying its exact date and time. Finally, the picture of the evil servant abusing his position became a warning for unworthy churchmen.

Chapter 24, and especially verses 29-31 and 40-41, are Matthew's contribution to a doctrine that some fundamentalist Christians call "the rapture." More fully described by Paul (1 Thess. 4:13-18) and with borrowings from Revelation, it tells how Jesus will unexpectedly appear "in heaven" to sweep the elect, both living and dead, up into the sky to abide with him until he returns to defeat the antichrist. This will be somewhat unsettling for the unbelievers left behind, especially if the cars around them are suddenly bereft of their drivers (one bumper sticker read, reassuringly, "In case of the rapture, this car will self-destruct") or, even worse, if they are in planes whose pilots are "raptured" out of their cockpits. And for those who must remain on earth to deal with the antichrist, there is a series of *Left Behind* novels by two Christian writers, Tim F. LaHaye and Jerry B. Jenkins, that began to appear in the 1990s and have now sold more than thirty million copies.

Chapter 25 begins with the parable of the Ten Virgins. Five were wise and five foolish, and since the number five does not have many significant occurrences in Scripture, the church's numerologists had to settle for the five senses, which can be put to good or bad ends. In a typical explication of number symbolism, one was for God, two for the tablets of Moses, three for the patriarchs (or the Trinity), four for the evangelists, five for the wise virgins, six for the water pots at the marriage in Cana (John 2:6), seven for the sacraments, eight for the Beatitudes, nine for the (nonbiblical) choirs of angels, ten (which "contains" all other numbers) for the Commandments, eleven for the eleven thousand virgins (martyrs borrowed from the St. Ursula legend), and twelve for the apostles. But the classic country song, "Deck of Cards," where playing cards are used as a "bible," also assigns five to the wise and foolish virgins as it proceeds to the jack (Satan), the queen (the Virgin Mary), and the king (God). As for the parable itself, most commentators agree that its point is spiritual preparedness for the end time: the bridegroom is the Messiah; the sleep is the waiting for the second coming; the midnight cry its angelic announcement; the marriage is the (delayed) Parousia; and the virgins represent prudent and imprudent Christians, their slumbering a sign of spiritual apathy. But there is no consensus on the oil, which Augustine took as charity. In a book-length "sermon" on the parable, the noted Puritan preacher Thomas Shepard (1605–49) insisted that "by Oil should be meant Faith," and not, as "Popish interpreters" claimed, good works; and the light referred to the watchful waiting "for the coming of Christ," while "by lamps may be meant minds enlightened and kindled by the word."[89]

Since this parable alludes to the end time, an anonymous sculptor included the leaders of the two groups in his *Last Judgment* sculpture on the cathedral of the French kings, St. Denis outside Paris. And verse 6 was quoted by Tom just before Little Eva's death in Harriet Beecher Stowe's *Uncle Tom's Cabin* (1852), as he explained why he "would not sleep in his room, but lay all night in the outer verandah" near Eva's sickroom.[90] In *The Woman's Bible* (1895–98) Elizabeth Cady Stanton offered an early feminist interpretation: it is a parable, she explained, urging "the duty of self-development," the wise virgins being those women "who burn oil in their vessels for their own use, who have improved every advantage for their own education, secured a healthy, happy, complete development, and entered all the profitable avenues of labor, for self support, so that when the opportunities and the responsibilities of life come, they may be filled fully to enjoy the one and ably to discharge the other."[91]

Two other parables in this chapter are the parables of the Unprofitable Servant (14-30) and the Separation of the Sheep from the Goats (31-46). The first is a judgment parable, with the large sums indicating that Matthew's community was familiar with finances and investments. A talent corresponded to six thousand denarii, containing around seventy-five pounds of silver, or about twenty years of wages. So the absent master (Jesus) was entrusting his slaves (the church) with enormous wealth (spiritual gifts and responsibilities). The five talents were often allegorized as the five carnal senses, or, if the first servant represents the Jews, the five books of the Pentateuch, doubled when he became a Christian. In this reading, the second servant stands for Gentile converts who add good works to faith, whereas the fearful servant who buried his lord's money was seen as restricting his abilities to earthly things. But more often this has been taken as a proof text for stewardship within the church, in that those who have been given gifts have the obligation to increase and expand them—though in what direction is not stated. The KJV was responsible for shifting the meaning of "talent" from a weight of money to an individual gift or ability, and the parable recurs regularly in secular literature as a warning to those who neglect to develop their natural abilities, as do the terms for the two servants, one "good and faithful," the other "unprofitable."[92]

The second parable (31-44) is popular with liberation theologians, who stress Jesus' identification with the poor, but it has also served as a proof text for the Last Judgment, which apparently will be conducted without the participation of God the Father. It raises some other difficult questions. Since "all nations" (32) suggests a universal judgment, will non-Christians be judged too? On what basis? Presumably on their works, which makes Matthew not only the "Jewish Gospel" and the "Church's Gospel," but also the gospel for all of those who have never heard of Jesus. If this judgment will not take place until "the Son of man shall come in his glory," what will be the fate of those who die before that day? One answer was the Augustinian doctrine of the "Particular Judgment" meted out to each soul at the point of death, as Jesus had promised the good thief, "Today shalt thou be with me in paradise" (Luke 23:43). Augustine formulated what became the accepted understanding, that at death the soul is judged but will not be reunited with its body until the "General Judgment," when, at the second coming of Jesus at the end of the world, body and soul will be rewarded with eternal happiness or punished with eternal suffering. Cardinal Newman commented on the Particular Judgment: "Oh, what a moment for the poor soul, when it comes to itself, and finds itself suddenly before the judgement-seat of Christ! Oh what a moment, when breathless with the journey and dizzy with the brightness, and overwhelmed with the strangeness of what is happening to him, and unable to realise where he is, the sinner hears the voice of the accusing spirit, bringing up all the sins of his past life, which he has forgotten or which he has explained away, which he would not allow to be sins, though he suspected that they were . . . And, oh!, still more terrible, still more distressing, when the Judge speaks and consigns it to the jailors, till it shall pay the endless debt which lies against it!"[93]

As to how that "endless debt" shall be paid, Matthew 25 has also given the world much of what it knows, in fear and trembling, about the eternal fires of hell, with its "weeping and wailing and gnashing of teeth," a subject that Jesus speaks about more than anyone else in Scripture (both Jesus and Matthew have somewhat less to say about the joys of heaven). Although it offers one of the most explicit proof texts for a *poena sensus,* a hell of painful fire, it makes no mention of the devils' role in inflicting punishments, nor does it remind us, as do the theologians, that hell's greatest punishments are the sting of conscience and, especially, the *poena damni,* the loss of the Beatific Vision, the total experience of God's love. It also leaves out its location, traditionally an infernal "down there," a "bottomless pit" (Rev. 9:1, 2, 11), but somehow at the center of the earth, farthest away from heaven and the light and warmth of God's love (=Sun), its black fires accompanied by foul smells, cacophonous noises, and total darkness—details first offered by the anonymous composers of the *Apocalypse of Peter* (2c) and the *Apocalypse of Paul* (4c). Hell has two general names in Scripture: the Hebrew *sheol* (Greek *hades*), which accepts all the dead, both good and bad; and *gehenna,* favored by Matthew, which is a place of punishment that is retributive but not specifically eternal. Unlike heaven's pearly gates, its imagined entrance was the gaping mouth of a monstrous beast, a spectacular setting for art and theater and derived from Leviathan in Job 41:21: "His breath kindleth coals, and a flame goeth out of his mouth."

An eternity of fire is not an aspect of Scripture that soothes the sensibilities of the Bible's modern readers (Bertrand Russell: "It is a doctrine that put cruelty into the world"),[94] and it has often been noted that without Matthew and his commentators, readers would have missed out on most of hell's terrors. The Old Testament had scattered references to Sheol, and the final verse of Isaiah, 66:24, speaks of an unquenchable fire for those who "have transgressed against me"; but Judaism had no developed doctrine of the afterlife, and pagan writers had various versions of its rewards and penalties. That Christian notions of heaven and hell are much like classical notions of the Elysian Fields and the Underworld (such as those in the sixth book of Virgil's *Aeneid*) did not trouble those Christians convinced that pagans had been given access to incomplete and garbled versions of the truth. Mark mentions being "cast into hell fire" (9:47), while Luke offers the piquant story of the rich man in the torment of hades who looked up and across a "great gulf" saw the beggar Lazarus in "Abraham's bosom" (16:19-31). But it is Matthew (the "ethical gospel") that offers us here and elsewhere—a warning against an erring body's consignment to hell (5:30), the broad way that leads to destruction (7:13), body and soul destroyed in hell (10:28)—that the mighty opposite of salvation is "that awful doctrine" (Newman), eternal punishment. So there is a long history in Christianity (and in Islam) of preaching hell and its unquenchable fires—flames that do not light or warm but only burn without consuming—and with no hope of relief for the condemned, not even through annihilation.

In the notorious chapter 5 of his *Decline and Fall of the Roman Empire,* Gibbon quoted Tertullian on the "greatest of all spectacles," the joy and exultation of the saved as they look down into hell and see "so many proud monarchs, and fancied gods, groaning in the lowest abyss of darkness; so many magistrates, who persecuted the name of the Lord, liquefying in fiercer fires than they ever kindled against the Christians; so many sage philosophers blushing in red hot flames, with their deluded scholars; so many celebrated poets trembling before the tribunal, not of Minos, but of Christ; so many tragedians, more tuneful in the expression of their own sufferings; so many dancers—!" Here Gibbon breaks off. "But the humanity of the reader will permit me to draw a veil over the rest of this infernal description, which the zealous African pursues in a long variety of affected and unfeeling witticisms."[95] Gibbon might well have mentioned Aquinas (and others), though St. Thomas attributed the pleasure of the viewers to their sense of divine justice.

For this frightening picture almost all the scriptural references come from Matthew and the theology from Augustine, though interpreters have also tried, wherever possible, to mitigate its fearful message (the freethinker Robert Ingersoll said: "It has cast a shadow upon every cradle and upon every grave") by invoking God's love, mercy, and forgiveness and expanding on the Christian virtue of hope. Eloquent was Thomas Browne (1605–82), who in his classic *Religio Medici* argued that God's fiery judgments are "the forced and secondary method of His wisdom, which He useth but as the last remedy, and upon provocation: a course rather to deter the wicked than incite the virtuous to His worship. I can hardly think there was any scared into Heaven."[96] But God can reveal Himself in judgment and anger as well as in love and care, however difficult it is to do justice to these contraries. And there is also accountability for our actions, especially our sins. Thus, one theological basis for hell is that offenses against an infinite God require an infinite, retributive, and irreversible punishment, just as Adam's sin required Christ's redemptive sacrifice. Another argument is that hell, a life without God in the next world, is an appropriate—and freely chosen—fate for those who deliberately elected a life without God in this world. Anything less would trivialize and sentimentalize sin and devalue the atonement. And it has always been felt that without the ultimate ethical sanction of hell, Christianity would dilute its moral seriousness and humanity would no longer be deterred from sin and crime. But others, believing in "eternal hope" and "universal restoration," have countered that sin is also a finite evil committed by finite beings and that the punishments of hell demonstrate God's vengeance, not His justice. In a letter, Benjamin Rush (1746–1813), one of the signers of the Declaration of Independence, described a "polar truth" of Christianity: "A belief in God's universal love to all his creatures, and that he will finally restore all those of them that are miserable to happiness."[97]

That hell's punishments are eternal (even though hell itself is timeless) and irreversible was confirmed for early Christians at the Second Council of Constantinople (553), which also condemned Origen for having claimed that its torments could not be eternal, but rather ameliorative, since for him punishments inflicted by a good God should purify souls and prepare them for eventual restoration to divine favor. This optimistic theory, that the next world is not the final state of mankind and that its sufferings are disciplinary and therapeutic, not punitive, has been persistent in Christian thought. Thus, the liberal Boston clergyman Charles Chauncy (1705–87) wrote: "And there may be yet other states, before the scheme of God may be perfected, and mankind universally cured of their moral disorders, and in this way qualified for, and finally instated in, eternal happiness."[98] But an eternity of suffering concluded the fifth-century Athanasian Creed ("Those who have done evil will enter eternal fire"), and in 1530 it was restated for Protestants in Article XVII of the *Augsburg Confession*—though Calvin took it as a metaphor, like the worm of Mark 9:44, "to convey to us a sense of dreadful torment which we can neither imagine nor express properly with our words,"[99] and others have argued that the fires may be eternal but that those consumed by them are not.

All of this was a lively subject in Victorian England and was one of the subjects raised at the heresy trials that followed the 1860 publication of a notorious volume entitled *Essays and Reviews*. A contributor named Henry Bristow Wilson, a liberal Anglican theologian, ventured to suggest that upon death "all shall find a refuge in the bosom of the Universal Parent, to repose, or be quickened into higher life, in the ages to come, according to his Will." Since this opinion seemed to contravene the Apostles', Nicene, and Athanasian Creeds, as well as the *Book of Common Prayer*, within a year Wilson was found guilty of heresy by an ecclesiastical court. His appeal to the secular Judicial Committee of the Privy Council was successful, and the Lord Chancellor ruled that Wilson had expressed a hope, not an opinion, and that his interpretation of "everlasting" (the controversial Greek *aionion*, which some have wanted to take as "age-long" and hence limited) was within the boundaries of legitimate discussion. In his *Memoir* (1897), Tennyson's son Hallam recalls how "one day towards the end of his life he bade me look into the Revised Version and see how the Reviser had translated the passage 'Depart from me, ye cursed, into everlasting fire.' His disappointment was keen when he found that the translators had not altered 'everlasting' into 'aeonian' or some such word; for he never would believe that Christ could preach 'everlasting punishment.'"[100]

Unfortunately, much is still left unexplained here. Luke's rich man and the virtuous beggar Lazarus seem able to see one another, so hell must be a place in view of heaven, whose fortunate inhabitants have the further satisfaction, even pleasure, of watching the damned suffer their punishments (so Tertullian, though the "zealous African" says nothing of those looking down on the torments of their loved ones), the smoke from hell's fires being, it was said, incense in the nostrils of the saved. But how did Abraham already get into a Christian paradise? One solution—now abandoned—was the creation of limbo, a painless afterlife without the joys of heaven or the "Beatific Vision" and reserved for unbaptized infants, virtuous pagans, and Hebrew patriarchs. For Catholics there was the modification of purgatory, where the temporal punishment due to venial sins was expiated (the Eastern church saw it as a process without time or place). Since both churches endorsed praying for the dead (pagans prayed *to* the dead), and All Souls Day was a traditional observance, there had to be some sort of intermediate area where the departed could benefit from these prayers as they purged themselves of their remaining guilt. There were even earthly entrances to purgatory, one being on Station Island in Lough (Lake) Derg in Ireland, said to have been revealed by Jesus to St. Patrick and long a popular pilgrimage site.

The sufferings of purgatory's sinners were hellish, but its fires both punish and purify, so their victims were sustained by hope (even, some said, consoled by angels) as they awaited admission to the joys of heaven. And since Mary was seen as the supreme intercessor, one strain of Mariology made her the "Queen of Purgatory." Luther accepted the doctrine of purgatory, but many Protestants found it damned by its abuses and too closely connected with indulgences, requiem masses, and intercessory prayers for the dead. Its lack of any basis in canonical Scripture and the fact that it had not been established as doctrine until 1274 at the Second Council of Lyons made it an early casualty of the Reformation. But without purgatory, Protestants had no way to deal with the fate of worthy but imperfect souls, which more or less included everyone on earth, though its abolition relieved the faithful of worries about being punished for minor sins. Another modification of the afterlife was eventual and universal salvation ("restorationism"), based on God's limitless mercy; and both the Seventh-day Adventists and Jehovah's Witnesses deny the existence of hell (and heaven) and argue for a "soul-sleep" before an earthly resurrection at the advent of Jesus. Still others have speculated that sinners' souls might be "annihilated" after death or—so that justice would be served—following an appropriate period of punishment. In fact, it was one theological basis for Universalism, the nineteenth-century Protestant denomination that professed universal salvation. But the problem remains: how to minimize hell without minimizing sin and divine justice and undermining Christ's incarnation and salvific mission.

Hell did not figure in early Christian art, but it was memorably described in Dante's *Inferno* (1310), where for the sake of his narrative Dante had to relieve the darkness, enlist hordes of demons, and vary the punishments to fit the crimes. At the center of his hell it is not fire but ice—the cold of a traitor's heart—that imprisons Christianity's worst betrayer, Lucifer, who gnaws on the heads of his competitors, Judas, Brutus, and Cassius. Moreover, hell became a feature, often in harrowing detail, of the west entrance of some French churches, notably in Paris, Bourges, and Amiens. At the cathedral of St. Lazare in Autun in Burgundy, huge hands lift the dead from the earth, and angels and devils operate a scales that has frightened souls hanging in the balance. At the twelfth-century Gothic cathedral of Saint-Denis outside Paris, the *Last Judgment* tympanum over the central portal features Jesus holding two banners, one with the "Come, ye blessed of my Father" of verse 34, the other with the "Depart from me, ye cursed" of 41.[101] In art it is pictured in Giotto's fresco above the western wall of the Scrovegni Chapel (1305; Padua) and by Michelangelo in the lower right-hand corner of his *Last Judgment* in the Sistine Chapel (1536–41). Giotto's treatment is conventional, at least as compared with Michelangelo's greater work, where it appears that Christ is not really judging anyone. In Luca Signorelli's relief-like fresco *The Damned Cast into Hell* (1499–1502; Orvieto), there are no monsters, tortures, or fire, so the agonies of the condemned are expressed only by the contortions of their muscled bodies. But there is a long and sadistic tradition of imaging the sufferings of the damned. St. Francis Liguori wrote in 1758: "He will be in fire like a fish in water. This fire will not only surround the damned, but it will enter into his bowels to torment him. His body will become all fire."[102] A nineteenth-century writer describes a tormented child "in the red-hot oven. Hear how it screams to come out; see how it turns and twists itself about in the fire. It beats its head against the roof of the oven. It stamps its little feet upon the floor."[103]

The sermon of Jonathan Edwards (1703–58) "Sinners in the Hands of an Angry God" has become a classic of fire-and-brimstone preaching. On divine "justice," he said: "The God that holds you over the pit of hell, much as one holds a spider, or some loathsome insect, over the fire, abhors you and is dreadfully provoked: his wrath towards you burns, like fire; he looks upon you as worthy of nothing else, but to be cast into the fire."[104] But contemporary readers can find the eternity of hell most memorably described in James Joyce's "Hell-fire Sermon" preached at a retreat in his *Portrait of the Artist,* as the retreat master describes its everlasting pains by the image of a little bird that every million years takes away a grain from a mountain of sand that reaches "from the earth to the farthest heavens, and a million miles broad, extending to remotest space, and a million miles in thickness." And yet, "at the end of that immense stretch of time not even one instant of eternity could be said to have ended. At the end of all those billions and trillions of years eternity would have scarcely begun."[105] An unsettling prospect, but in the comfortable opti-

mism of the contemporary world, hell seems a doctrine to be acknowledged—
and ignored. Its darkness has faded; its fires have been banked.

Chapter 25 then ends with an apocalyptic discourse (31-46), origin of the
now-familiar "sheep and goats" disjunction, with Jesus no longer the "good
shepherd" of John 10, and goats, always less valuable than sheep, cast in the
ignominious role of condemned souls. It is also a proof text for the Last (or
General) Judgment, when all humanity will be judged, with God the Father
or Son appearing in one scenario on a cloud above the valley between the
Temple Mount and the Mount of Olives. Another legend had it that when the
twelve apostles met at Pentecost and formulated the Apostles' Creed, each providing one "belief," it was Matthew who was responsible for the Last Judgment ("from thence He shall come to judge the living and the dead"). But in
its few—and imaginative—verses, the passage raises serious subjects: the divinity of Jesus as Christ the King (34); his equality with the Father as the Son
of man (31); his ascendancy over Satan and the rebellious angels (41); predestination (34b); and the eternity of heaven's joys and hell's fires (46). It also
raises some difficult questions. Do "all nations" and "the least of these my
brethren" refer to humanity in general (the modern understanding, particularly for those who favor "social Christianity")? Or does *ethna,* the Greek word
for "nations," refer here, as usually in Matthew, to Gentiles, with the point
being that they will be judged, separately from the Jews, on how they treated
Jesus' disciples?

As is so often the case, a single word, "For" (35a; *gar* in Greek), was at the
center of a Reformation dispute. For Catholics it was causal, the reason why
acts of charity can merit heavenly rewards; for Protestants it was consequen-
tial, denoting the acts of charity that result from faith, signs of gratitude for
God's grace. John Locke found it "remarkable" that 31-46 is "without any
mention of believing or not believing."[106] Hence, John Wesley, in his commentary on Matthew, warned against isolating charitable services: "All these
works of outward mercy suppose faith and love, and must needs be accompanied with works of spiritual mercy."[107] But Benjamin Franklin, as a deist,
thought that "vital Religion had always suffer'd, when Orthodoxy is more regarded than Virtue. And the Scripture assures me, that on the last Day, we shall
not be examin'd what we *thought,* but what we *did* "[108]—though it is important
to note that for Jesus in 42-43 worse than the evil men do is the good that they
fail to do. Another proof text for the Reformers was that the left-right disjunction left no middle space for purgatory or limbo. But these dogmatic difficulties aside, Jesus' words have been an inspiration for all the institutions
devoted to works of Christian charity, not only among fellow believers (if Matthew is here referring to his own community), but for all who are needy and
suffering.

The Last Judgment will also see the reuniting of souls with their bodies, though there has been little certainty of how and where the disembodied souls would exist from the time of death until the Great Assize. It was of some consolation for the saved that their bodies would be recognizable but freed of all imperfections. With this doctrine in mind, Franklin composed his epitaph: "The Body of / B. Franklin Printer / (like the Cover of an old Book / Its Contents torn out / And stript of its Lettering and Gilding) / Lies here, Food for Worms. / But the Work shall not be lost; / For it will (as he believ'd) appear once more, / In a new and more elegant Edition / Revised and Corrected / By the Author."[109] The resurrection of the body on the day of General Judgment also encouraged Christians to honor the physical remains of saints, especially martyrs, and to turn their burial places into centers of pilgrimage. If their bodily parts were not available, then material objects associated with them, such as bits of clothing, provided believers with visible links to sanctity, an access to divinity for those uneducated in Scripture and theology.

Verse 35 was cited by St. Benedict in his *Rule* (53) in ordering that his monks should treat guests "as Christ himself," and Jesus' words have provided the source for the "Seven Corporal Works of Mercy," with burying the dead added to the six listed (35-40). The "Seven Spiritual Works of Mercy" are instructing the ignorant, counseling the doubtful, admonishing sinners, bearing wrongs patiently, forgiving offenses willingly, comforting the afflicted, and praying for the needs of others. These comprise the social matrix of Christianity, its faith in action and service (and although Herod imprisoned John the Baptist at 14:3, there is no record in Scripture of prison visits), and "everlasting fire" (41) for those who neglected these works. They had no counterpart in ancient paganism. But since 31-46 seem to promise rewards for good works, Calvin stressed that the "kingdom" is not the wages of a worker but the inheritance (v. 34) of a son.[110] William Penn quoted verse 45 in "A Persuasion to Moderation to Church Dissenters in Prudence and Conscience" (1686) as he expanded these acts of charity to include religious toleration.[111] Emily Dickinson alluded to this verse and to a similar sentiment in 25:40-42 in the last two stanzas of her lyric 132, "I bring an unaccustomed wine." "And so I always bear the cup / If, haply, mine may be the drop / Some pilgrim thirst to slake— / If, haply, any say to me, 'Unto the little, unto me,' / When I at last awake."[112] This was also a favored passage in the American civil rights movement, and Martin Luther King Jr. quoted 42-45 ("When saw we thee . . . ?") in his last sermon, on Passion Sunday, March 31, 1968, in Washington's National Cathedral, concluding with "That's the question facing America today."[113]

Chapter 25 concludes with 40-46, and there is a long dispute over the identity of the "brethren" (v. 40). Are they other Christians (implied by Jesus' words at 12:50, "whosoever shall do the will of my Father") or, more likely, anyone who is needy (implied by his words at 7:3-5, "thy brother")? Jesus later recalled this verse when he appeared in a dream vision to the twenty-year-old St. Martin of Tours (316–400). Jesus was wearing the cloak that Martin, despite his poverty, had shared with a poor man he had met at the Amiens city gate. Martin at once received baptism and began his long career in Gaul as monk, bishop, and miracle-worker.[114]

But for those who responded less charitably, there was prepared an "everlasting fire" (also at 18:8). This fate was also decreed for "Jews, heretics, and schismatics" and anyone else outside "the bosom and unity of the Catholic Church," according to the "Decree for the Jacobites" (1442; the Jacobites were Coptic Christians and Monophysites in Egypt) issued at the General Council of Florence (1431–45) convened to seek union between the Eastern and Western churches. The Reformed creed, the Second Helvetic Confession (1566), invoked a familiar precedent: "For as without the ark of Noah there was no escaping when the world perished with floods," so "such as would be saved must in no wise separate themselves from the true Church of Christ."[115] But this refers to apostates, and despite such sentiments, allowance has traditionally been made for those living according to their own lights, a state sometimes described as "implicit desire" or "invincible ignorance" (which can surprise or irritate those so designated) of the true church. Hence, in 1949 Pope Pius XII condemned Fr. Leonard Feeney, the Boston priest who insisted on a literal application of *extra ecclesiam nulla salus* ("Outside the Church there is no salvation"). But it can also be understood more inclusively as "No well-being outside God's family."

8

Passion, Death, and Resurrection

Here we move from Jesus as teacher and preacher to Jesus as sufferer and victim, and, for Christians, as Messiah and Redeemer. Matthew's passion and resurrection account generally follows Mark's, though he adds such details as the thirty pieces of silver (alluded to at Zech. 11:12), the suicide of Judas, the dream of Pilate's wife and Pilate's famous handwashing, the setting of a guard at Jesus' tomb, and a final Great Commission to his disciples. The ordeals of Matthew's passion narrative also recall elements of his infancy narrative: death, birth; Pontius Pilate, Herod; a journey to Galilee, a journey from Galilee; a dream by Pilate's wife, a dream by Mary's husband; darkness over the earth, a star in the sky; Roman soldiers, foreign wise men; Joseph of Arimathea, Joseph, husband of Mary. Finally, the title "King of the Jews," along with the presence of angels and an abundance of OT "fulfillment" allusions in both narratives remind readers that for Matthew the troubling story of the passion is actually the culmination of a divine plan.

> There is no religion without *mysteries;*
> these, with *sacrifices,* constitute the
> essential part of worship.
> —Chateaubriand

> And Caiaphas was in his own mind
> A benefactor to mankind.
> —William Blake

Chapter 26 begins with the announcement of the Passover feast and Jesus' betrayal and crucifixion.[1] The evangelists themselves disagree on the order of events in Passion Week, and there is still no modern consensus on the exact date or site of the Last Supper and its coordination with the Jewish seder, or Passover Supper, which was normally held within families. Matthew and Luke, following Mark, identify the two suppers, though they both omit significant details such as the eating of lamb and unleavened bread, the sprinkling of blood on the house door, and the recollection of the Exodus experience; and Jesus' family is now his disciples. The identification of the Last Supper with the Passover Seder may reflect the concern of the early church to exploit the feast's sacrificial and redemptive symbolism, its evocation of the Jews' liberation from Egypt, in order to suggest the new "salvation" preached by Jesus and ratified by his resurrection. But John's passion account, which places the crucifixion before Passover, is probably closer to the historical truth, since it is unlikely that Jewish officials would conduct a trial and crucifixion during Passover. But if there is no agreement on situating the events recorded during that fateful week, there is even less agreement—indeed, often bitter disputes—about their meaning both for the original participants and for Christians reenacting them in their liturgies and their lives. (This should not be surprising when one reflects on the factual, evidential, and ideological disputes that still rage over the assassination of John F. Kennedy, an event widely witnessed, recorded on film, and painstakingly investigated with all the resources of modern technology.)

The problem faced by the Jewish officials in verses 3-4 of how they are to capture and kill Jesus is solved by the appearance of Judas in 14-16 and his agreement to deliver Jesus in return for thirty pieces of silver—a combination of treachery and greed that recalls how the similarly named Judah sold Joseph to the Ishmaelites for twenty pieces of silver (Gen. 37:28). It is a basic source of Western civilization's anti-Semitic stereotype, and in the early church, Wednesday, the day of Judas' betrayal, ranked just behind Friday as a day of fasting and penitence. Judas was traditionally shown as red-haired and red-bearded (like the devil). His name, the Greek form of Judah, meaning "Judean" or "Jew," added to the anti-Semitic resonance of the story; and, as the thirteenth at the table of the Last Supper, he would forever stigmatize that number. The verb customarily translated as "betray" in describing Judas's action also has the more neutral meaning of "hand over," but there is still no consensus on why Judas handed Jesus over to the authorities (who really did not need his services to find and capture Jesus). Speculations include simple greed (complicated by the unknown denomination and value of the "thirty pieces of silver"), disappointment that Jesus refused to be the messiah who would organize the Jews and liberate Israel, and even a noble role in furthering God's plan in the "Suffering Servant" scenario that would redeem the world. The extent to which Judas's will was free in implementing what can be seen as a divine plan was argued by Erasmus and Luther, with the former insisting that he could have changed his mind, the latter that his will was fixed by God's foreknowledge.[2]

Christians later accumulated more Jewish blame through a canard connected with the Eucharist, that Jews "recrucified" Christ by stealing and mutilating consecrated hosts, though the favorite charge was that they kidnapped and sacrificed Christian children, using their blood in Passover ceremonies, an ironic slander since the Old Testament so persistently denounces child-sacrifice. It is well to remember that anti-Semitism of a sort existed in pagan antiquity (though the term was not coined until the nineteenth century), even if it rarely provoked the bloody persecutions that have disfigured subsequent history and culminated in the Holocaust. Many Greeks and Romans seem to have been simply contemptuous of Jews, regarding them as misanthropic atheists (because they refused to acknowledge the humanized gods of Mt. Olympus) who mutilated themselves (circumcision—though also practiced by Egyptians) and were addicted to a weekly observance (instead of seasonal festivals) and eccentric dietary laws (avoiding pork and shellfish); and in 137 BC and AD 19 they were expelled from Rome, though under obscure circumstances. But others admired their imageless worship of a single deity, their ancient lineage, their austere morality, and their social cohesiveness; and the Roman government permitted them to avoid military service and court appearances on the Sabbath, to finesse emperor worship by sacrificing for his health, to send their annual half-shekel tax to Jerusalem to support the temple, and generally to conduct their own affairs. Later Christian regimes would not always be so tolerant, though their religious prejudices were usually fueled by other, less noble resentments; and the worst act of anti-Semitism, the Holocaust of Nazi Germany, was perpetrated by people who were violently anti-Christian.

In verses 6-13, Jesus is in Bethany on the eastern side of Jerusalem at the house of Simon the leper, who is otherwise unknown, leading to speculation that he might have earlier been healed by Jesus. The Western church, beginning with Gregory the Great (540–604), has traditionally identified the unnamed woman who anoints his head as Mary Magdalene, thus making this episode part of the Magdalene legend. (At Luke 7:37-50, where the setting is a Pharisee's house, the woman anoints his feet, since he was not sitting but reclining at table in the Greco-Roman manner.) This service made her the patron of hairdressers and perfumers, and the alabaster box was said to have been preserved in Constantinople inside the base of the Column of Constantine, along with the ax Noah used in constructing the Ark, the stone from which Moses drew water, and loaves of the bread served at the Wedding Feast in Cana. Since Mary's service, anointing the "Anointed One," an act that suggests both a royal coronation and a preparation for burial (12), provided a precedent for the display of Catholic ceremonials, Calvin stressed that such extravagances were justified only while Jesus was present on earth.

Also seen as the Magdalene was Mary, the sister of Martha at Luke 10:38-42, who was commended because, unlike her busy sister, she only "sat at Jesus' feet, and heard his word," as well as the Mary of Bethany of John 11:1-2 and 12:1-8, the sister of Lazarus and Martha, who "anointed the feet of Jesus, and wiped his feet with her hair." These identifications, taken cumulatively, created an imposing and multifaceted female presence in the scriptural tradition. Mary Magdalene became a Christian counterpart of the mother goddess of pagan fertility cults, her tearful presence at Christ's empty tomb (John 20:13) replicating, if only faintly, Isis's search for Osiris or Aphrodite's weeping over the dead Adonis. She was seen as prefigured in the anonymous maiden of the Song of Solomon ("I sought him whom my soul loveth. I sought him but I found him not," 3:1), and she became the feminine embodiment of both the flesh and the spirit in gnostic heresies of the early church. This role was revived for her in Cecil B. DeMille's *The King of Kings* (1927), where she is Judas's lover, and in Kazantzakis's *Last Temptation of Christ* (filmed in 1988 by Martin Scorsese), where she is Jesus' cousin and fantasized lover. She reappears as a harlot in a popular musical, Andrew Lloyd Webber's *Jesus Christ Superstar* (1970, filmed in 1973), and in a number of other films and modern novels based on the NT narrative and requiring a provocative woman.

There was also an elaborate and romantic legend, beginning in the eighth century and popularized in the *Golden Legend* (1.374–83), whereby Mary Magdalene became "the first Apostle" or the "Apostle to the Apostles" and a counterpart to Peter, since it was she who would be the first witness to the risen Christ and would report his resurrection to the disciples (28:9-10). The legend then made of her the beautiful and appropriately long-haired daughter of wealthy parents ("Magdalene," from Magdala, a fishing village on the Sea of Galilee, was etymologized as "castle tower," and it is a persistent feature of saints' lives that they be heirs to worldly riches which they can renounce) and was the sister of Martha and of Lazarus, the "Count of Bethany." In the twelfth century a legend conflated her story with that of St. Mary of Egypt, a converted prostitute whose cult was popular in the Eastern church. "Mary" is Hebrew for "bitter," and "Magdalene" has lingered on as a benign term for a prostitute. Another story had her losing her betrothed, John the Evangelist, to Jesus' service; but she was healed of her afflictions, moral and/or physical, by Jesus, joined his entourage (in what capacity?), and was a privileged participant in the events of the passion. (Kazantzakis and Scorsese made her the abandoned fiancée of Jesus himself.) She then commenced a career as a quasi-apostle ("apostylesse" in medieval lyrics) that took her first to Ephesus, the cult center of the mother goddess Artemis, and then, along with Saints Lazarus and Martha, to Marseilles to preach the faith in France. There the *Golden Legend* reports that she converted the local ruler and his wife from paganism and enabled them to conceive a child; while her brother Lazarus, meanwhile, became the city's first bishop.

A variant tradition had her also spending thirty years in penance and contemplation in a grotto at Saint-Maximin-la-Sainte-Baume near Marseilles, said to have been a cult center of Diana, Artemis's Roman counterpart, but now named after St. Maximinus, one of the seventy-two disciples who had come with her to Marseilles. She died there after receiving her last Communion from angels, and her remains were subsequently interred at Vézelay in Burgundy, reportedly to protect them from invading Saracens. Her corpse became a prime source of relics (her bones benefiting Duke Gerard, another ruler in need of a son), and the saintly Hugh of Lincoln, a great collector of sacred souvenirs, was discovered trying to bite off a piece of her arm. In Vézelay the twelfth-century Basilique de la Madeleine became, like the Sainte-Baume grotto, a pilgrimage center competing even with Compostela in northern Spain.

Mary Magdalene's success with infertile women suggests she retained some of the powers of a mother goddess, but by Christians she was identified as an intermediary between Eve and the Virgin Mary, sharing the flesh's weaknesses with the former (she is sometimes represented partially nude in art) and serving her Savior along with the latter. As a result, her life story became in all its amalgamations a compendium of the Christian virtues of faith and repentance, hence commended by both Catholics and Protestants. Divinely healed, she was a model of service and, paradoxically, in contrast with her busy sister Martha, a model of the contemplative life. She was reborn from her own lowly past into a new life of sanctity and was also a witness to Christ reborn from his human state. Like the church, she served Christ humbly (anointing his feet) and proudly (anointing his head); and she who as a prostitute knew the perversions of love aspired to a greater love and heard her Lord say of her, "Her sins, which are many, are forgiven; for she loved much" (Luke 7:47). On the other hand, feminist commentators see her story as part of what they take to be the Bible's demeaning of female sexuality, her personal sinfulness and repentance an object lesson on the perils of physical beauty and carnal appetites in a patriarchal society.

The artistic tradition portrays the Magdalene first as an attractive but sorrowful penitent blessed with an abundance of hair (St. Mary of Egypt was covered with hair after her clothes wore out while she was doing penance in the desert). It was the source of her beauty and vanity but also of her humility, since she did not raise her head from Jesus' feet (Donatello's 1460 statue of a haggard and toothless "Penitent" is exceptional). Later, she appears as a Renaissance courtesan, hence sinner and lover; and since she has experienced carnal and divine passion, she becomes a Christian counterpart of the Aphrodite of Greek myth and the Eros of Platonic philosophy, both of whom had spanned the range of love from earthly to heavenly. In Titian's sensual portrait (ca. 1535) the crossing of her arms over her body, barely concealing her nakedness, recalls similar gestures in classical statues of Venus. Some portraits also show the cave of her penitence, and almost all include the urn holding her ointments.

In recent times Mary Magdalene has become a kind of icon for Christian feminists, and "for a memorial of her" is echoed in the title of one foundational text, Elisabeth Schüssler Fiorenza's *In Memory of Her* (1983). She is celebrated as the heroine of the brief and fragmentary *Gospel of Mary*, and for many feminists she is an example of the woman's voice lost or suppressed in the male-dominated structures of the early church. In this "gospel," which is hardly more than an anecdote, Mary has received a private—and gnostic— vision from Jesus according to which at life's end the soul ascends through seven successive levels that represent the powers of sin, the flesh, and the world. Peter is upset that Jesus has spoken privately to Mary, for which he is reprimanded by Levi as the story ends. Like many such writings, it appears to be a work of the late second century at the earliest.

Chapter 26 also tells the story of the Last Supper (17-30), known sacramentally as the Eucharist ("giving thanks"). For Matthew it is a version of the Passover meal and a foreshadowing of the messianic banquet that was an important feature of the end time in the Jewish tradition (reflected in Rev. 19:9: "Blessed are they which are called unto the marriage supper of the Lamb"), which is alluded to in verse 29 when Jesus speaks of drinking again with his apostles in "my Father's kingdom." So the narrative has also moved symbolically from the moneychangers' tables that were overthrown in the temple to the table of the Last Supper; and the table used for the Passover meal ceremony is now the table used for the institution of the Eucharistic ritual. The Koran (5:112-13) also mentions a table that the disciples want God to send down "from heaven" so that they can eat with Jesus and "reassure our hearts and know that what you said to us is true," but it makes no reference to the Eucharist.

In archetypal terms of hero-myth, a feast and a marriage traditionally end a success story, so Jesus' life can also be seen—with some effort of the imagination—as a reenactment of a hero's progress to kingship in which he survives an imperiled infancy; is initiated in the desert; takes a journey in the course of which he performs marvelous deeds; overcomes various foes, including a dragon (Satan) and death itself; and emerges victorious as a new king with his bride, the church. This he celebrates with a banquet. In his *Life of Constantine,* Eusebius thought that the lavish banquet the emperor gave for the attendant bishops toward the end of the Council of Nicaea to celebrate the twentieth year of his reign was a foretaste of the messianic banquet: "One might have thought that a picture of Christ's kingdom was thus foreshadowed, and that it was a dream rather than a reality."[3]

In the early church there seems to have been a single *agape* ("love" or "fellowship") meal, concluding with a Eucharist service and celebrated at first in private homes. St. Paul complained about abuses in 1 Corinthians 11; and by the second century, as Christian communities expanded, there were two Sunday services: the Communion "meal" in the morning, by now connected with Scripture readings, prayers, and a sermon; and the *agape* meal among smaller groups in the evening. The latter was often represented among the banquet scenes popular in early Christian art but was discontinued by the fourth century. By the Middle Ages the morning Communion came to be seen not only as a memorial of the Last Supper but also as a ritual reenactment of Jesus' sacrifice on the cross, a combination that was hotly debated throughout the Reformation. And in a parallel development, by the end of the second century the wooden Eucharistic table had become an altar, appropriate for performing a sacrifice and also commemorating the custom of celebrating the Eucharist at the tombs of local martyrs. This custom began in the mid-second century with Eucharistic ceremonies held at the tomb of the martyred St. Polycarp, an adaptation of the Roman custom of gravesite banquets held on the anniversaries of deceased relatives. Hence, the altar was early shaped like a coffin (West) or funerary urn (East, where martyrs were burned at the stake). In Catholic churches it came to enclose the remains or at least a relic of a saint (sometimes housed in a crypt below the main altar), the Eucharist table now becoming what Whittier in his poem "Worship" called "the priestly altar and the saintly grave."[4] To accommodate priests saying private masses, churches not only had "high altars" but also a number of side altars. At first altars were made of wood, but by 506 the Council of Albion declared stone the appropriate material for these tomb-like structures. This development, from freestanding table to fixed altar, was deplored and reversed by the Reformers, from stone altar to wooden table. Modern Catholic liturgies have restored the scriptural table, so most Catholic worshipers now receive Communion as sharers in a common meal, though behind it often stands the traditional altar with its saint's relic.

In Orthodoxy the Communion service became known as the "liturgy"; and in Roman Catholicism, as the "mass," from its final words, *Ite, missa est,* "Go, the mass is finished." Since Luke adds, "This do in remembrance of me" (22:19), suggesting that the Eucharist, the first of all the sacraments, should continue to be performed in memory of Jesus, these words also provided a scriptural basis for the liturgical rites, those external exercises and ceremonies through which Christians perpetuate the priesthood of Jesus and (for Catholics) acquire sacramental graces. The Eastern church's liturgy emphasized the "mystery" of the Eucharist through the iconostasis, a screen dividing the priest from the faithful. It was decorated with icons and had doors and windows that could be opened and closed at appropriate times. The Western equivalents were the rood screen and the communion rail, both removed by the Reformers, who also gave prominence to the pulpit, so that the faithful—now a priesthood of all believers—could actively participate in the Eucharist and hear the Word of God. In Mormonism, Jesus institutes the Eucharist outdoors and after the crucifixion (3 Nephi 18), and he later miraculously provides bread and wine and administers the sacrament to "the multitude" (3 Nephi 20:1-7).

Traditionally, the Last Supper took place on a Thursday, the crucifixion on a Friday; and Christians have always seen in Jesus the paschal lamb, his blood the ratification of the "new testament." John makes this explicit both at 1:29,

36 ("Behold the Lamb of God") and in having the crucifixion take place on the day when the Passover lambs were being sacrificed in the temple (19:14). Hence, Jesus is both the priest and the sacrifice. Its traditional site is on Mt. Zion as part of a complex of buildings that supposedly includes the "House of Caiaphas" and the "Tomb of David," but the "upper room" (Mark 14:15) shown to visitors today is a twelfth-century Crusader construction that was later decorated in Gothic style by its Franciscan owners, and there has been no effort to make it a site of pilgrimage or worship. So the actual site remains as mysterious as the identity of the man in 26:18 who owns the house.

The Last Supper also evokes the OT covenant ceremony celebrated by Moses at Exodus 24:4-8, where he sprinkled half the blood of the sacrificial oxen on the altar of God and half on the people, thus symbolizing that they were bound together in a mutual commitment. In Catholic tradition it represents a clear break with the Jewish sacrificial system, since it is an unbloody "sacrifice" that is performed outside the temple and that precedes the bloody sacrifice of the cross; and the communal meal is held before, not after, the "sacrifice." Jesus uses wine/blood to enact a similar bonding between himself and his followers in a new covenant—and, since this Eucharist ceremony may be repeated, he not only bonds with the twelve disciples but with all future Christians. One crucial difference is that this time the food they share is bread and wine, not the flesh of sacrificed animals; another, that it will not be the shedding of animal blood but his own as he, the "lamb of God," takes the place of the sacrificial victim. Again, one notices the importance of sacrifice, of giving up something of one's own, and the importance of eating (recall the fruit of Eden) and of sharing food together.

So the sacrifice that happened historically in the temple and on the cross now happens sacramentally in the mass—the altar is Golgotha. This equation of Eucharist and sacrifice was also reinforced universally by the presence on the altar of a crucifix, a practice begun in the Middle Ages and later mandated by the church. The sacrifice on Calvary was also suggested by the priest's "breaking" of the bread, technically known as "fraction." This was celebrated in the early church by the breaking and distribution of the loaves for the Eucharist ceremony, but it also anticipated and symbolized the "breaking" of Christ's body on the cross. The word "sacrifice" for the Eucharist first appeared in "Letter 51" by Ambrose when in 390 he temporarily excommunicated the Roman emperor Theodosius ("I dare not offer the Holy Sacrifice if you intend to be present"[5]); its perpetuation has continued to characterize the Roman Catholic mass. For Aquinas, "The altar is representative of the cross . . . the priest also bears Christ's image. . . . And so, in a measure, the priest and victim are one and the same." Furthermore, "for the remission of sins" (v. 29), added by Matthew to Mark's account, implies that Jesus' death will not be an ordinary death but a substitutionary and expiatory sacrifice that will bring spiritual gifts to his people. Aquinas: "By this sacrament, we are made partakers of the fruit of Our Lord's Passion."[6]

All of this was overwhelmingly rejected by the Reformers on the ground that there was—and could be—only one perfect and unrepeatable sacrifice, that of Christ on the cross, and that the "sacrifice of the mass" deflected attention from the passion. Hence, they rejected the title "priest," with its suggestion of sacrificial rites, in favor of "minister," "pastor," or "preacher." Luther called the traditional concept of the mass as "a good work and a sacrifice" a "most wicked abuse" of the Lord's Supper. He contended instead that the Eucharist was a promise, a "testament" that God bequeathed to the faithful.[7] And Calvin wrote: "We are indignant that in the room of the sacred Supper has been substituted a sacrifice, by which the death of Christ has been emptied of its virtues."[8] But since that happened on Calvary, not at the Last Supper, some radical Reformers were convinced that the Eucharist was not even a sacrament, but a memorial, a ceremony of remembrance. Nevertheless, England's Elizabeth I, for all her Protestant convictions, refused to remove a crucifix from the communion table in her Chapel Royal, and its presence along with her lighted candles was a constant irritant to her more militant bishops, who feared their sovereign would set an example for her people and undo their work of dismantling "popish" altar furnishings.

The "Holy Eucharist" is the only sacrament expressly instituted by Jesus and with instructions that it be continued in his remembrance. Its celebration then evolved: what began as part of an evening meal was later moved to a morning ritual; from Sunday alone it was also performed by the fourth century on Wednesday and Friday, then every day. Once a communal liturgy, by the eleventh century it was also being celebrated privately by individual priests; and participants, who originally offered, by way of "sacrifice," the bread and wine, later substituted money. This sacrament is still celebrated in the Communion services of Christian churches, although the relation of the bread and wine to Jesus' body and blood is variously understood—as, for example, reenactment, perpetuation, recollection—by the various denominations. There are serious disagreements about what Jesus meant by saying "This is my body" and "This is my blood" and that his blood "is shed for many," along with the Matthean "for the remission of sins." For their first millennium, Christians generally agreed that the "presence" of Jesus in the bread and wine was "real," not merely spiritual or symbolic or commemorative, and that his death "for many" meant that its celebration made the mass a kind of sacrificial ritual, though one that was variously modified over the centuries.

Its central event, the words spoken over the bread and wine, was surely part of the liturgy before being recorded by the Synoptics, but it was codified by the Catholic doctrine of transubstantiation, a tradition formulated by Aquinas and affirmed in 1215 at the Fourth Lateran Council and then reaffirmed in

1551 at the Council of Trent. This doctrine maintains that in the sacrifice of the mass the internal and invisible substance of the bread and wine, once consecrated by the priest, is changed into Christ's body and blood, while their accidents, that is, their material and perceptible characteristics, remain intact. This was a formulation influenced by the physics of Aristotle (384–22), which held that all things are composed of matter and form, hence the Eucharist exhibits the external forms of bread and wine while the underlying matter has been transformed by divine power. But in the Reformation this understanding of the mass and the Eucharist became a great source of controversy. And when as a young monk Luther visited Rome, he was shocked to hear that some Italian priests were quietly murmuring, "*Panis es, panis manebis; vinum es, vinum manebis*" ("Thou are bread and will remain bread; thou art wine and will remain wine").⁹

Most Reformers, beginning with Wycliffe, acknowledged the real presence of Jesus in the Eucharist, though they could not agree on how it came to be there or if it resided in the host or in the believers, and they were unanimous in rejecting Aquinas's Aristotelian theory of transubstantiation. It was a word, they claimed, not found in Scripture or the Fathers (though the Council of Trent [1545–63] later found that it described the Eucharistic presence "properly and appropriately"),¹⁰ and a doctrine they variously disparaged as "scholastical," "papistical," and "romish" (and one that enhanced the power of priests, who alone could perform this ritual). It was also considered a kind of blasphemy that the priest, even a wicked one, could appear to be converting bread into God Himself—a creature creating his Creator. They further contended that Catholic insistence on the omnipresence of Jesus' body and blood in all the world's masses tended to undermine the incarnation, which has Jesus taking on humanity only once in history, though the orthodox theory of the "communication of properties" maintains that Jesus' divine attributes can be transferred to his humanity, and vice versa.

Luther considered transubstantiation unnecessary, arguing, as had Wycliffe, for what has been called "consubstantiation" (bread *and* body, wine *and* blood), whereby both the bread and wine, materially, and Christ's body and blood, spiritually, were substantially present, just as fire and metal are equally present in molten iron. Calvin, following Plato rather than Aristotle, offered "virtualism" ("by the *arcana virtus* of the Holy Spirit"): that in the ritual the Holy Spirit conferred the transcendent virtue, or power, of Christ's body and blood, through the materials of bread and wine, but in a way that is beyond human understanding (similar views are held today even by some Catholic theologians): "We hold that there must be no local limitation, that the glorious body of Christ must not be degraded to earthly elements; that there must be no fiction of transubstantiating the bread into Christ, and afterward worshiping it as Christ."¹¹ Zwingli, favoring Calvary over the Last Supper, saw the presence not as "real" but as "spiritual," and less meaningful than the atonement: "The flesh of Christ profiteth . . . by being slain, not eaten."[12] An uncompromising dualist, he also appealed to John 6:63 ("It is the spirit that quickeneth; the flesh profiteth nothing")—a verse, he told Luther, that will "break your neck."[13] He argued that the Eucharist was more symbolic than sacramental, since for him the bread was only a visible species of "flesh" and could not render the spiritual reality of faith; and the true body was the assembly of believers. Hence, he regarded "This is my body" as figurative, meaning little more than, for example, "I am the true vine" (John 15:1). His position has been called "Real Absence," but unfairly, since he did acknowledge that Jesus communicated himself spiritually through the Eucharist— "The true body of Christ is present by the contemplation of faith." Luther, on the other hand, argued that the spirit can act only through the flesh (as in the incarnation); hence, he maintained that Jesus' flesh is not only spiritually but also really present in the Eucharist. Voltaire said of their disagreements: "The Papists ate God, not bread; the Lutherans ate bread and God; the Calvinists came soon after and ate bread, not God."[14] Most Anglicans are in agreement with Chapter XXIX of the *Westminster Confession* (1646) in accepting Christ's spiritual presence in the sacrament—a kind of "real" though not corporeal presence—but without presuming to understand or explain how this *mysterium tremendum* happens.[15] Similarly, Eastern Orthodoxy accepts the divine presence as incomprehensible, noting that the process whereby Jesus' body and blood are turned, supernaturally, into bread and wine is analogous to the process whereby the bread and wine are turned, naturally, into the body and blood of the communicants.

These were the positions taken at the Marburg Colloquy, convened on October 1, 1529, by the Landgraf Philip of Hesse so that the Germans Luther and Melanchthon, who accepted the "Real Presence," could settle their differences with the Swiss Zwingli and Oecolampadius. Zwingli, citing Luke's "This do in remembrance of me" (22:19), argued that "the mass is not a sacrifice but a remembrance," particularly since the setting here is the Last Supper, not the sacrifice of the cross; and Luke, unlike Mark (10:45) and Matthew (20:28), says nothing here or elsewhere of Jesus' death being a "ransom" or a sacrificial atonement for sin. He also cited Jesus' words at 26:11, "Me ye have not always," as a proof text that Jesus was not physically present in subsequent celebrations of the Holy Eucharist. And taking "is" (in "This is my body") as "signifies" or "represents," he contended that it was only a ritual of remembrance, not a quasi-cannibalistic ritual; a sign, not an instrument of grace; and that its effectiveness was not objective but subjective, depending on the presence of Christ in the hearts of the communicants ("receptionism"). Luther said in reply: "God can make a body be in one place alone or in several places at the same time or in no place at all." But Oecolampadius supported Zwingli:

"Christ rose; He sits at God's right hand; thus He cannot be in the bread." There was also the problem of the bread and wine left over after the Eucharistic celebration. Should they be reserved since they remained Christ's body and blood (Luther)? Or should only the consumed elements be considered as consecrated (Melanchthon)? Still, they all agreed that the Eucharistic meal had been illegitimately transformed into a propitiatory sacrifice, partly under the influence of Anselm's theory that the atonement entailed the voluntary self-sacrifice of Jesus in order to appease an angry God. Hence, they refused to allow that a "priest" could offer the "sacrifice of the mass" not only for himself but for others, contending that it would be blasphemous for a sinful human to presume to enact a sacrifice that had been offered "once for all" (so Heb. 10:10) on Calvary, and that the spiritual condition of Christians depends, not on such works as attendance at mass, but on their relationship to the sacrificed Christ.[16]

Landgraf Philip hoped the participants could provide the Reformation with a common theological foundation for the Eucharist. They could not. Zwingli maintained that Luther was interested not in what the Bible means, but only in what it says (Luther was reported to have chalked *Hoc est corpus meum*, "This is my body," on the table in their meeting room). At the conclusion of their debate, Luther refused to shake Zwingli's hand, later taking grim satisfaction from his death in battle: "If God has saved him, he has done so above and beyond the rule."[17] He wrote to his wife on October 4 that "we are in perfect union in all points except that our opponents insist that there is simply bread and wine in the Lord's Supper, and that Christ is there only in a spiritual sense."[18] But he remained so troubled that after the failed colloquy, he regularly branded his opponents as "fanatics," "false prophets," and "ministers of Satan," abuse he normally reserved for Catholics. He was particularly hard on Andreas Karlstadt for his suggestion that when saying "This is my body," Jesus was pointing at himself, not at the bread. And Zwingli, for his part, derided Luther's "countless inconsistencies, the absurdities and follies which he bleats out," and he gloated over his "defeat."[19] These disagreements were also a great source of distress for their English counterparts, who proposed a great ecumenical synod at which their disputes could be resolved. The synod never took place, and another colloquy at Regensburg in 1541 also failed; the differences remained irreconcilable.

The Reformers' inability to agree on a counter-theory apart from refocusing their emphasis on the faith of the recipients and spiritualizing the Communion as nourishment for the soul was an early example of the difficulty of establishing authoritative interpretations of scriptural passages that were vague or ambiguous. Ironies abounded: their "paper pope" (a Catholic jibe at their reverence for the Bible) turned out to be as enigmatic and inconsistent as its flesh and blood counterpart; the "plain sense" of Scripture turned out to be not so plain after all; they disagreed with each other as much and as violently as with Rome; they often found themselves appealing to church traditions they theoretically rejected; and through their writings, beginning with Luther's *Lesser Catechism* (1529) and Calvin's *Institutes* (1536), they built up their own traditions of scriptural interpretation, liturgical worship, and ecclesiastical organization that their successors would apply, modify, or reject.

Both transubstantiation and the real presence were further devalued in the Enlightenment. Voltaire, on what he called the "sensitive subject" of the Eucharist wrote: "One half of Europe anathematizes the other on the subject of the Eucharist; and blood has flowed in torrents from the Baltic Sea to the foot of the Pyrenees for nearly two centuries on account of a single word, which signifies 'gentle charity' ["eucharist" is actually closer to "giving thanks"]." Voltaire was careful not to appear to be speaking for himself when he wrote, "That Jesus Christ did not take his body in his two hands to give his disciples to eat; that a body cannot be in a hundred thousand places at once in bread and wine; that the God who formed the universe cannot consist of bread which is converted into feces, and of wine which flows off in urine." But he added with customary irony, "I repeat that I have nothing to do with controversy. I believe with a lively faith all that the Catholic apostolic religion teaches on the subject of the Eucharist, without comprehending a single word of it."[20]

Later Emerson, writing on "The Lord's Supper" for those Unitarians who would reject bread and wine altogether said, "We are not accustomed to express our thoughts or emotions by symbolical actions. Most men find the bread and wine no aid to devotion, and to some, it is a painful impediment. To eat bread is one thing; to love the precepts of Christ and resolve to obey them is quite another."[21] It was these sentiments, preached in 1832 at the Second Church in Boston, that brought Emerson to resign his Unitarian ministry, and Protestantism has traditionally shifted the emphasis in Christian worship from the performance of the Eucharist liturgy, as it had evolved over the centuries, to the preaching of the Word of God as found in Scripture. With the Quakers the Eucharist has been entirely abandoned, since they regard Jesus' language as figurative, analogous to his calling himself "the bread of life." Similarly, in a valedictory essay, "Are We Still Christians?" (1872), David Friedrich Strauss, whose *Life of Jesus* (1835) had caused many to lose faith in the Gospels' historical Jesus, rejected what he called the "repulsive Oriental metaphor" of bread for flesh and wine for blood and foresaw a time when the Eucharist liturgy would yield to a "fraternal feast of humanity, with a common draught from a single cup."[22] If there can be a minimum of agreement salvaged from these disagreements, it is that the "change" should take place, not in the elements of bread and wine, but in the hearts of the recipients, that they receive as much as they believe they receive. Some contemporary theologians, concerned to overcome these denominational differences, now prefer to speak of the Eucharist less in objective terms than as a subjective encounter with God through the undeniable—if unexplainable—presence of Jesus Christ.

In popular Catholicism the real presence was enhanced by elevating the host and chalice and by the ringing of bells to signal the climax of the mass and to enable those not receiving communion to benefit spiritually by gazing on them both, particularly on the host.[23] This theory was more metaphysical than theological, but it seemed confirmed by some of the most commonly reported Eucharistic miracles, when the matter overcame the form and the elements were turned back into flesh and blood, sometimes causing the host to bleed (in Martin Scorsese's film *Last Temptation of Christ,* the wine turns into clotted blood). One rumor had the hosts bleed because they were sacrilegiously stabbed by Jews to get blood for their rituals, and there were reports of the Virgin and Christ child appearing in hosts. A typical story was told of a German priest who harbored doubts about the doctrine. While on his way to Rome in 1263, he stopped to say mass at a church near Orvieto and fainted when he saw blood pour from the consecrated wafer. This is the subject of Raphael's fresco, the "Miracle of Bolsena" (1508) in the Heliodorus Room of the Vatican (although scientists might attribute it to a bacterium, *serratia marcescens,* which causes a red, blood-like substance to appear on bread products that are stored under damp conditions). Devotion to the real presence was also the origin of the summer Feast of Corpus Christi ("Body of Christ"), officially instituted in 1264 by Pope Urban IV, and one of the most popular holy days in Catholic Christianity. Organized and conducted by laymen, it featured plays, tableaux without dialogue, and elaborate processions in which the host, removed from the context of the mass, was conspicuously displayed as if it were a saint's relic. Place was even made for Mary at the Eucharist, since the presence of Jesus in the bread was analogous to his prenatal presence in her human body. St. Catherine of Siena had papal permission to receive communion more than once a day, and stories were told of holy women who subsisted for years on communion wafers alone. At the same time, the Catholic Church has always invoked the "natural resemblance" of a male priest to Jesus in forbidding the ordination of women.[24]

The veneration of the host in Corpus Christi processions, its elevation by the priest at mass, introduced in the thirteenth century (it was said that one would not die on the day one had gazed at an elevated host), and its "exposition" in monstrances at specific times in the liturgical year, all traditional practices, were denounced by the Reformers.[25] Luther once referred to the mass itself as "a work of evil scoundrels" and "this dragon's tail," and the *Heidelberg Catechism* (1563) called it "an accursed idolatry."[26] In Luther's lifetime the mass was the subject of *l'affaire des placards,* when on the night of October 17–18, 1534, posters inscribed with slogans attacking the "papal mass" ("You can't hide a twenty- or thirty-year-old man in a morsel of bread") appeared in

Paris, some even on the bedroom door of the king, Francis I, who retaliated with arrests, imprisonments, and burnings. But the attacks continued, and Calvin called the mass impious, blasphemous, and idolatrous, and denounced such venerations as worshiping "the gifts instead of the Giver."[27] In an interview with the Catholic Mary Queen of Scots in 1561, John Knox dared to call it "an abomination before God, and no sacrifice that ever God commanded."[28] The Puritan theologian William Fulke (1538–89) argued that it was by hearing the gospel preached, not by attending mass, that Christians' "conscience is galled, their wickedness and hypocrisy discovered, their damnation threatened," and they are thereby "called to repentance" and "to holiness and innocency of life."[29] And the fact that the communion host could be held in one's mouth and taken out of church made it indispensable for all sorts of miraculous cures, magical rites, and bizarre abuses, particularly the so-called Satanic Black Mass, in which the celebrant, preferably a defrocked priest, dips the host in the vagina of a nude woman lying prone to serve as a human altar.

Another controversy had to do with the distribution of communion wine. The drinking of blood, with its suggestion of cannibalism, was normally offensive to Jewish sensibilities (Lev. 7:27, condemns whoever "eateth any manner of blood," a verse still used by Jehovah's Witnesses to refuse blood transfusions), and in John 6 Jesus' call to "eat my flesh and drink my blood" even caused some of Jesus' followers to desert him (6:66). It was almost unknown in the classical world, so its very unexpectedness is an authentication of the Eucharist tradition. "Cannibalism" was one of pagan antiquity's favorite vilifications of Christians, along with "unnatural sexual unions," since they met at night and called each other "brother" and "sister." But although Jesus consecrated both bread and wine, the distribution of wine to the laity was uncommon. The Reformers noted the irony of Jesus' giving wine to his disciples while speaking words they could understand, whereas his church withheld the wine and spoke an incomprehensible language. Thus, they insisted on the observance of Jesus' words, "Drink ye all of it" (26:27), as representing the blood Jesus shed during the passion. It was a significant moment in the Reformation when on Christmas Day, 1521, Andreas Karlstadt celebrated the first Reformation mass, not wearing traditional vestments, pronouncing the words of Eucharistic institution in German, not Latin, and letting his Wittenberg communicants take in their hands both the bread and the cup of wine. Within a month the Wittenberg city council endorsed these changes, and when Luther objected that such sudden innovations could cause scandal and offense, Karlstadt replied that the fulfillment of a divine command permits no delay, citing the uncompromising 18:8, "Wherefore if thy hand or thy foot offend thee, cut them off," and 15:13, "Every plant, which my heavenly Father hath not planted, shall be rooted up."[30]

Protestant translators in France preferred to render "cup" as *coupe,* Catholics as *calice* (chalice), suggesting the Reformers' interest in a vessel large enough to hold wine not just for the priest but for all communicants. Nonetheless, until recently the Catholic Church distributed only consecrated bread at communion, maintaining that here wine is being offered to the apostles, who were in effect "ordained," and that in any case Jesus' body and blood are both present under either species ("concomitance"). There was also the prudential consideration that the wine might easily be spilled. Hence the veneration of the consecrated host became the center of the mass, particularly when raised high at the elevation to the ringing of bells or displayed on special occasions, such as the Corpus Christi processions, in monstrances lavishly decorated with gold and precious stones. In response, the Protestant rejection of transubstantiation led to abusive terms for the consecrated host in the tabernacle ("Jack-in-the-box"), and survives in "hocus-pocus," a parody of *Hoc est corpus meum* ("This is my body").

Proponents of offering both bread and wine were known as Utraquists ("both forms") and Calixtones ("chalices"); they were preeminently the Hussites of fifteenth-century Bohemia and were condemned at the Council of Constance in 1414 on the ground that Jesus was wholly present in both bread and wine. On July 6, 1415, their leader, John Hus, who had been heavily influenced by the writings of the English Reformer John Wycliffe, was burned at the stake, after being imprisoned and tried despite a promise of safe conduct to present his case. When King Wenceslas IV of Bohemia (1361–1419) tried to suppress Utraquism in Prague and other towns in his jurisdiction, militant leaders gathered peasants at a hill they named "Tabor," thought to be the mountain where Jesus underwent his transfiguration. This was the beginning of the "Taborites," radical reformers whose insistence on the lay chalice extended to greater use of the Czech language in place of Latin; a Scripture-centered mass without ornaments, vestments, or ceremony; and the abolishment of the cult of saints, private confession, and the doctrine of purgatory. Taborite armies, under a flag featuring a red chalice on a black background, raged through Central Europe—the "Hussite Wars"—until the middle of the fifteenth century, incited by apocalyptic furies and visions of a new society and a common possession of goods. They were finally reconciled with the church in 1436, though the Hussites were the last major reform movement—or heresy—before the appearance of Martin Luther. That so minor a point, though enjoined by Scripture, led to such an overreaction indicates the late-medieval church's zeal in prosecuting, and persecuting, "heretics"; it also shows that the mass had moved from a Eucharistic meal to a meritorious sacrifice subject to church discipline. After the Second Vatican Council (1962–65) wine became optional for Catholics, but teetotaling Protestants, such as Baptists, use grape juice, first developed in 1869 when Dr. Thomas Welch, a Methodist dentist, pasteurized Concord grape juice to make an unfermented wine. The Mormons use water.

The Last Supper has always been a staple of Christian art, and it was a favorite wall decoration in monastery refectories. The two most compelling moments in chapter 26 were conjoined by Leonardo da Vinci in his celebrated *Last Supper* (1495–98; Milan) as Jesus, a calm, almost solemn figure among the agitated apostles, points with his left hand to the bread ("This is my body"), while with his right hand he reaches out to dip his hand in the dish with Judas. The apostles, in four groups of three, numbers repeated in the four wall hangings on each side and the three rear windows, react with varied gestures of shock and innocence. In sharp contrast is Tintoretto's Mannerist version (1594; Venice), where a dark room crowded with servants and angels is illumined by Jesus' brilliant halo (Judas has none). Veronese's version (1573; Venice), which made the Last Supper only the central part of a festive scene that also showed a clown and a dog (even German soldiers, undoubtedly Lutherans!), was so unacceptable to the Inquisition that he changed its title to "The Feast in the House of Levi" (Luke 5:29). Significantly, Judas calls Jesus, not "Lord," as do the other disciples, but "Master" ("Master, is it I?"), that is, "Rabbi," the title used by Jesus' foes. His greeting, "Hail, master," at verse 49 is recalled by Shakespeare's Richard II as he thinks of the followers who have abandoned him: "Did they not sometimes cry 'All hail' to me? / As Judas did to Christ: but he in twelve / Found truth in all but one; I in twelve thousand none" (4.1). And in a dramatic scene painted by Jacques-Louis David (1748–1825) twelve "disciples" gather around a Christ-like Socrates as he points upward—though the "chalice" he is about to drink contains hemlock.

In two classics of German literature there are remarkable versions of the Last Supper. Toward the end of Thomas Mann's *Magic Mountain* ("the hour is at hand"), a kind of god-king named Mynheer Peeperkorn presides over a table of twelve, with bread and wine, like "an elderly priest of some oriental cult."[31] As his exhausted guests nod off, he recites the story of Gethsemane and Jesus' rebuke (26:40-41). It is not his life that is ending (though he will soon die), but his vitality, his potency. He is Jesus and also Bacchus; his passion is a loss of passion. Almost two hundred years earlier, the romantic hero of Goethe's *Sufferings of Young Werther* (and in German the word for sufferings also means passion) dramatized his suicide—and himself—by first dining on bread and wine and then visiting a garden. He had earlier felt himself forsaken by God (27:46), and he was persuaded that he was sacrificing himself to spare his beloved Lotte his obsessive attentions and "save" her marriage to Albert. He dies as a martyr to unhappy love. Ignazio Silone (1900–78), in his novel *Bread and Wine* (1936), invoked the traditional interpretation of these two foods as a symbol of unity: the bread "made from many ears of grain," the wine "made from many grapes."[32] For the novel's hero, Pietro Spina, this sharing serves as an authentic—though secularized—ritual of brotherhood and solidarity, the only values he can affirm after becoming disillusioned with the dogmas of Communism.

The rest of chapter 26 takes place at night, and its darkness, along with the "darkness over all the land" at 27:45, is commemorated by the Tenebrae (Latin for "shades") services in some Christian churches, in which candles are successively extinguished during Holy Week to symbolize the disciples' abandonment of Jesus and to dramatize the darkness of a world without God. The next scene is the "Agony in the Garden," with its depiction of a humanly apprehensive, if not fearful Jesus, who falls "on his face" (reminiscent of the Muslin prayer position), though artists preferred to follow Luke 22:41, which has Jesus kneeling, not prostrate (39). (Here the 1611 KJV had "Judas" for "Jesus" in 36, another reminder that modern readers do not have the original—and sometimes erroneous—text of the Authorized Version.) Since the divine plan appears to connect the two gardens, Eden and Gethsemane, and Adam's sin in Eden was disobedience, it is appropriate that Jesus be shown in Gethsemane as obedient to God's will; in Bach's *St. Matthew Passion* the bass soloist connects Jesus' "fall" with Adam's. One oddity of this scene is that the words of his acceptance (39: "not as I will, but as thou wilt"), along with "enter not into temptation" in 41, recall the Lord's Prayer. Another is that Jesus' three prayers—which are heard by the sleeping disciples!—seem balanced by Peter's three denials at 69-75. This event distressed many patristic and medieval commentators, who were concerned with the spirituality of Scripture and so would have preferred that he exhibit more confidence in the face of death, though their distress is evidence for its authenticity. Aquinas said: "Since Christ could do all things, it does not seem becoming to Him to ask anything from anyone." Since the episode resists allegorization, one solution was to sharply divide Jesus' human from his divine nature (Aquinas: "To pray belongs to Christ as man"), a division that they in theory rejected.[33] Hence, his revulsion from death is another sign of his human nature, and since death is the legacy of sin, and as Jesus opposed sin, so must he also oppose death. Similarly, his resurrection, which represents a victory over death, is also a victory over sin. Still, some have invidiously compared the "agony" of this scene with Socrates' calm acceptance of his approaching death. But for Renan it was part of *une grande tristesse* that he saw afflicting Jesus in his last days: "Did he remember the clear fountains of Galilee where he was wont to refresh himself: the vine and the fig-tree under which he had reposed, and the young maiden who, perhaps, would have consented to love him?"[34]

Judas then leads a mob to arrest Jesus, identifying him with a kiss—the only such gesture in Matthew—but it is a "kiss of betrayal," a blasphemous perversion of the "kiss of peace" that is supposed to unite Christian souls in Christ by conveying through their lips the love that is in their hearts. So the liturgical "kiss of peace" is omitted from the mass on Holy Thursday. This incident is the subject of a Giotto fresco in the Scrovegni Chapel (1305) in Padua, where Judas seems to trap Jesus in his cloak, their gazes hypnotically interlocking. The Garden of Gethsemane ("oil press") on the Mount of Olives is now marked by the Church of All Nations, or Church of the Agony (1919–24). Built over previous churches, it contains part of what is said to be the rock on which Jesus knelt to pray.

Next a disciple (Peter, in John 18:10) cuts off the ear of one of the high priest's servants, though some have been alarmed that a follower of Jesus should be so heavily armed. This is a well-known episode because of the proverbial—though ambivalent—quality of Jesus' statement: "They that take the sword shall perish with the sword" (52; also at Rev. 13:10). Usually taken as condemning violence, it has also been used to justify capital punishment or even interpreted to mean that "you who take up your sword against me will perish by my sword." It was one of the Quakers' standard proof texts against bearing arms, and in his *Journal* (1664) their founder, George Fox, quoted 52, adding: "Here is the faith and patience of the saints, to bear and suffer all things, knowing vengeance is the Lord's."[35] Like many others, the Anabaptist Reformer Balthasar Hubmaier cited this text as an argument for pacifism, though he expected the "authorities" to use the sword to protect its citizens, noting that Jesus did not tell Peter to throw the sword away. "For Christ rebuked him because he drew it, not because he had a sword at his side."[36] But even this detail of the passion was also interpreted symbolically, so since the "Annunciation" to Mary in Luke was sometimes taken to mean that Jesus was conceived through her ear, this cutting off of the servant's ear came to symbolize deafness to the word of God. Finally, Jesus' submissiveness here became a clear warrant for the authority of secular rulers.

In the second century Celsus noted that the Christians' "Most High, or whatever name you prefer," did not intervene to help His people, just as He seemed to have neglected His Chosen People, who "instead of being masters of the whole world . . . have been left with no land or home of any kind" (8.69, 505). But here Jesus chooses not to resist, though he evokes a kind of apocalyptic scenario when he reminds his captors that he could enlist the aid of angelic hosts. Shaw said of the mixed messages given him as a child: "He was a man who could be persecuted, stoned, scourged, and killed; and he was a god, immortal and all-powerful, able to raise the dead and call millions of angels to his aid. It was a sin to doubt either view of him."[37] Here the fulfillment of the Scriptures (54) is not further specified (nor was the "it is written" of 24), but it must refer to the sufferings described in the "messianic" Psalm 22 and Isaiah 53, as well as to Zechariah 13:7 ("Smite the shepherd, and the sheep shall be scattered"). Finally, the flight of the apostles seemed more prudent than cowardly, and for William of Ockham (1285–1347) it offered a salutary lesson: we should not in our human weakness bind ourselves with obligations we are not equipped to fulfill. Hence for him, kings and princes were not obligated to offer the popes perfect obedience.[38]

Luke and John omit the next episode, the night trial, or hearing, before the Jewish council, usually given the Hellenized name "Sanhedrin" ("sitting together"). In the *Inferno* section of his *Divine Comedy*, Dante has Caiaphas punished for hypocrisy (23.112–17), but readers can well understand how difficult it was for him to preserve Jewish freedoms while reassuring the Roman authorities and how anxious he was that Jesus not destabilize this precarious relationship. Caiaphas, who was high priest from AD 18 to 36, may be the only figure in the Passion Narrative to have bequeathed material remains, for in 1990 excavators in Jerusalem discovered a family ossuary, beautifully decorated and inscribed with (translated) "Joseph of the family of Caiaphas," that contained the bones of a sixty-year-old man who may have been the high priest. Perhaps even more remarkable is an ossuary dated 63 and found in 2002 in a private collection that bears the inscription "James, son of Joseph, brother of Jesus," for this may be the first mention of Jesus outside the Scriptural tradition. Ossuaries were limestone boxes in which bones were preserved after the flesh had decomposed, and their use at the time of Christ is another indication of the belief by some Jews in the physical resurrection of the body. For unknown reasons they were no longer used after the fall of the Temple in 70.

The Sanhedrin was an informal group of prominent Jews, some seventy in number and mostly Sadducees, who superintended the temple and acted on occasion as the high priest's "privy council." Like him, its members would be concerned to maintain good relations with the Romans, and Matthew wants to emphasize that it was these Jewish officials who were chiefly responsible for Jesus' crucifixion. John's account (18:24, 28) suggests that its nighttime gathering was an ad hoc hearing or interrogation, not a formal meeting, since the full council had other things to do on the first day of Passover than to crowd into Caiaphas's house. Here it brings two charges against Jesus: threatening to destroy the temple; and blasphemy, that is, misuse of the divine name by making messianic claims. (The threat to the temple would later be restated in an anti-Jesus comment in the *Hadith*, a seventh-century collection of Muslim writings, with "mosque" substituted for "temple" and no mention of its being rebuilt.) The accusation of blasphemy is not new, since it had been raised by "certain of the scribes" when Jesus forgave the sins of the palsied man at 9:2; and Deuteronomy 13:5 decreed death for any such deceiving prophet or "dreamer of dreams." Both charges were potentially explosive despite the scantiness of the evidence, and they were given credibility by Jesus' silence or his noncommittal replies. The case against Jesus was weak, and although it may not have been blasphemous to claim to be a human messiah, given the diversity of contemporary Judaism (there was an old saying: "Two Jews, three opinions"), the report that Jesus also claimed to be the "Son of God" and personally empowered to bring about the "kingdom of God" was the kind of blasphemy that could well cause the high priest to rend his garments. But the council, which had jurisdiction only in Judea, could condemn Jesus for blasphemy (the penalty was death by stoning, Lev. 24:16), though it probably could not have him executed, particularly if the religious offense had a political dimension ("king of the Jews"). But little is known of their rules for evidence and their procedures and powers or of how at this time they chose judges for their court. Still, they had good reason to be hostile toward a figure they saw as another demagogue trying to subvert their faith and cause them trouble with their Roman masters.

The Roman prefect, Pontius Pilate from 26 to 37, had the right to inflict capital punishment, and he could invoke the *Lex Julia Majestatis* directed against conspirators such as self-designated "kings," but he must have been reluctant, understandably, to exercise it in what he saw as a police action designed to end an internal squabble among his quarrelsome Jewish subjects. The appropriateness and legality of these procedures (it would be an exaggeration to call either a "trial") have been a rich source of discussion among commentators, since not enough data are available for adequate analysis. How, for example, did others hear of the statements Jesus made privately to his disciples, such as 24:2 regarding the temple? How did the gospel writers learn of the exchange between Jesus and Caiaphas? Why, for example, was Christ required, under oath, to make a self-incriminating statement—if, indeed, it was a crime to claim to be the messiah? At what point would a sectarian movement become a threat to public order? When it enlisted volatile crowds? Where were the Pharisees? And why was no attempt made to round up Jesus' disciples? Or is this account more theological than historical?

Jesus' silence "fulfills" what was said of the "Suffering Servant" in Isaiah 53:7: "He opened not his mouth" (though when Jesus did, he probably spoke Greek to Pilate, not the Palestinian dialect of Aramaic that was his usual language). It is odd that Matthew does not mention this fulfillment allusion, which Jews generally interpret as referring to the nation of Israel itself. Porphyry, who was a Neoplatonist, was perhaps thinking of Socrates' speech in Plato's *Apology* when he criticized Jesus' silence: "And even if Christ's suffering was carried out by divine command, even if he was not meant to suffer punishment—at least he might have faced the suffering nobly and spoken words of power and wisdom to Pilate, his judge, instead of being made fun of like a peasant boy in the big city."[39] Shaw was often asked to dramatize Jesus' trial. But he wrote, "The trial of a dumb prisoner, at which the judge who puts the crucial answers to him remains unanswered, cannot be dramatized unless the judge is to be the hero of the play."[40] Instead, he recast the subject in the trial scene of *Saint Joan* (1923), and it was not until the preface of his minor play *On the Rocks* (1933) that he attempted a sketch of their exchange.

Jesus' "Thou has said" (v. 64) is evasive and not a clear yes, since Jesus does not understand that appellation in the same terms as Caiaphas or, later, as Pilate did (27:11). Hebrew messiah or "Christian" messiah? The high priest will charge Jesus with blasphemy, an indictment that is not specified in any detail, but it must cover his assertion that as the "Son of man" he sits at the right hand of God (v. 64, words later proclaimed by James, the leader of the Jerusalem church, before being pushed to his death from a temple parapet). It must also include the messianic claims of his followers, his actions in the temple and his implied prophecy of its destruction, his attitude toward parts of the law (however it might have been reported), and his purported forgiveness of sins. A key issue at the interrogation seems to have been Jesus' claims to authority, both with the people (which upset the Romans) and with God (which upset the Jews), as expressed in such potentially subversive titles as "king," "Christ," and "Son of God." Supporting a preemptive action was the apocalyptic strain in Jesus' preaching, since authorities do not like to hear that their societies are doomed to destruction. Still, Jesus' interrogation, held at night in a private house on the eve of a festival, does not conform with Jewish legal procedures, though there is much uncertainty about how scrupulously the Jews or Romans observed what rules they had, particularly in the face of what they perceived as sedition. So the apportionment of blame to the two sides has generated a vast and inconclusive literature, and while Christians must remember that Jesus was innocent, the charges were themselves very serious ones and not simply frivolous or malicious complaints by gratuitously wicked Jews.

Chapter 26 concludes with a second interrogation—of Peter by a lowly servant. The first had ended with Jesus being "buffeted" (67), and there was an Easter custom in eleventh-century Toulouse obliging a member of the local Jewish community to submit to a blow from a priest or bishop. At the very moment that Jesus' prophetic powers are being derided, his prophecy about Peter's denial is becoming true. The seriousness of Peter's denial is confirmed, ominously, by Jesus' words at 10:33: "But whosoever shall deny me before men, him will I also deny before my Father which is in heaven." Augustine saw Peter as a symbol of the church in both its virtues and defects, and Anglicans like to see in Peter's denial and subsequent repentance a foreshadowing of Thomas Cranmer, Archbishop of Canterbury, who tried to avoid a death sentence in 1556 during the Marian persecutions by recanting his Protestantism. But on learning that he must still burn, he retracted his recantation. Earlier Thomas More, executed in 1535, worried about his own constancy in the face of martyrdom when he meditated on St. Peter, the "Prince of the Apostles," who "so suddenly fainted at a woman's word and so cowardly forsook his master."[41] And for Calvin, human weakness was confirmed in that it took only the words of a "damsel" (69) to bring down the Prince of the Apostles.[42]

The story of Peter's lapse is told with varying details in all four gospels, and its potential for embarrassment suggests that it is authentic. The weeping Peter—as contrasted with the impenitent Judas—became a model in the Catholic Counter-Reformation for the sacrament of penance that the Reformers had abolished. And Peter's story was also the centerpiece of one of Christianity's oldest debates, between the competing claims of divine grace and human effort—the one emphasizing God's power and providence, the other combining His love with human freedom. It was raised again by the Jesuits and the rigorist Jansenists in seventeenth-century France, with the Jesuits preaching "sufficient grace": that God always supplies the grace needed by believers to take advantage of Jesus' sacrifices and serve Him, that is, to turn— or not, as they wish—"sufficient" into "efficacious grace." The Jansenists contended that man, in bondage to original sin, does not even have the power to cooperate with God, but needs "efficient grace" (which is not given to all); hence they allowed little room for free choice. Their position was endorsed by Pascal (1623–62) in "Letter II" of his *Provincial Letters* (1656–57), in which he accused the Jesuits of casuistry and moral laxity with such verve and eloquence that in the process he created modern French prose. But like the reconciliation of free will with predestination, the harmonizing of divine and human initiatives remains something of a balancing act.

Legend has it that Peter died in Rome on the same day as Paul, both victims of Nero's persecutions of 64. According to a fourth-century story, he was escaping from Rome when he met Christ at the city gate and asked him, "*Domine, quo vadis?*" ("Lord, where are you going?"). When Jesus told him that he was going to Rome to "be crucified again" and take his place as a martyr, Peter returned to the city and was crucified upside down, since he dared not presume to rival Jesus. The church of "Domine, quo vadis" on the Appian Way in Rome marks their meeting place, and in the nearby catacomb church of San Sebastiano is a stone purporting to show Jesus' footsteps. But in another story, told in the *Acts of Peter* (2c), his preaching of purity so impressed Roman women that they refused to have sex with their husbands, whose wrath then drove Peter out of Rome.

The chapter ends with a cock's crow. The cock is memorialized by the weathervane on church steeples, and its reminder of Peter's denial as it heralds the dawn has made its crowing a signal of the passage from the darkness of evil to the light of grace, truth, and virtue. It also ends T. S. Eliot's *The Waste Land,* where a crowing cock announces the coming of the rains that will revivify the parched land. This leads to the three affirmations—give, sympathize, control—that seem to constitute the poem's message.

On the day he was to be hanged, January 30, 1649, Charles I of England was pleased to learn that the second lesson for that day's mass was from chapter 27, which begins with Jesus' trial, a coincidence noted and publicized by his royalist followers. When Charles pursued this connection in his defense in *Eikon Basilike* (1649), his opponents, notably Milton in *Eikonoklastes* (1649), responded that his life had been less than Christlike and that their "regicide" was an act of self-defense by the British people. This chapter also introduces Pontius Pilate, who had probably come to Jerusalem with a detachment of auxiliaries from his headquarters at Caesarea Maritima on the coast (not the northern inland city of Caesarea Philippi), since AD 6 the Roman capital of Palestine, to make sure that there was no trouble from the crowds gathered to celebrate Passover. Since it was a springtime pilgrimage feast, there would be many visitors in Jerusalem; there would be recollections of their Egyptian subjugation and their liberation under Moses; and there might well be talk of freedom in the air. Pilate had already had trouble with his Jewish subjects, once in AD 26 for displaying military standards in Jerusalem ornamented with "graven images" of the Emperor Tiberius. When the people violently protested, he had the images removed and returned to Caesarea. Another time he defied their protests and used temple funds to pay for the construction of an aqueduct. Officially, Pilate was the "prefect" of Judea (so identified by an inscription found in 1961 in the ruins of a theater at Caesarea), though the Roman historian Tacitus used the civilian title "procurator" (*Annals* 15.44) assigned in AD 44, so he was of lower rank than the Roman legate of the province of Syria. It would be part of his responsibility to eliminate local nuisances before they became threats to Roman authority, and he was authorized even to execute potential troublemakers. The Romans were tolerant of their subjects' customs and religions, but they could hardly be expected to distinguish between religious and political messianism, and they would brutally suppress any potential sedition. They were particularly sensitive to the word "king" (*rex*) ever since they drove out the Etruscan kings in the sixth century BC—the traditional date is 510—and made Rome a republic, and Pilate was probably made aware of a local rabble-rouser who was carrying on about a new "kingdom."

The cord that binds Jesus at the beginning of chapter 27 is recalled in the "maniple," a silken band sometimes worn on the left arm of a priest while celebrating mass. Similarly, the "clean linen cloth" used to cover Jesus' body (59) is symbolized by the "pall," a stiff white square of cardboard that is faced with linen and covers the chalice at the Eucharist; it is also the word for the covering of a coffin.

The scene now switches to Judas and his suicide (3-10). His repentance is defective in Christian terms, since it is not accompanied by a saving faith in Jesus, though nothing is said of his being condemned to eternal punishment. Furthermore, the other account of Judas' death (Acts 1:18-19; that he fell, probably from a roof, and "all his bowels gushed out") does not agree with this one. In his *St. Matthew Passion,* Bach has an emotional Judas cry out, "Give me back my Jesus" (Aria 51), and he also echoes Luke's parable of the Prodigal Son in calling Judas "a lost son" (as the Prodigal Son is known in German). Suicide is uncommon in Scripture; the only other biblical character to hang himself was Ahithophel, David's counselor who conspired with David's son Absalom to rebel against his father. In medieval tradition the tree that Judas used was the elder; it has also given its name to "Flowering Judas" by Katherine Anne Porter (1890–1980), a celebrated story of faith, betrayal, and disillusionment set in Mexico during the Obregón revolution of 1920–21.

How did Matthew learn about Judas' repentance and confession? From chief priests and elders who later became Christians? An old tradition has it that Pilate's wife (sometimes named Claudia Procla), who calls Jesus "that just man," became a Christian and converted her husband, for which she was canonized by the Eastern church. This is not surprising, since Jewish monotheism and morality impressed many wives of Roman provincial officials. In general, Romans and other Gentiles were more receptive than Jews to the message of Christianity, which did not correspond to Israel's conventional expectations of a messiah who would usher in an era of peace under the universal rule of God. Their receptiveness, along with the desire of Jewish Christians to be seen as good citizens, creates an understandable pro-Roman bias in the New Testament (Revelation being a striking exception).

The potter's field (7-8) was in the Valley of Hinnom, once Jerusalem's refuse dump, and its smoldering fires made it an image of hell (gehenna). It was later the site of a charnel house with a great pit into which were consigned the bodies of strangers who died while in Jerusalem. According to Acts 1:19, the field was called Akeldama, "field of blood," and was purchased by Judas. Its soil was said to dissolve bodies, so it became another item on the shopping lists of Christian pilgrims, beginning with Helena, and later of the Crusaders. In the fulfillment at verse 9, "Jeremiah" should be Zechariah (11:12), unless Matthew knew of a Jeremiah text now lost, or Zechariah was drawing on Jeremiah. For those maintaining the inerrancy of the Bible, this is a mistake, not an error, since there is no intent to deceive; and a number of scribes, made aware of the mistake, omitted it from their manuscripts. In any case, the fulfillment helps answer the question of why Jesus had so misjudged Judas's character when making him an apostle.

The Barabbas episode (15-21) shows a conciliatory Pilate. There is no record of this custom, although Roman officials had considerable latitude in dealing with their foreign subjects, and there may have been a kind of "paschal privilege" or Passover amnesty for prisoners in memory of the Israelites' liberation from Egypt. It was also shrewd of Pilate to evade responsibility and curry favor by appearing to go along with popular opinion. Barabbas, whom Mark calls a murderer and a rebel—and whose name may mean, ironically, "son of the Father" (his real name may have been Jesus, which appears in some Greek manuscripts)—offered a message to Christians: the true and innocent "Son of the Father" dies so that the false and guilty one may live. A further irony: the criminal Barabbas is the first sinner "freed" by Jesus' death. These multiple ironies cause some scholars to feel that Barabbas belongs more to legend than to history.

Pilate's wife has a dream (19), invariably in Matthew a source of divine guidance. But in his *Piers Plowman* (18.300–10), William Langland has the devil inspire her dream in the hope that Jesus will not die—and therefore not descend into hell and vanquish Satan. Still, it was important for the later church that Gentiles like Pilate's wife and Roman soldiers (54) instinctively bear witness to the innocence of Jesus. Pilate's declaring that he "washed his hands" of Jesus' fate has made this saying proverbial. The scene itself was painted by Tintoretto in his *Christ Before Pilate* (1566; Venice). His is a Mannerist treatment, centered on an elongated Jesus all in white who is standing while the seated Pilate turns his head away. Later, Shakespeare's murderous Macbeth will ask: "Will all great Neptune's ocean wash this blood / Clean from my hand?" (2.2.60). As she was about to be beheaded on February 12, 1554, the sixteen-year-old Lady Jane Grey, England's "nine day queen" used Pilate's expression in denying any involvement in the plot against Mary Tudor. And Charles I used Pilate's expression in disavowing responsibility for the 1641 massacre of English settlers by Irish rebels who wanted to restore his powers ("God knows, as I can with truth wash my hands in innocency as to any guilt in that rebellion.").[43] Still, it is unlikely that a Roman official would invoke a traditional Jewish purification practice "before the multitude," though it could be an effective way to disassociate himself—and the Romans—from Jesus' condemnation. Pilate's motivations are so sketchily characterized in the New Testament that an array of later writers have been inspired to fill in the spaces. One story, popularized in the *Golden Legend* (1.213), had him committing suicide in Rome and his body thrown into the Tiber, only to be rejected by its waters. The presence of his corpse brought such floods and storms on the Romans that they shipped it off to northern Europe, where, after various failed interments it ended finally in a lake under the cloud-covered peak of Mt. Pilatus near Lucerne, Switzerland. This mountain was a traditional lair of dragons, and it is said that Pilate's body emerges from the lake waters on every Good Friday, when he can be seen trying to wash Jesus' blood from his hands.

At verse 25 the so-called "Cry of the People," which is found only in Matthew, echoes 2 Samuel 1:16, where David describes the slaying of Saul, also "the Lord's anointed." Matthew now broadens the "multitude" (20, 24) to include "all the people" who invoke on themselves "and on our children" a kind of divine curse. This has led to a tragic confusion of individual responsibility, which some Jews shared, and collective guilt, which all Jews did not share. The specific curse is probably a retrojected reference to the destruction of the temple, still almost thirty years in the future and directly affecting the next generation of Palestinians. But it has been perfidiously extended even further to implicate all Jews in subsequent ages, and the marginal gloss in the Geneva Bible (1560) notes: "This curse taketh place to this day." As a result, this exculpation of the Romans became, tragically, the Bible's most notorious warrant for anti-Semitism, although John 8:44 ("Ye are of your father the devil") and Revelation 2:9, 3:9 ("synagogue of Satan") provide some competition. Such is the notoriety of this line in the terrible history of Jewish sufferings that in 1984 its removal was one of the changes made in the script of the Oberammergau Passion Play. It has also been omitted from most "Jesus" films, and both Cecil B. DeMille in the *King of Kings* (1927) and Franco Zeffirelli in his *Jesus of Nazareth* (1977) invented a wicked high priest whom they could hold personally and singularly responsible for Jesus' fate.

Some like to distinguish between anti-Judaism (or "Judeophobia"), caused by the inevitable tension between Jewish and early Christian leaders, most of whom considered themselves Jewish, and historical anti-Semitism, explaining—without seeking to justify—sentiments such as these as the evangelist's desire to distance Christians from Jews in the aftermath of the Jewish revolt of AD 66–73; and both Luke and John minimize Pilate's role in condemning Jesus—after all, he had washed his hands. But it is important, too, to note that Jesus himself never attacks the Jewish people, and it is often overlooked that the Nicene Creed, the one Christian foundation document that is accepted by Catholics and Protestants and by the Orthodox with only one change (the omission of "from the Son"), says nothing of the Jews and mentions only Pontius Pilate. Moreover, theologically, it is human sin that is responsible for Jesus' death.

The passion begins in earnest with verse 26, when Jesus is scourged and delivered to be crucified. In the twelfth century, under the influence of Franciscan spirituality and its emphasis on Jesus' humanity, the sufferings on the cross invaded art and literature. The five wounds of the "Man of Sorrows," said to expiate the sins committed by our five senses, with the gash in his side claiming pride of place, were represented—often in morbid detail and at the expense of the church's central mystery, the Trinity, and its central event, the resurrection. Such details also encouraged pilgrims to visit the sites of Jesus' sufferings. They begin with a preliminary scourging—a fancy word for a beating. This was a Roman practice, and apart from offering another public spectacle of torture, it would hasten death on the cross through a preliminary loss of blood. It also reminds readers that Gentiles had their own cruel part in Jesus' sufferings. The scourging, probably with hard-tipped leather straps, was reported in the popular *Meditations on the Life of Christ* (late 13th century) to have taken place at the "Holy Pillar," a marble column parts of which were said to have been brought back by the Crusaders in the thirteenth century and are now found in the Church of Santa Prassede in Rome.[44] The site is marked today in Jerusalem by the Franciscan Chapel of the Flagellation. Scourging also provided a precedent for the ascetic and penitential practice of self-flagellation. The Flagellant Movement that began in northern Italy in the thirteenth century and spread throughout Europe was particularly prevalent among monks, who already had a tradition of self-mortification, and for whom it provided instant, if violent, identification with the suffering Jesus. Some would whip themselves for thirty-three days, the years of Jesus' life, later to atone for the sins that they thought had brought on the Black Death in 1348–49. All classes participated, organized into companies clad in white robes with red crosses (though women were reluctant to strip to the waist), marching barefoot in procession from town to town, singing hymns and wielding iron-tipped scourges. When scourging did not seem to stop the dying, many turned to Christianity's usual scapegoats, with rumors that Jews had poisoned the wells. "Therefore everyone, great and small, was so aroused against them that they were all burned and put to death in the market place where the Flagellants were met by the lords and justices of those places." The Flagellants' lay leadership and their growing independence of the church led to their suppression by Pope Clement VI in 1349, but public flagellation is still practiced by the Mexican Pentitentes sect.[45]

The "common hall" (v. 27) where Jesus was dressed in a scarlet robe and crown of thorns is the *praetorium* or governor's chambers located in Herod's palace, the official residence of Pilate while in Jerusalem (unless, as tradition has it, he was in the Antonia Fortress on the northwestern corner of the Temple Mount), and the trial was conducted on a tribunal, a speaking platform open to the public. The palace was destroyed in September of 66 by Jewish insurrectionists, but the twenty-eight marble steps Jesus ascended are said to have been brought to Rome by the zealous Helena, where, as the Scala Santa ("Holy Stairs"), they were installed in the Lateran Palace and can be climbed only by pilgrims on their knees. They have been so worn by use that they are now covered with wood.

Here may be interposed one version of the medieval legend of the Wandering Jew. As Jesus was being led out of Pilate's presence, a gatekeeper named Cartaphilus struck him from behind with his fist and mocked him, "Move faster, Jesus, keep going, what are you waiting for?" With a stern look in his eye, Jesus turned to him and said, "I am going, and you will wait until I return." And so, just as the Lord foresaw, Cartaphilus is still awaiting his return. He was about thirty at the time of the passion, and whenever a hundred years pass, he returns to the same age he was at the time of Christ's suffering. But after the passion, with the growth of the Catholic faith, he was baptized by Ananias (who also baptized Paul at Acts 9:18) and took the name Joseph. He continues to live in the East, where he is a model of Christian faith and a great source of information about the times of Jesus. In other versions the Wandering Jew is a shoemaker named Ahasuerus who abused Jesus while he was resting under the weight of the cross. Unconverted, he now wanders incessantly, constantly awaiting the second coming of Jesus and forever recalling his words, "I am standing and resting, but you shall not." He would like to die, but try as he might he cannot. Mark Twain said of him: "He is old, now, and grave, as becomes an age like his; he indulges in no light amusements save that he goes sometimes to executions, and is fond of funerals."[46]

Jesus came into the world naked, and here (28) he is stripped naked; hence, the nakedness of candidates in the baptism ceremonies of the early church as they put on a new self and achieved the Edenic innocence of their first parents. Here the robe is taken from one of the soldiers, its scarlet color symbolizing Jesus' flesh; in John 19:2 it is purple, symbolizing his kingship, which is, for Christians, ironically mocked by passersby. The victims of crucifixion were naked, but it was an artistic convention in the West, and mandated by the sixteenth-century Council of Trent, to show Jesus wearing a loincloth (said to be among the relics preserved in the cathedral in Aachen), thus avoiding the indignity of nakedness. In the East (less often) he was depicted wearing a sleeveless tunic lest the physical features of his body detract from his divinity. Still, nakedness could symbolize his innocence and poverty, just as the loincloth recalls the "apron" (Gen. 3:7) of the first Adam. Stripping Jesus of his clothes fulfilled for Matthew Psalm 22:18, "They part my garments among them," and symbolically reversed the situation of Adam and Eve, who put on clothes after they had sinned. It is evoked liturgically by stripping the altar of its cloth covering on Holy Thursday. That it was not divided (unlike the torn cloak of Ahijah, which symbolized the just-divided kingdom at 1 Kgs. 11:30) made it a visible symbol of church unity and indivisibility for Cyprian, the third-century bishop of Carthage, in arguing in 251 against the easy readmission of Christians who had yielded to Roman persecution or had been baptized into heretical factions.

Matthew's "garments" is in John "a seamless cloak" (19:23), unusual in that a tunic normally consisted of two cloth panels seamed together but with openings for head and arms. For Christians it is the climactic appearance of cloak symbolism in the Bible, and John's seamlessness added to its unity symbolism. According to the *Golden Legend* (1.212–13), Pilate wore it when he was summoned to Rome to explain to an outraged Tiberius why he had not acceded to the emperor's request to send Jesus to him to cure his sickness. (Actually, he was recalled to Rome to account for his ordering the slaughter of some Samaritans in 35, but Tiberius died before he arrived and the matter seems to have been dropped.) When Tiberius's eyes fell on the cloak, his rage abated; but on the suggestion of a Christian bystander, he had Pilate stripped of his cloak, then angrily imprisoned him.

For Calvin, Jesus' nakedness meant that Christians too must be stripped of their worldly raiment before they can "appear with God's angels in his presence" in heaven. But for the anonymous author of *The Play of the Dice,* one of the Towneley cycle of medieval mystery (biblical) dramas, the "lots" offered an opportunity for the soldiers to roll dice for Jesus' garment with Pilate ("I commaunde not to cutt it"), which leads to a message about the evils of gambling (no good "commys of dysyng").[47] The winner, according to Lloyd Douglas's novel *The Robe* (1942; film, 1953), was a hardened Roman tribune named Marcellus. The robe and the memories of Jesus that it recalls obsess Marcellus and eventually bring him to Christianity.

The crown worn by Orthodox priests when celebrating their liturgies is meant to recall the crown of thorns (29). So does a monk's tonsure, which in turn recalls, ironically, the spikes radiating like sunbeams from imperial crowns as well as the wreaths of leaves and flowers awarded to victors in ancient games and also shown gracing the brows of artists and rulers. Its circularity symbolizes perfection. The monk's shorn hairs represent superfluous thoughts, and his bare skull shows that our thoughts cannot be concealed from God. Mary's counterpart is a crown of roses, recalled in the beads of the rosary, which she was said to have given to St. Dominic (1170–221), who used them to defeat the Albigensian heretics. The thorns episode is recalled in the great twelfth-century hymn attributed to St. Bernard of Clairvaux, "O Sacred Head, Now Wounded." It was subsequently translated into German and English, and its singing is one of the supreme moments of Bach's *St. Matthew Passion.* The Crusader Baldwin (1058–1118), the first Latin king of Jerusalem, chose Bethlehem for his consecration because he felt he could not let it happen in a city where Jesus had been crowned with thorns. What was thought to be the crown itself became a prized relic, eventually acquired by St. Louis (1214–70), the king of France, who built the elegant Sainte-Chapelle in Paris to enshrine it. It was lost in the desecrations of the French Revolution.

Instead of his being mocked, some gnostic Christians had Jesus laugh at his tormentors, even while on the cross. This is a version of the "docetic" heresy, that Jesus only "seemed" to be a man, but it is not the biblical record. In fact, the Greek imperfect tense indicates that the soldiers repeatedly "smote" Jesus. Still, it enabled gnostics to rescue Jesus as a divine "illuminator" from physical sufferings and justified their own distaste for the pains of martyrdom. Islam too rejects Jesus' crucifixion: "They declared: 'We have put to death the Messiah, Jesus, the son of Mary, the apostle of God.' They did not kill him, nor did they crucify him, but he was made to resemble another. . . . God lifted him up to Him" (Koran 4.157). The source for this belief may also have been gnostic speculation that God cannot suffer and die, hence one theory: "It was Simon of Cyrene who was mistakenly sacrificed, since he had been transformed by Jesus to look like himself." Commentators on the Koran have no dogmatic version of how this occurred, but Muslims generally consider Jesus a human prophet who died a natural death and hold that it was Muhammad who delivered the final revelation of God.

At verse 32 the soldiers force Simon, probably a pilgrim in Jerusalem for Passover, to share the burden of the crossbeam, not, as so often in art, the whole cross, since the upright beam would have already been in place. This makes for a nice contrast between Simon Peter, who fled Jesus' sufferings, and Simon of Cyrene, who helped to relieve them. That Cyrene was in northern Africa has suggested to some that Simon was black, hence hallowing the sufferings of slaves by making them sharers in Christ's passion. Countee Cullen, noting the contrast with the denials of Simon Peter wrote: "Yea, he who helped Christ up Golgotha's track, / That Simon who did *not* deny, was black."[48]

Simon's assistance is Episode 5 of the fourteen "Stations of the Cross" that are signed along the Via Dolorosa, the 765-yard-long "Way of the Cross" from the Antonia Fortress to Calvary, which is now occupied by the Church of the Holy Sepulcher (for Eastern Christians the Church of the Resurrection), built by twelfth-century Crusaders over Constantine's basilica. What should be the most inspiring edifice in Christianity, at the site of Jesus' crucifixion and resurrection, is for many visitors an uncomfortable and depressing experience— dark, crowded, noisy, confusing, and shared by six different and mutually mistrustful denominations. The Via Dolorosa, so called since the sixteenth century, is not historically tenable if the praetorium where Pontius Pilate interrogated Jesus was not at the Antonia Fortress but at Herod's palace on the western side of the Old City. Jesus would have then been taken from what is now the Citadel inside the Jaffa Gate north to the site of Calvary, an abandoned stone quarry that at that time was just outside the city walls.

The "Stations of the Cross" devotion was a practice introduced by pilgrims who returned from the Holy Land and wanted to install around their local churches pictures or reliefs that would memorialize the stages of Jesus' last walk. They were part of a circuit of holy places localized in Jerusalem by its Franciscan custodians that pilgrims could visit as they followed "in the footsteps of Jesus," stopping to pray at each. The "stations" varied between five and thirty before Pope Clement XIII in 1731 stabilized their number at fourteen— nine scriptural and five from popular tradition, where three "falls" serve to emphasize Jesus' sufferings. In 1975 the Vatican replaced the popular stations with biblical events, beginning with the Last Supper, and in 1991 Pope John Paul II added the resurrection. What was formerly the sixth station came from a Latin interpolation in the fifth-century *Gospel of Nicodemus,* and it showed Seraphica, a wealthy woman living on the Via Dolorosa, giving the burdened

Jesus her veil to wipe his brow and receiving it back imprinted with the image of his face. This woman came to be known as Veronica ("True Image"?), and was also identified with the woman of 9:20-22, whose faith cured her when she touched the hem of Jesus' garment. She was later brought to Rome with her veil to cure an illness of the Emperor Tiberius, and it is now said to be among the relics kept in St. Peter's Basilica in Rome. There Bernini has done a statue of Veronica, which has given its name to one of the four massive piers supporting Michelangelo's dome.

The crucifixion site is Golgotha (33), and one "reversal" legend made it refer to the skull of Adam (often seen below the cross in medieval representations), his sin now to be washed away by Christ's redeeming blood. Similarly, the Friday on which Jesus died was said in the *Golden Legend* to be the day of Adam's creation; and "the ninth hour" (46), the time of Adam's fatal fall (1:208–209). Another legend said that the crucifixion took place on the site of the Garden of Eden and that the wood of the cross came from the Tree of Life (Gen. 2:9) or that it grew from the seeds of the apple eaten by Adam. John Donne wrote: "We think that Paradise and Calvarie, / Christs Cross and Adams tree, stood in one place; / Looke, Lord, and finde both Adams met in me; / As the first Adams sweat surrounds my face, / May the last Adams blood my soule embrace."[49] Islam also associates Jesus with Adam, seeing them both specially chosen by God in a succession of prophets that culminated with Muhammad. The popular *Meditations on the Life of Christ* (333–34) offered two versions of the actual crucifixion: one with ladders for Jesus and his crucifiers, the other that he was nailed to the cross while it lay on the ground.[50]

The skull is reproduced in a rock formation outside the Damascus Gate on a site known as "Gordon's Calvary" after a British general, Charles George Gordon, who became convinced during a visit there in 1883 that this was Jesus' tomb. It is now listed in guidebooks as the "Garden Tomb" and is much favored for its pleasant surroundings by some conservative Christians uncomfortable with the dark and cluttered interior of the Church of the Holy Sepulcher. But although it might have once been a necropolis in the ninth century, there is no archaeological evidence that it was a burial place in the first century, much less the one that belonged to Joseph of Arimathea. So it does appear that the aedicule inside the Church of the Holy Sepulcher, though dating from the early nineteenth century and enclosing the remains of earlier such structures from the fourth, eleventh, and sixteenth centuries, is above the tomb cut into the rock of an abandoned limestone quarry. The memory of its location was probably preserved by local Christians and marked with their graffiti before being covered by the Emperor Hadrian's second-century temple, then to be uncovered in 325 by the Emperor Constantine for the erection of the present church.

All four evangelists mention a vinegar-like drink (vv. 34, 48), but, typically, Matthew alone preserves the "gall" specified in Psalm 69:21, which could hardly have served as a narcotic. According to the *Golden Legend:* "Since Adam had stretched out his greedy hands toward the forbidden fruit, it was fitting that the second Adam should open his guiltless hands on the cross. Since Adam had tasted the sweetness of the apple, Jesus had to taste the bitterness of gall" (1.17). Understandably, the reed and sponge never attained the relic status reserved for the more durable nails and cross. But that "those prophane souldiers" did kneel, if only in mockery, before Jesus was noted by James I (1566–1625) of England in his essay, "A Pattern for a King's Inauguration" (1619), in complaining of "our foolish superstitious Puritanes," who refused to "kneele at the receiving of the blessed Sacrament."[51]

The words at verse 37, often capitalized, are usually portrayed in art by a scroll with the initials *INRI,* the "King of the Jews"—the title lending ironic confirmation to the expectations of a royal messiah. It is probably historically authentic, since the mockery of its "royal" title was not how the early church wanted Jesus to be regarded and remembered. It might have been affixed to the upper part of the vertical (as so often in art) or else to the spike that nailed the crossbar to the upright of a T-shaped cross (known as the "tau" cross after the Greek letter for "t"). The RI (*Rex Iudaeorum*) was combined with VE (*Vetus Evangelium,* "Old Testament") and TAS (*Testamentum Aeternae Salvationis,* "Testament of Eternal Salvation") to form VERITAS ("Truth"), the Latin motto of Harvard University. Across from Harvard Yard, St. Paul's Catholic Church countered with its own inscription, from 1 Timothy 3:15, that it is the church that is "the pillar and ground of the truth," adding, for good measure, on its bell, "a voice crying in the wilderness" (Isa. 40:3).

Matthew does not preserve the Lukan tradition of the "good thief" (23:39-43). Instead, both thieves revile him, and Matthew's readers should be grateful to Tyndale and the KJV translators for preferring "dynamic equivalence" to "formal correspondence" by putting "teeth" into the Greek's colorless "insulted." Their traditional names, Dismas and Gestas, are from the apocryphal *Gospel of Nicodemus.* And Matthew oddly neglects a "fulfillment" citation that is preserved by Mark (15:28) and Luke (22:37): the "Suffering Servant" was "numbered with the transgressors" (Isa. 53:12).

Jesus' "Last Words" have caused a problem. Either they are these, as also reported by Mark (15:34), or Luke's "Father, into thy hands I commend my spirit" (23:46, often invoked by Christian martyrs), or John's "It is finished" (19:30). With the addition of John's "Woman, behold thy son!" and, to his beloved disciple, "Behold thy mother!" (19:26-27), as well as "I thirst" (28) and Luke's "Today shalt thou be with me in paradise" (23:43, to the penitent thief), their number was put at seven and then popularized in the *Meditations.* They are also his first words since the trial before Pilate. The "cry of derelic-

tion" (v. 46) also raises a question: Why this sense of desolation and abandonment if Christ was a perfect being fulfilling God's will? Matthew once more
underscores the importance of the Old Testament for Jesus at critical junctures,
and here again it is Psalm 22, where, however, the psalmist's initial despair leads
to confidence in God's righteousness and triumph ("All the ends of the world
shall remember and turn unto the Lord"). For orthodox Christians it is Jesus'
last expression of the human nature he assumed when in the incarnation he
"emptied" himself of his divinity (the theory of *kenosis* or "emptying," based
on Phil. 2:5-11), though there is much dispute over the intermingling of Jesus'
divine and human properties. But for some, such as the gnostics and the adoptionists, who denied that Jesus was "eternally begotten of the Father," it was a
proof text that the divinity that had entered Jesus, probably at his baptism, and
had inspired his miracles and teachings was now returning to heaven, and that
it was the human Jesus, not the divine Christ, who suffered and died on the
cross. The apparent despair in these words persuaded Reimarus that "it was
then clearly not the intention or object of Jesus to suffer and to die," and that
his was the story of a failed mission.[52] On this basis he initiated the Enlightenment's "critical" tradition of gospel interpretation. Finally, the onlookers' misunderstanding of "Eli" as "Elias" (Elijah) derives from their general expectation
of the prophet's return, as promised in the last two verses of the Old Testament
(Mal. 4:5-6).

The date of the crucifixion is traditionally given as March 25 or April 6
or 7 of the year 30, with Jesus' nativity three months before, hence his conception on the same date as his death. Crucifixion itself was a Roman custom,
reserved for slaves, army deserters, the worst of criminals, and insurrectionists
until it was finally forbidden by Constantine in 337. It was unknown to the
Old Testament (apart from hanging an executed offender "on a tree" [Deut.
21:22-23]), but other literary sources have recorded thousands of crucifixions,
some of women, in first-century Palestine. Six thousand slaves had been crucified along the Appian Way after the failure of a revolt led by Spartacus in
73–71 BC. There were no established procedures, but victims' arms were probably tied, not nailed, to the cross bar, since wood and nails were scarce and had
to be reused. When nails were used, they probably had wooden strips beneath
their heads so that a desperate victim could not pull his hands free. Their bodies could be left hanging as a deterring example to passersby and prey to animals and vultures, or they could be given, as here, to friends and relatives for
burial. As for the physiological processes typical of crucifixion, there is no certainty about how they operate, much less of how they affected Jesus. Loss of
blood (although the Synoptics do not mention nails), shock, and heart failure
make a plausible sequence, though some have argued that the hanging posture
would make exhalation so difficult that the victims would be asphyxiated, particularly if their legs had been broken (John 19:31-33). But those who like to

think that Jesus survived the crucifixion by "swooning" claim that the traditional three (or six) hours does not allow enough time for a crucified man to expire. Archaeologists have found the physical remains of only one such victim, dating from the first century AD, a young man named Yehochanan with a nail still embedded in his right ankle bone where it had been affixed to the upright bar.

There is a legend that the wood of the cross was from the dogwood tree, which once grew as tall and strong as the oak. The dogwood was grieved by this use of its wood, so out of pity Jesus saw to it that it would never happen again. Hence, its wood is now thin and twisted, while its blossoms take the form of a Greek cross with red-stained nail markings and a crown of thorns in the middle of each flower. The dogwood blossoms in the spring, its colors sometimes pink for shame or red for blood; and the "weeping dogwood" testifies to its sadness. Jewelry makers like to design crosses with the distinctive appearance of dogwood branches.

Although simple crosses often occur in the early church, there is an odd discontinuity between Christian literature, where the crucifixion is a significant subject, and art, where it is surprisingly absent until the middle of the fifth century. Then it appeared, carved on a panel of the wooden doors of the Santa Sabina Church in Rome, though in a curious representation that shows Jesus still alive and only hints at his hanging on the cross. Apparently the ignominy of crucifixion was still so widespread that artists were reluctant to show the shameful end of their incarnate God and Savior, preferring instead such symbols as the lamb, the fish, or the vine—or else a beardless Christ in a long tunic, blending the imagined features of David and a Greek god and shown as a wondrous healer, a wise teacher, or the Good Shepherd (John 10). But since the triumph of the resurrection is also absent from early art (as is the nativity), artists may have felt a more general inhibition about the representation of divinity in its most sacred mysteries.

By the sixth century, however, Venantius Fortunatus, a Roman and Christian poet, was composing the great hymn *Pange lingua* ("Record, O tongue"), in which he sang of the "sweet rod bearing a sweeter burden fastened tightly with sweet nails." And in the eighth century the anonymous author of the Old English poem "The Dream of the Rood" imagined the rood (cross) appearing to him to tell him that after once holding "the young warrior" it had been transformed from a device of torture to an instrument of salvation. Medieval scribes often regarded the initial Greek and Latin capitals T and X as images of the cross to be stylized and decorated in their manuscripts. In the later Middle Ages the crucifix was a standard element in Christian churches, partly as a result of Franciscan theology and other emphases on Jesus' humanity, and partly as a result of pilgrimages to Jerusalem and the Crusades, which awakened interest in the details of Christ's passion.

Unfortunately, the scriptural record is scanty, but painters have generally shown Jesus upright against the cross, with outstretched arms parallel to the crossbeam, his head turned upward to heaven and to the right toward the Lukan "Good Thief," or else with his body slumped and hanging, his head below the level of his hands, with his legs bent. His feet are either nailed separately to the footrest or with one nail piercing his crossed feet. The agonies of crucifixion were reserved for the two thieves (exceptional is the ravaged Jesus of Matthias Grünewald's *Crucifixion* for the Isenheim Altarpiece [1515; Colmar]), whose bodies, especially their arms, were usually grotesquely twisted around their crosses. Often the "tau" crosses are shown without the upper vertical and they are held by ropes for a more protracted suffering, whereas Jesus is almost always shown held by nails, under the influence of Psalm 22:16, "They pierced my hands and my feet," and the theological importance of Jesus' "atoning" blood. The nails are mentioned only in the story of "Doubting Thomas" in John 20:25 ("Except I shall see in his hands the print of the nails . . . I will not believe"), but they were said to have been recovered by Helena, and they—or even shavings from them—became Christendom's most precious relics. The cross is sometimes imagined as facing toward Rome, away from Jerusalem, with St. John, the "beloved disciple," to Jesus' left at its foot, and to the right the Virgin Mary, who in her constancy symbolized the church.

Since artists have traditionally shown nails piercing Jesus' hands, this is where stigmatics, such as St. Francis of Assisi and St. Catherine of Siena, have experienced their wounds. Others have felt the shoulder and back wounds associated with the scourging and carrying the cross. Although Paul alludes to them at Galatians 6:17 ("I bear in my body the marks of the Lord Jesus"), Francis was the first individual to have these five wounds appear on his body. It happened while he was receiving a vision of the crucified Christ on September 12, 1224, at a time of increasing devotion to Jesus' human sufferings. When he was reluctant to reveal his stigmata, a fellow Franciscan, "who realized that some miracle had taken place," reminded him of the "wicked and slothful" servant in the Matthean parable (25:24-28) who was condemned by the lord for burying his talent.[53] The moment of St. Francis's stigmatization, amid plants and animals, is shown in Bellini's mysterious masterpiece, *St. Francis in Ecstasy* (mid-1470s; New York). Of the 425 recorded cases of stigmata, most have been women, and some have had only certain wounds. The most recent stigmatic was Padre Pio (1887–1968), an Italian Capuchin priest, a popular confessor, and a reputed miracle-worker, who bore them for fifty years. The Catholic Church has taken no position on the subject, and explanations have ranged from the miraculous to the psychosomatic.

Some have speculated that Jesus was tied to the cross with ropes, or that the nails mentioned by John actually pierced Jesus' wrists, as is shown in the *Book of Kells* (800), since hands alone are not solid enough to support the weight of a suspended body. But apparently there is an area near the upper part of the palm on the thumb side that is strong enough and may have been known to Jesus' crucifiers. In either case, the piercings are said to be symbolized by the doors in the transepts of Gothic cathedrals.

Jesus' death is followed by a series of portents. The rending of the veil that curtained off the holy of holies suggests the sorrow that leads to the rending of clothes. It anticipates the historical end of the temple in 70 and tells Christians that from now on Jesus is to be their access to God, his flesh also "rent" on the cross. For Protestants, so the marginal note of the Geneva Bible (1560), it also meant an end to "all the ceremonies of the Law," meaning the ritualism they saw persisting in Catholic liturgies. According to the apocryphal *Protevangelium of James* (10:2), it was Mary herself who as a child had woven the veil; and when a needle accidentally pricked her finger, she was given a foretaste of the pain she would feel at the crucifixion. Later, the Reformers saw another version of the obstructing veil in the Catholic priesthood. And for those fundamentalist Christians known as "dispensationalists," the rending of the temple veil ended the "dispensation of law" and inaugurated the "dispensation of grace," that sixth and last division of history that will culminate in the final dispensation, which is the second coming. Dispensationalism began with J. N. Darby (1800–82), a nineteenth-century British leader of the nonconformist Plymouth Brethren, and was propagated in the United States by Cyrus I. Scofield (1845–1921), the author and editor of the influential *Scofield Reference Bible* (Oxford, 1909). It divides human history into seven dispensations or ages, with each representing a distinctive change in God's way of dealing with the human race. Surprisingly, Scofield found the age of grace beginning, not with Jesus' birth but with his death, and the doctrines of grace, not in the Gospels but in the Epistles, since for him Jesus was still preaching the previous dispensation of law.

The earthquake in verse 51 is often taken as nature's proclamation of a new age; and as for the "rent" rocks, a cleft called "Rock of the Knoll" is shown to visitors at the Church of the Holy Sepulcher. According to legend, since the aspen tree alone did not join in nature's mourning, its leaves have been forever condemned to tremble. In his "Good Friday" poem, John Donne described the earthquake and the darkness. The crucifixion made God's "owne Lieutenant Nature shrinke, / It made his footstoole crack, and the Sunne winke."[54] The darkness, the torn veil, the earthquake, and the resurrection of the dead (Dan. 12:2) are phenomena suggesting the apocalypse, appearing here in a kind of anticipation of the future and final coming of God's kingdom.

It is uncertain if "darkness over all the land" (45) means Judea, Israel, or the whole world; but it is these three hours of (symbolic? apocalyptic?) darkness, also recorded by Mark (15:33) and Luke (23:44), that have long animated the Bible's critics—in the event that they do not attribute it to storm clouds that benefited from a pious exaggeration. Since it was the time of Passover, it could not have been a solar eclipse, which takes place only at the time of a new moon. Gibbon, who attributed much of Rome's demise to Christian fanaticism, wondered with "grave and temperate irony" why this, like other "innumerable prodigies" in Scripture, went unremarked by the pagan world: "The lame walked, the blind saw, the sick were healed, the dead were raised, daemons were expelled, and the laws of Nature were frequently suspended for the benefit of the church. But the sages of Greece and Rome turned aside from the awful spectacle, and, pursuing the ordinary occupations of life and study, appeared unconscious of any alterations in the moral or physical government of the world. Under the reign of Tiberius the whole earth, or at least a celebrated province of the Roman Empire, was involved in a preternatural darkness of three hours. Even this miraculous event, which ought to have excited the wonder, the curiosity, and the devotion of mankind, passed without notice in an age of science and history."[55] The dark was also the source for the title *Darkness at Noon* (1940) that Arthur Koestler chose for his anti-Communist novel. The allusion is to the novel's sacrificial hero, Rubashov, whom the Party has condemned for crimes he did not commit. He accepts his fate with the faith that his death will lead to the "resurrection" of a new society.

Only Matthew mentions the opening graves, although he situates this "after his resurrection" (53). This passage, along with Ezra 37:1-14, 1 Peter 3:19, and Romans 10:6-7, offers a kind of preview of Jesus' own resurrection, complete with matching earthquakes and women witnesses. It is also a basis for the popular story of the "Harrowing of Hell"—that Jesus descended into a limbo-like "hell" during his three-day interment and brought back Adam and Eve, the Hebrew patriarchs, prophets, martyrs, and even those virtuous pagans who by their "predictions" of the coming of a "savior" (Virgil in his *Eclogue* 4) had indirectly contributed to Christianity and deserved heaven but had to wait for Jesus' atoning work. Whittier: "The dead are waking underneath! / Their prison door is rent away! / And ghastly with the seal of death / They wander in the eye of day."[56] Thus, Jesus' resurrection is not just a personal "victory over death," but leads to a violent confrontation with Satan that liberates an array of worthies who date back to Creation itself. This event, narrated in the apocryphal *Gospel of Nicodemus,* distinguishes Jesus from Enoch and Elijah, who were taken directly into heaven at the end of their lives; and it may have meant no more than that Jesus was (in the land of the) dead while awaiting his resurrection, though it has been understood as Jesus' opening "the gates of heaven," closed since the fall of Adam.

The story also strikes many modern readers as a Christian version of the many descents of Greek mythic heroes, such as Odysseus, Theseus, Heracles, Aeneas—and especially Orpheus, the prophet and musician (recall David) whose picture often appears in early Christian art and who entered the underworld and overcame the powers of death. But the legend made its way into a creed formulated at a 359 council, became part of the Apostles' Creed ("he descended into hell, and on the third day he arose again"). And it served as a proof text for the geography of hell as being "down there"; for the existence of those intermediate areas, purgatory and limbo; and for the bodily resurrection of the dead. It appeared prominently in medieval art and literature, telling how Jesus, no longer the passive victim of the crucifixion, broke down the gates of hell to the sounds of Psalm 24:7-10 ("Lift up your heads, O ye gates"), captured Satan, and handed him over to hades to keep until he came again. Some of the "saints" he liberated went to paradise (which may or may not be the same as heaven), and others returned to the world to testify to Jesus' resurrection and defeat of sin and death. But then where did they go? Calvin thought it "nothing strange" that they might have returned to their tombs, though it is unclear to what extent the OT figures, who had been excluded from heaven as a result of Adam's sin, acknowledged Christ as their Messiah and Redeemer.[57] And if Satan was captured, how can he still be operating in the world?

None of this was as important as the usefulness of the "Harrowing of Hell" as an example of Christ's triumph over death and the devil or as an extension of his redemptive mission to all those who lived before the incarnation, including righteous pagans. Germanic converts could see in Christ's attack on Satan the kind of heroic militancy they admired, and the ninth-century Anglo-Saxon poet Cynewulf described its "clash of weapons" as the "king of glory, the helm of heaven, waged battle on his olden enemies."[58] Aquinas saw it as the completion of Christ's triumph over the devil in that he invaded Satan's kingdom and robbed him of his prisoners, or at least those worthy of liberation.[59] Although the Reformers were concerned to purge Christianity of superstitions and mythical accretions, they did not dispute the "Harrowing," and Question 44 of the *Heidelberg Catechism* (1563) has it mean "that in my severest tribulations I may be assured that Christ my Lord has redeemed me from hellish anxieties and torment by the unspeakable anguish, pains, and terrors which he suffered in his soul both on the cross and before."[60] Calvin saw it as a necessary completion of Jesus' redemptive death, by his going on to suffer, in his soul and invisibly, "that death which the wrath of God inflicts on transgressors." For only by "contending with the power of the devil and overcoming it" could he "appease the wrath of God and satisfy His justice," thereby enabling Christians to "no longer dread those things which our Prince has destroyed."[61]

In the Eastern church the "Harrowing" is a popular subject for church wall paintings, since it illustrates Orthodoxy's doctrine of *theiosis,* or deification, whereby the sinner is raised up by divine influence—and, with its vanquished Satan and joyful "saints," it makes a more dramatic composition than the empty tomb. Visitors to Venice can see a version on the west vault of St. Mark's central dome, where Jesus is astride a goggle-eyed Satan who lies bewildered among hell's keys, locks, and door panels; those to Istanbul can see a mosaic (1310–20) in St. Savior in Chora (later the mosque of Kariye), where a white-robed Jesus literally yanks Adam and Eve out of their graves. In Orthodoxy the word for resurrection, *anastasis,* refers not only to Christ's rising from the dead but also to his "raising up" of the dead, beginning with Adam, after his "Descent into Hell"; and it is the latter subject that was preferred by Byzantine artists, since for them it initiated the era of redemption for mankind. Celsus complained that "He ought to have appeared to the very men who treated him despitefully" (2.63). Thomas Paine was skeptical: "The writer . . . should have told us who the saints were that came to life again and went into the city . . . and what became of them afterward, and who it was that saw them . . . whether they came out naked . . . he-saints and she-saints . . . whether they went to their former habitations, and reclaimed their wives, their husbands, and their property, and how they were received."[62] And Markham Sutherland, the anguished hero of J. A. Froude's epistolary novel *The Nemesis of Faith* (1849), uses it as an argument against eternal punishment ("He went down to hell, but it was to break the chains, not bind them"),[63] as he questions the Christian faith that as an Anglican priest he was ordained to preach. Others have also felt that if Jesus descended "into hell" to free its captives, there is hope that he will eventually do the same for those condemned to its flames.

It is unclear what the centurion and his soldiers, who were probably local auxiliaries, not Roman legionaries, meant by the famous words of verse 54 ("Truly, this was the Son of God"), drawled by John Wayne in the film *The Greatest Story Ever Told* (1965), and apparently spoken in response to the portents. Readers can only wonder if his tone of voice was dismissive, ironic, or sarcastic. In Mark 15:39 the centurion includes the word "man," and in Luke 23:47 he calls him a "righteous man." He is sometimes identified as the soldier whose spear pierced Jesus' side at John 19:34, a certain Longinus, who, according to legend, was afflicted with poor vision but had his sight restored when he touched his eyes with the blood from his spear. He was converted and later martyred, and the weapon is said to be in St. Peter's in Rome, where Bernini's statue of St. Longinus fronts another of the four piers supporting Michelangelo's dome.

The next event, the "Descent from the Cross" (55-60) or "Deposition," is a favorite subject in art and has been much elaborated by artists, who drew on the *Meditations* in adding ladders, backgrounds, and bystanders, notably St. John the Evangelist, the Virgin Mary, Mary Magdalene, "the other Mary" (there were five women named Mary among Jesus' followers), and even the artists' patrons. Unfortunately, there is no basis in the evangelists for another of art's most popular subjects, the "Lamentation" over Jesus' body, particularly Giotto's in the Scrovegni Chapel in Padua and Michelangelo's better-known

Pietà sculpture (1500) in the Vatican, where Mary holds in her lap the dead body of Jesus, a scene that poignantly recalls her holding the infant Jesus. This theme was so influential that it even informed the death scenes of secular heroes, notably *The Death of General Wolfe* (1770) by Benjamin West. These events feature the "women at the cross," both in the Gospels and in art, recalling their traditional roles in preparing the dead for burial. Sometimes Mary is accompanied only by St. John the Evangelist, usually at Jesus' right side.

Joseph of Arimathea (v. 57) was a wealthy member of the Sanhedrin, and there is a legend that he was a tin merchant and the uncle of Jesus, taking his nephew on business trips to the tin mines of Cornwall. This is the story behind William Blake's remarkable lyric, "And did those feet in ancient time / Walk upon England's mountains green?" Like Simon of Cyrene, Joseph enters the narrative when many of those closer to Jesus choose to be absent. He is foreshadowed in Isaiah 53:9 ("And he made his grave with the wicked [the two thieves?], and with the rich in his death"), and here he fulfills the Jewish law of burial before sundown (Deut. 21:23). He later passed into legend as a missionary to Britain and founder of the English church, building in AD 60 the first of the churches that became Glastonbury Abbey. The Abbey was controlled by the Benedictines and served as a great pilgrimage center as well as the legendary burial place of King Arthur and Queen Guinevere. There it is said the hawthorn tree that grew from Joseph's staff, the "Glastonbury thorn," still blossoms in spring and at Christmas. Though uprooted by Oliver Cromwell's soldiers in 1653 during the Civil War, cuttings were made and can still be found on the grounds of the local church. Joseph also brought along the Holy Grail, either the cup Jesus drank from at the Last Supper or the one Joseph used to catch his blood at the crucifixion (the same?), concealing it in the local "Chalice Well," from which has ever since flowed reddish water (of high iron content). When human sinfulness caused the Grail to disappear from Glastonbury, various knights set out to obtain salvation by recovering or at least viewing it, their quests the subjects of stories told in Malory's *Morte d'Arthur* (15th century) and Tennyson's *Idylls of the King* (1859–85). Another legend has Jesus using a cup that was originally given to Solomon by the Queen of Sheba. It is now supposed to be in Italy in the treasury of the Church of San Lorenzo in Genoa, though it has some competition from a small cup of green agate in the cathedral of Valencia, Spain.

The "clean linen cloth" in which Jesus' body was wrapped (59), strikingly white in Rembrandt's dark *Deposition* (1634; Munich) is said to have survived as the notorious "Shroud of Turin," roughly 14 x 3.5 feet and long venerated as Jesus' bloodstained burial shroud—although John 20:7 distinguishes between a head "napkin" and "linen clothes" for the body—because of its image resembling the figure of a naked, bearded, and long-haired man. In 1988 scientists from the Shroud of Turin Research Project did a radiocarbon test on pieces of the shroud and dated the flax plants used in its linen to between 1260 and 1390, though this has been disputed by zealous sindonologists, sometimes called "shroudies," who argue that the swatch sample used for the test was not representative and that other kinds of tests, such as for the presence of Middle Eastern pollen grains, show its authenticity. But the pollen test procedures have in turn been contested, so there is still no consensus on how the image, whatever its date, was created and transferred to the shroud. The Catholic Church, while recognizing it as a relic, has taken no official stand on its genuineness. Oddly, no one at the time of Jesus' burial noticed the image on the shroud, and it was never listed among passion relics. It was first mentioned in the late fourteenth century by a French bishop, Henry of Poitiers, who had doubts about its authenticity. It eventually became the property of the House of Savoy, where it was damaged by a fire and repaired. It was later presented to the Vatican and is now kept in a silver casket in a chapel of the Turin Cathedral in Italy and periodically exhibited, in 1998 for the first time in two years and again during the Holy Year 2000. Meanwhile, the biblical cloth is represented by the altar's linen covering.

The entombment of Jesus is the last verse included in Thomas Jefferson's *The Life and Morals of Jesus* (1820), a compilation of verses from the Gospels which, like his earlier *Philosophy of Jesus* (1804), was a "demythologized" collection of Jesus' words and deeds designed to present him as a great moralist and not as a divine and resurrected redeemer. The two works, reflecting Jefferson's deistic Christianity, were unpublished in his lifetime and did not become available until the middle of the nineteenth century. Considering his other intellectual accomplishments, Jefferson had a narrow and simplistic conception of Jesus' ministry, which he thought was corrupted by the "Platonisms" of the early church. These he did not describe, nor did he identify the "priests" who, he claimed, had inserted them into the Gospels.[64]

Matthew's Passion Narrative ends with the resurrection account of chapter 28, which is divided into three parts: the "empty tomb" narrative (1-8); the bribery of the guards, who managed to sleep through a tomb robbery (11-15, unique to Matthew); and the "appearances" accounts (9-10, 16-20). With regard to one piece of resurrection evidence, the empty tomb, the evangelists disagree on who visited the tomb and when or why; on whether or not the stone had already been rolled back (sometimes fancied as the very stone on which was inscribed the Hebrews' law, and a favorite of preachers who like to offer it as a symbol of the stoniness that keeps Christians from the resurrected Christ); on the presence of a guard; on how many men were there and if they were angels; and on describing the women's reactions. Nor is the empty tomb mentioned by Paul or other early church writers. So for Christians the evidence for the resurrection is credible, even persuasive, if not historically verifiable, and they see these discrepancies outweighed by a basic agreement on the tomb's emptiness, a fact not disputed by critics of the resurrection (who speculated that the body had been stolen) and hence of no concern to the church's first apologists. Another argument for the historicity of this controversial event was the inability, or at least failure, of the Jewish authorities to produce the body of Jesus. It also seems unlikely that if the story had been deliberately crafted by Jesus' followers, they would have burdened it with so many divergent details and left the evangelists with traditions that were so inconsistent and contradictory. A fragment of the *Gospel of Peter* (2nd century), a passion narrative mingling Matthew with popular traditions, does tell of the emergence from the tomb of a man, presumably Jesus, supported by two others and with a cross behind them. The head of the Jesus figure "reached beyond the skies."[65] In his eighteenth-century attack on Matthew's credibility, Reimarus revived the ancient claim that the story of the "bribed" guards, recorded only here (with a surprise appearance by Pharisees), was a fabrication designed by Matthew (or the disciples) to anticipate and forestall Jewish assertions that the disciples had stolen Jesus' body. For Reimarus this theft was to be the disciples' first move in creating the resurrection story and further exploiting their dead leader's reputation.[66] Others have found that it is only a short step from noting the many discrepancies to denying the resurrection altogether or else transforming it into some sort of spiritual energy animating Jesus' followers. Or, as Reimarus also noted, even if the resurrection were admitted, this does not of itself establish Jesus as mankind's Redeemer.

The day of the resurrection became for Christians the eighth day, completing the seven days of the Old Creation and beginning a New; it eventually superseded the Sabbath, particularly among Christians concerned to differentiate themselves from Jews. In 321 Constantine made the "day of the sun" (*dies solis*) an official day of rest; symbolically, it prefigures the repose of eternity. It is still observed, with varying levels of solemnity, by all Christians except Sabbatarians such as Seventh-day Adventists and Quakers, who traditionally refer to it simply as "first day." The eighth day is sometimes reproduced in eight-sided church buildings, especially baptismal fonts. But Easter Sunday itself usually falls on different dates in the Western and Eastern churches. Both follow the Council of Nicaea (325) in celebrating it on the first Sunday after the first full moon following the spring equinox; but in 1582 the West changed from the Julian to the Gregorian calendar, and for the Orthodox, Easter must follow the Jewish Passover, which also changes its dates from year to year. Still, the resurrection, supremely important in Christian theology, lacks the homely details (and lavish gift-giving) that marks the nativity, so Easter has never had the popular appeal of Christmas. Another custom connected with Easter is the "Forty Hours" devotion that originated in the Middle Ages and is still observed in Catholic churches. In this devotion, church members volunteer to spend forty hours before the altar on which the host is exposed in a monstrance, this in commemoration of the watch at the sepulcher from Good Friday to Easter Sunday

Some sort of bodily resurrection was also accepted by the Pharisees (compare Ezra 37:12: "I will open your graves, and cause you to come up out of your graves"), but there is no recorded Jewish expectation of a crucified and resurrected messiah, so it is understandable that Matthew has his own "doubting Thomases" (17). That Christ first appeared to Mary Magdalene has been interpreted (with assistance from the Magdalene legend) as further evidence that he died for sinners. And that so many women were listed—and by name!—as witnesses to the resurrected Christ was a two-fold argument for its historicity, since a woman's testimony would be regarded as less trustworthy than a man's (because of their "levity and temerity"). Moreover, the story of their fidelity was an embarrassment for the disciples, who had fled the scene. The reaction of Celsus to witnesses of the risen Jesus was: "A hysterical female . . . and perhaps some other one of those who were deluded by the same sorcery, who either dreamt in a certain state of mind and through wishful thinking had a hallucination due to some mistaken notion (an experience which has happened to thousands), or, which is more likely, wanted to impress others by telling this fantastic tale" (2.55, 109). He also complained that Jesus' resurrection would have been more credible if he had "appeared to those who had mistreated him, to him who had condemned him, and to people in general." Although at 23:39 Jesus seems to have ruled out any public appearances, Porphyry also regretted the absence of disinterested witnesses. "Had he shown himself to people who could be believed, then others would have believed through them."[67] Thomas Paine later sneered at the evangelists' agreement that Mary Magdalene was the first to meet the risen Christ: "She was a woman of a large acquaintance, and it was not an ill conjecture that she might be upon the stroll."[68] But at 21:31 Jesus had said harlots would "go into the kingdom of God" before the chief priests and elders, and since Eve had been the Old Testament's messenger of death, it was only appropriate that Mary Magdalene should bring the message of life.

Similar reactions have persisted through the centuries among those who question or deny the Gospels' accounts of the resurrection (often calling it, dismissively, "the Easter event"), preferring a kind of apostolic cabal or mass delusion or, at best, Jesus as a vision or apparition, or suggesting that "resurrection" is somehow a way to describe the continuing life of the church after the death of its founder. At the same time these kinds of theories do not rule out the resurrection; they could just as readily indicate only the unavailability of the kinds of witnesses who might persuade skeptics. The absence of evidence is not always evidence of absence. And if there had really been no resurrection as it was proclaimed by the early church, it would be hard to explain why Jesus' disciples would conspire to create a hoax that might well endanger their lives.

Equally puzzling would be the missionary energy that galvanized followers who after the crucifixion were fearful and disorganized. Without that overwhelming event they might have been as lost to history as the disciples of John the Baptist.

Still, there have been alternative interpretations claiming that the crucifixion was a "crucifiction," that Jesus the Messiah was actually Jesus the Mastermind, and that his death and resurrection involved some sort of trance and resuscitation. Typical was one 1960s bestseller, which caused John Lennon to declare at a 1966 press conference, "My views on Christianity are directly influenced by *The Passover Plot* by Hugh J. Schonfield." For Schonfield, Jesus wanted to suffer on the cross but not die, so he arranged for a drug to simulate his death (the "vinegar" of 27:48) and plotted with Joseph of Arimathea to have his body taken from the cross before sundown in accordance with Jewish law and his wounds bandaged (the "clean linen cloth" of 27:50) before he could be spirited from the tomb to commence his "afterlife." But Jesus had not reckoned with the spear thrust (John 19:34), which caused him to die. Who then appeared to his disciples? Here the conspiracy theorists run into difficulties, and it is interesting that Schonfield simply ignores the story of doubting Thomas (John 20:24-29).[69]

It is odd that there is no account of the resurrection itself in the New Testament; that Matthew, unlike Mark (16:7), does not mention Peter; and that the risen Jesus does not appear to Mary (unless she was among the "other women" mentioned by Luke at 24:10)—although there was a tradition that an appearance did take place but was not reported by the evangelists since a mother's testimony in behalf of her son would not seem credible. As for the apostles, their disbelief indicates how unprepared they are for Jesus' bodily resurrection—even after his miracles and his explicit predictions. This is not what they might recognize as resuscitation, something they had experienced with Jairus's daughter (9:18-26); this is their experience of someone who has passed beyond life and death. There had been other "messiahs" in Jewish history, but none who had been resurrected. Finally, the "divine passive" translation of verse 6, "he has been raised" (*NEB, NRSV,* following the Greek passive voice, whereas the Vulgate's Latin *surrexit* is active), is the basis for the popular hymn "Jesus Christ Is Risen Today," originally a fourteenth-century Latin hymn, but this rendering has been criticized as detracting from the divinity of Jesus.

The evangelists disagree on the location of the resurrection appearances, with Luke and John placing them in and around Jerusalem; and they are vague about their times. Discrepancies on so important a matter have long preoccupied the Bible's critics, especially when it was believed that the authors of Matthew and John were both apostles and hence eyewitnesses to the events they describe. It is interesting, too, that Matthew indicates no knowledge of the earlier list of appearances recorded by Paul (1 Cor. 15:5-8). In older versions of the Catholic mass, where the priest regularly had his back to the worshipers (known as the "eastward position"), he would turn to them five times in recollection of Jesus' five resurrection appearances. Regarding the resurrection, H. L. Mencken noted that "though it wars upon every rationality that enlightened men cherish, the most civilized section of the human race has erected a structure of ideas and practices so vast and powerful in scope that the whole range of history showeth nothing the like!"[70]

The mention of Jesus' "feet" (9) is an odd detail, but its homeliness underscores the corporeality of Jesus' resurrected body, and it is at variance with the theories of the resurrection as a series of "mystical visions" or spiritual awakenings. It also opposes the gnostic and docetist heresies that Jesus only *seemed* to be human. "Flesh" in the sense of human life is also the theme of D. H. Lawrence's "resurrection" story, *The Escaped Cock* (1929; also known as *The Man Who Died*), in which the resurrected god is an Osiris figure returning to the world, not ascending into heaven: "And he said: This is the great Atonement, the being in touch. The grey sea and the rain, the wet narcissus and the woman I wait for, the invisible Isis and the unseen sun are all in touch, and art one."[71] Lawrence's story takes its place with George Moore's novel *The Brooke Kerith* (1916), another survival story, in which Joseph of Arimathea rescues Jesus from the cross. He then lives on as an Essene intellectual, repenting the harshness of his teaching (e.g., the "not peace, but a sword" of 10:34): "My sin was not to have loved men enough." He also regrets that he has deluded so many Israelites—and even himself—into believing he was the messiah, and he even considers returning to Jerusalem to set matters straight. Instead, he heads off for India. Paul appears toward the end of the novel, again in the familiar— and unsympathetic—role of the creator of orthodoxy, only to be told by Jesus, "All things are God, Paul: thou art God and I am God."[72]

As Matthew's gospel ends, Jesus has died on the cross and been resurrected (the ascension will not be described until Acts 1:9-11); Jesus' ministry has been vindicated; and, theologically, Satan's power over humankind has been broken and everyone on earth has been "redeemed"—that is (according to one theory), Jesus has paid, vicariously, the debt of punishment that humanity owes to God for sin. But at the same time, the Jewish people he was to deliver had rejected him, and it seemed that Satan, in the form of death, had indeed triumphed. For most of its population the world went on much as before, and in Palestine the unrest of the Jewish-Roman War (AD 66–73) would make life even more difficult. In the light of these continuing calamities, Jews might well have wondered why Christians could feel that Jesus had "redeemed" the world. Voltaire, with his customary irony said: "He left the greater part of mankind a prey to error, to crime, and to the devil. This, to our weak intellects, appears a fatal contradiction. But it is not for us to question Providence; our duty is to humble ourselves in the dust before it."[73]

One way for Jesus' less humble followers to deal with this anomalous situation was to regard their time as transitional, a brief and troubled present that was but a prelude to another advent, the imminent second coming of their Lord and Savior that would see a general judgment, the final vanquishing of Satan (whose powers had been defeated by the cross but not destroyed), and the end of human history. This might have been the ending the evangelists wanted for their gospels. But it did not happen, so the victory over Satan was spiritualized: man was reconciled to God, the gates of heaven were opened, and the good news of salvation through Jesus Christ was now to be promulgated throughout the world.

The Great Commission of 16-20 offers a summary of Matthew's theology. Jesus' final appearance, recalling Daniel 7:14 ("dominion" over "all people, nations and languages"), is a kind of minor Parousia, anticipating the second coming; but it also looks back to Moses, since it takes place on a mountain, perhaps the "mountain" of the Sermon and the transfiguration. Like Moses with Joshua, Jesus can look into the future as he delegates authority for his disciples' worldwide mission—though he says nothing here of their passing on this power to others. "Teach," because converts must be taught how to live new lives; "baptizing," because their repentance of sin must be ritualistically demonstrated (and this initiation rite became distinctive of Christianity); and "observe," because they must follow the new laws of Christ (and this last injunction became a Reformation proof text against Roman "additions"). A similar version appears in Mark (16:15-18), where the baptism in the name of the Trinity is omitted and Jesus speaks of the faith of new Christians and the wonders they will be able to perform. In the "Hebrew Matthew" it is simply "Go and teach (them) to carry out all the things which I have commanded you forever." This is the "short form" of the Great Commission, thought by some to have been the original conclusion to which Matthew added the Trinitarian baptism formula.

The invocation "in the name of the Father, and of the Son, and of the Holy Ghost," called the "Baptismal Affirmation," is unique in the New Testament, where baptisms are usually in the name of Jesus (Acts 8:16, 10:48, 19:5), and may reflect a baptismal formula from the early church. Or it may be a post-Nicene interpolation, since there is some evidence for a "short ending" without these words. It is a kind of embryonic creed, and it serves as the supreme scriptural basis for the "developed" doctrine—and the mystery—of the Holy Trinity, three Gods in one divine person, with the Son and the Holy Spirit eventually defined as of "one being" or "substance" or "essence" (Greek: *homoousios;* Latin: *substantia*) with the Father, their mutual indwelling technically known as "circumincession." This is a doctrine better experienced mystically than explained logically, much less cogently. But for early Christians it accounted for the God of the Old Testament, the divinity of Jesus, and their own sense of spiritual empowerment. Still, it has been a difficult doctrine historically since Christianity, like Judaism, distinguished itself from paganism by its uncompromising monotheism, and Scripture even has Jesus admitting that "my Father is greater than I" (John 14:28). But now in addition to God the Creator, there was the fact of Jesus Christ, Lord and Redeemer, Son of the Father, and the problem of God's presence within him, as well as a sense of the inspiring and sanctifying Spirit, the Comforter, who came to be united with Jesus in baptismal formulas and other liturgical invocations.

Although it often alludes to three aspects—word/power, love, spirit—of divinity, the New Testament says nothing of the doctrine of the Trinity as such, and it is odd that so important a concept should appear only in Matthew and so belatedly in Jesus' teachings. This has created problems for Trinitarian Protestants who objected to doctrines not firmly anchored in Scripture, and it has not been a popular subject with their preachers. The problem of defining the relations, particularly of the Father and the Son, among the three equal but distinct realities or "persons" of the Trinity was to preoccupy thinkers of the early church, who had to clarify the Trinitarian references in Scripture and liturgy. It was Tertullian who first used the term in the early third century, although other church fathers had used Trinitarian language, and in the late second century Irenaeus had come close to formulating what would become an orthodox consensus.

They relied heavily on Proverbs 8:22 ("The Lord possessed me [wisdom] in the beginning"), which seemed to distinguish between God's power and wisdom in His creation, and on imperfect analogies of unity and separation, such as the light and heat of the sun ("light from light" came to be enshrined in the Nicene Creed). Wisdom they could identify with Jesus as the pre-existent agent of creation (who by his redemptive act "recreated" a fallen world), since he is named in John 1 as God's creative *logos*. As for the Holy Spirit, this they saw operating in the inspiration that animated the prophets and apostles and worked within believers for their sanctification. It was first named, though more as power than person, at Genesis 1:2 as moving "upon the face of the waters"; it made a notable appearance at Jesus' baptism (3:16); it was known in the church's creeds as "the Lord" and "giver of Life"; and it would be a prominent force in the inspirational, prophetic, miraculous, and mystical lives of Christians, a constant counterweight to the authority of church and Bible. Such speculations inevitably required definitions and clarification, and they also engendered heresies, versions of which are still held by many who regard themselves as Christians.

Finally, an orthodox doctrine was developed and formulated, largely the creation of Origen and the three Cappadocian Fathers of the fourth century, Basil the Great, Gregory of Nazianzus, and Gregory of Nyssa. They developed the "one substance/essence" formula, rejecting the subordination implied by the terms "Father" and "Son," and specifying that whereas God "created" the world as something new and different from Himself, He "generated" the Son and the Holy Spirit and eternally "subsists" with them as separate but shared and co-equal parts of Himself, not merely as modes or functions of His being, succeeding Him in time. This was proclaimed at the ecumenical councils of Nicaea in 325 and Constantinople in 381, and finally established by Augustine in the fifth century and endorsed at the Fourth Lateran Council (1215). It was a balancing act, trying to reconcile the oneness of God with the lordship of Jesus while avoiding an emphasis on unity that would lead to modalism and an emphasis on distinctiveness that would lead to tritheism. For Christians it amounted to nothing less than a definition—if not an explanation—of God; and since the twelfth century, the Trinity has been celebrated on the first Sunday after Pentecost. Its popular understanding is that God is the Creator, Jesus the Redeemer, and the Holy Spirit the Sustainer (Whittier wrote of the Spirit: "A bodiless Divinity, / The still small voice that spake to thee / Was the Holy Spirit's mystery").[74] The paradox of unity within multiplicity (and vice versa) is everywhere in life. Imperfect analogies have been St. Patrick's shamrock; the three aisles that lead to the one altar in Gothic churches; the Free Masons' equilateral triangle, a version of which appears on the dollar bill enclosing the "eye of God"; and Dorothy Sayers' example of a book: the author (God the Father), the material book itself (Jesus Christ), and the effect of its message on the reader (Holy Spirit).[75] In Graham Greene's novel *Monsignor Quixote* (1982), the title character compares it to wine in a bottle, with the taste of the wine serving as "the extra spark of life" that is the Holy Spirit.[76] And Augustine maintained that since we have been created in God's image, we have the Trinity within us in our memory, understanding, and will.[77] But for artists it has been a challenging subject, since three-headed or three-faced figures, though occasionally found, are repulsive, or else they recall Cerberus, the three-headed Underworld dog of classical mythology. The Trinity can also be suggested by such triads as the Holy Family or the three "angels" that visited Abraham at Mamre (Gen. 18:2). In the *Trinity* done by Masaccio (1401–28) in 1426 for the Dominican Church of Santa Maria Novella in Florence, a white dove descends from Father to Son to represent the incarnation. In Albrecht Dürer's *Adoration of the Trinity* (1508–11; Vienna) the crucified Jesus dominates the composition, with God the Father behind him as a crowned king, and the Holy Spirit above them as a dove.

The Trinity is a difficult concept (Donne: "Bones to philosophy, but milke to faith"),[78] and Reimarus wondered why so important a doctrine should be revealed so late in the gospel and then as only part of a baptismal formula.[79] So as usual, not all have been persuaded or been content to rest in paradox, mystery, or faith. Islam regards it as a species of polytheism (Koran 3.74), and for Jews the wisdom and power that Christians claimed for Jesus and the Holy

Spirit were simply attributes of the one God. And why not, they asked, add a fourth or fifth "Person" to account for other attributes? But among other Christians, anti-Trinitarianism probably ranked with Sabbatarianism, infant baptism, and the incarnation as a staple of controversy, schism, and heresy, as the Bible's readers searched the stories of Scripture for the formulas of theology. In the early church some heterodox versions were adoptionism, that God divinized the man Jesus at his baptism and then adopted him into His Godhead; monarchianism, that God is one, and as the Father is dominant; Sabellianism, that the Son and Holy Spirit are successive modes of the one God; and, most influentially, Arianism, that the Son was begotten by the Father in time, hence neither eternal nor fully divine, and that Jesus and the Holy Spirit are not co-equal with Him. In the Reformation it was Michael Servetus who argued most forcefully that Father, Son, and Holy Spirit were all names for one God, that Jesus was God's word, given divinity when he was made man, while the Holy Spirit was the "activity of God" in the human heart, his divinity a creation of the "philosophers." For this he incurred the wrath of Calvin, who testified against him at a trial in Geneva for gross blasphemy but later pleaded in vain that he be beheaded rather than burned at the stake. On October 28, 1553, he became anti-Trinitarianism's first martyr.[80]

The seventeenth-century Socinians, endorsing Jesus' full humanity, were the first organized anti-Trinitarians, and although precise distinctions are difficult, Arians, Arminians, and deists all rejected the Trinity. In his *Christian Doctrine* (Bk. I, chs. 5 and 6), Milton noted the persistent disjunction of Father and Son in the New Testament and argued that this formula was meant only to characterize the Father as savior, Jesus as redeemer, and the Holy Spirit as sanctifier. Voltaire simply dismissed it as irrelevant: "What does it matter to human society, morality, and duties that there is one person in God, or three, or four thousand?"[81] When John Locke endorsed "the reasonableness of Christianity" in his 1695 book, he simply ignored the Trinity; Kant thought it of no practical value; and Thomas Jefferson complained about "the hocus-pocus phantasm of a god like another Cerberus with one body and three heads."[82] William Ellery Channing, in his classic exposition of modern Socinianism "Unitarian Christianity" (1819), noted that it was more theological than scriptural and was rejected by "the three greatest and noblest minds of modern times," Milton, Locke, and Newton: "This doctrine, were it true, must, from its difficulty, singularity, and importance, have been laid down with great clearness, guarded with great care, and stated with all possible precision. But where does this statement appear? From the many passages which treat of God, we ask for one, one only, in which we are told, that he is a threefold being."[83] Christian Scientists have also rejected the Trinity, which they see as unscriptural tritheism; and the Mormons, who baptize with this formula, are in fact tritheists, though for them the "great secret" is that God Himself is what they call an "exalted man" who once lived a mortal life. Furthermore, even those denominations that accept the orthodox tradition seem to show little interest in its propagation.

The order to "teach all nations" (19) is a proof text for the apostolic succession and for Christianity's universalism, and the latter has been used against the idea of national churches. That Jesus wants his teachings propagated is also the warrant for the Christian church's proselytizing activities and is well illustrated in a tympanum relief on the Cathedral of St. Madeleine (1120–32) in Vézelay, France, where each of the apostles holds a copy of the Scriptures they will be using "to teach all nations." Unfortunately, after Paul and until the time of Constantine, the names of the faith's first missionaries are imperfectly recorded, and there is no evidence that the early church created a missionary organization. Nor is anything said about those whom the Christian message does not reach or who for whatever reason choose to reject it. Because teaching here precedes baptism, this verse was a basic proof text, often cited, for Anabaptists and others who favored a "believer's baptism," since newborn infants could hardly be taught. But Calvin and others pointed out that this baptism refers to the conversion of adult pagans, not to the situation of children in Christian communities. Later this mandate was a powerful stimulus for English colonists to America, particularly since so many of them were Puritan exiles aspiring to realize the millennium in a theocratic New England. Along with the Genesis command to "replenish the earth" (9:1), it was regularly invoked to rationalize their settlements in America and the conversion of the Indians, whose presumed descent from the "lost tribes" of Israel ("they agree in rites, they reckon by moons; they offer their first-fruits, they have a kind of feast of tabernacles") meant that their accepting Christianity would be a step toward the conversion of the Jews that would precede the second coming.[84] Less often mentioned was the hope that English colonialism could also curb the aggressive expansion of Catholic Spain and France (French priests, said Cotton Mather, had taught the Indians "that the Mother of our Blessed Saviour was a French lady, and that they were Englishmen by whom our Saviour was Murdered; and that it was therefore a Meritorious thing to destroy the English Nation"[85]), advance the Protestant faith, and thereby preserve peace on earth. These verses recur constantly in the Puritan writings and preaching of the times together with the larger OT precedent of the Israelites' appropriation of Canaan, but it is important to note that there is no suggestion of religious coercion in the Great Commission.

This was also a key text for William Carey (1761–1834), founder of the Baptist Missionary Society and often called the father of Protestant missions. He argued that the Great Commission was not restricted to the apostles, and he invoked this text to support his postmillennial theology that Christ would not return until after a thousand years of peace and harmony achieved through universal conversion, hence the urgency and importance of the missionary enterprise.

The provision that the apostles were to teach "whatsoever I have commanded you" was a Protestant proof text (so the Geneva Bible's marginal note) that "men may not teach their own doctrine." Jesus also promises to be "with you always, even unto the end of the world" (v. 20) or to the "end of the age," with the translation depending on how one understands the extent of the Greek *aionos* and the Latin *saeculi*. This is the great proof text for the Catholic insistence on the validity of tradition, as witnessed by its unbroken existence since the time of Christ. Still, some prefer "unto the end of the age," that is, the time of the apostles' missionary activity. Much depends here, as in the "everlasting fire," on how to translate the Greek and Latin. But this promise created a problem for some Reformers, for they had to acknowledge that Christ had to have been and must still be (somehow) with the church they were disowning and attacking, and they had to prove that the Roman Church was false enough to abandon and yet true enough to provide them with valid sacraments and an apostolic succession. They also had to explain what happened to the souls of those Christians who for fifteen hundred years lived and died in a faith that for them had now been proved false—pious souls who may have perished secure in the belief they had earned salvation by purchasing indulgences. But these words also served as a proof text for Luther that Jesus, not the pope, was the head of the church; and he used this verse at the outset of the "Leipzig Disputation" (1519) with John Eck on the question of papal supremacy. This Eck did not deny, responding that Jesus was talking about the church on earth and reasserting the familiar words of 16:18 ("Thou are Peter . . . I will build my church"), perhaps the most controverted verse in all of Scripture and typical of Matthew's impact on the history of the world.

Notes

It is another witness to the popularity and influence of Matthew that portions of his gospel are continually being reprinted in commentaries, readers, anthologies, and source books. Hence, first reference in these notes will often be to these secondary sources, which have the further advantage of being more readily available than the primary sources.

Preface

1. Jon Nielson and Royal Skousen, "How Much of the King James Bible Is William Tyndale's?" *Reformation* 3 (1998):48–74. As for its emendations, one nineteenth-century study reviewed six KJV printings and found some twenty-four thousand variations, though it claimed none affected "the integrity of the text." Harold P. Scanline, "Bible Translations by American Individuals," in *The Bible and Bibles in America*, ed. Ernest S. Frerichs (Atlanta, Ga.: Scholars' Press, 1988), 51.

2. Walter Scott, *Monastery* (New York: Houghton Mifflin, 1913 [1820]), 140.

3. Matthew Arnold, "Aberglaube Invading," *Literature and Dogma* (New York: AMS, 1970 [1883]), 70.

Introduction

1. Samuel Taylor Coleridge, Letter VI, *Confessions of an Inquiring Spirit* (London, 1849), 76; *Critics of the Bible, 1724–1873,* ed. John Drury (Cambridge: Cambridge University Press, 1989), 111.

2. In fact, just such a chronological order, beginning with Thessalonians, is suggested by Sue Bridehead to the hero of Hardy's *Jude the Obscure* (1895) in the "Melchester" section. It would be, she said, a "*new* New Testament . . . twice as interesting as before, and twice as understandable."

3. Peter DeVries, *The Mackerel Plaza* (Boston, Mass.: Little, Brown, 1958), 7.

4. Origen, *Commentary on Matthew, Ante-Nicene Fathers,* ed. Allan Menzies (Grand Rapids, Mich.: Eerdmans, 1978), 10:413; John Chrysostom, Homily 1.6, *Homilies on the Gospel of Saint Matthew, Nicene and Post-Nicene Fathers,* ed. Philip Schaff (Grand Rapids, Mich.: Eerdmans, 1975), 10:3.

5. William Paley, *A View of the Evidences of Christianity* [1794], 3.8, in *Classical Readings in Christian Apologetics, AD 100–1800,* ed. L. Rush Bush (Grand Rapids, Mich.: Zondervan, 1983), 369.

6. Joseph Butler, *Analogy of Religion Natural and Revealed* (New York: Dutton, 1901 [1736]), xxvii.

7. *The Complete Gospels,* ed. Robert Miller (Sonoma, Calif.: Polebridge, 1992).

8. Irenaeus, *Against Heresies,* 3.11.8, in *Early Christian Fathers,* ed. Cyril C. Richardson, trans. Edward Rochie Hardy (New York: Macmillan, 1970), 382.

9. Voltaire, "Apostles," *Philosophical Dictionary* (New York: Coventry House, 1952 [trans. 1901]), 1:120.

10. All Matthew commentaries are good, but best of all is *The Gospel According to Saint Matthew,* W. D. Davies and Dale C. Allison Jr., *International Critical Commentary,* 3 vols. (Edinburgh: T & T Clark, 1988–97).

11. John Updike, "Matthew," *Incarnation: Contemporary Writers on the New Testament*, ed. Alfred Corn (New York: Viking, 1990), 1.

1. The Infancy Narrative

1. Tyndale's gloss is illustrated in David Norton, *A History of the English Bible as Literature* (Cambridge: Cambridge University Press, 2000), Pl. 1. On the Infancy Narratives, there is the detailed and authoritative Raymond E. Brown, *Birth of the Messiah* (New York: Doubleday, 1977, 1993).

2. On Joachim, see Marjorie Reeves, *Joachim of Fiore and the Prophetic Future* (Princeton, N.J.: Princeton University Press, 1993).

3. A traditional argument against the doctrine of the Virgin Birth. See *Origen: Contra Celsum*, 1.32, ed. and trans. Henry Chadwick (Cambridge: Cambridge University Press, 1965), 31. Further references to this edition will be in the text. Celsus was well versed in Jewish and Christian scriptures, particularly Matthew, and many of his criticisms were preserved in Origen's response, *Contra Celsum* (ca. 240). On "German Christians" and their Institute for the Study and Eradication of Jewish Influence on German Church Life, see Doris L. Bergen, *Twisted Cross: The German Christian Movement in the Third Reich* (Chapel Hill: University of North Carolina Press, 1996), and Leander Keck, *Who Is Jesus? History in Perfect Tense* (Columbia: University of South Carolina Press, 2000), 22.

4. Justin Martyr, *Dialogue with Trypho*, 67, *Ante-Nicene Fathers*, 1:231.

5. Joseph Butler, *Analogy of Religion Natural and Revealed* (New York: Dutton, 1901 [1736]), 215.

6. Justin Martyr, *Apology* 1.54, *Ante-Nicene Fathers*, 1:181.

7. Clement, *Protrepticus (Exhortation to the Heathen)*, 1, *Ante-Nicene Fathers*, 2:172–74. See also John Warden, *Orpheus: The Metamorphoses of a Myth* (Toronto: University of Toronto Press, 1982), xi–xii, 51–59.

8. Origen, "Letter to Thaumaturgus," in *Treasury of Early Christianity*, ed. Anne Freemantle (New York: Viking, 1953), 66–67.

9. Thomas Paine, *The Age of Reason* (1794, 1796), *The Complete Writings of Thomas Paine*, ed. Philip S. Foner (New York: Citadel, 1945), 1:597.

10. Chrysostom, *Homily* 4.12, *Nicene and Post-Nicene Fathers*, 10:25.

11. *Joseph's Trouble About Mary*, in *York Mystery Plays*, ed. Richard Beadle and Pamela M. King (Oxford: Clarendon Press, 1984), 50.

12. Jacobus deVoragine, *The Golden Legend*, trans. William Granger Ryan (Princeton, N.J.: Princeton University Press, 1993), 2:153. Further references will be in the text.

13. "I should myself call the Incarnation the central aspect of Christianity," John Henry Cardinal Newman, *An Essay on the Development of Christian Doctrine* (New York: Longmans, Green, 1949), 33; "the central truth of the Gospel," ibid., 302.

14. Celsus, *On the True Doctrine: A Discourse Against the Christians*, trans. R. Joseph Hoffmann (New York: Oxford University Press, 1987), 70.

15. Adolf Harnack, *What Is Christianity?* trans. Thomas Bailey Saunders (New York: Harper, 1957 [1923]), 207.

16. *Porphyry's Against the Christians: The Literary Remains*, ed. and trans. R. Joseph Hoffmann (Buffalo, N.Y.: Prometheus, 1994).

17. *The Papal Encyclicals, 1939–1958*, ed. Claudia Carlen (Raleigh, N.C.: McGrath, 1981), 73.

18. Otto, Bishop of Freising, "History of the Two Cities," in *The High Middle Ages 1000–1300*, ed. Bryce D. Lyon (New York: Free Press, 1964), 196–97.

19. Pseudo-Bonaventure, *Meditations on the Life of Christ,* ed. Isa Ragusa and Rosalie B. Green, trans. Isa Ragusa (Princeton, N.J.: Princeton University Press, 1961), 33.

20. *Dialogue with Trypho* 78, *Ante-Nicene Fathers,* 1:237.

21. *Koran,* trans. N. S. Dawood (London: Penguin, 1956), 19.21. Further references will be in the text.

22. Henry Adams, "The Dynamo and the Virgin," *Education of Henry Adams* (New York: Random House, 1931 [1900]), 388.

23. James I, *A Premonition to All Most Mighty Monarchs, Kings, Free Princes, and States of Christendom,* in *Works,* ed. James Montague (1616), in *Anglicanism,* ed. Paul Elmer More and Frank Leslie Cross (London: Society for the Promotion of Christian Knowledge, 1962), 4.

24. *Ineffabilis Deus,* Pius IX, 8 December 1854, in *Documents of the Christian Church,* ed. Henry Bettenson and Chris Maunder, 3rd ed. (Oxford: Oxford University Press, 1999), 286; Apostolic Constitution, *Munificentissimus Deus* (1 November 1950), ibid., 297–98.

25. On the star and on biblical dates in general, basic is Jack Finegan, *Handbook of Biblical Chronology,* rev. ed. (Peabody, Mass.: Hendrickson, 1998).

26. Ignatius, "To the Ephesians," 19, 2–3, *Early Christian Fathers,* 93.

27. Giovanni Boccaccio, *Decameron,* trans. Richard Aldington (Garden City, N.Y.: Doubleday, 1930), 323–33.

28. *Dante's Monarchia,* 3.7.1–2, trans. Richard Kay (Toronto: Pontifical Institute of Medieval Studies, 1998), 243. Further references to book and chapter will be in the text.

29. "Orientalium Dignitas" (30 November 1894), <http://www.papalencyclicals.net/Leo13/113orient.htm>.

30. Tertullian, *Adversus Marcionem* 3.13, *Ante-Nicene Christian Library,* ed. Alexander Roberts and James Donaldson (Edinburgh: Clark, 1867), 7:145.

31. Letter to Lady Jane Henrietta Swinburne, 18 July 1855, *The Swinburne Letters,* ed. Cecil Y. Lang (New Haven, Conn.: Yale University Press, 1959–62), 1:2–4.

32. *Travels of Marco Polo,* trans. Ronald Latham (Baltimore, Md.: Penguin, 1958), 58.

33. St. Basil, *Treatise on the Holy Spirit,* 27, *The Church at Prayer,* V. 1, *Principles of the Liturgy,* ed. Irénée Henri Dalmais et al., trans. Matthew J. O'Connell (Collegeville, Minn.: Liturgical Press, 1986), 181; Germanos I, Patriarch of Constantinople, 715–30, *Ecclesiastical History,* cited in Hugh Wybrew, *The Orthodox Liturgy* (London: SPCK, 1989), 124.

34. "A View of Popish Abuses Yet Remaining in the English Church" (1572), in *Religion and Society in Early Modern England: A Sourcebook,* ed. David Cressy and Lori Ann Ferrell (London: Routledge, 1996), 84.

35. Yeats, "The Magi" (1914), *Collected Poems* (New York: Macmillan, 1959), 124.

36. Eliot, "Journey of the Magi" (1927), *Complete Poems and Plays, 1909–1950* (New York: Harcourt, Brace & World), 68.

37. Prudentius, trans. John Mason Neale, in *Treasury,* 601.

38. Paine, "Examination of the Prophecies," *Writings,* 2:856.

39. W. H. Auden, "For the Time Being: A Christmas Oratorio," *Collected Poetry* (New York: Random House, 1945), 459.

40. Mark Twain, *Innocents Abroad* (New York: Harper & Brothers, 1899), 2:537–38.

2. The Ministry Begins

1. John Calvin, *Commentary on a Harmony of the Evangelists, Matthew, Mark, and Luke,* trans. William Pringle (Grand Rapids, Mich.: Eerdmans, 1949), 1:118.

2. "The wetter the better," wrote Robert Ingersoll. Letter to Mark M. Aiken, 20 November 1890, *The Letters of Robert Ingersoll,* ed. Eva Wakefield Ingersoll (New York: Philosophical Library, 1951), 321.

3. Voltaire, "Baptism," *Philosophical Dictionary,* trans. Peter Gay (New York: Basic Books, 1962), 1:110.

4. Augustine, "On Baptism," *Documents,* 85.

5. Menno Simons, *The Complete Writings of Menno Simons (c. 1496–1561),* ed. John Christian Wenger, trans. Leonard Verduin (Scottsdale, Pa.: Herald Press, 1956), 513–14.

6. "Zurich edict against Anabaptism" (7 March 1526), *Documents on the Continental Reformation,* ed. and trans. William G. Naphy (New York: St. Martin's, 1996), 94; also in *The Reformation: A Narrative History Related by Contemporary Observers and Participants,* ed. Hans J. Hillerbrand (New York: Harper & Row, 1964), 232–33.

7. William Penn, "The Rise and Progress of the People Called Quakers," *The Witness of William Penn,* ed. Frederick B. Tolles and E. Gordon Alderfer (New York: Macmillan, 1953 [1694]), 15; Voltaire, *Quaker Reader,* ed. Jessamyn West (New York: Viking, 1962), 276.

8. Letter to Melanchthon, 13 January 1522, in *Martin Luther,* ed. E. G. Rupp and Benjamin Drewery (New York: St. Martin's, 1970), 78. See also "Concerning Rebaptism" (1528), *Martin Luther's Basic Theological Writings,* ed. Timothy F. Lull (Minneapolis, Minn.: Fortress, 1989), 368–69.

9. John Calvin, *Institutes of the Christian Religion,* 4.19.4–13, trans. Ford Lewis Battles (Philadelphia: Westminster, 1960), 2:1453, 1461.

10. Voltaire, "End of the World," *Philosophical Dictionary,* 1:429.

11. George Foote, *Bible Handbook for Freethinkers and Inquiring Christians,* ed. G. W. Foote and W. P. Ball, 11th ed. (New York: Arno Press, 1972 [1888]), 161.

12. Robert Blatchford, *God and My Neighbour* (London: Clarion, 1911), 37.

13. Arnold, "The New Testament Record," *Literature and Dogma,* 137.

14. Origen, "Prayer," *Ancient Christian Writers,* trans. John O'Meara (Westminster, Md.: Newman, 1954), 95.

15. Augustine, *City of God against the Pagans,* 20.5, ed. and trans. R. W. Dyson (Cambridge: Cambridge University Press, 1998), 971–75.

16. Friedrich W. Nietzsche, *The Antichrist,* trans. H. L. Mencken (Torrance, Calif.: Noontide Press, 1980 [1918]), 104.

17. Thomas Hobbes, *Leviathan* (New York: Dutton, 1950), 4.44, 533.

18. Edward Gibbon, *A History of the Decline and Fall of the Roman Empire,* ed. J. B. Bury (New York: Heritage Press, 1946), 364.

19. Immanuel Kant, *Religion Within the Limits of Reason Alone,* ed. and trans., Thomas Hoyt Hudson and T. M. Greene (New York: Harper & Row 1960 [1793]), 113.

20. "Augsburg Confession," in *Creeds of the Churches,* rev. ed., ed. John H. Leith (Richmond, Va.: John Knox Press, 1973), 73.

21. Albert Schweitzer, *The Quest of the Historical Jesus* (New York: Macmillan, 1910), 201.

22. Martin Luther King Jr., "Pilgrimage to Nonviolence," *Christian Century* 77 (1960): 440.

23. Walter Rauschenbusch, "The Kingdom of God," *A Theology for the Social Gospel* (New York: Abingdon, 1981 [1917]), 131–45.

24. John Bunyan, *The Pilgrim's Progress* (Oxford: Clarendon Press, 1960 [1678]), 10.

25. "The Nature, Design, and General Rules of the United Societies" (1743), *Works of John Wesley* (Nashville, Tenn.: Abingdon, 1989), 9:70.

26. "Repentance" (Thesis 12), Augsburg Confession, in *Creeds of the Churches,* 71.

27. "Life of St. Remigius," in *A Dictionary of Miracles,* ed. E. Cobham Brewer (Detroit, Mich.: Gale, 1966 [1885]), 108.

28. John Calvin, "Clear Explanation of Sound Doctrine" (1561), *Theological Treatises,* ed. J. K. F. Reid (Philadelphia, Pa.: Westminster, 1954), 269–70.

29. Origen, *On First Principles,* trans. G. W. Butterworth (New York: Harper & Row, 1966), 289. On the temptation narrative as parable, see David Friedrich Strauss, *The Christ of Faith and the Jesus of History: A Critique of Schleiermacher's Life of Jesus* (1865), ed. and trans. Leander E. Keck (Philadelphia: Fortress, 1977), 77.

30. Voltaire, "The Questions of Zapata" (1767), *Toleration and Other Essays,* trans. Joseph McCabe (New York: Putnam's, 1912), 201–202.

31. *Geneva Bible* (1560), intro. Lloyd E. Berry (Madison: University of Wisconsin Press, facsimile, 1969), 3. Further references to this edition will be in the text.

32. John Calvin, *Commentaries,* ed. and trans. Joseph Haroutunian (Philadelphia: Westminster, 1958), 165.

33. Robert Gundry, *Matthew: A Commentary on His Literary and Theological Art* (Grand Rapids, Mich.: Eerdmans, 1983), 55.

34. John Milton, *Eikonoklastes,* ch. 5 (1649). *Complete Poems and Major Prose,* ed. Merritt Y. Hughes (New York: Odyssey Press, 1957), 799.

35. Chrysostom, *Homily* 13.4, *Nicene and Post-Nicene Fathers,* 10:82.

36. *The Muslim Jesus: Sayings and Stories in Islamic Literature,* ed. and trans. Tarif Khalidi (Cambridge, Mass.: Harvard University Press, 2001), 72.

37. Henry Wadsworth Longfellow, "Mount Quarantina," *The Divine Tragedy,* in *The Complete Poetical Works of Longfellow* (Boston: Houghton, Mifflin, 1922), 365.

38. "Witchcraft at Salem," in *A Documentary History of Religion in America to the Civil War,* ed. Edwin S. Gaustad (Grand Rapids, Mich.: Eerdmans, 1983), 137.

39. Chrysostom, *Homily* 13.3, *Nicene and Post-Nicene Fathers,* 10:81.

40. John Lightfoot, *Harmony of the Gospels* (1654), *Works,* ed. J. R. Pitman (London, 1822–25), 3:42. Quoted in Elizabeth Pope, *Paradise Regained, The Tradition and the Poem* (Baltimore: Johns Hopkins University Press, 1947), 59.

41. Joachim Jeremias, *New Testament Theology,* trans. John Bowden (New York: Scribner's, 1971), 75.

42. Athanasius, *Life of Antony and the Letter to Marcellinus,* trans. Robert C. Gregg (New York: Paulist Press, 1980), 34.

43. Pseudo-Bonaventure, *Meditations on the Life of Christ,* 117.

44. Letter of Pope Gregory VII to Hermann, Bishop of Metz, 15 March 1081, in *Church and State Through the Centuries,* ed. and trans. Sidney Z. Ehler and John B. Morrall (London: Burns and Oates, 1954), 33.

45. *Book of Common Prayer 1559: The Elizabethan Prayer Book,* ed. John E. Booty (Charlottesville: University of Virginia Press, 1976), 273.

46. Augustine, "Letter to Januarius," *Treasury,* 375.

47. John Knox, "First Temptation of Christ," *Twenty Centuries of Great Preaching,* ed. Clyde E. Fant Jr. and William M. Pinson Jr. (Waco, Tex.: Word Books, 1971), 2:205; "Exposition upon Matthew IV, Concerning the Temptation of Christ in the Wilderness," *Works of John Knox,* ed. David Laing (Edinburgh, 1855; New York: AMS Press, 1966), 4:99.

48. *Institutes of the Christian Religion,* ed. John T. McNeill, trans. Ford Lewis Battles (Philadelphia: Westminster, 1960), 4.12.15–21, 1242–48.

49. Voltaire, *Philosophical Dictionary,* 2:157.

50. Thomas More, *A Dialogue of Comfort* (New York: E. P. Dutton, 1946), 194.

51. Martin Luther, *The Sermon on the Mount,* in *Luther's Works,* ed. and trans. Jaroslav Pelikan (Saint Louis, Mo.: Concordia, 1956), 21:159.

52. John Milton, *Paradise Regained,* in *Complete Poems and Major Prose,* ed. Hughes, 470–530.

53. T. S. Eliot, *Murder in the Cathedral,* in *The Complete Poems and Plays, 1909–1950* (New York: Harcourt, Brace & World, 1961), 191, 193.

54. Charles Dickens, *The Life of Our Lord* (New York: Simon and Schuster, 1934 [1846–49]), 23.

55. Somerset Maugham, *Of Human Bondage* (New York: Penguin, 1992 [1915]), 118.

56. Leo Tolstoy, *A Confession, The Gospel in Brief, and What I Believe*, ed. Aylmer Maude (London: Oxford University Press, 1974), 139–40.

57. Fyodor Dostoevsky, *The Brothers Karamazov*, trans. Constance Garnett (New York: Random House, 1950), 2.5.5, 299–300, 305, 311.

58. Thomas Jefferson, *Jefferson's Extracts from the Gospel*, in *Papers of Thomas Jefferson*, Second Series, ed. Dickinson W. Adams (Princeton, N.J.: Princeton University Press, 1983).

59. William Barclay, *The Gospel of Matthew* (Louisville, Ky.: Westminster/John Knox Press, 1956, 2001), 1:86–88.

60. "Penitential of Bede," in *How to Read Church History*, ed. Jean Comby (London: SCM Press, 1985), 1:146.

61. "Decrees of the Fourth Lateran Council," *Documents*, 147; *Basic Documents in Medieval History*, ed. Norton Downs (Princeton, N.J.: Van Nostrand, 1959), 75.

62. Eamon Duffy, *The Stripping of the Altars: Traditional Religion in England 1400–1580* (New Haven, Conn.: Yale University Press, 1992), 289.

63. Erasmus, Letter to J. Botzheim, *Documents on the Continental Reformation*, 35.

64. Hillerbrand, ed., *Reformation*, 44–46.

65. Luther, Letter to John Staupitz, 30 May 1518, *Reformation Writings*, 1:58.

66. "Calvin's Reply to Sadoleto" (1539), in *A Reformation Debate*, ed. John C. Olin (New York: Harper, 1966), 72.

67. Athanasius, *Life of Antony*, 31.

68. Harriet Martineau, *Eastern Life, Present and Past* (Philadelphia: Lea and Blanchard, 1848), 462.

3. The Sermon on the Mount

1. John Wesley, *Journals and Diaries II (1738–42)*, in *Works* (Nashville, Tenn.: Abingdon, 1990), 19:46.

2. Clarence Bauman, *The Sermon on the Mount: The Modern Quest for Its Meaning* (Macon, Ga.: Mercer University Press, 1985), 3–4.

3. Henry J. Cadbury, *The Peril of Modernizing Jesus* (New York: Macmillan, 1937), 116.

4. Friedrich Nietzsche, *Beyond Good and Evil*, 46, in *The Philosophy of Nietzsche* (New York: Random House, 1927), 432.

5. D. H. Lawrence, *Kangaroo*, ed. Byron Steele (Cambridge: Cambridge University Press, 1994 [1923]), 267. See T. R. Wright, *D. H. Lawrence and the Bible* (Cambridge: Cambridge University Press, 2000), 107.

6. Augustine, *Commentary on the Lord's Sermon on the Mount*, trans. Denis J. Kavanagh (Washington, D.C.: Catholic University Press, 1951), 17–199.

7. Aquinas, *Summa Theologica*, Question 108, Article 4 (New York: Benziger Brothers, 1947–48), 1118–19

8. *Didache*, in *Early Christian Fathers*, 177–79.

9. Justin Martyr, "First Apology," 15, 16, in *Early Christian Fathers*, 250–52.

10. Tolstoy, *My Religion*, 81.

11. *The Book of Mormon* (Salt Lake City, Utah: Herald Press, 1986 [1830]), 430–38.

12. G. K. Chesterton, *The Everlasting Man* (New York: Dodd, Mead, 1925), 324.

13. Baron Paul Tiry d'Holbach, *Ecce Homo!: An Eighteenth Century Life of Jesus*, ed. Andrew Hunnick, trans. George Houston (New York: Mouton de Gruyter, 1995), 148.

14. James Doelman, *King James I and the Religious Culture of England* (Cambridge: D. S. Brower, 2000), 85.

15. Augustine, Letter 189, *From Irenaeus to Grotius: A Sourcebook in Christian Political Thought,* ed. Oliver O'Donovan and Joan Lockwood O'Donovan (Grand Rapids, Mich.: Eerdmans, 1999), 135.

16. *Works of John Locke,* reprint (Aulen, Germany: Scientia, 1963), 6:15.

17. Wesley, *Works,* 9:70.

18. Nicolas Cop, "Academic Discourse," *Institutes* (1536), ed. and trans. Ford Lewis Battles (Grand Rapids, Mich.: Eerdmans, 1975), Appendix III, 371. Unless otherwise noted, further references will be to this edition.

19. Luther, *Sermon on the Mount,* 21:56–57.

20. Martin Niemöller, "The Salt of the Earth," *Religion from Tolstoy to Camus,* ed. Walter Kaufman (New York: Harper & Row, 1961), 322–38.

21. Pius XI, *Nos es muy conocido* (1937), in *Church and State Through the Centuries,* ed. and trans. Sidney Z. Ehler and John B. Morrall (London: Burns and Oates, 1954), 583.

22. Quoted in *The Puritans: A Sourcebook,* ed. Perry Miller and Thomas H. Johnson (New York: Harper & Row, 1963), 199; Joseph M. McShane, "Winthrop's 'City on a Hill' in Recent Political Discourse," *America* 159 (1988): 194–98.

23. "General Admonition," *Documents of the Christian Church,* 106.

24. William Penn, "The Natives of Pennsylvania," *Witness,* 123–24.

25. Irenaeus, "Against Heresies," 27.2, *Ante-Nicene Fathers,* 1:352.

26. John Toland, *Christianity Not Mysterious* (New York: Garland, 1978 [1696]), 160–63.

27. R. S. Sugirtharajah, *The Bible and the Third World: Precolonial, Colonial and Postcolonial Encounters* (Cambridge: Cambridge University Press, 2001), 232–33.

28. "Trial and Martyrdom of Michael Sattler" (Rottenburg, 1527), *Martyrs' Mirror* (1660, trans. 1886), in *Spiritual and Anabaptist Writers: Documents Illustrative of the Radical Reformation,* ed. George Huntston Williams and Angel M. Mergal (Philadelphia, Pa.: Westminster, 1957), 140.

29. Luther, *Sermon on the Mount,* 78.

30. Mark Twain, "Bible Teaching and Religious Practice," *A Pen Warmed-Up in Hell,* ed. Frederick Anderson (New York: Harper & Row, 1972 [1890]), 142.

31. "Catholic-Orthodox Declaration," *Documents of Vatican II,* ed. Walter M. Abbott (New York: America Press, 1966), 726.

32. Camilo Torres, "Message to Christians," *Revolutionary Priest: The Complete Writings and Messages of Camilo Torres* (New York: Random House, 1971), 368.

33. Kant, *Religion Within the Limits of Reason Alone,* 72.

34. Athenagoras, "A Plea for the Christians," 32, *Classical Readings,* 58.

35. Augustine, *Commentary on the Lord's Sermon on the Mount,* 53.

36. Gregory, *Morals on the Book of Job,* trans. J. H. Parker (Oxford, 1844–50), in *Traditions of the Western World,* ed. J. H. Hexter (Chicago: University of Chicago Press, 1967), 166–67.

37. *Fox's Book of Martyrs* (Philadelphia: Winston, 1926), 249.

38. Voltaire, "Adultery," *Philosophical Dictionary,* 1:38.

39. Tertullian, *De Cultu Feminarum,* 2.6, in *Ante-Nicene Fathers,* 4:21.

40. Augustine, Letter to Publicola, in *Treasury,* 133.

41. Calvin, "Commentary 5:34," *Reformed Reader: A Sourcebook in Christian Theology,* ed. William Stacy Johnson and John J. Leith (Louisville, Ky.: Westminster/John Knox Press, 1993), 1:345.

42. George Fox, *Journal* (Leeds: Pickard, 1836), 2:61.

43. "Memorandum Submitted to Chancellor Hitler, June 4, 1936," in Arthur C. Cochrane, *The Church's Confession under Hitler* (Philadelphia: Westminster, 1952), 276.

44. Thomas More, *Utopia,* in *Complete Works,* ed. Edward Surtz and J. H. Hexter (New Haven, Conn.: Yale University Press, 1963), 4:101.

45. Benjamin Jowett, *Essays and Reviews: The 1860 Text and Its Reading,* ed. Victor Shea and William Whitla (Charlottesville: University of Virginia Press, 2000), 496.

46. Kant, *Religion Within the Limits of Reason Alone,* 147.

47. Letter 47.5, *Letters,* in *The Works of Saint Augustine,* ed. John E. Rotelle (Hyde Park, N.Y.: New City Press, 2001), 2:190.

48. Thomas Aquinas, *Summa,* Q. 64, Art. 1, 1219.

49. Letter to William Lenthall, Speaker of the Parliament, 11 October 1649, *Letters and Speeches of Oliver Cromwell,* ed. Thomas Carlyle and S. C. Lomas (London: Methuen, 1904), 3:486.

50. *Luther and Calvin on Secular Authority,* ed. and trans. Harro Höpfl (Cambridge: Cambridge University Press, 1991), 20.

51. Calvin, *Commentaries,* ed. and trans. Joseph Haroutunian and Louise Pettibone Smith (Philadelphia: Westminster, 1958), 334.

52. *Creeds of the Churches,* 287, 304.

53. Tolstoy, *My Religion* (1884), 83, 134.

54. *The Holy Scriptures. Translated and corrected by the Spirit of Revelation by Joseph Smith Jr., the Seer* (1867); also *An Inspired Revision of the Authorized Version, by Joseph Smith Jr., A new corrected edition* (Independence, Mo.: Herald Press, 1944), 432.

55. "Speeches and Writings of M. Gandhi," *The Message of Jesus Christ,* ed. Anand T. Hingorani (Bombay: Bharatiya Vidya Bhavan, 1971), 5.

56. Jefferson, *Jefferson's Extracts,* 333.

57. *Reimarus: Fragments,* ed. Charles H. Talbert, trans. Ralph S. Fraser (Philadelphia: Fortress, 1970).

58. David Friedrich Strauss, *The Life of Jesus Critically Examined,* trans. George Eliot, 2nd ed. (New York: Macmillan, 1892 [1835]).

59. Ernest Renan, *The Life of Jesus* (New York: Belmont/Tower, 1972).

60. Aquinas, *Summa,* Q. 96, Art. 4, 1020.

61. Luther, *Sermon on the Mount,* 21:117.

62. Calvin, *Commentary on a Harmony* (Grand Rapids, Mich.: Eerdmans, 1949), 1:301.

63. *Boswell's Life of Johnson,* 28 April 1783 (London: Oxford University Press, 1982), 1228.

64. Elihu Palmer, *Principles of Nature,* in *American Deists,* ed. Kerry S. Walters (Lawrence: University Press of Kansas, 1992), 257.

65. Tertullian, *Apology* 31, *Documents,* 8.

66. Thomas Paine, *Complete Writings,* 1:598.

67. Quoted in Taylor Branch, *Pillar of Fire: America in the King Years* (New York: Simon & Schuster, 1998), 336.

68. Kant, *Religion Within the Limits of Reason Alone,* 158.

69. Martin Luther King Jr., *The Strength to Love* (New York: Harper & Row, 1963), 49–57.

70. Calvin, *Institutes* (1536), 3.15.7, 38.

71. John Wesley, "On Perfection, *Works of John Wesley,* ed. Albert C. Outley (Nashville, Tenn.: 1986), 3:70:87; see also Barrie W. Tabraham, *The Making of Methodism* (London: Epworth, 1995), 38–39.

72. George Fox, *Journal,* 27.

73. William Ellery Channing, "Likeness to God" (1828), in *Selected Writings,* ed. David Robinson (New York: Paulist Press, 1985), 149.

74. Quoted in Spencer Klaw, *Without Sin: The Life and Death of the Oneida Community* (New York: Allen Lane, 1993), 26.

75. *Letters of Abelard and Heloise,* ed. and trans. Betty Radice (Harmondsworth, U.K.: Penguin, 1974), 191.

76. In *Advocates of Reform,* ed. Matthew Spinka (Philadelphia: Westminster, 1953), 302–303.

77. St. Ambrose, "The Sacraments," *Theological and Dogmatic Works,* trans. Roy J. DeFerrari (Washington, D.C.: Catholic University of America Press, 1963), 322–23.

78. Dietrich Bonhoeffer, *The Cost of Discipleship,* trans. R. H. Fuller, rev. Irmgard Booth (New York: Macmillan, 1963), in *A Testament to Freedom: The Essential Writings of Dietrich Bonhoeffer,* ed. Geffrey B. Kelly and F. Burton Nelson (San Francisco: HarperSanFrancisco, 1990), 146.

79. Luther, Letter to Peter Biskendorf, 1535, *Letters of Spiritual Counsel,* ed. Theodore G. Tappert (Philadelphia: Westminster, 1955), 128.

80. Clarke Garrett, *Respectable Folly: Millenarians and the French Revolution in France and England* (Baltimore: Johns Hopkins University Press, 1975), 18.

81. Frank Paul Bowman, *Le Christ Romantique* (Geneva: Droz, 1973), 97.

82. Erasmus, "The Complaint of Peace" (1517), *From Irenaeus to Grotius,* 575.

83. Luther, *Reformation Writings,* 92.

84. George Bernard Shaw, Letter to Gilbert Murray, 22 September 1913, in Sidney P. Albert, "The Lord's Prayer and Major Barbara," 107. See also *Shaw and Religion,* ed. Charles A. Berst (University Park: Penn State Press, 1981), 107–28.

85. Calvin, *Institutes* (1536), 3.20.42, 79.

86. Pius X, *Readings in Church History,* 3:109.

87. Voltaire, "Books," *Philosophical Dictionary,* 1:219–20.

88. Benjamin Franklin, Letter to Benjamin Vaughan, 9 November 1779, "The Lord's Prayer," in *American Deists,* 89–91.

89. Ola Elizabeth Winslow, *John Eliot, "Apostle to the Indians"* (Boston: Houghton Mifflin, 1968), 95.

90. Origen, *Prayer, Ancient Christian Writers,* trans. John O'Meara (Westminster, Md.: Newman, 1954), 115.

91. Luther, "Short Exposition," in *Reformation Writings,* 98.

92. Augustine, *Commentary on the Sermon on the Mount,* 139–40; "Letter to Probus," 412, *Treasury,* 427.

93. Franklin, *American Deists,* 89–91.

94. Wesley, "A Meditation on the Lord's Prayer," *Selected Prayers, Hymns, Journal Notes, Sermons, Letters and Treatises* (New York: Paulist Press, 1981), 119.

95. Calvin, "Catechism of the Church of Geneva" (1545), *Theological Treatises,* 129.

96. Mary Baker Eddy, *Science and Health with Key to the Scriptures* (Boston: First Church of Christ Scientist, 1971 [1875]), 17.

97. Walter Rauschenbusch, "The Social Meaning of the Lord's Prayer," in *Invitation to Christian Spirituality: An Ecumenical Anthology,* ed. John R. Tyson (New York: Oxford University Press, 1999), 373–75.

98. *The Book of Mormon,* trans. Joseph Smith Jr. (Salt Lake City, Utah: Church of Jesus Christ of Latter-day Saints, 1986 [1830]), 434.

99. *Complete Short Stories of Ernest Hemingway* (New York: Macmillan, 1987), 291.

100. St. Jerome, *Treasury,* 96–97.

101. Knox, *Reformed Reader,* 1:355.

102. "Sermon LVIII," *Complete Sermons of Ralph Waldo Emerson,* ed. Teresa Toulouse and Andrew Delbanco (Columbia: University of Missouri Press, 1989), 2:97

103. Quoted in David Norton, *A History of the Bible as Literature* (Cambridge: Cambridge University Press, 2000), 2:87.

104. Thomas Paine, *Writings,* 1:486.

105. Shaw, "Christianity and Equality" (1913), *Religious Speeches,* 56.

106. Elihu Palmer, *Principles of Nature* (1801), "That the Immorality of the Christian Religion Proves That It Is Not of Divine Origin," in *Varieties of Unbelief: From Epicurus to Sartre,* ed. J. C. A. Gaskin (Englewood Cliffs, N.J.: Prentice Hall, 1989), 108.

107. *Treatise III,* "Of the Lapsed," *Ante-Nicene Fathers,* 5:444.

108. St. Ambrose, "Letter 17," in *Early Latin Theology,* ed. S. L. Greenslade (Philadelphia: Westminster, 1956), 197.

109. Tertullian, *De Spectaculis,* 21; *De Cultu Feminarum,* 7.2, *Disciplinary, Moral and Ascetical Works* (New York: Fathers of the Church, Inc., 1959), 96–97.

110. Bertrand Russell, *Why I am not a Christian* (New York: Simon & Schuster, 1963 [1930]), 15.

111. "Second Inaugural Address," *Collected Works of Abraham Lincoln,* ed. Roy P. Basler (New Brunswick, N.J.: Rutgers University Press, 1953), 8:333.

112. John Stuart Mill, "In the Golden Rule of Jesus of Nazareth, we read the complete spirit of the ethics of utility" ("Utilitarianism"), *Essays on Ethics, Religion, and Society,* in *Collected Works,* ed. J. M. Robson (Toronto: University of Toronto Press, 1969), 10:218.

113. Jonathan Edwards Jr., "The Injustice and Impolicy of the Slave Trade, and of Slavery" (1791), *Works,* 2:75–82, in *Reformed Reader,* 1:370.

114. Augustine, *De Doctrina Christiana,* trans. R. P. H. Green (Oxford: Clarendon Press, 1995), 2.62, 85.

115. Bunyan, *Pilgrim's Progress,* 25.

116. Kierkegaard, *Attack upon Christendom,* in *A Kierkegaard Anthology,* ed. Robert Bretall (Princeton, N.J.: Princeton University Press, 1946), 57f.

117. "Calvin's Reply to Sadoleto" (1539), 85.

118. "Allan of Lille: A Scholar's Attack on Heresies," in *Heresies of the High Middle Ages,* ed. Walter L. Wakefield and Austin P. Evans (New York: Columbia University Press, 1969), 215–16.

119. Luther, "The Freedom of a Christian" (1520), *Basic Theological Writings,* 613–14.

120. Erasmus, Letter to Duke John, Elector of Saxony, 2 March 1526, *Documents on the Continental Reformation,* 27–28.

121. "Answer of King Henry VIII," *Reformation,* ed. Hillerbrand, 314–15.

122. Nietzsche, *Will to Power,* 192, in *Complete Works of Friedrich Nietzsche,* ed. Oscar Levy (New York: Russell & Russell, 1964), 14:114.

123. Mary Baker Eddy, "Fruitage," *Science and Health,* rev. ed. (Boston: Christian Science Publishing Co., 1971 [1875]), 600–700.

124. John Locke, *The Reasonableness of Christianity* (1695), ed. John C. Higgin-Biddle (Oxford: Clarendon Press, 1999), 55–56.

125. Franklin, "Dialogue between Two Presbyterians" (1735), in *American Deists,* 82.

126. Emerson, "Sermon XLVIII," *Complete Sermons,* 2:48.

127. John Ruskin, Letter to J. J. Laing (mid-1850s), *Works* (New York: Jefferson Press, 1900), 36:179–80. See also Michael Wheeler, *Ruskin's God* (Cambridge: Cambridge University Press, 1999), 156.

128. Edna St. Vincent Millay, "Second Fig," *Collected Lyrics* (New York: Harper & Brothers, 1943), 127.

129. Locke, *Reasonableness of Christianity,* 151, 163.

130. Melba Berry Bennett, *The Stone Mason of Tor House: The Life and Work of Robinson Jeffers* (Los Angeles: Ward Ritchie, 1966), 135–36. See also Wayne Cox, "Robinson Jeffers and the Conflict of Christianity," *Robinson Jeffers and a Galaxy of Writers* (Columbia: University of South Caroline Press, 1995), 123.

4. Miracles

1. Reimarus, *Fragments,* 234.

2. Jean-Jacques Rousseau, "The Profession of the Savoyard Vicar," *Emile, or On Education,* Bk. 4, ed. and trans. Allan Bloom (New York: Basic Books, 1979), 299. See also "Letters from the Mountain," *Rousseau's Religious Writings,* ed. Ronald Grimsley (Oxford: Clarendon Press, 1970), 350.

3. Thomas Woolston, *A Discourse on the Miracles of our Saviour* (New York: Garland, 1979 [1728]), 5.

4. Johnson, *Boswell's Life,* 21 July 1765, 315.

5. Julian, "Against the Galileans," 213B, *Works,* trans. Wilmer Cave Wright (New York: Putnam's, 1923), 3:381.

6. John Wesley, *Journal,* 5 March 1769, *Works,* ed. Reginald Wald (Nashville, Tenn.: Abingdon, 1993), 22:172.

7. David Hume, "Of Miracles," *Enquiry Concerning Human Understanding* (LaSalle, Ill.: Open Court, 1949), 127, 145.

8. *The Complete Poetical Works of Percy Bysshe Shelley,* ed. Thomas Hutchinson (London: Oxford University Press, 1947), 823.

9. Renan, *Life of Jesus,* 138.

10. Calvin, *Institutes,* 3.4.4 (1536), 135.

11. John England, *Letters* (1840–41), in *American Christianity,* ed. H. Shelton Smith, Robert T. Handy, and Lefferts A. Loetscher (New York: Scribners, 1963), 2:201.

12. "The Capuchin Constitution of 1536," in *The Catholic Reformation: Savonarola to Ignatius Loyola,* ed. John C. Olin (New York: Harper & Row, 1969), 157.

13. Henry Wadsworth Longfellow, *Complete Poetical Works* (Boston: Houghton, Mifflin, 1902), 2.

14. George Moore, *The Brook Kerith* (London: Macmillan, 1916), 361

15. James Joyce, *Portrait of the Artist as a Young Man* (New York: Viking, 1957 [1916]), 248–49. That Jesus might have been referring to a second burial, that is, the transfer of bones from a grave to an ossuary, is argued by Byron R. McCane. "'Let the Dead Bury Their Own Dead': Second Burial and Matt. 8:21–22," *Harvard Theological Review* 83 (1990): 31–43.

16. Baron d'Holbach, *Ecce Homo!* 122.

17. *Porphyry's Against the Christians,* 43.

18. Voltaire, *The Sermon of the Fifty,* trans. J. A. R. Séguin, 2nd ed. (Jersey City, N.J.: Ross Paxton, 1965 [1749]), 25; also in *Voltaire, Toleration, and Other Essays,* trans. Joseph McCabe (New York: G. P. Putnam's Sons, 1912), 178.

19. Quoted in Peter Hinchliff, "Ethics, Evolution and Biblical Criticism in the Thought of Benjamin Jowett and John William Colenso," *Journal of Ecclesiastical History* 37 (1986), 108.

20. Mark Twain, *Innocents Abroad,* 2:356.

21. Mary Baker Eddy, "One Cause and Effect," *Miscellaneous Writings 1883–1896* (Boston, 1899), 24.

22. Mikhail Bulgakov, *The Master and Margarita,* trans. Michael Glenny (New York: Harper & Row, 1967), 22.

23. Bruce Barton, *The Man Nobody Knows* (Indianapolis: Bobbs-Merrill, 1925), 130.

24. *Rule of St. Benedict,* 27, in *Documents of the Church,* 130.

25. Luther, "Thesis 28," Heidelberg Disputation, *Martin Luther,* 29.

26. "Clement's Second Letter," 2.4, *Early Christian Fathers,* 194.

27. Joseph Smith, "Teachings, 9–11," *"A Plainer Translation": Joseph Smith's Translation of the Bible. A History and Commentary,* Robert J. Matthews (Provo, Utah: Brigham Young University Press, 1975), 247.

28. Calvin, *Commentaries,* 255.

29. The Venerable Bede, *Ecclesiastical History of the English People,* ed. Bertram Colgrave and R. A. B. Mynors (Oxford: Clarendon Press, 1969), 93.

30. Bernhard Lang, *Sacred Games: A History of Christian Worship* (New Haven, Conn.: Yale University Press, 1997), 336–41.

31. Reimarus, *Fragments,* 143.

5. Disciples

1. Albert Schweitzer, *Out of My Life and Thought,* trans. C. T. Campion (New York: Holt, 1949), 6–8.

2. Ulrich Zwingli, "The Clarity and Certainty of the Word of God" (1522), in *Reformed Reader,* 1:18.

3. Richard Fletcher, *The Barbarian Conversion: From Paganism to Christianity* (New York: Holt, 1997), 130, 236–37.

4. Quoted in *Advocates of Reform: From Wyclif to Erasmus,* ed. Matthew Spinka (Philadelphia, Pa.: Westminster, 1963), 203.

5. William Penn, "Preface to George Fox's Journal," in *Quaker Reader,* 109.

6. "Advice on Reforming the Church," in *Catholic Reformation: Savonarola to Ignatius Loyola,* 188.

7. Thomas of Celano, *Life of St. Francis,* 9.22, ed. and trans. Placid Hermann (Chicago: Franciscan Herald Press, 1963), 12. See also Elizabeth Goudge, *St. Francis of Assisi* (London: Duckworth, 1959), 58.

8. Deno John Geanakoplos, *Byzantium: Church, Society, and Civilization Seen through Contemporary Eyes* (Chicago: University of Chicago Press, 1984), 208–12.

9. *Epistolae ad Virgines,* trans. Benjamin P. Pratten, *Ante-Nicene Christian Library* (Edinburgh: 1969), 14:2.3 ff. in *Paganism and Christianity, 100–425 C.E.: A Sourcebook,* ed. Ramsay MacMullen and Eugene N. Lane (Minneapolis: Fortress, 1992), 170–72.

10. Germain Marc'hadour, *The Bible in the Works of Thomas More* (Nieuwkoop: DeGraaf, 1969), 2:34.

11. St. Ambrose, "Epistle 40," in *Early Latin Theology,* 230.

12. *Rule of St. Benedict,* 7.36, ed. Timothy Fry (Collegeville, Minn.: Liturgical Press, 1981), 197.

13. *Mark Twain's Notebook,* ed. Albert Bigelow Paine (New York: Harper, 1935), 99.

14. Sam J. Ervin Jr., *The Whole Truth: The Watergate Conspiracy* (New York: Random House, 1980), 311.

15. Calvin, *Institutes,* 1.16.1–2.

16. *The Writings of Benjamin Franklin,* ed. Albert Henry Smythe (London: Macmillan, 1905–1907), 9:94.

17. *Documents of the English Reformation,* ed. Gerald Bray (Cambridge: J. Clarke, 1994), 58. How these ruptures shaped the lives of the saints, particularly women, is described by Thomas J. Heffernan, *Sacred Biography: Saints and their Biographers in the Middle Ages* (New York: Oxford University Press, 1988).

18. Augustine, *Exposition of the Psalms* 33–50, trans. Maria Boulding, *The Works of St. Augustine,* ed. John E. Rotelle (Hyde Park, N.Y.: City Press, 2000), 3:289–91.

19. Thomas Müntzer, "Sermon Before the Princes," in *Spiritual and Anabaptist Writers,* 65.

20. John Knox, "Letter to the Regent," *On Rebellion*, ed. Roger A. Mason (Cambridge: Cambridge University Press, 1994), 57, 71.

21. *Voltaire on Religion*, trans. Kenneth W. Applegate (New York: Ungar, 1974), 83.

22. *Critical Remarks on the Truth and Harmony of the Four Gospels . . . By a Free Thinker* (New York: Kraus, 1970 [1836]), bound together with Ethan Allan's *Reason, the Only Oracle of Man* (1836), 95.

23. Percy Bysshe Shelley, "A Refutation of Deism," *Shelley's Prose*, ed. David Lee Clarke (Albuquerque: University of New Mexico Press, 1954 [1814]), 124.

24. Bertrand Russell, "Has Religion Made Useful Contributions to Civilization?" *Why I Am Not a Christian*, 34–35.

25. Chesterton, *Everlasting Man*, 225–27.

26. Charles M. Sheldon, *In His Steps* (Nashville, Tenn.: Broadman, 1963 [1896]), 15.

27. Schweitzer, *Out of My Life and Thought*, 85.

28. Thomas More, *A Dialogue Concerning Heresies*, ed. Thomas M. C. Lawler, Germain Marc'hadour, and Richard C. Marius (New Haven, Conn.: Yale University Press, 1981), 1:48–49.

29. Augustine, "On Grace and Free Will," *Works of Aurelius Augustine*, ed. Marcus Dods (Edinburgh: T & T Clark, 1886), 15:33.

30. William R. Shea, "Galileo and the Church," in *God and Nature: Historical Essays on the Encounter Between Christianity and Science*, ed. David C. Lindberg and Ronald L. Numbers (Berkeley and Los Angeles: University of California Press, 1986), 118.

31. Flannery O'Connor, letter to Dr. T. R. Spivey, 16 March 1960, in *The Habit of Being*, ed. Sally Fitzgerald (New York: Farrar, Strauss, Giroux, 1979), 382.

32. *Luther's Works*, ed. Helmut T. Lehman, trans. John W. Doberstein (Philadelphia: Muhlenberg Press, 1959), 51:391.

33. Socrates, *Church History*, 1.9, *Documents of the Christian Church*, 44.

34. John Cassian, *Third Conference of Abbot Chaeremon*, in *Readings in the History of Christian Theology*, ed. William C. Placher (Philadelphia: Westminster, 1988), 1:134.

35. See also Heinz Bluhm, *Martin Luther, Creative Translator* (St. Louis, Mo.: Concordia, 1965), 28.

36. John Wesley, "Sermon 128," in *Readings in Christian Humanism*, ed. Joseph Shaw, R. W. Franklin, Harris Kaasa, and Charles W. Buzicky (Minneapolis, Minn.: Augsburg, 1982), 431.

37. Gilbert Burnet, *Discourse* (1688), in *Anglicanism*, 243.

38. Owen Watkins, *The Puritan Experience: Studies in Spiritual Autobiography* (New York: Schocken, 1972), 41.

39. William Fitz Stephen, *Life of St. Thomas Beckett* (1170), in *Those Who Prayed: An Anthology of Medieval Sources*, ed. Peter Speed (New York: Italica Press, 1997), 246.

40. Baron d'Holbach, *Ecce Homo!* 140.

41. Franklin, in *American Deists*, 340–41.

42. Rauschenbusch, *Theology for the Social Gospel*, 102.

43. Ulrich Luz, *The Theology of the Gospel of Matthew*, trans. J. Bradford Robinson (Cambridge: Cambridge University Press, 1993), 65–66.

44. Leo Tolstoy, *The Kingdom of God and Peace Essays*, trans. Aylmer Maud (London: Oxford University Press, 1951), 254.

45. Jacques-Benigne Bossuet, "On Authority," in *Politics Drawn from the Very Words of Holy Scripture*, ed. Patrick Riley (Cambridge: Cambridge University Press, 1990), 41.

46. Kant, *Religion Within the Limits of Reason Alone*, 113.

47. Catherine Albanese, *Natural Religion in America: From the Algonkian Indians to the New Age* (Chicago: University of Chicago Press, 1990), 113–14.

48. Robert Peel, *Mary Baker Eddy: The Years of Authority* (New York: Holt, Rinehart and Winston, 1977), 234. See Robert Peel, "Science and Health with a Key to the Scriptures," *The Bible and Bibles in America*, 196.

49. John Henry Cardinal Newman, *Tracts for the Times* (New York: AMS, 1969 [1833–41]), 4.

50. Hosea Ballou, "Treatise on Atonement" (1805), in *Universalism in America*, ed. Ernest Cassara (Boston: Beacon, 1971), 96.

51. Gregory of Nazianzus, *Fifth Theological Oration: On the Holy Spirit*, 29–30, in *Nicene and Post-Nicene Fathers*, 7:319.

52. Luther, "Confession Concerning Christ's Supper," *Basic Theological Writings*, 400.

53. C. S. Lewis, *Surprised by Joy* (London: G. Bles, 1955), 224.

54. Stephen L. Wailes, *Medieval Allegories of Jesus' Parables* (Berkeley and Los Angeles: University of California Press, 1987), 101.

55. *Readings in Church History*, 3:421.

56. *Reformation*, ed. Hillerbrand, 60.

57. Augustine, "On Baptism," in *Documents of the Christian Church*, 85.

58. Aquinas, *Summa*, Q. 11, Art. 3, 1226; also in *Documents of the Christian Church*, 147.

59. Thomas More, *Utopia*, ed. Edward Surtz (New Haven, Conn.: Yale University Press, 1964), 2:134.

60. Sebastian Castellio (?), *Concerning Heretics*, ed. Roland D. Bainton (New York: Columbia University Press, 1935), 126.

61. Milton, *Areopagitica* (1644), *Milton*, ed. Hughes, 747.

62. Hus, "The Church," ch. 5, in *Forerunners of the Reformation: The Shape of Medieval Thought*, ed. Heiko A. Obermann (New York: Holt, Rinehart and Winston, 1966), 225.

63. John Wesley, *Sermons*, 5.106–107, quoted in Barrie W. Tabraham, *The Making of Methodism* (London: Epworth, 1995), 31.

64. Mark Twain, *A Pen Warmed-Up in Hell*, 142.

65. George Bernard Shaw, *Complete Prefaces*, ed. Dan H. Laurence and Daniel J. Leary (Harmondsworth, U.K.: Penguin, 1995), 1:237.

66. Origen, "On First Principles," 4.1, *Ante-Nicene Fathers*, 4:373.

67. Nathaniel Hawthorne, *The Scarlet Letter*, ed. Kenneth S. Lynn (New York: Harcourt, Brace & World, 1949), 49.

68. Dietrich Bonhoeffer, *The Cost of Discipleship*, trans. R. H. Fuller, rev. Irmgard Booth (New York: Macmillan, 1963), 45–48.

69. Martin Luther, *Lectures on Romans*, ed. and trans. Wilhelm Pauck (Philadelphia: Westminster, 1961), 102.

70. Kent P. Jackson, "The Sacred Literature of the Latter-day Saints," *The Bible and Bibles in America*, 163–91.

71. Lionel Lambourne, *Victorian Painting* (London: Phaidon, 1999), 237–38.

72. Pius XI, *Divini Redemptoris*, in *Papal Encyclicals*, 3:544.

73. Josephus, *Jewish Antiquities*, 18.5.2; Elizabeth Cady Stanton, *The Woman's Bible* (New York: Arno Press, 1972 [1895]), 119.

74. Gustave Flaubert, "Hérodias," *Three Tales*, trans. Robert Baldick (Harmondsworth, U.K.: Penguin, 1961), 121.

75. Joris Karl Huysman, *Against Nature*, trans. Margaret Malden (New York: Oxford University Press, 1998), 46. See also Helen Zagona, *The Legend of Salome* (Geneva: Droz, 1960).

76. Oscar Wilde, *Salome*, trans. Lord Alfred Douglas (London: Faber and Faber, 1989 [1894]), 26.

77. Voltaire, "Epistle to the Romans," *Toleration, and Other Essays*, 135.

78. Bertolt Brecht, *Mother Courage,* in *Collected Plays,* trans. Ralph Manheim (New York: Random House, 1972), 5:145.

79. Lloyd C. Douglas, *The Robe* (New York: Houghton, Mifflin, 1999 [1942]), 282.

80. Erasmus, "Preface," *Latin New Testament,* in *The Praise of Folly and Other Writings,* ed. Robert M. Adams (New York: Norton, 1989), 138–39.

81. Mark Twain, *Innocents Abroad,* 2:305.

82. Thomas Cowper, "Light Shining out of Darkness" (1779), *Olney Hymns, Verses and Letters* (Cambridge, Mass.: Harvard University Press, 1968), 154.

83. For the *Heliand* text, see <http://titus.uni-frankfurt.de/texte/etcs/germ/asachs/heliand>. For a partial translation and commentary, see G. Roland Murphy, *The Saxon Savior: The German Transformation of the Gospel in the Ninth-Century Heliand* (New York: Oxford University Press, 1989).

84. St. Ambrose, "On the Death of Theodosius," in *Treasury,* 114.

85. Calvin, *Tracts and Treatises on the Reformation of the Church,* ed. Thomas Torrance, trans. Henry Beveridge (Grand Rapids, Mich.: Eerdmans, 1985), 1:303–305.

6. Jesus and the Pharisees

1. *American Folk Gospel,* ed. Thomas E. Q. Williams (Greenfield, Ind.: Coiny, 1999), 289.

2. Zwingli, in *Reformation,* ed. Hillerbrand, 140.

3. Roger Williams, *The Bloudy Tenent of Persecution,* 124.

4. Thomas Woolston, *A Discourse,* in *Six Discourses,* 53.

5. Augustine, *Eighty-three Different Questions,* trans. David L. Mosher (Washington, D.C.: Catholic University Press, 1982), 120–21.

6. *Documents of Vatican II,* ed. Walter M. Abbott (New York: America Press, 1966), 201–202.

7. Calvin, *Commentary on a Harmony,* 2:289.

8. John Wesley, *Explanatory Notes Upon the New Testament* (London: Kelly, 1905 [1754]), 81.

9. Quoted in *Reformation,* ed. Hillerbrand, 323.

10. Luther, "Why the Books of the Pope and His Followers Were Burned," *Reformation Writings,* 2:82.

11. Luther, "Appeal to the Ruling Class," *Reformation Writings,* 1:120.

12. Cyprian, "On the Unity of the Catholic Church," in *Treasury,* 360; *Documents of the Christian Church,* 78.

13. *The Bloudy Tenent Yet More Bloudy,* ed. Samuel L. Caldwell, *Complete Writings of Roger Williams* (New York: Russell & Russell, 1963), 4:442.

14. *Documents of the Christian Church,* 89–90.

15. Ibid., 25.

16. *Church and State,* 11.

17. "Dictatus Papae" (1075), *Basic Documents in Medieval History,* ed. Norton Downs (Princeton, N.J.: Van Nostrand, 1959), 58.

18. *Documents of the Christian Church,* 127.

19. Vatican Council 1, 1870, "First Dogmatic Constitution of the Church of God," 18 July 1870, in *Readings in Church History,* 3:74–79.

20. William of Ockham, *A Short Discourse on the Tyrannical Government,* ed. Arthur Stephen McGrade, trans. John Kilcullen (Cambridge: Cambridge University Press, 1992), 23, 29, 106–107.

21. Luther, "Appeal to the Ruling Class," *Reformation Writings,* 191.

22. *Documents of the Christian Church,* 106.

23. Ibid., 109.

24. John Wycliffe, "On the Church and Her Members," in Ray Petry, *History of Christianity* (Englewood Cliffs, N.J.: Prentice-Hall, 1962–64), 521.

25. Calvin, *Commentary on a Harmony,* 2:296.

26. Aquinas, *Summa,* Q.17–20, Supplement, 2626–40.

27. H. L. Mencken, *Treatise on the Gods* (New York: Knopf, 1946), 211.

28. *Documents of the Christian Church,* 147.

29. *Creeds of the Churches,* 288.

30. Lactantius, *On the Deaths of the Persecutors,* 44.1–10, in *Pagans and Christians in Late Antiquity: A Sourcebook,* ed. A. D. Lee (New York: Routledge Press, 2000), 82.

31. Mark Twain, *Letters from the Earth,* ed. Bernard DeVoto (New York: Harper & Row, 1962), 44.

32. John Donne, "The Crosse," *Divine Poems,* ed. Helen Gardner, 2nd ed. (Oxford: Clarendon Press, 1978), 26.

33. Justin Martyr, *Apology,* 1.55, in *Early Christian Fathers,* 278–79.

34. Athanasius, "Incarnation of the Word," 25, in *Nicene and Post-Nicene Fathers,* 4:49.

35. Tertullian, "The Chaplet," *Disciplinary, Moral, and Ascetical Works,* 237.

36. "Apology: An Attack on Veneration of Relics," trans. A. Cabaniss, in *Early Medieval Theology,* ed. G. E. McCracken and A. Cabaniss, 241–48; *Medieval Saints: A Reader,* ed. Mary-Ann Stouck (Petersborough, Ont.: Broadview, 1999), 371.

37. "The Conduct of the Inquisition of Heretical Depravity," in *Heresies of the High Middle Ages,* 374.

38. John Adams, *Great Quotations,* ed. George Seldes (New York: Lyle Stuart, 1960), 45.

39. Friedrich Nietzsche, *Daybreak: Thoughts on the Prejudices of Morality,* 84, ed. Maudmarie Clark and Brian Lester, trans. R. J. Hollingdale (Cambridge: Cambridge University Press, 1997), 49–50.

40. George Bernard Shaw, *Platform and Pulpit* (New York: Hill and Wang, 1961), 209.

41. Schweitzer, *Out of My Life,* 85.

42. Ignatius, "On Martyrdom," in *Invitation to Christian Spirituality,* ed. John R. Tyson (1999), 54–55.

43. Robert Bolt, *A Man For All Seasons* (New York: Random House, 1962), 158.

44. Calvin, *Institutes* (1536), 3.18.2, 40.

45. *Boswell's Life,* 30 July 1763, 324.

46. D. F. Strauss, *The Life of Jesus Critically Examined,* 2.10.107.

47. St. Gregory Palamas (1296–1359), *Triads* 1.3.43, in *A History of Christian Doctrine,* ed. Hubert Cunliffe-Jones (Edinburgh: Clark, 1978), 222.

48. Woolston, *Discourses,* 44.

49. Origen, *Commentary on Matthew,* 13.12, in *Ante-Nicene Fathers,* 10:482.

50. Aquinas, *Summa,* Q. 104, Art. 6, 1646.

51. Luther, "The Freedom of a Christian" (1520), *Reformation Writings,* 377.

52. "Conrad Grebel and the Zurich Anabaptists: Letter to Thomas Muentzer" (1524), in *Spiritual and Anabaptist Writers,* 81; *Protestant Reformation,* 128.

53. Tolstoy, "My Religion" (1884), in *Religion from Tolstoy to Camus,* 50.

54. Pius XI, in *Church and State,* 475.

55. Andreas Karlstadt, "Whether one should proceed slowly," in *The Radical Reformation,* ed. Michael G. Baylor (Cambridge: Cambridge University Press, 1991), 65.

56. *Foxe's Christian Martyrs of the World* (Chicago: Moody, 1960), 506.

57. Edmund Burke, "Speech on Clerical Subscription," *The Writings and Speeches of Edmund Burke,* ed. Paul Langford (New York: Oxford University Press, 1981), 2:362.

58. Luther, *Documents of the Christian Church,* 217.

59. *Creeds of the Churches,* 285; Michael Sattler, *The Schleitheim Articles* (1527), in *Radical Reformation,* 174–75.

60. Luther, in *Karlstadt's Battle with Luther: Documents in a Liberal-Radical Debate,* ed. Ronald J. Sider (Philadelphia, Pa.: Fortress, 1978), 35.

61. Innocent III, *How to Read Church History,* ed. Jean Comby, John Bowden, and Margaret Lydamme, 1:138; Decretal "Novit Ille," *Church and State,* 70.

62. Joseph Priestley, "An Essay on the First Principles of Government" (1771), *Political Writings,* ed. Peter N. Miller (Cambridge: Cambridge University Press, 1993), 75.

63. *Church and State,* 526.

64. John of Paris, *Tractate on Royal and Papal Power,* in *From Irenaeus to Grotius,* 407.

65. *Church and State,* 535.

66. Calvin, *Institutes* (1536), 4.11.2, 144–45.

67. John Greenleaf Whittier, *Complete Poetical Works* (Boston, Mass.: Houghton, Mifflin, 1909), 101.

68. Joseph DeMaistre, "Du Pape" ("The Pope"), trans. Aeneas McDawson, in *Romance and the Rock,* ed. Joseph Fitzer (Philadelphia: Fortress, 1989), 196.

69. Castellio, in *Reformation,* ed. Hillerbrand, 291.

70. Rabanus Maurus, *Medieval Allegories,* 135–36.

7. Jerusalem

1. *Letters of Abelard and Heloise,* 4, 148.

2. Laura Engelstein, *Castration and the Heavenly Kingdom* (Ithaca, N.Y.: Cornell University Press, 1999).

3. Tolstoy, "An Afterword to 'The Kreutzer Sonata,'" *The Lion and the Honeycomb: The Religious Writings of Tolstoy,* ed. A. N. Wilson (London: Collins, 1987), 70.

4. Henry Ware, "Letters Addressed to Trinitarians and Calvinists" (1820), in *American Christianity, 1607–1820,* ed. H. Shelton Smith (New York: Scribners, 1960–63), 1:507.

5. Joyce, *Portrait of the Artist,* 236.

6. Aquinas, *Summa,* Q.109, Art.5, *Basic Readings,* 132.

7. Calvin, *Commentaries,* 105–106.

8. "On Free Will" (1527), *Spiritual and Anabaptist Writers,* 112–35.

9. William Ware, "Antiquity and Revival of Unitarian Christianity" (1831), in *An American Reformation: A Documentary History of Unitarian Christianity,* ed. Sydney E. Ahlstrom and Jonathan S. Carey (Middletown, Conn.: Wesleyan University Press, 1985), 138.

10. Clement of Alexandria, "The Rich Man's Salvation," 12, in *Documents in Early Christian Thought,* ed. Maurice Wiles and Mark Santer (Cambridge: Cambridge University Press, 1975), 203.

11. Melanchthon, "On the Vows of Monks," *Melanchthon and Bucer,* ed. Wilhelm Pauck (Philadelphia: Westminster, 1969), 60.

12. Athanasius, *Life of Antony,* 2.31.

13. *Church and State,* 334–35.

14. Porphyry, *Against the Christians,* 44–45.

15. *Los Angeles Times,* 17 March 2001, A-13.

16. Letter to John Colet, 29 October 1511, in J. Huizinga, *Erasmus and the Age of the Reformation* (New York: Harper, 1959), 211–13.

17. Voltaire, *Zapata's Questions,* #63, in *Voltaire on Religion,* 36.

18. Branch, *Pillar of Fire,* 359.

19. Barclay, *Gospel of Matthew,* 1:332.

20. Calvin, *Institutes* 3.23.1, 948.

21. John Wesley, "Sermon 110," *Works* (Nashville, Tenn.: Abingdon, 1986), 3:551.

22. G. K. Chesterton, *What's Wrong with the World,* 153, in David W. Fagerberg, *The Size of Chesterton's Catholicism* (South Bend, Ind.: Notre Dame Press, 1998), 168.

23. Milton, *Christian Doctrine,* ed. Hughes, 941.

24. *Barmen Declaration,* in *Between Caesar and Christ,* ed. Charles Villa-Vicencio (Grand Rapids, Mich.: Eerdmans, 1986), 98.

25. Augustine, "Sermon 130," *Sermons, The Works of Saint Augustine,* 7:311.

26. Gregory of Nyssa, "An Address on Religious Instruction," in *Christology of the Latin Fathers,* ed. Edward Rochie Hardy and C. C. Richardson (Philadelphia: Westminster, 1954), 301.

27. Anselm, *Documents,* 153; see also "Why God Became Man," in *A Scholastic Miscellany: Anselm to Ockham,* ed. and trans. Eugene R. Fairweather (Philadelphia: Westminister, 1966), 100–183.

28. Aquinas, *Summa,* Q.48, 2283–87. See also Philip L. Quinn, "Aquinas on Atonement," 153–77, in *Trinity, Incarnation, and Atonement,* ed. Ronald J. Feenstra and Cornelius Plantinga Jr. (South Bend, Ind.: Notre Dame Press, 1989), 162.

29. Abelard, *Commentary on the Epistle to the Romans 3:21–26,* in *Basic Readings in Theology,* 107.

30. William Ellery Channing, "Unitarian Christianity" (1819), in *Unitarian Christianity and Other Essays,* ed. Irving H. Bartlett (New York: Liberal Arts Press, 1957), 93.

31. Calvin, *Institutes,* 2.16.2, 505.

32. Locke, *Reasonableness of Christianity,* 145–51.

33. Kant, *Religion Within the Limits of Reason,* 107.

34. Joseph Priestley, "The Doctrine of Atonement," *History of the Corruptions of Christianity* (New York: Garland, 1974 [1782]), 2:152–280.

35. Paine, *Writings,* 1:497.

36. Baron d'Holbach, *Ecce Homo!* 77–78.

37. Hosea Ballou, "Treatise on Atonement"(1805), *Universalism in America,* 101–102.

38. *Bible Handbook for Freethinkers and Inquiring Christians,* 126.

39. George Bernard Shaw, "Preface on the Prospects of Christianity," *The Crime of Imprisonment* (New York: Philosophical Library, 1949), 92. See Anthony S. Abbott, *Shaw and Christianity* (New York: Seabury Press, 1965), 54–55.

40. Letter to Jas. E. Gould, 31 July 1879, *Letters of Robert G. Ingersoll,* 32.

41. Nietzsche, *Antichrist,* 174.

42. René Girard, *Things Hidden From the Foundation of the World,* trans. S. Bann and M. Metteer (London: Athlone, 1987), 182.

43. Letter to John Henry Weltch, 4 February 1867, *Letters and Diaries of John Henry Newman,* ed. Charles Stephen Dessain and Thomas Gornall (Oxford: Clarendon Press, 1973), 23:52.

44. Origen, *Commentary on John,* 10:18, in *Ante-Nicene Fathers,* 10:396–97.

45. G. K. Chesterton, *Collected Poems* (New York: Dodd, Mead, 1932), 54.

46. Tolstoy, *The Gospel in Brief,* trans. Aylmer Maude, 147.

47. Origen, *Commentary on John,* 10.16, in *Ante-Nicene Fathers,* 10:394–95.

48. John Hus, "On Simony," in *Advocates of Reform,* 204.

49. Voltaire, "Miracles," *Philosophical Dictionary,* 2:90. Many of Voltaire's objections to biblical miracles (and prophecies) were taken from the works of Jean Meslier (1664–1729) and from those of the English deists Thomas Woolston, Anthony Collins, and Matthew Tindal. See Andrew R. Morehouse, *Voltaire and Jean Meslier* (New Haven, Conn.: Yale University Press, 1936).

50. Woolston, in Rupp, *Religion in England, 1688–1791,* 274.

51. Maugham, *Of Human Bondage,* 52.

52. Robert Naunton (1563–1635), *Fragmenta Regalia,* ed. John S. Cerovski (Washington, D.C.: Folger, 1985), 40.

53. Voltaire, "An Important Study by Lord Bolingbroke," *Voltaire on Religion,* 127.

54. John Stuart Mill, "On Liberty" (1859), *Collected Works,* 18.255.

55. *Documents of the Christian Church,* 21.

56. *Church and State,* 11.

57. *Celsus: On the True Doctrine,* 124–25.

58. *Documents of the Christian Church,* 9.

59. Jerome, "Preface to Commentary on Ezekiel," in *Nicene and Post-Nicene Fathers,* 6:444.

60. Thomas Hobbes, *Leviathan* (New York: E. P. Dutton, 1950), 614.

61. *Documents of the Christian Church,* 123.

62. John of Paris, *On Royal and Papal Power,* in Petry, *History,* 506.

63. Luther, "Against the Robbing and Murdering Hordes of Peasants," *Martin Luther,* 121–22.

64. King James VI and I, *Political Writings,* ed. Johann P. Somerville (Cambridge: Cambridge University Press, 1984), 72.

65. Jacques-Benigne Bossuet, "The Duties of Subjects," Bk. 6, *Politics drawn from the very words of Holy Scripture,* 174.

66. Mark Allan Powell, "Do and Keep What Moses Says," *Journal of Biblical Literature* 114, no. 3 (1995): 419–35.

67. *Creeds of the Churches,* 70.

68. Frederick Douglass, "Appendix," *Narrative of the Life of an American Slave* (New York: Viking Penguin, 1982 [1845]), 155–56.

69. William Fulke, "A Brief and Plain Declaration" (1577), in *Elizabethan Puritanism,* ed. Leonard J. Trinterud (New York: Oxford University Press, 1971), 255.

70. Tolstoy, "Reply," in *Religion from Tolstoy to Camus,* 133, 136.

71. Elisabeth Schüssler Fiorenza, *In Memory of Her: A Feminist Theological Reconstruction of Christian Origins,* rev. ed. (New York: Crossroad, 1998), 150–51.

72. *Reformation Writings,* 1:337.

73. E. V. Rieu, trans., *The Four Gospels* (New York: Penguin, 1953).

74. *Reformation Writings,* 1:48.

75. *Documents of the Christian Church,* 22.

76. François-René de Chateaubriand, *Génie du christianisme,* 4.3 (Paris: Garnier, 1920), 144.

77. *Luther and Erasmus: Free Will and Salvation,* ed. E. Gordon Rupp (Philadelphia: Westminster, 1969), 45.

78. John Wesley, *Works,* ed. Albert C. Outler (Nashville, Tenn.: Abingdon, 1986), 3:554–55.

79. Michael Wigglesworth, *Day of Doom* (New York: American News, 1867), 21, 25, 27, 36, 37, 82, 84.

80. Henry Grattan Guinness, *The Approaching End of the Age, Religion in Victorian Britain, The Sources,* ed. James R. Moore (New York: St. Martin's, 1988), 3:192.

81. *Book of Prophecies edited by Christopher Columbus,* ed. Robert Rusconi, trans. Blair Sullivan (Berkeley and Los Angeles: University of California Press), 157.

82. Quoted in M. A. Screech, *Laughter at the Foot of the Cross* (New York: Penguin, 1997), 190.

83. Luther, "An Appeal to the Ruling Class," *Reformation Writings,* 1:169.

84. Jean Danielou, *The Bible and the Liturgy* (South Bend, Ind.: Notre Dame Press, 1956), 31.

85. Voltaire, "An Important Study by Lord Bolingbroke," *Voltaire and Religion,* 147.

86. Shelley, "A Refutation of Deism," *Shelley's Prose,* 127.

87. The classic in this field is Lindsey's *The Late Great Planet Earth* (Grand Rapids, Mich.: Zondervan, 1970). A Bantam paperback went through thirty-six printings by 1981, selling more than fifteen million copies.

88. Augustine, *The City of God against the Pagans,* 20.30, ed. R. W. Dyson (Cambridge: Cambridge University Press, 1998), 1042–43.

89. Thomas Shepard, "The Parable of the Ten Virgins," Section I, in *Salvation in New England,* ed. Phyllis M. Jones and Nicholas R. Jones (Austin: University of Texas Press, 1977), 133–34.

90. Harriet Beecher Stowe, *Uncle Tom's Cabin* (Cambridge, Mass.: Belknap Press), 165.

91. Cady Stanton, *Woman's Bible,* 126.

92. For other examples of allegory and literary allusions, see "Parable of the Unprofitable Servant," *Dictionary of Biblical Tradition in English Literature,* ed. David Lyle Jeffrey (Grand Rapids, Mich.: Eerdmans, 1992), 799–801.

93. John Henry Newman, "Particular Judgment," *Discourses to Mixed Congregations* (London: Burns, Oates, 1876), 38.

94. Bertrand Russell, *Why I am not a Christian,* 18.

95. Gibbon, *Decline and Fall,* 366.

96. Thomas Browne, *Religio Medici,* ed. R. H. A. Robbins (Oxford: Clarendon Press, 1972), 55.

97. Benjamin Rush, Letter to Jeremy Belknap, 6 June 1791, in *Universalism in America,* 92.

98. Charles Chauncy, "The Mystery Hid from Ages and Generations, made manifest by the Gospel-Revelation: or, The Salvation of All Men" (London, 1784), in *American Christianity,* 1:492.

99. Calvin, *Commentaries,* 402.

100. Hallam Tennyson, *Alfred Lord Tennyson: A Memoir* (London: Macmillan, 1897), 2:65.

101. Brian Young, *The Villein's Bible: Stories in Romanesque Carving* (London: Barrie & Jenkins, 1990), 126–27.

102. Francis Liguori, *The Eternal Truths: Preparation for Death,* quoted in Geoffrey Rowell, *Hell and the Victorians* (Oxford: Oxford University Press, 1974), 155–56.

103. Joseph Furniss, *Sight of Hell* (1921), in *Hell and the Victorians,* 172.

104. Jonathan Edwards, in *Reformed Reader,* 1:157.

105. Joyce, *Portrait of the Artist,* 131–32. Joyce took many of his details from Giovanni Pietro Pinamenti, *Hell Opened* (1868). See Elizabeth F. Boyd, "Joyce's Hell Fire Sermons," *Modern Language Notes* 75 (1960): 561–71; reprinted in *Portraits of an Artist: A Casebook on James Joyce's A Portrait of the Artist as a Young Man,* ed. William E. Morris and Clifford A. Nault (New York: Odyssey, 1962), 253–63.

106. Locke, *Reasonableness,* 134.

107. John Wesley, *Explanatory Notes Upon the New Testament* (1754), 57.

108. Benjamin Franklin, Letter to Josiah and Abiah Franklin, 13 April 1738, in *American Deists,* 88.

109. *Benjamin Franklin's Autobiographical Writings,* ed. Carl Van Doren (New York: Viking, 1945), 29.

110. Calvin, *Institutes,* 3.18.2, 822.

111. *The Select Works of William Penn,* in *A Documentary History of Religion in America,* ed. Edwin S. Gaustad (Grand Rapids, Mich.: Eerdmans, 1982), 1:119.

112. *Poems of Emily Dickinson,* 126, ed. R. W. Franklin (Cambridge, Mass.: Belknap Press, 1999), 65.

113. *A Testament of Hope: The Essential Writings of Martin Luther King Jr.,* ed. James Melvin Washington (New York: Harper & Row, 1986), 275.

114. "Life of Martin" 3, in Petry, *History,* 1:136.

115. *Creeds of the Churches,* 147.

8. Passion, Death, and Resurrection

1. Papyrus fragments of chapter 26, acquired in Egypt in 1901 and dated toward the end of the second century (now in Oxford and known as P64), are among the oldest NT manuscripts. Since they were written on both sides, they came from a book-like codex, not from a roll. Two Barcelona fragments, from chapters 3 and 5 and known as P67, were subsequently identified as being from the same codex, named P4, and are now in Paris. Christians popularized the codex over the papyrus roll because it was capacious enough to contain the four Gospels and facilitated the search for specific passages. Earlier than the codex was a wooden tablet coated with wax that was useful for notes and messages, since it could be erased and reused.

2. *Luther and Erasmus: Free Will and Salvation,* 68, 246–48.

3. Eusebius, *Life of Constantine,* ed. and trans. Averil Cameron and Stuart G. Hall (Oxford: Clarendon Press, 1999), 127.

4. Whittier, "Worship," *Complete Poetical Works,* 429.

5. *Saint Ambrose, Letters,* trans. Mary Melchior Beyenka (Washington, D.C.: Catholic University Press, 1954), 24.

6. Aquinas, *Summa,* Q. 83, Art. 1, 2512.

7. Luther, in *Reformation Writings,* 1:231, 233.

8. "Calvin's Reply to Sadoleto" (1539), 74.

9. *Reformation,* ed. Hillerbrand, 25.

10. *Creeds of the Churches,* 432.

11. Calvin, *Institutes,* 4.17.10, 1370.

12. Huldrych Zwingli, *Commentary on True and False Religion,* 18.5, ed. Samuel Macauley Jackson and Clarence Nevin Heller (Durham, N.C.: Labyrinth, 1989 [1525]), 95. See also "On the Nature of the Sacraments," in *Account of Faith, Sources of Protestant Theology,* ed. William R. Scott (New York: Bruce, 1971), 53.

13. *Documents on the Continental Reformation,* 99.

14. Voltaire, *Essai sur les moeurs,* in *Oeuvres Complètes* (Paris, 1785), 2:219.

15. *Creeds of the Churches,* 225–26.

16. "Marburg Colloquy," *Documents on the Continental Reformation,* 94–100; *Great Debates,* 71–107.

17. Martin Luther, *Table Talk* (1451), ed. and trans. Theodore G. Tappert, *Luther's Works* (Philadelphia: Westminster, 1967), 54:152.

18. Rupp and Drewery, eds., *Martin Luther,* 136.

19. Letter to Vadian, 20 October 1529, ibid., 137–38.

20. Voltaire, "Eucharist," *Philosophical Dictionary,* 1:444.

21. Ralph Waldo Emerson, *Essays and Lectures* (New York: Viking, 1983), 1137.

22. David Friedrich Strauss, "Are We Still Christians?" *The Old Faith and the New* (1872, trans. 1873), in *The New Christianity,* ed. William Robert Miller (New York: Delacorte, 1967), 130.

23. Lang, *Sacred Games,* 336–41.

24. "Declaration on the Question of the Ordination of Women to the Ministerial Priesthood," 1976, *Documents,* 391.

25. M. Rubin, *Corpus Christi: The Eucharist in Late Medieval Culture* (Cambridge: Cambridge University Press, 1991).

26. Smalcald Articles, 2.2 (1538), *Basic Theological Writings*, 503–505; *Reformed Catechisms of the Sixteenth Century*, ed. Arthur C. Cochrane (Philadelphia: Westminster, 1966), 320.

27. John Calvin, "The Geneva Confession," in *The Protestant Reformation*, ed. Lewis W. Spitz (Englewood Cliffs, N.J.: Prentice-Hall, 1966), 119. See also *Institutes* 4.17.37, 1413.

28. John Knox, *History of the Reformation in Scotland*, Bk. 4, *Works*, ed. David Laing, 2:276.

29. William Fulke, "A Brief and Plain Declaration," in *Elizabethan Puritanism*, 270.

30. Sider, ed., *Karlstadt's Battle with Luther*, 82.

31. Thomas Mann, *Magic Mountain*, trans. H. T. Lowe-Porter (New York: Knopf, 1960), 572.

32. Ignazio Silone, *Bread and Wine*, trans. Harvey Fergusson II (New York: New American Library, 1963 [1937]), 270.

33. Aquinas, *Summa*, Q. 21, Art. 1, 2138.

34. Renan, *Life of Jesus*, 202.

35. George Fox, *Journal* (1664), 2:52–53.

36. Hubmaier, "On the Sword" (1527), in *Radical Reformation*, 185.

37. Shaw, *Complete Prefaces*, 1:163.

38. William of Ockham, *A Short Discourse on the Tyrannical Ascendancy of the Pope*, Bk. 2, in *From Irenaeus to Grotius*, 471–72.

39. Porphyry, *Against the Christians*, 40.

40. George Bernard Shaw, *Three Plays* (New York: Dodd, Mead, 1934), 217.

41. Thomas More, *Dialogue of Comfort Against Tribulation*, ed. Frank Manley (New Haven, Conn.: Yale University Press, 1977), 251.

42. Calvin, *Commentaries*, 322.

43. Charles I, *Eikon Basilike, The Portraiture of His Sacred Majesty in His Solitude and Suffering* (1648), ed. Philip A. Knachel (Ithaca, N.Y.: Cornell University Press, 1966), 64.

44. Pseudo-Bonaventure, *Meditations*, 328–29.

45. Jean le Bel, Canon of Liege (1290–1370), *Vrayes Chroniques* (1326–31). Jean Comby, *How to Read Church History*, 1:282.

46. Mark Twain, *Innocents Abroad*, 2:352.

47. *Play of the Dice*, in *The Towneley Plays*, ed. Martin Stevens and A. C. Cawley (New York: Oxford University Press, 1994), 318, 322. See also Rosemary Woolf, *The English Mystery Plays* (Berkeley and Los Angeles, Calif.: University of California Press, 1972), 267.

48. Countee Cullen, "Colors," *My Soul's High Song: The Collected Writings of Countee Cullen* (New York: Doubleday, 1991), 145.

49. "Hymne to God my God, in my sicknesse," *Divine Poems*, 50.

50. Pseudo-Bonaventure, *Meditations*, 333–34. For a review of theories suggested for the absence of the crucifixion from early Christian art, see Robin Margaret Jensen, *Understanding Early Christian Art* (London: Routledge, 2000), 133–37.

51. King James VI and I, *Political Writings*, 234.

52. Reimarus, *Fragments*, 150.

53. *The Official Life of St. Francis*, in *Medieval Saints: A Reader*, 500.

54. Donne, "Goodfriday, 1613. Riding Westward," *Divine Poems*, 31.

55. Edward Gibbon, *The History of Christianity* (New York: Arno Press, 1970), 200.

56. Whittier, "The Crucifixion," *Complete Poetical Works*, 418.

57. Calvin, *Commentary on a Harmony*, 3:212.

58. "Christ's Ascension," *The Poems of Cynewulf*, ed. and trans. Charles W. Kennedy (London: Routledge, 1910), 196.

59. *The Sermon-Conference of St. Thomas Aquinas on the Apostles' Creed*, ed. and trans. Nicholas Ayo (Notre Dame, Ind.: Notre Dame Press, 1988), 81.

60. *Reformed Catechisms*, 312.

61. Calvin, *Institutes* 2.16.8–12.

62. Paine, *Writings,* 1:576.

63. J. A. Froude, *Nemesis of Faith,* 2nd ed. (London: Chapman, 1849), 19.

64. Jefferson, *Jefferson's Extracts,* 297.

65. *Complete Gospels,* 405.

66. Reimarus, *Fragments,* 152.

67. Porphyry, *Against the Christians,* 19.

68. Paine, *Writings,* 1:578.

69. Hugh J. Schonfield, *The Passover Plot* (New York: Random House, 1965).

70. Mencken, *Treatise on the Gods,* 224.

71. D. H. Lawrence, *The Escaped Cock,* ed. Gerald M. Lacy (Los Angeles: Scarecrow Press, 1973 [1928]), 58–59.

72. Moore, *Brooke Kerith,* 365–66, 385.

73. Voltaire, "Christianity," *Philosophical Dictionary,* 1:273.

74. Whittier, "Trinitas," *Complete Poetical Works,* 344.

75. Dorothy Sayers, *The Mind of the Maker* (reprint, Cleveland, Ohio: World, 1964), 113–15.

76. Graham Greene, *Monsignor Quixote* (New York: Simon & Schuster, 1982), 42–43.

77. Augustine, "The Trinity," *Works,* 175, 289. See also "On the Trinity," 9.1.1–5, 8, *Documents,* 41.

78. Donne, "Trinity," *Divine Poems,* 17.

79. Reimarus, *Fragments,* 95–96.

80. *Two Treatises of Servetus on the Trinity,* 3, in *Reformation,* ed. Hillerbrand, 276.

81. Voltaire, "An Important Study by Lord Bolingbroke," *Voltaire on Religion,* 190.

82. Letter to James Smith, 8 December 1822, *Jefferson's Extracts,* 409.

83. Channing, "Unitarian Christianity," 13.

84. Penn, *Witness of William Penn,* 134.

85. Cotton Mather, *Magnalia Christi Americana,* 2.17 (Hartford, Conn.: Silas Andrus, 1853 [1702]), 216.

Index

HOWARD CLARKE is Professor Emeritus of Classics at the University of California at Santa Barbara, and author of studies on Homer and Vergil, including *The Art of the Odyssey* and *Homer's Readers*.